Mobile Development with .NET

Second Edition

Build cross-platform mobile applications with Xamarin.Forms 5 and ASP.NET Core 5

Can Bilgin

BIRMINGHAM—MUMBAI

Mobile Development with .NET
Second Edition

Copyright © 2021 Packt Publishing

All rights reserved. No part of this book may be reproduced, stored in a retrieval system, or transmitted in any form or by any means, without the prior written permission of the publisher, except in the case of brief quotations embedded in critical articles or reviews.

Every effort has been made in the preparation of this book to ensure the accuracy of the information presented. However, the information contained in this book is sold without warranty, either express or implied. Neither the author, nor Packt Publishing or its dealers and distributors, will be held liable for any damages caused or alleged to have been caused directly or indirectly by this book.

Packt Publishing has endeavored to provide trademark information about all of the companies and products mentioned in this book by the appropriate use of capitals. However, Packt Publishing cannot guarantee the accuracy of this information.

Associate Group Product Manager: Pavan Ramchandani
Senior Editor: Hayden Edwards
Content Development Editor: Aamir Ahmed
Technical Editor: Shubham Sharma
Copy Editor: Safis Editing
Project Coordinator: Kinjal Bari
Proofreader: Safis Editing
Indexer: Tejal Daruwale Soni
Production Designer: Vijay Kamble

First published: June 2018
Second edition: April 2021

Production reference: 1080421

Published by Packt Publishing Ltd.
Livery Place
35 Livery Street
Birmingham
B3 2PB, UK.

ISBN 978-1-80020-469-0

www.packt.com

To my beloved wife and best friend for life, Sanja.

– Can Bilgin

Contributors

About the author

Can Bilgin is a solution architect, working for Authority Partners Inc. He has been working in the software industry for almost two decades on various consumer- and enterprise-level engagements for high-profile clients using technologies such as BizTak, Service Fabric, Orleans, Dynamics CRM, Xamarin, WCF, Azure services, and other web/cloud technologies. His passion lies in mobile and IoT development using modern tools available to developers. He shares his experience on his blog, on social media, and through speaking engagements at local and international community events. He was recognized as a Microsoft MVP for his technical contributions between 2014 and 2018.

I want to thank my wife and daughter for their tremendous support during this project.

About the reviewer

Ahmed Ilyas has 18 years of professional experience in software development.

After leaving Microsoft, he ventured into setting up his own consultancy company, offering the best possible solutions for a number of industries and providing real-world answers to those problems. He uses the Microsoft stack to not only build these technologies to be able to provide the best practices, patterns, and software to his client base to enable long-term stability and compliance in the ever-changing software industry but also to improve the skills of software developers around the globe as well as pushing the limits of technology.

This has led to him being awarded MVP in C# by Microsoft three times for "providing excellence and independent real-world solutions to problems that developers face." His great reputation has resulted in him having a large client base for his consultancy company, Sandler Ltd (UK) and Sandler Software LLC (US), which includes clients from different industries. Clients have included him on their "approved contractors/consultants" list as a trusted vendor and partner.

Ahmed Ilyas has also been involved in the past in reviewing books for Packt Publishing and wishes to thank them for the great opportunity once again.

> *I would like to thank the author/publisher of this book for giving me the great honor and privilege of reviewing the book, as well as, especially, Microsoft Corporation and my colleagues for enabling me to become a reputable leader as a software and solutions developer in the industry.*

Table of Contents

Preface

Section 1: Understanding .NET

1
Getting Started with .NET 5.0

Technical Requirements	4	Developing with .NET 5.0	9
Exploring cross-platform development	4	Creating a runtime-agnostic application	9
Developing fully native applications	5	Defining a runtime and self-contained deployment	14
Hybrid applications	5	Defining a framework	17
Native cross-platform frameworks	6	Summary	19
Understanding .NET Core	7		

2
Defining Xamarin, Mono, and .NET Standard

Understanding Xamarin	22	Using .NET with Xamarin	35
Setting up Your Development Environment	22	Xamarin.Forms	37
Creating your First Xamarin Application	25	Extending the reach	42
Xamarin on Android – Mono Droid	26	Summary	43
Xamarin on iOS – Mono Touch	32		

3
Developing with Universal Windows Platform

Introducing Universal Windows Platform	46	Native with UWP	54
Creating UWP applications	47	Working with Platform extensions	55
Understanding XAML Differences	51	Summary	57
Using .NET Standard and .NET			

Section 2: Xamarin and Xamarin.Forms

4
Developing Mobile Applications with Xamarin

Technical Requirements	62	implementation	72
Choosing between Xamarin and Xamarin.Forms	62	Architectural Patterns for Unidirectional Data Flow	81
Organizing Xamarin.Forms application projects	64	Useful architectural patterns	83
Selecting the presentation architecture	67	Inversion of Control	83
		Event aggregator	84
Model-View-Controller (MVC) implementation	68	Decorator	85
Model-View-ViewModel (MVVM)		Summary	86

5
UI Development with Xamarin

Technical Requirements	88	Implementing navigation structure	94
Application layout	88		
Consumer expectations	88	Single-page view	94
Platform imperatives	91	Simple navigation	100
Development cost	93	Multi-page views	103

Master/detail view	109	**Creating data-driven views**	**128**
Implementing Shell Navigation	**113**	Data binding essentials	128
Using Xamarin.Forms and		Value converters	130
native controls	**116**	Triggers	133
Layouts	116	Visual states	135
Xamarin.Forms view elements	123	**Collection Views**	**138**
Native components	126	**Summary**	**139**

6
Customizing Xamarin.Forms

Technical Requirements	**142**	Platform specifics	159
Xamarin.Forms development		Xamarin.Forms effects	160
domains	**142**	Composite customizations	164
Xamarin.Forms shared		**Creating Custom Controls**	**168**
domains	**144**	Creating a Xamarin.Forms control	168
Using styles	144	Creating a custom renderer	172
Creating behaviors	148	Creating a custom Xamarin.Forms	
Attached properties	154	control	178
XAML markup extensions	156	**Summary**	**182**
Customizing native domains	**159**		

Section 3:
Azure Cloud Services

7
Azure Services for Mobile Applications

An overview of Azure services	**186**	Azure storage	202
An introduction to distributed systems	186	Cosmos DB	204
Cloud architecture	190	Azure Cache for Redis	205
Azure service providers and resource		**Azure Serverless**	**205**
types	198	Azure functions	205
Data stores	**201**	Azure Logic apps	208
Relational database resources	201	Azure Event Grid	209

Development services	**209**	Visual Studio App Center	211
Azure DevOps	210	**Summary**	**212**

8
Creating a Datastore with Cosmos DB

Technical Requirements	**214**	Creating and accessing documents	225
The basics of Cosmos DB	**214**	Denormalized data	231
Global distribution	216	Referenced data	234
Consistency spectrum	216	**Cosmos DB in depth**	**236**
Pricing	219	Partitioning	236
Data access models	**220**	Indexing	239
The SQL API	220	Programmability	241
The MongoDB API	220	The change feed	245
Others	224	**Summary**	**245**
Modeling data	**224**		

9
Creating Microservices Azure App Services

Technical requirements	**248**	Implementing a soft delete	267
Choosing the right app model	**248**	**Integrating with Redis cache**	**268**
Azure virtual machines	249	**Hosting the services**	**271**
Containers in Azure	250	Azure Web App for App Service	271
Microservices with Azure Service Fabric	251	Containerizing services	274
Azure App Service	252	**Securing the application**	**277**
Creating our first microservice	**253**	ASP.NET Core Identity	279
Initial setup	253	Azure AD	280
Implementing retrieval actions	256	Azure AD B2C	285
Implementing update methods	264	**Summary**	**286**

10
Using .NET Core for Azure Serverless

Understanding Azure Serverless	**288**
Developing Azure Functions	**288**
Using Azure Function Runtimes	289
Function triggers and bindings	294
Configuring functions	295
Hosting functions	296
Creating our first Azure function	297
Developing a Logic App	**300**
Implementing Logic Apps	301
Using connectors	304
Creating our first Logic App	305
Workflow execution control	310
Integration with Azure services	**313**
Repository	313
Queue-based processing	314
Event aggregation	315
Summary	**316**

Section 4:
Advanced Mobile Development

11
Fluid Applications with Asynchronous Patterns

Utilizing tasks and awaitables	**320**
Task-based execution	321
Synchronization context	327
Single execution guarantee	329
Logical tasks	331
The command pattern	332
Creating producers/consumers	335
Using observables and data streams	337
Asynchronous execution patterns	**342**
Service initialization pattern	342
Asynchronous event handling	344
The asynchronous command	346
Native asynchronous execution	**349**
Android services	349
iOS backgrounding	350
Summary	**352**

12
Managing Application Data

Improving HTTP performance with transient caching	354	SQLite.NET	361
		Entity Framework Core	363
Client cache aside	355	**Data access patterns**	**364**
Entity tag (ETag) validation	357	Implementing the repository pattern	365
Key/value store	359	Observable repository	367
Persistent relational data cache	**361**	**Summary**	**373**

13
Engaging Users with Notifications and the Graph API

Understanding Native Notification Services	376	Device registration	384
		Transmitting notifications	388
Notification providers	376	Broadcasting to multiple devices	390
Sending notifications with PNS	377	Advanced scenarios	391
General constraints	378	**The Graph API and Project Rome**	**393**
Azure Notification Hubs	**379**		
Notification Hubs infrastructure	379	The Graph API	393
Notifications using Azure Notification Hubs	381	Project Rome	393
		Summary	**396**
Creating a notification service	**383**		
Defining the requirements	383		

Section 5:
Application Life Cycle Management

14
Azure DevOps and Visual Studio App Center

Using Azure DevOps and Git	400	Branching strategy	402
Creating a Git repository with Azure DevOps	400	Managing development branches	404

Table of Contents vii

Creating Xamarin application packages	**408**	Setting up distribution rings	420
Using Xamarin build templates	409	**Distributing with App Center**	**422**
Environment-specific configurations	416	App Center releases	422
Creating and utilizing artifacts	416	AppCenter distribution groups	423
		App Center distribution to production	424
App Center for Xamarin	**417**	**App Center telemetry and diagnostics**	**425**
Integrating with the source repository and builds	418		
		Summary	**427**

15
Application Telemetry with Application Insights

Collecting insights for Xamarin applications	**430**	Application Insights data model	443
The telemetry data model	430	Collecting telemetry data with ASP.NET Core	444
Advanced application telemetry	435	Collecting telemetry with Azure Functions	449
Exporting App Center telemetry data to Azure	440	**Analyzing data**	**451**
Collecting telemetry data for Azure Service	**443**	**Summary**	**454**

16
Automated Testing

Maintaining application integrity with tests	**456**	Implementing platform tests	473
Arrange, Act, and Assert	456	**Automated UI tests**	**473**
Creating unit tests with mocks	462	Xamarin.UITests	474
Fixtures and data-driven tests	466	Page Object Pattern	477
Maintaining cross-module integrity with integration tests	**469**	**Summary**	**481**
Testing client-server communication	469		

17
Deploying Azure Modules

Creating an ARM template	484	Deploying .NET Core applications	499
ARM template concepts	491	Summary	503
Using Azure DevOps for ARM templates	495		

18
CI/CD with Azure DevOps

Introducing CI/CD	506	Testing	519
CI/CD with GitFlow	508	Static code analysis with SonarQube	520
Development	509	Creating and using release templates	525
Pull request/merge	510		
The CI phase	512	Azure DevOps releases	525
Release branch	515	Xamarin release template	531
Hotfix branches	516	Azure web application release	533
Production	517	Summary	534
The QA process	517	Why subscribe?	537
Code review	518		

Other Books You May Enjoy

Index

Preface

In this book, you will learn how to design and develop highly attractive, maintainable and robust mobile applications for multiple platforms, including iOS, Android and UWP, with the toolset provided by Microsoft using Xamarin, .NET 5 and the Azure cloud services. The book will not only provide practical examples and walkthroughs but also useful insights about cloud and mobile architectural patterns. You will also learn about most effective ways to manage the lifecycle of your mobile projects using the latest tools and platforms modern DevOps ecosystem has to offer.

Who this book is for

This book is for mobile developers who wish to develop cross-platform mobile applications. Programming experience with C# is required. Some knowledge and understanding of core elements and cross-platform application development with .NET is required.

What this book covers

Chapter 1, Getting Started with .NET 5.0, gives you a brief introduction to .NET Core while explaining the different tiers of the .NET infrastructure. Languages, runtimes, and extensions that can be used together with .NET will be discussed and analyzed.

Chapter 2, Defining Xamarin, Mono, and .NET Standard, explains the relationship between .NET Core and Xamarin. You will learn about how the Xamarin source code is executed with MonoTouch on iOS and the Mono runtime on Android.

Chapter 3, Developing with Universal Windows Platform, discusses the components that allow UWP apps to be portable within the Windows 10 ecosystem and how they are associated with .NET Core.

Chapter 4, Developing Mobile Applications with Xamarin, explains Xamarin and Xamarin.Forms development strategies, and we will create a Xamarin.Forms application that we will develop throughout the remainder of the book. We will also discuss the architectural models that might help us along the way.

Chapter 5, *UI Development with Xamarin*, takes a look at certain UI patterns that allow developers and user experience designers to come to a compromise between the user expectations and product demands in order to create a platform and product with a consistent user experience across platforms.

Chapter 6, *Customizing Xamarin.Forms*, goes through the steps and procedures of customizing Xamarin.Forms without compromising on the performance or user experience. Some of the features that will be analyzed include effects, behaviors, extensions, and custom renderers.

Chapter 7, *Azure Services for Mobile Applications*, discusses the fact that there are a number of services that are offered as services (SaaS), platform (PaaS), or infrastructure (IaaS), such as Notification Hubs, Cognitive Services, and Azure Functions, that can change the impressions of users regarding your application with little or no additional development hours. This chapter will give you a quick overview of using some of these services when developing .NET Core applications.

Chapter 8, *Creating a Datastore with Cosmos DB*, explains how Cosmos DB offers a multi-model and multi-API paradigm that allows applications to use multiple data models while storing application data with the most suitable API for the application, such as SQL, JavaScript, Gremlin, and MongoDB. In this chapter, we will create the datastore for our application and implement the data access modules.

Chapter 9, *Creating Microservices Azure App Services*, goes through the basics of Azure App Service, and we will create a simple, data-oriented backend for our application using ASP.NET Core with authentication provided by Azure Active Directory. Additional implementation will include offline sync and push notifications.

Chapter 10, *Using .NET Core for Azure Serverless*, shows how to incorporate Azure Functions into our infrastructure to process data on different triggers, and how to integrate Azure Functions with a logic app that will be used as a processing unit in our setup.

Chapter 11, *Fluid Applications with Asynchronous Patterns*, explains that when developing Xamarin applications and ASP.NET Core applications, both the task's framework and the reactive modules can help distribute the execution threads and create a smooth and uninterrupted execution flow. This chapter will go over some of the patterns associated with these modules and apply them to various sections of the application.

Chapter 12, *Managing Application Data*, explains that in order to avoid data conflicts and synchronization issues, developers must be diligent regarding the procedures implemented according to the type of data at hand. This chapter will discuss the possible data synchronization and offline storage scenarios using products such as SQLite and Entity Framework Core, as well as the out-of-the-box offline support provided by Azure App Service.

Chapter 13, *Engaging Users with Notifications and the Graph API*, briefly explains how notifications and the graph API can be used to improve user engagement by taking advantage of push notifications and the graph API. We will create a notification implementation for cross-platform applications using Azure Notification Hubs. We will also create so-called activity entries for our application sessions so that we can create a timeline that is accessible on multiple platforms.

Chapter 14, *Azure DevOps and Visual Studio App Center*, shows how to use Visual Studio Team Services and App Center to set up a complete, automated pipeline for Xamarin applications that will connect the source repository to the final store submission.

Chapter 15, *Application Telemetry with Application Insights*, explains how Application Insights is a great candidate for collecting telemetry from Xamarin applications that use an Azure-hosted web service infrastructure because of its intrinsic integration with Azure modules, as well as the continuous export functionality for App Center telemetry.

Chapter 16, *Automated Testing*, discusses how to create unit and coded UI tests, and the architectural patterns that revolve around them. Data-driven unit tests, mocks, and Xamarin UI tests are some of the concepts that will be discussed.

Chapter 17, *Deploying Azure Modules*, demonstrates how to configure the ARM template for the Azure web service implementation, as well as other services (such as Cosmos DB and Notification Hubs) that we used previously so that we can create deployments using the Visual Studio Team Services build and release pipeline. Introducing configuration values into the template and preparing it to create staging environments are our primary focuses in this chapter.

Chapter 18, *CI/CD with Azure DevOps*, explains how developers can create fully automated templates for builds, testing, and deployments using the toolset provided with Visual Studio Team Services. In this chapter, we will set up the build and release pipeline for Xamarin in line with the Azure deployment pipeline.

To get the most out of this book

The book is primarily aimed at .NET developers with slim to moderate experience with Xamarin and .NET. The cloud infrastructure-related sections heavily use various services in the Azure cloud infrastructure. However, familiarity with the basic management concepts of the Azure portal should be enough for the more advanced topics.

For the code samples, a combination of Windows and macOS development environments is used throughout the book. The ideal setup to utilize the samples would be to use macOS together with a Windows 10 virtual machine. This way, samples from both environments can be used.

Software/hardware covered in the book	OS requirements
.NET 5.0 and above	Windows, macOS X, or Linux
Xamarin.Forms 5.0	Windows, macOS X, or Linux
Python	Windows, macOS X, or Linux
Docker	macOS X or Linux

The IDE of choice for implementing the code walk-throughs is Visual Studio 2019 on Windows and Visual Studio for Mac on macOS. Visual Studio Code, which supports both platforms, can be used to create the scripting and Python examples.

If you are using the digital version of this book, we advise you to type the code yourself or access the code via the GitHub repository (link available in the next section). Doing so will help you avoid any potential errors related to the copying and pasting of code.

Download the example code files

You can download the example code files for this book from GitHub at `https://github.com/PacktPublishing/Mobile-Development-with-.NET-Second-Edition`. In case there's an update to the code, it will be updated on the existing GitHub repository.

We also have other code bundles from our rich catalog of books and videos available at `https://github.com/PacktPublishing/`. Check them out!

Conventions used

There are a number of text conventions used throughout this book.

`Code in text`: Indicates code words in text, database table names, folder names, filenames, file extensions, pathnames, dummy URLs, user input, and Twitter handles. Here is an example: "The `IObserver` and `IObservable` interfaces, which form the basis for observables and so-called reactive patterns."

A block of code is set as follows:

```
namespace FirstXamarinFormsApplication
{
    public partial class MainPage : ContentPage
    {
        InitializeComponent();
        BindingContext = new MainPageViewModel();
    }
}
```

When we wish to draw your attention to a particular part of a code block, the relevant lines or items are set in bold:

```
public App()
{
    InitializeComponent();
    MainPage = NavigationPage(new ListItemView())
}
```

Any command-line input or output is written as follows:

```
$ docker run -p 8000:80 netcore-usersapi
```

Bold: Indicates a new term, an important word, or words that you see onscreen. For example, words in menus or dialog boxes appear in the text like this. Here is an example: "Both the ALM process and the version control options are available under the **Advanced** section of the project settings."

> **Tips or important notes**
> Appear like this.

Get in touch

Feedback from our readers is always welcome.

General feedback: If you have questions about any aspect of this book, mention the book title in the subject of your message and email us at `customercare@packtpub.com`.

Errata: Although we have taken every care to ensure the accuracy of our content, mistakes do happen. If you have found a mistake in this book, we would be grateful if you would report this to us. Please visit `www.packtpub.com/support/errata`, selecting your book, clicking on the Errata Submission Form link, and entering the details.

Piracy: If you come across any illegal copies of our works in any form on the Internet, we would be grateful if you would provide us with the location address or website name. Please contact us at `copyright@packt.com` with a link to the material.

If you are interested in becoming an author: If there is a topic that you have expertise in and you are interested in either writing or contributing to a book, please visit `authors.packtpub.com`.

Reviews

Please leave a review. Once you have read and used this book, why not leave a review on the site that you purchased it from? Potential readers can then see and use your unbiased opinion to make purchase decisions, we at Packt can understand what you think about our products, and our authors can see your feedback on their book. Thank you!

For more information about Packt, please visit `packt.com`.

Section 1: Understanding .NET

The fundamental requirement for implementing cross-platform applications with Xamarin is to understand the .NET ecosystem and the supporting Microsoft stack. This part of the book specifically walks you through the evolution of .NET and how it can efficiently be utilized for mobile projects.

This section comprises the following chapters:

- *Chapter 1, Getting Started with .NET 5.0*
- *Chapter 2, Defining Xamarin, Mono, and .NET Standard*
- *Chapter 3, Developing with Universal Windows Platform*

1
Getting Started with .NET 5.0

.NET Core (previously known as .NET vNext) is the general umbrella term used for Microsoft's cross-platform toolset that aims to solve the shortcomings of centralized/machine-wide frameworks (classic .NET Framework) by creating a portable, platform-agnostic, modular runtime and framework. This decentralized development platform, which is replacing the classic .NET Framework starting with v5.0, allows developers to create applications for multiple platforms using the common .NET base class libraries (implementation of the .NET standard), as well as various runtimes and application models, depending on the target platforms.

This chapter will give you a brief introduction to the new .NET Framework while explaining different tiers of the .NET Core infrastructure. The combination of .NET Core, .NET Standard, and Xamarin is the key to cross-platform projects and opens many doors that were previously only available to Windows developers. The ability to create web applications that can run on Linux machines and containers, and the implementation of mobile applications that target iOS, Android, Universal Windows Platform (UWP), and Tizen, are just a couple of examples designed to emphasize the capabilities of this cross-platform approach.

In this chapter, we will analyze cross-platform development tools and frameworks for mobile applications and take an initial look at .NET Core development.

The following sections will guide you through getting started with .NET 5.0:

- Exploring cross-platform development
- Understanding .NET Core
- Developing with .NET 5.0

Technical Requirements

You can find the code used in this chapter through the following GitHub link: https://github.com/PacktPublishing/Mobile-Development-with-.NET-Second-Edition/tree/master/chapter01/src.

Exploring cross-platform development

The term **cross-platform application development** refers to the process of creating a software application that can run on multiple operating systems. In this book, we will not try to answer the question of *why*, but *how* to develop cross-platform applications – more specifically, we will try to create a cross-platform application using the toolset provided by Microsoft and .NET Core.

Before we start talking about .NET Core, let's take a look at the process of developing an application for multiple platforms. Faced with the cross-platform requirement, the product team can choose multiple paths that will lead the developers through different application life cycles.

Throughout this book, we will have hypothetical user stories defined for various scenarios. We will start with an overall user story that underlines the importance of .NET Core:

> "I, as a product owner, would like to have my consumer app running on iOS and Android mobile platforms, as well as Windows, Linux, and macOS desktop runtimes, so that I can increase my reach and user base."

In order to meet these demands, we can choose to implement the application in several different ways:

- Fully native applications
- Hybrid applications
- Cross-platform

Let's take a look at each of these methods.

Developing fully native applications

Following this path would create probably the most performant application, with increased accessibility to platform APIs for developers. However, the development team for this type of development would require a wider range of skills so that the same application can be created on multiple platforms. Development on multiple platforms would also increase the developer hours that need to be invested in the application.

Considering the scenario presented in the previous section, we would potentially need to develop the client application in Cocoa and CocoaTouch (macOS and iOS), Java (Android), .NET (Windows), and C++ (Linux), and finally build a web service infrastructure using another development platform of our choice. In other words, this approach is, in fact, implementing a multi-platform application rather than a cross-platform one.

Hybrid applications

Native hosted web applications (also known as hybrid applications) are another popular choice for (especially mobile) developers. In this architecture, a responsive web application would be hosted on a thin native harness on the target platform. The native web container would also be responsible for providing access to the web runtime on native platform APIs. These hybrid applications wouldn't even need to be packaged as application packages, but as **Progressive Web Apps (PWAs)** so that users can access them directly from their web browsers. While the development resources are used more efficiently than in the native cross-platform framework approach, this type of application is generally prone to performance issues.

In reference to the business requirements at hand, we would probably develop a web service layer and a small **Single - Page Application (SPA)**, part of which is packaged as a hybrid application.

Native cross-platform frameworks

Development platforms such as React Native, Xamarin, and .NET Core provide the much-required abstraction for the target platforms, so that development can be done using one framework and one development kit for multiple runtimes. In other words, developers can still use the APIs provided by the native platform (for example, the Android or iOS SDK), but development is executed using a single language and framework. This approach not only decreases development resources, but also saves you from the burden of managing multiple source repositories for multiple platforms. This way, the same source is used to create multiple application heads.

For instance, using .NET Core, the development team can implement all target platforms using the same development suite, thereby creating multiple client applications for each target platform, as well as the web service infrastructure.

In a cross-platform implementation, architecturally speaking, the application is made up of three distinct tiers:

- **Application model** (the implementation layer for the consumer application)
- **Framework** (the toolset available for developers)
- **Platform abstraction** (the harness or runtime to host the application)

In this context, we, in essence, are in pursuit of creating a platform-agnostic application layer that will be catered for on a platform abstraction layer. The platform abstraction layer, whether we are dealing with a native web host or a native cross-platform framework, is responsible for providing the bridge between the single application implementation and the polymorphic runtime component.

.NET Core and Mono provide the runtime, while .NET Standard provides the framework abstraction, which means that cross-platform applications can be implemented and distributed on multiple platforms. Using Xamarin with the .NET Standard framework on mobile applications and .NET Core on the web infrastructure, sophisticated cloud-supported native mobile applications can be created.

As you can easily observe, native cross-platform frameworks offer the optimal compromise between development costs, performance, and the nativeness of the target application, providing developers with an ideal option for creating applications for multiple platforms. From this perspective, .NET (Core) and Xamarin, which together evolved into a cross-platform framework and runtime, has become one of the most prominent development platforms for mobile applications.

We have discussed different ways to implement cross - platform applications and identified the pros and cons of these methodologies. We can now start exploring the .NET ecosystem and cross-platform toolset.

Understanding .NET Core

In order to understand the origins of, and motivation for, .NET Core, let's start with a quote:

> *"Software producers who maximize their product's potential for useful combination with other software, while at the same time minimizing any restrictions upon its further re-combination, will be the survivors within a software industry that is in the process of reorganizing itself around the network exchange of commodity data."*
>
> *– David Stutz – General Program Manager for Shared Source Common Language Infrastructure, Microsoft, 2004.*

.NET Core dates back as early as 2001 when **Shared Source Common Language Infrastructure (SSCLI)** was shared sourced (not for commercial use) under the code name **Rotor**. This was the ECMA 335, that is, the **Common Language Infrastructure (CLI)** standard implementation. Rotor could be built on FreeBSD (version 4.7 or newer) and macOS X 10.2. It was designed in such a way that a thin **Platform Abstraction Layer (PAL)** was the only thing that was needed to port the CLI to a different platform. This release constitutes the initial steps to migrate .NET to a cross-platform infrastructure.

2001 was also the year the Mono project was born as an open source project that ports parts of .NET to the Linux platform as a development platform infrastructure. In 2004, the initial version of Mono was released for Linux, which would lead to ports on other platforms such as iOS (MonoTouch) and Android (MonoDroid), and would eventually be merged into the .NET ecosystem under the Xamarin name.

One of the driving forces behind this approach was the fact that the .NET framework was designed and distributed as a system-wide monolithic framework. Applications that are dependent on only a small portion of the framework required the complete framework to be installed on the target operating system. It did not support application-only scenarios where different applications can be run on different versions without having to install a system-wide upgrade. However, more importantly, applications that were developed with .NET were implicitly bound to Windows because of the tight coupling between the .NET Framework and Windows API components. .NET Core was born out of these incentives and opened up the doors of various platforms for .NET developers.

Finally, in 2020, .NET Core replaced classic .NET. The unified .NET platform now provides developers with a single runtime and framework that can be used to create cross-platform applications using a single code base.

Semantically speaking, .NET now describes the complete infrastructure for the whole set of cross-development tools that rely on a common language infrastructure and multiple runtimes, including .NET Core Runtime, .NET, also known as Big CLR, the Mono runtime, and Xamarin:

Figure 1.1 – .NET Ecosystem

In this setup, the .NET CLI (Common Language Infrastructure) is made up of the base class library implementation, which defines the standards that need to be provided by the supported runtimes. The base class library is responsible for providing the PAL, which is provided by the hosting runtime under the name of the Adaption Layer. This infrastructure is supported by compiler services such as Roslyn and **Mono Compiler (MCS)**, as well as **Just-In-Time (JIT)** and **Ahead-of-Time (AOT)** compilers such as RyuJIT (.NET Core), mTouch, and LLVM (for Xamarin.iOS) in order to produce and execute the application binaries for the target platform.

Overall, .NET Core is a rapidly growing ecosystem with a large number of supported platforms, runtimes, and tools. Most of these components can be found on GitHub as open source projects under the supervision of the .NET Foundation. This open source growth is one of the key factors behind .NET Core reaching its peak today, where the implemented APIs almost fully match those of .NET Framework. This is why the .NET 5.0 release marks the end of the .NET era (as we know it) since the two .NET frameworks are being merged into one in this release, where .NET Core, de facto, replaces .NET itself. Let's now, without further ado, start developing in .NET 5.0.

Developing with .NET 5.0

.NET applications can be developed with Visual Studio on the Windows platform and Visual Studio for Mac (inheriting from Xamarin Studio) on macOS. Visual Studio Code (an open source project) and Rider (JetBrain's development IDE) provide support for both of these platforms, as well as Unix-based systems. While these environments provide the desired user-friendly development UI, technically speaking, .NET applications can be written with a simple text editor and compiled using the .NET Core command-line toolset.

The only intrinsic runtime in the .NET Core CLI is the .NET Core runtime, which is primarily used for creating console applications with access to the complete base class library.

Without further ado, let's create our first cross-platform application with the CLI tools and see how it behaves on multiple target platforms. In this example, we will develop a simple calculator with basic arithmetic operations support as a console application.

Creating a runtime-agnostic application

When developing our calculator, our main goal is to create an application that we can run on multiple platforms (in other words, Windows and macOS). To begin with, we will create our console application on macOS with .NET Core installed:

```
$ mkdir calculator && cd $_
$ dotnet --version
5.0.100-preview.7.20366.6
$ dotnet new solution
The template "Solution File" was created successfully.
$ dotnet new console --name "calculator.console" --output "calculator.console"
The template "Console Application" was created successfully.
$ cd calculator.console
```

> **Important note**
>
> In this example, we have used the console template, but there are many other templates available out of the box, such as a class library, unit test project, ASP.NET Core, and more specific templates, such as Razor Page, MVC ViewStart, ASP.NET Core Web App, and Blazor Server App.

10   Getting Started with .NET 5.0

The `calculator.console` console application should have been created in the folder that you specified.

In order to restore the NuGet packages associated with any project, you can use the `dotnet restore` command in a command line or terminal window, depending on your operating system.

> **Important note**
> Generally, you don't need to use the `restore` command, as the compilation already does this for you. In the case of template creation, the final step actually restores the NuGet packages.

Next, copy the following implementation into the created `program.cs` file, replacing the `Main` method:

```
static char[] _numberChars = new[] { '0', '1', '2', '3', '4', '5', '6', '7', '8', '9' };
static char[] _opChars = new[] { '+', '-', '*', '/', '=' };
static void Main(string[] args)
{
    var calculator = new Calculator();
    calculator.ResultChanged = (result) =>
    {
        Console.Clear();
        Console.WriteLine($"{Environment.NewLine}{result}");
    };
    // TODO: Get input.
}
```

Here, we have delegated the calculator logic to a simple calculator state machine implementation:

```
public class Calculator
{
    private int _state = 0;
    string _firstNumber;
    string _currentNumber = string.Empty;
    char _operation;
```

```csharp
    public Action<string> ResultChanged = null;

    public void PushNumber(string value)
    {
        // Removed for brevity
    }
    public void PushOperation(char operation)
    {
        // Removed for brevity
    }
    private int Calculate(int number1, int number2, char operation)
    {
        // Removed for brevity
    }
}
```

The `Calculate` method is the actual calculator implementation, and this needs to be added to the `Calculator` class as well:

```csharp
private int Calculate(int number1, int number2, char operation)
{
    switch(operation)
    {
        case '+':
            return number1 + number2;
        case '-':
            return number1 - number2;
        case 'x':
            return number1 * number2;
        case '/':
            return number1 / number2;
        default:
            throw new NotSupportedException();
    }
}
```

Finally, we just need to expand our `Main` method to retrieve the user inputs. You can now replace the placeholder in the `Main` method for user input with the following:

```
while (true)
{
    var key = Console.ReadKey().KeyChar;
    if (key == 'e') { break; }
    if (_numberChars.Contains(key))
        { calculator.PushNumber(key.ToString()); }
    if(_opChars.Contains(key))
        { calculator.PushOperation(key); }
}
```

Now that our application project is ready (after editing the `program.cs` file), we can build and run the console application and start typing the input as follows:

```
$ dotnet run
123+1=124
```

Here, we used the `run` command to compile and run our application in the current platform (macOS). If you were to navigate to the `build` folder, you would notice that, instead of an executable, the CLI actually created a **Dynamic Link Library (DLL)** file. The reason for this is that, since no other compilation option was defined, the application was created as a **framework-dependent** application. We can try running the application with the `dotnet` command, which is called the driver:

```
$ cd bin/Debug/net5.0/
$ ls
        calculator.console.deps.json
        calculator.console.pdb
        calculator.console.runtimeconfig.json
          calculator.console.dll
           calculator.console.runtimeconfig.dev.json
$ dotnet calculator.console.dll
```

Here, it is important to note that we used the description *framework-dependent* (in this case, the .NET Core App 5.0 runtime). If we were discussing the .NET Framework prior to .NET Core, this would strictly refer to the Windows platform. In this context, however, it refers to an application that is only dependent on the framework itself while being platform-agnostic. In order to test our application on Windows, we can copy the `bin` folder to a Windows machine with the target framework installed and try running our application:

Figure 1.2 – Running a .NET Core Application

The application binary on Windows Console gives the exact same result as the macOS terminal given that both systems have the .NET 5.0 runtime installed.

> **Important note**
> In order to verify that the required framework is installed on the target machine, you can use the `dotnet --info` or `dotnet --list-runtimes` commands, which will list the installed runtimes on the target machine.

In order to test the runtime independence of the created `demo.dll` file, we can try running it with the Mono runtime. On macOS, you can try the following command to execute our application:

```
$ cd bin/Debug/net5.0/
$ mono calculator.console.dll
```

14   Getting Started with .NET 5.0

If we were to analyze what really is happening in the context of the clean architecture onion diagram, you would notice that the dotnet runtime would represent the infrastructure of the application, whereas the console with the net core app abstraction provided would make up the application UI. While the infrastructure is provided by the target platform, the UI and the application core are portable across platforms:

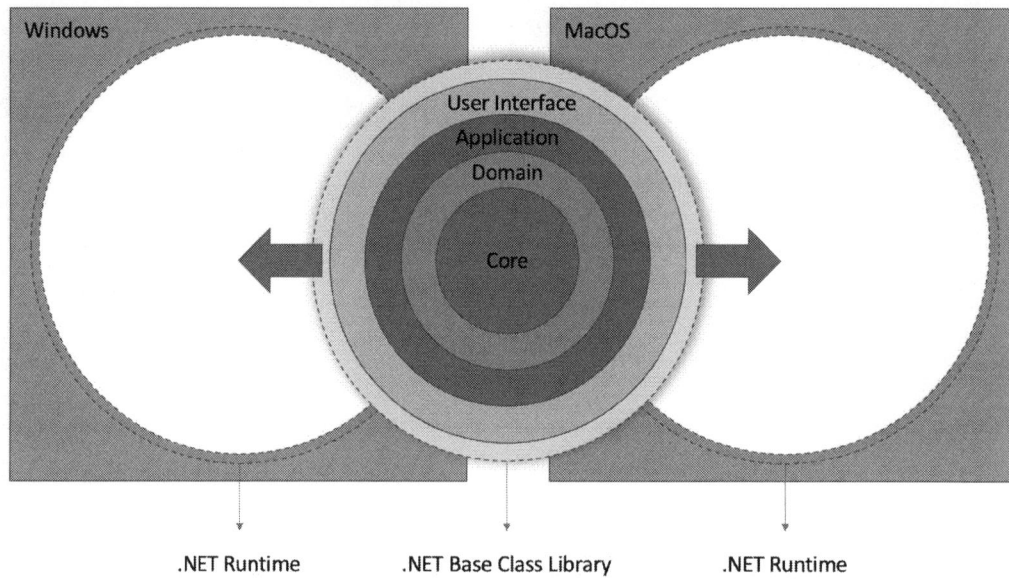

Figure 1.3 – A Platform - Agnostic .NET Application

In this diagram, the two operating systems have the .NET Runtime installed, which provides the implementation for the .NET BCL, allowing the same binary package to be executed on both platforms.

Taking it one step further, let's now try to package the infrastructure input in the application and prepare a platform-dependent package as opposed to a framework-dependent one.

Defining a runtime and self-contained deployment

In the previous example, we created a console application that is operating system-agnostic. However, it had a dependency on the NETCore.App runtime. What if we want to deploy this application to a target system that doesn't have the .NET Core runtime and/or SDK installed?

When the .NET Core applications need to be published, you can include the dependencies from the .NET Core framework and create a so-called **self-contained** package. However, by going down this path, you would need to define the target platform (operating system and CPU architecture) using a **Runtime Identifier** (**RID**) so that the .NET CLI can download the required dependencies and include them in your package.

The runtime can be defined either as part of the project file or as a parameter during `publish` execution. Instead of a command parameter, let's modify our project file to include the runtime identifier:

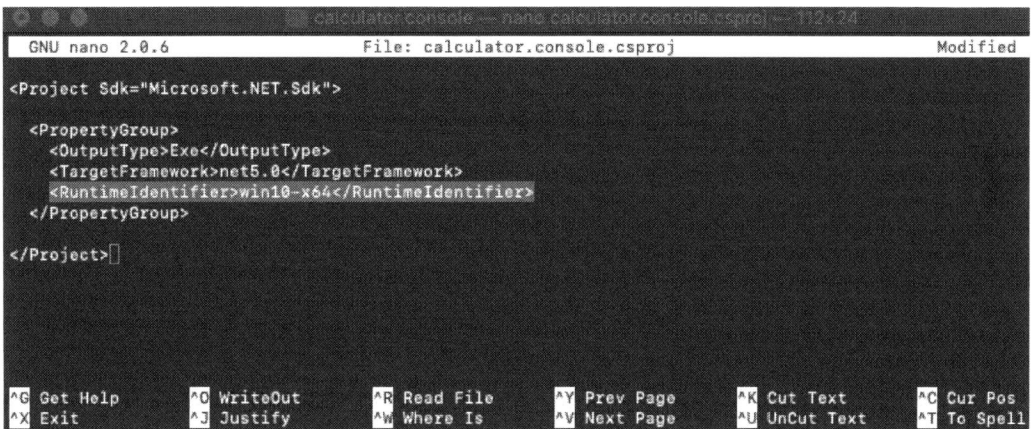

Figure 1.4 – Setting the Runtime Identifier

Here, we have edited the project file to target Windows 10 with the x64 architecture, which would mean that the packaged application would only be targeting this platform.

Now, if we were to publish the application (note that the publishing process is going to take place on macOS), it would create an executable for the defined target platform:

```
$ nano calculator.console.csproj
$ dotnet publish
Microsoft (R) Build Engine version 16.7.0-preview-20360-
03+188921e2f for .NET
Copyright (C) Microsoft Corporation. All rights reserved.

  Determining projects to restore...
  Restored /Users/can/Work/Book/calculator/calculator.console/
calculator.console.csproj (in 6.87 sec).
  calculator.console -> /Users/can/Work/Book/calculator/
calculator.console/bin/Debug/net5.0/win10-x64/calculator.
console.dll
```

```
calculator.console -> /Users/can/Work/Book/calculator/
calculator.console/bin/Debug/net5.0/win10-x64/publish/
```

Here, we have used the terminal editor to modify the project file with the runtime requirements. Once the `dotnet publish` command execution is finalized, the `publish` folder will include all the necessary packages from the .NET Core runtime and framework targeting the Windows 10 runtime:

Figure 1.5 – .NET Self-Contained Publish Package

Notice that, once the deployment target platform is defined, an executable file is created and there is no more need for the driver. In fact, the executable's sole purpose here is to act as the access point (host) to the dynamic class library that is created by .NET Core.

In comparison to the previous application package, this package contains the infrastructure content as well as the application core:

Figure 1.6 – Platform-Specific Deployment

Some of the most notable runtimes include Windows 7 to Windows 10 on three different architectures (x86, x64, and ARM), multiple macOS versions, and various distributions and versions of Linux, including OpenSuse, Fedora, Debian, Ubuntu, RedHat, and Tizen. However, considering our goals of creating a cross-platform application, the target framework definition of a .NET project helps us to package platform-agnostic application binaries with only a dependency on the target runtime, not the platform. Let's now take a closer look at possible target framework options.

Defining a framework

In the previous examples, we have been using .NET 5.0 as the target framework. While, as regards the self-contained deployment for this console application, this has proven to be sufficient, if we were preparing a Xamarin or a UWP application, we may potentially need to use .NET Standard for the core application and a platform-specific target for the infrastructure, such as Xamarin.iOS.

18 Getting Started with .NET 5.0

The target platform framework can be changed using the `<TargetFrameworks>` project property. We would have to use the moniker assigned to the desired framework:

Target framework	Latest	Moniker	.NET Standard
.NET Standard	2.1	netstandard2.1	N/A
.NET 5 (and .NET Core)	5.0	netcoreapp3.1 net5.0	2.1
.NET Framework	4.8	net48	2.0
Universal Windows	10	uap 10.0	2.1

Figure 1.7 – Platform Monikers

In this section, using .NET 5.0, we developed a cross-platform console application that can run on both Windows and macOS platforms. We have looked at both runtime- and framework-dependent versions of the same application. The execution of the same console application on Windows' Command Prompt and the macOS terminal, as well as Linux Bash, is an impressive sight:

Figure 1.8 – The .NET console calculator on multiple platforms

As you can see in this sample, the same source code and even the same binary is executed on multiple platforms with the same outcome. This portability of .NET applications should demonstrate the flexibility of the .NET ecosystem, which expands beyond desktop and console applications to mobile development with Xamarin.

Summary

The .NET ecosystem is growing at an exponential pace with the new, open source-oriented approach being adopted by Microsoft. Various runtimes and frameworks are now part of community-driven projects that cover bigger portions of the original .NET Framework, which was, ironically, destined to be part of Windows itself.

We have thus far only taken a brief look at the .NET application model and infrastructure. In order to demonstrate the portability of .NET, we have created a simple calculator application, which was then compiled for different runtimes and platforms.

In the following chapter, we will move on to Xamarin, which is the provider of the runtime and the implementation of .NET Standard for mobile platforms. We will implement our first classic Xamarin as well as Xamarin.Forms applications.

2
Defining Xamarin, Mono, and .NET Standard

Xamarin is the app model implementation for the modern .NET infrastructure. As part of the cross-platform infrastructure, Xamarin uses the Mono runtime, which, in turn, acts as the adaption layer for the .NET Standard base class library/libraries. By means of the abstraction provided by the Mono runtime (MonoTouch and MonoDroid), Xamarin can target mobile platforms such as iOS and Android.

This chapter will try to define the relationship between .NET and Xamarin. You will start by preparing the Xamarin development environment and create your first Xamarin application. You will then discover how the .NET source code is executed with MonoTouch on iOS and the Mono runtime on Android. This will help you understand the cross-platform nature of .NET better and how it is run on mobile platforms.

The following sections will walk you how to implement your first Xamarin application:

- Understanding Xamarin
- Setting up Your Development Environment
- Creating your first Xamarin application
- Developing with Xamarin.Forms
- Extending the reach

Let's get started!

Understanding Xamarin

Xamarin, as a platform, can be identified as the legacy of the Mono project, which was an open source project that was led by some of the key people that later established the Xamarin group. Mono was initially a **Common Language Infrastructure (CLI)** implementation of .NET for Linux that allowed developers to create Linux applications using the .NET (2.0) framework modules. Later on, Mono's runtime and compiler implementation were ported to other platforms until Xamarin took its place within the Microsoft .NET Core ecosystem. The Xamarin suite is one of the flagships of .NET Core and the key technologies for cross-platform development.

Setting up Your Development Environment

As a developer planning to create native mobile applications using Xamarin, you have several options for setting up your development environment. In terms of development, both macOS and Windows can be utilized, using either Visual Studio or Rider IDEs.

As a .NET developer, if you are looking for a familiar environment and IDE, the best option would be to use Visual Studio on Windows.

In order to use the Xamarin-related templates and available SDKs, the first step would be to install the required components using the Visual Studio installer:

Setting up Your Development Environment   23

Figure 2.1 – Visual Studio installer

When you install the **Mobile Development with .NET** component, the required SDKs (for Android and iOS) are automatically installed, so you don't need to do any additional prerequisite installation.

Once the setup is complete, various project templates become available under the **Cross Platform App** section, as well as platform-specific sections, namely **Android** and **iOS**. The multi-project template for the cross-platform Xamarin app will help guide you through the project creation process using Xamarin.Forms, while the available **Android App** and **iOS App** templates create application projects using the classic Xamarin infrastructure:

Figure 2.2 – Cross Platform App

Using this template, Visual Studio will create a common project (shared or .NET Standard) and a project for each selected platform (selected platforms out of iOS, Android, and UWP). For this example, we will be using the **Shared Project** code sharing strategy and selecting iOS and Android as target platforms.

> **Important Note**
>
> It is important to note that if you are developing on a Windows machine, a macOS build service (a macOS device with Xamarin.iOS and Xcode installed) is required to compile and use the simulator with the iOS project.
>
> If you, in the first compilation of the iOS project, receive an error pointing to missing Xcode components or frameworks, you need to make sure that the Xcode IDE is run at least once manually so that you can agree to the terms and conditions. This allows Xcode to complete the setup by installing additional components.

In this solution, you will have platform-specific projects, along with the basic boilerplate code and a shared project that contains the `Main.xaml` file, which is a simple XAML view. While the platform-specific projects are used to host the views that are created using the declarative XAML pages, the `MainActivity.cs` file on an Android project and the `Main.cs` file on an iOS project are used to initialize the Xamarin.Forms UI framework and render the views.

This XAML view tree is rendered on the target platforms using the designated renderers. It uses the page, layout, and view hierarchy:

Figure 2.3 – Xamarin.Forms Boilerplate Application

In this section, we set up our development environment and tested it using the boilerplate application that was generated for us. Assuming that your development environment is ready, we can move on and start implementing our cross-platform calculator application from the previous chapter – first as a classic Xamarin application and then as a Xamarin.Forms application.

Creating your First Xamarin Application

The project that we created in the previous section used the Xamarin.Forms UI rendering. While this can be the most efficient way to implement a cross-platform application, in some cases, you might need to implement a very platform-specific application (this includes many platform APIs and specialized UI components). In these types of situations, you can resort to creating a classic Xamarin.iOS and/or Xamarin.Android application. Let's implement the calculator application for both.

Xamarin on Android – Mono Droid

We will start our implementation with Xamain.Android. The application will use a single view with a standard calculator layout, and we will try to reuse the calculator logic from the console calculator we created in the previous chapter. Without further ado, let's start creating our application:

1. For the Android application, we will add a new project to our calculator solution, namely `calculator.android`. For this example, we will use the **Blank Android App** template:

Figure 2.4 – Blank Android App

This will create a standard boilerplate application project for Xamarin.Android with a single view and associated layout file. If you open the created `Main.axml` file, the designer view will be loaded, which can be used to create our calculator:

Figure 2.5 – Xamarin.Android Designer View

2. Now, let's start designing our calculator view by creating the result. When handling the Android XML layout files, you are given the option to either use the designer or the source view. When using the designer view to create the welcome view, you have to drag and drop the text view control and adjust the alignment, layout, and gravity properties for the label.

Using the source view, you can also paste the following layout declaration to see what the application looks like when it's run on the Android platform:

```xml
<?xml version="1.0" encoding="utf-8"?>
<LinearLayout xmlns:android="http://schemas.android.com/apk/res/android"
    xmlns:app="http://schemas.android.com/apk/res-auto"
    xmlns:tools="http://schemas.android.com/tools"
    android:layout_width="match_parent"
    android:layout_height="match_parent"
    android:orientation="vertical">

    <TextView
        android:id="@+id/txtResult"
        android:layout_width="match_parent"
```

```
        android:layout_height="100dp"
        android:gravity="center|right"
        android:textSize="30sp"
        android:layout_margin="5dp"
        android:text="0"
        />
</LinearLayout>
```

This will be the upper view that we will use to display the calculation results.

3. Next, let's create the number pad. In order to create the rows of buttons, we will be using a `LinearLayout` with a horizontal orientation. You can insert the following row right under the result `TextView` so that it contains the first row of buttons:

```
<LinearLayout
    android:layout_width="match_parent"
    android:layout_height="0dp"
    android:layout_weight="1"
    android:orientation="horizontal">
    <!-- The buttons will sit here >
</LinearLayout>
```

4. Next, you can use simple `Button` controls within the horizontal `LinearLayout` to create the number pad:

```
<Button android:id="@+id/number7" android:text="7"
    android:layout_width="0dp"
    android:layout_height="match_parent"
    android:layout_weight="1"
    android:textSize="20sp" />
<Button android:id="@+id/number8" android:text="8"
    android:layout_width="0dp"
    android:layout_height="match_parent"
    android:layout_weight="1"
    android:textSize="20sp" />
<Button android:id="@+id/number9" android:text="9"
    android:layout_width="0dp"
    android:layout_height="match_parent"
    android:layout_weight="1"
```

```
        android:textSize="20sp" />
<Button android:id="@+id/opDivide" android:text="/"
        android:layout_width="0dp"
        android:layout_height="match_parent"
        android:layout_weight="1"
        android:textSize="20sp"   />
```

Repeat this for the other rows, changing the `android:id` attribute depending on the button text label until you reach the last row (that is, 4 5 6 * and 1 2 3 -). Each row will use a separate `LinearLayout` with a horizontal orientation. The last row will only have three buttons (that is, 0 = +). In order to make button 0 span for two columns, you can use a `layout_weight` of 2.

The final layout should look similar to the following:

Figure 2.6 – Android Calculator Layout

5. Next, we will modify the generated Android activity code to introduce the calculator logic, while keeping the IDs of the controls we have added to the layout in mind.

   In order to keep references to the controls that we have added, we should create private fields:

   ```
   Button _btnNumber0, _btnNumber1, _btnNumber2, _
   btnNumber3, _btnNumber4, _btnNumber5, _btnNumber6, _
   btnNumber7, _btnNumber8, _btnNumber9;
   Button _btnOpAdd, _btnOpSubstract, _btnOpMultiply, _
   btnOpDivide, _btnOpEqual;
   TextView _txtResult;
   ```

6. During this code's execution, once the content view has been set to the layout, we can retrieve the view and assign it to the private fields using the `FindViewById` function. In order to intercept this activity life cycle event and assign the respective references, you can use the `OnCreate` method:

   ```
   protected override void OnCreate(Bundle
   savedInstanceState)
   {
       base.OnCreate(savedInstanceState);
       Xamarin.Essentials.Platform.Init(this,
   savedInstanceState);
       SetContentView(Resource.Layout.activity_main);

       _btnNumber0 = FindViewById<Button>(Resource.
   Id.number0);
       // ...
       // Removed for brevity
   }
   ```

7. Now, copy the `Calculator` class from the console application and instantiate it within the `OnCreate` method.

8. After this, we can assign the event handlers to the buttons to execute the calculation logic:

   ```
   _btnNumber0.Click += (_, __) => _calculator.
   PushNumber("0");
   // ...
   ```

```
// Removed for brevity

_btnOpAdd.Click += (_, __) => _calculator.
PushOperation('+');

// ...
// Removed for brevity
```

9. Finally, for the resulting delegate of the calculator logic, we can simply assign the result value to the _txtResult field:

```
_calculator.ResultChanged = (result) =>
{
    _txtResult.Text = result;
};
```

You can now run the application and test the calculator's implementation.

The Xamarin.Android platform functions a little more like .NET Core. Unlike Xamarin.iOS, there are no restrictions on code generation, so the Mono Droid runtime execution is done using the JIT compiler, which is responsible for providing the IL packages that are part of the application package. The Mono Droid runtime exists in the application package in the form of native code that replaces the .NET Core runtime:

Figure 2.7 – Xamarin Android runtime

After this exploration of the Android platform, let's re-create our calculator application on iOS platform using Mono Touch.

Xamarin on iOS – Mono Touch

As you have seen in the Android example, in a classic Xamarin application, views are created using native SDK components and toolsets. This way, custom native controls can be introduced into views without you having to create instructions (that is, custom renderers) for the common UI infrastructure. In the case of Xamarin.iOS, developers can create application views either using an iOS namespace and UI elements using code or using XIBs or storyboards with backing controllers.

Now, let's recreate the implementation of the calculator app that we did on Xamarin. Android for Xamarin.iOS:

1. We will start by creating our project. Use the **iOS Single View App** application template listed under the iOS section:

Figure 2.8 – Creating a Xamarin.iOS Project

This template will create a simple Xamarin.iOS application with a single view, an associated storyboard, and a controller for the main view that was created.

2. Once the project has been created, open the `Main.storyboard` file to start creating the user interface. With either Visual Studio on Windows or macOS, use the Visual Studio designer, as well as the Xcode designer, depending on your development environment setup. If you are using Windows, you will need to have a Xamarin build agent that has XCode and Xamarin installed and has been paired with your Windows environment.

3. To create the button controls, drag and drop the button control from the toolbox. To begin with the layout, you can use a size of **90** for the width and height of the buttons. In this example, we are using the dark background color and black for the tint color.

4. To complete the UI, we will need to introduce a label control that should appear on top of the keypad layout.

Now, if we compile and run the application, you will get a similar view to that of Xamarin.Android in the previous section:

Figure 2.9 – Calculator Layout for iOS

5. Now that our UI is ready, we can start introducing the calculator logic. We will start by creating the so-called outlets for our UI controls, so that they can be referenced from within the view controller. You can create an outlet by simply assigning a name to a UI Control. While naming the controls, we will be using the same field names that we used in our Android application (thatis, . _btnNumber0 and _btnOpAdd). After naming all the controls on the UI, you can open the `ViewController.designer.cs` file to verify whether outlets have been created for all the controls.

6. Next, we will introduce the calculator logic. In order to import the application logic, copy and paste the calculator class into the `ViewController.cs` file. Now, in the `ViewDidLoad` method, we can copy and paste the same event handling logic that we had for the Android sample:

```
base.ViewDidLoad();

_calculator = new Calculator();

_btnNumber1.TouchDown += (_, __) => _calculator.PushNumber("0");
// ... Removed for brevity

_calculator.ResultChanged = (result) =>
{
    _txtResult.Text = result;
};
```

As you can see, the only change here would be to use the `TouchDown` event instead of the `Click` event to propagate the action to the application logic.

You can now build and run the application. The behavior will be the same as it is for the Android version of the application.

Using Xamarin.iOS, during the compilation process, the project that we created with the C# and .NET (standard) modules is first compiled into a **Microsoft Intermediate Language** (**MSIL**), just like any other .NET project, and is then compiled into native code with AOT compilation. At this point, one of the most crucial components is the monotouch runtime, which acts as the adaption layer that sits on top of the iOS kernel, allowing the .NET Standard libraries to access the system-level functions. During compilation, just like the application code, the monotouch runtime libraries, together with the .NET Standard packages, are linked and trans(com)piled into native code.

> **Important Note**
> AOT compilation is only a requirement when the compiled package is being deployed to a real device because of the code generation restrictions on iOS. For other platforms or when running the application on an iOS simulator, a JIT compiler is used to compile MSIL into native code – not at compile time, but at runtime.

The following diagram outlines the transcompilation process of APT and LLVM for Xamarin.iOS applications:

Figure 2.10 – Xamarin.iOS Compilation

At this point, you have probably noticed the similarities between the Xamarin.Android and Xamarin.iOS platforms, one of which is the application domain implementation. In both examples, we have used the same application logic that was previously implemented for the console application sample. In order to reuse this logic, we have copied the calculator class implementation. For the maintainability of our solution, it would be helpful if we could reuse this implementation. In the next section, we will discuss the possibility of using .NET as a common ground between these platforms to create reusable components.

Using .NET with Xamarin

Even though the Xamarin and/or .NET Core target platforms (Platform APIs) are treated as if they have the same setup, capabilities, and functionalities as a platform-agnostic framework, each of these target platforms are different from each other. The adaption layer (implementation of .NET Standard) allows us, as developers, to treat these platforms in the same way.

Before the unification and standardization of .NET modules, together with shared projects, cross-platform compatibility was maintained by common denominators of implemented functionality on target platforms. In other words, the available APIs on each selected platform made up a profile that determined the subset of functionality that could be used for these platforms. These platform-agnostic projects that were used to implement the application logic were then packaged into so-called **Portable Class Libraries** (**PCLs**). PCLs were an essential part of cross-platform projects, since they could create and share application code that would be executed on multiple platforms:

Figure 2.11 – Portable Class Library

At some point, since .NET API implementations on various platforms have all converged into (almost) the same subset, a standard set of .NET APIs were defined as the common implementation ground for cross-platform implementation – .NET Standard. As a simple analogy, .NET Standard can be considered the interface that's used to access the platform APIs that are implemented by target platform runtimes. With .NET 5, this subset is now defined as .NET platform, making it a truly cross-platform framework.

Using .NET (Standard), we can create a shared application core project that can be referenced by the Xamarin classic and our .NET console application. This allows us to create a testable platform-agnostic logical application, which can then be tested as a standalone library.

You can create a .NET Standard Library using the *.Net Library* project template. Once you've selected this template, you will also need to select **net5.0** as the target framework. You can now copy and paste the `Calculator` class implementation into this project and reference it from our .NET calculator, as well as the Xamarin.iOS and Xamarin.Android applications.

As much as this helps with the maintainability of the business logic, in Xamarin classic implementations, we will still need to take care of two separate UIs. In order to create and manage a common declarative UI for multiple platforms, we can use Xamarin.Forms.

Xamarin.Forms

In the Android and iOS examples, we followed almost the same implementation methodology, which is composed of three steps, as follows:

1. Declare the UI Elements.
2. Create the Application Domain logic.
3. Integrate the Application Logic to the UI.

The main difference between the two platforms was how the first step was executed. This is exactly where Xamarin.Forms comes to the aid of developers.

Xamarin.Forms greatly simplifies the process of creating UI mobile applications on two complete different platforms using the same declarative view tree, even though the native approaches on these platforms are, in fact, almost completely different.

From a UI renderer perspective, Xamarin.Forms provides native rendering with two different ways of using the same toolset at compile time (compiled XAMLs) and at runtime (runtime rendering). In both scenarios, page-layout-view hierarchies that are declared in XAML layouts are rendered using renderers. Renderers can be described as the implementations of the view abstractions on target platforms. For instance, the renderer for the label element on iOS is responsible for translating label control (as well as its layout attributes) into a UILabel control.

Nevertheless, Xamarin.Forms can't just be categorized as a UI framework, since it provides various modules out of the box that are essential to most mobile application projects, such as dependency services and messenger services. Being among the main patterns for creating SOLID applications, these components provide the tools for creating abstractions on platform-specific implementations, thus unifying the cross-platform architecture to create application logic that spans across multiple platforms.

Additionally, the **data binding** concept, which is the heart and soul of any **Model-View-ViewModel** (**MVVM**) implementation, can be directly introduced at the XAML level, saving developers from having to create their own data synchronization logic:

1. In order to demonstrate the capabilities of Xamarin.Forms, we will implement our calculator application using Xamarin.FormFirst step will be to create the Xamarin.Forms application using the multi-project template for a *Blank Forms App*:

Figure 2.12 – Creating a Xamarin.Forms application

2. This will create three projects called `calculator.forms` (a Xamarin.Forms common application), `calculator.forms.Android`, and `calculator.forms.iOS`.

3. Now that the projects have been created, we can add a reference to the `calculator.core` project (from the previous section) from the `calculator.forms` project. This will allow us to reuse the calculator logic.

4. Next, we need to create the `MainPageViewModel` class under the common application project. We will integrate the calculator logic inside this class:

```
public class MainPageViewModel : INotifyPropertyChanged
{
    private Calculator _calculator = new Calculator();
```

```
        private string _result;

    public event PropertyChangedEventHandler
PropertyChanged;

    public MainPageViewModel()
    {
    }
}
```

5. The view-model will need to have two commands that will handle the number push and operation push actions. Add these two declarations to the class:

```
public Command<string> PushNumberCommand { get; set; }
public Command<char> PushOperationCommand { get; set; }
```

6. Finally, the view-model should also declare a `Result` field. This should propagate the changes to the view using the `PropertyChanged` event handler:

```
    public string Result
    {
        get => _result;
        set
        {
            _result = value;
            PropertyChanged?.Invoke(this, new
PropertyChangedEventArgs(nameof(Result)));
        }
    }
```

7. We can now initialize the commands and assign the result delegate to the calculator instance within the constructor:

```
PushNumberCommand = new Command<string>(_ => _calculator.
PushNumber(_));
PushOperationCommand = new Command<char>(_ => _
calculator.PushOperation(_));

_calculator.ResultChanged = _ => { Result = _; };
```

8. Now, let's assign this view model as our binding context to the main view:

```
public partial class MainPage : ContentPage
{
    public MainPage()
    {
        InitializeComponent();
        BindingContext = new MainPageViewModel();
    }
}
```

9. We can now create our UI elements and bind the appropriate commands to our buttons. We will start by creating our `Grid` layout (copy and paste the following XAML into `MainPage.xaml`):

```
<?xml version="1.0" encoding="utf-8"?>
<ContentPage
    xmlns="http://xamarin.com/schemas/2014/forms"
    xmlns:x="http://schemas.microsoft.com/winfx/2009/xaml"
    x:Class="calculator.forms.MainPage">
    <Grid>
        <Grid.RowDefinitions>
            <RowDefinition />
            <RowDefinition />
            <RowDefinition />
            <RowDefinition />
            <RowDefinition />
        </Grid.RowDefinitions>
        <Grid.ColumnDefinitions>
            <ColumnDefinition />
            <ColumnDefinition />
            <ColumnDefinition />
            <ColumnDefinition />
        </Grid.ColumnDefinitions>
    </Grid>
</ContentPage>
```

This will create a grid of five rows and four columns.

10. Insert the result label into the first row and make sure it spans for four columns:

    ```
    <Label FontSize="50" HorizontalTextAlignment="End" Grid.
     Row="0" Grid.ColumnSpan="4"
            Text="{Binding Result}" />
    ```

    Notice the binding setup for the `Result` property of the binding context.

11. Next, we will create the buttons for the calculator's keypad. Use the following example to create the buttons on the grid with the correct column and row values:

    ```
    <Button Text="7" BackgroundColor="DarkGray"
     TextColor="Black" Grid.Row="1" Grid.Column="0"
            Command="{Binding PushNumberCommand}"
     CommandParameter="7" />
    ```

    It is important to make sure that the `Command` property of each number button is bound to the `PushNumberCommand` property of the binding context.

12. Repeat this process for the operation buttons:

    ```
    <Button Text="7" BackgroundColor="DarkGray"
     TextColor="Black" Grid.Row="1" Grid.Column="0"
            Command="{Binding PushNumberCommand}"
     CommandParameter="7" />
    ```

This concludes the implementation of the calculator. Our application is now ready for its first test run.

By revisiting our onion structure, we can easily see how using Xamarin.Forms expands the portable part of the application between the platforms:

Figure 2.13 – Xamarin versus Xamarin.Forms

In this section, we created a cross-platform application that targets iOS and Android with a single declarative UI using Xamarin.Forms. In addition to the fact that the UI implementation is fully shared between the two platforms, using data bindings also substantially decreases the complexity of our application, thus creating a robust and maintainable mobile application. Here, we have only targeted iOS and Android, but it is possible to expand the platform coverage to other platforms using standard or extension SDKs while making minimal modifications to the UI layouts.

Extending the reach

Finally, since we are talking about Xamarin, it is important to mention that Xamarin and/or Xamarin.Forms do not bind the developers to Android and iOS phone or tablet devices. By using Xamarin and Xamarin.Forms, developers can target devices varying from simple wearables such as smart watches to IoT devices and home appliances.

When developing applications for iOS- or Android-based appliances, exactly the same toolset can be used, while more specialized platforms (such as Tizen) can constitute a target platform, given that the .NET Standard implementation exists natively:

Figure 2.14 – Additional Target Platforms
Source: (https://developer.tizen.org/development/training/overview#type/ [CC BY-SA 3.0 (https://creativecommons.org/licenses/by-sa/3.0)])

The Tizen implementation is also a good example of .NET being used by Xamarin.Forms and the Linux kernel.

As you can see, Xamarin and .NET provides the necessary infrastructure and abstractions so that cross-platform applications can be distributed to various platforms.

Summary

In this chapter, we learned about Xamarin, one of the main supported runtimes of .NET, and how to use it to create mobile applications for multiple platforms. We explored two distinct ways of cross-platform development using Xamarin. While the classic Xamarin approach allows developers to directly interact with native components, Xamarin.Forms provides a more generic and maintainable approach. We also saw how the Xamarin infrastructure can be extended to other platforms such as wearables and Tizen, as well **Universal Windows Platform** (**UWP**).

In the next chapter, we will take a deeper look at UWP and how it can contribute to .NET developers who are executing cross-platform development projects. UWP, being the most mature member of the cross-platform .NET initiative, can provide developers with a completely separate market for development.

3
Developing with Universal Windows Platform

Universal Windows Platform (**UWP**) is a common API layer that allows developers to create applications for various platforms, from desktop PCs to niche devices such as HoloLens. Compared to the Xamarin setup, UWP applications are a little more coupled with .NET Framework and runtime components. UWP makes use of two completely different sets of .NET Framework: .NET Native and .NET Core. Here, .NET Core acts as the BCL library, while .NET Native is part of the application model.

This chapter will discuss the components that allow UWP apps to be portable within the Windows 10 ecosystem and how they are associated with .NET. We will recreate the calculator example from the previous chapter for the Universal Windows Platform using Xamarin.Forms, and then try to identify the differences between Xamarin.Forms and UWP from a XAML perspective. We will also look at how .NET Native can be utilized for UWP.

The following sections will help you create your first Xamarin application:

- Introducing Universal Windows Platform
- Creating UWP applications
- Understanding XAML differences
- Using .NET Standard and .NET Native
- Working with Platform extensions

Let's get started!

Introducing Universal Windows Platform

Windows, prior to the release of Windows 8 (and Windows runtime), exposed a flat set of Windows APIs and COM extensions, allowing developers to access system-level functions. .NET modules that rely on these functions included the **Platform Invoke** (**P-Invoke**) statements for this API layer to make use of its operating system-level functionality.

Windows Runtime (**WinRT**) provided a more accessible and managed development interface that is available for a wide range of development languages. WinRT can be used in common .NET languages (including C# and VB), as well as C++ and JavaScript.

Using the common ground WinRT created, UWP provided the much-needed convergence of multiple platforms within the Microsoft ecosystem. Developers were able to create applications using the same SDK for various devices, which were esoteric targets. Using the UWP development tools, applications with shared modules and user interfaces can target desktop devices, game consoles, and augmented reality devices, as well as mobile and IoT implementations:

Figure 3.1 – Universal Windows Platform

Each device family allows a subset of APIs that are available within the UWP, and it is up to the developer to decide on the platform they want to implement. Additionally, each platform brings in extension APIs that are only available for that platform. These differences between the device families are handled with platform extensions that can be included in your projects at compile time, as well as possible device family checks that can be executed at runtime.

UWP should not only be evaluated as a set of development tools, but truly an application platform. As a platform, it imposes certain security policies regarding how the applications should be handled by the runtime environment. More specifically, the application sandbox model, which is a common concept on other mobile platforms, is also imposed by UWP. Even desktop applications written for UWP should abide by the installation and execution policies, in order to standardize the installation process for users and protect the runtime by compartmentalizing the applications. Finally, because of this platform standardization, the common application store can be used for multiple platforms.

Now that we understand what UWP is, we can look at its connection to Xamarin. In the next section, we will expand our Xamarin.Forms example with a UWP target.

Creating UWP applications

In a cross-platform and .NET Core context, UWP relies on the .NET Framework itself. However, the .NET Framework does implement .NET Standard and, as a result, the portable modules of cross-platform applications can be consumed by UWP applications. In other words, similar to the Xamarin implementation, shared (possibly platform-agnostic) application code can be extracted from UWP applications to leave only the native UI implementation as a UWP-specific module. In turn, UWP projects can be included as part of any mobile development endeavor involving .NET Standard and/or Xamarin.

When implementing the native UI, developers have two inherently similar options, depending on the existing project architecture in a Xamarin project:

- You can create the UWP UI using the native XAML approach (that is, create the user interface within the platform-specific project and share only the business logic).

- You can create a UWP target using Xamarin.Forms and reserve the platform-specific project for platform dependencies.

Using our previous Xamarin and Xamarin.Forms applications, we can add the UWP project so that we can deploy our application to Windows 10 devices:

Figure 3.2 – Creating a UWP Project

Now that the project has been created, we can reference the shared (or .NET Standard) platform-agnostic project (that is, `calculator.core`) and reuse the business logic. For Xamarin.Forms, we can also include the forms project (that is, `calculator.forms`) and bootstrap the Xamarin.Forms application. Bootstrapping the Xamarin.Forms application is as simple as installing the Xamarin.Forms NuGet package for UWP and loading the Xamarin.Forms application that was created previously.

For the UWP application to render the Xamarin.Forms views we created, we need to install the Xamarin.Forms package and make sure that all the target platform projects have the same version installed:

Figure 3.3 – Adding the Xamarin.Forms Nuget package

Now that the forms package has been installed, we can modify the `MainPage.xaml` file, as well as `MainPage.xaml.cs`, to bootstrap the forms layout. First, we will convert the `MainPage` view into a Forms page:

```xml
<uwp:WindowsPage
    x:Class="calculator.forms.uwp.MainPage"
    xmlns="http://schemas.microsoft.com/winfx/2006/xaml/presentation"
    xmlns:x="http://schemas.microsoft.com/winfx/2006/xaml"
    xmlns:local="using:calculator.forms.uwp"
    xmlns:d="http://schemas.microsoft.com/expression/blend/2008"
    xmlns:mc="http://schemas.openxmlformats.org/markup-compatibility/2006"
    xmlns:uwp="using:Xamarin.Forms.Platform.UWP"
    mc:Ignorable="d"
    Background="{ThemeResource ApplicationPageBackgroundThemeBrush}">
    <Grid />
</uwp:WindowsPage>
```

Here, we have used the `uwp` namespace from the Xamarin.Forms package to convert `MainPage` into a Xamarin.Forms platform-specific page.

Now, we will load the Xamarin.Forms application:

```
public sealed partial class MainPage : WindowsPage
{
    public MainPage()
    {
        this.InitializeComponent();
        LoadApplication(new calculator.forms.App());
    }
}
```

Running the application now may result in an exception, stating that Xamarin.Forms should have been initialized. The initialization can be included in the `OnLaunched` event override method, which can be found in the `App.xaml.cs` file:

```
protected override void OnLaunched(LaunchActivatedEventArgs e)
{
    Xamarin.Forms.Forms.Init(e);
    //... Removed for brevity
}
```

Now, running the application will display the same UI as on the previous platforms, but as a UWP application:

Figure 3.4 – Calculator on UWP Platform

As you can see, with a minimal amount of platform code, we were able to include the Windows platform as one of the targets for our application. The same could have been done either using the Xamarin classic approach and only using the view-model, as well as by creating a native UI using the UWP toolset.

However, what if we wanted to create a "fully" native application user interface using XAML for UWP? To create a UWP application UI in XAML, we need to use slightly different controls and layout structures.

Understanding XAML Differences

Both Xamarin.Forms and UWP can utilize declarative UI pages with the **EXtensible Application Markup Language** (**XAML**). It was initially introduced as part of Windows Presentation Foundation and has been extensively used in .NET applications, starting with .NET 3.0.

While both development platforms offer similar UI elements, they use a slightly different set of controls and layouts, which might cause UI inconsistencies while you are creating cross-platform applications that target iOS/Android (with Xamarin.Forms) and UWP.

Let's take a look at the layout structures:

UWP	Xamarin.Forms	Notes
StackPanel	StackLayout	Left-to-right or top-to-bottom infinite stacking
Grid	Grid	Tabular format (rows and columns)
Canvas	AbsoluteLayout	Pixel/coordinate positioning
WrapPanel	FlexLayout	Wrapping stack
RelativePanel	RelativeLayout	Relative rule-based positioning
UniformGrid	n/a	Provides a tabular grid of uniform size
ScrollViewer	ScrollView	Provides scrolling container for content

Figure 3.5 – UWP and Xamarin.Forms layouts

Similar to layouts, controls also exhibit slight variations. By looking at the controls that are used on these platforms, you can easily spot the subtle differences:

UWP	Xamarin.Forms	Notes
RichTextBox	Editor	Editor does not support rich text
TextBlock	Label	
TextBox	Entry	
ToggleSwitch	Switch	
RadioButton	n/a	Switch is used in most scenarios/or custom controls
Slider	Slider	
ScrollViewer	ScrollView	

Figure 3.6 – UWP and Xamarin.Forms Controls

The differences between the two XAML implementations stem from the fact that UWP carries the legacy of Windows Presentation Foundation, whereas Xamarin.Forms was developed independently to unify Android and iOS view hierarchies.

To demonstrate the differences between the two XAML syntax, we can consider the following Xamarin.Forms layout:

```
<StackLayout>
    <Label Text="{Binding Platform, StringFormat='Welcome to {0}!'}"
           HorizontalOptions="Center"
           VerticalOptions="CenterAndExpand" />
</StackLayout>
```

This view will display some welcome text in the center of the screen binding to a `Platform` parameter. This layout structure will be the same for iOS, Android, and UWP platforms, given that the Xamarin.Forms rendering engine is used.

Nevertheless, if we want to use the UWP native controls in order to achieve the same view we displayed on UWP platform, it would have to be translated as follows:

```
<StackPanel VerticalAlignment="Center">
    <TextBlock
        HorizontalAlignment="Center"
        VerticalAlignment="Center"
        Text="{Binding Platform,
            Converter={StaticResource FormatConverter},
            ConverterParameter='Welcome to {0}!'}" />
</StackPanel>
```

Notice that `StackLayout` was translated into `StackPanel`, while `TextBlock` was translated into `TextBlock`. Additionally, the `HorizontalOptions` and `VerticalOptions` attributes were changed to the `HorizontalAlignment` and `VerticalAlignment` attributes, respectively. Another big difference is the fact that the `StringFormat` property of the `Binding` markup extension is not supported on UWP. In order to support the string formatting, we would need to create our own value converter.

> **Important Note**
> The Window Community Toolkit is a collection of helper functions and custom controls that simplify a developer's tasks in regard to creating UWP apps. The toolkit already contains commonly used converters, one of which is called `StringFormatConverter`.

Using UWP XAML views, from an architectural standpoint, is similar to using native XML views for the Android applications or storyboards for iOS applications on Xamarin. While the two XAML syntax are similar, the infrastructures used to render these views are completely different. Each approach can be utilized based on the development strategy that's been selected (native versus forms), and yet considering the fact that UWP is inherently a .NET application model, using native UWP views within a Xamarin.Forms application could still be accommodated without much hassle. Similarly, UWP also has two .NET compiler variations that can be used for the application runtime during the compilation.

Using .NET Standard and .NET Native with UWP

As we saw previously, UWP using the .NET Framework conforms to .NET Standard. The implementation of .NET Standard within .NET Framework is used as the common **Base Class Library** (**BCL**) while the **Core Common Language Runtime** (**Core CLR**) is responsible for executing the modules that are implemented with .NET Standard definition. Besides .NET Core and .NET Standard, another .NET concept that is invaluable for Universal Windows Applications is .NET Native.

.NET Native provides a set of tools that are responsible for generating native code from .NET applications for UWP, bypassing the **Intermediate Language** (**IL**). Using the .NET Native toolchain, .NET Standard class libraries, as well as the common language runtime infrastructure modules such as garbage collection, are linked to smaller, dynamic link libraries (similar to the Xamarin build process for iOS and Android).

In order to enable the native compilation, you need to enable the .NET Native toolchain for the current configuration (for example, Release x64), which will be used for preparing the appx package in the application, as well as the appx bundle. This will need to be created for the supported architectures (**ARM**, **x86**, and **x64**):

Figure 3.7 – .NET Native Tool Chain

During the linking process, several actions are executed:

- Code paths that utilize reflection and metadata are replaced with static native code.
- Eliminates all metadata (where applicable).

- Links out the unused third-party libraries, as well the .NET Framework class libraries.
- Replaces the full common language runtime with a refactored version that primarily includes the garbage collector.

As a result, similar to .NET (Core) runtime applications (with a specified platform target), UWP applications can be cleaned up from direct dependencies to the .NET Framework by means of converting these dependencies into local references for the application itself. This, in turn, reflects on the application as performance and portability enhancements.

Another UWP feature that allows the core part of the UWP application model to be portable is its platform extensions. Next, we will take a look at UWP extensions that provide access to the platform-specific APIs within the UWP ecosystem.

Working with Platform extensions

As we mentioned previously, UWP supports a wide range of devices. Each of these devices executes its own implementation of .NET Standard and the UWP app model.

Nevertheless, the surface area of this complete API layer might not always apply to the target platform. The UWP app model contains certain APIs that are specific to only a subset of these devices. These types of API modules are, in fact, left as placeholder methods in the core UWP SDK, while the actual implementation is included in extension modules that can be referenced in your UWP applications:

Figure 3.8 – UWP Platform Extensions

Without adding the specific SDK, the developers are confined to only universal APIs. Without adding the extension modules, it is highly likely that certain platform-specific methods would throw `NotImplementedException` or similar, since the actual implementation of these methods only exists in the platform extensions libraries.

After including the target platform extension, the developers are also responsible for executing runtime checks for the methods and events to see whether these APIs are supported in the current device runtime. Developers can make use of various `ApiInformation` methods, such as `IsTypePresent`, `IsEventPresent`, `IsMethodPresent`, and `IsPropertyPresent`.

For instance, to check whether the current device supports the `CameraPressed` event (it might be present on a mobile device, though unlikely to be supported on a desktop PC), we would need to resort to `IsEventPresent`:

```
bool isHardwareButtons_CameraPressedAPIPresent = Windows.
Foundation.Metadata.ApiInformation.IsEventPresent ("Windows.
Phone.UI.Input.HardwareButtons", "CameraPressed");
```

This runtime check can also be executed at the contract level to see whether a group of events, or other class members that are used to execute a certain action, are supported or not:

```
bool isWindows_Devices_Scanners_
ScannerDeviceContract_1_0Present = Windows.Foundation.Metadata.
ApiInformation.IsApiContractPresent ("Windows.Devices.Scanners.
ScannerDeviceContract", 1, 0);
```

This way, developers can avoid situations where the application's behavior and compliance with requirements is neither predetermined nor predictable.

As you can see, UWP is not only an application model that is integrated into the Xamarin. Forms infrastructure as part of the cross-platform application model; it also provides extensibility options for various device-specific functionality through extensibility SDKs.

Summary

Overall, UWP is one of the most sophisticated members of the .NET family. While being quite similar to the Xamarin.Forms architecture in nature and utilizing a similar compilation/execution process, it differs in certain fundamental aspects such as the XAML syntax and application life cycle. However, as we saw when we implemented the calculator application, it can easily be included in, and executed with, Xamarin and Xamarin.Forms projects without increasing development timeline or maintenance costs. The extensibility SDKS we have looked at also showed us the added benefit of you being able to deliver your applications to various UWPs.

In the next chapter, we will concentrate on Xamarin and Xamarin.Forms and different architectural models that we can utilize.

Section 2: Xamarin and Xamarin.Forms

Xamarin as a platform provides various development models and strategies. Each model and framework can be used to meet different project requirements. Understanding these different development approaches will help developers cope with ever-changing customer demands. This part of the book concentrates on practical development examples on the Xamarin platform.

This section comprises the following chapters:

- *Chapter 4, Developing Mobile Applications with Xamarin*
- *Chapter 5, UI Development with Xamarin*
- *Chapter 6, Customizing Xamarin.Forms*

4
Developing Mobile Applications with Xamarin

When you're dealing with cross-platform development with Xamarin, it is important to understand that the application source cannot be completely cross-platform. The platform-agnostic modules of a Xamarin application vary, depending on the application's content, as well as the development approach that's used. Xamarin classic and Xamarin.Forms are two different approaches used to create native applications for (mainly) iOS and Android platforms. While Xamarin classic uses a more native approach, literally migrating the native platform implementation strategy to the .NET ecosystem, Xamarin.Forms delivers an additional abstraction layer for the native UI implementation.

In this chapter, we will learn about Xamarin and Xamarin.Forms development strategies and create a Xamarin.Forms application that we will develop throughout the remainder of this book. We will also discuss architectural models and design patterns that are relevant to the presentation layer, as well other tiers.

The following sections will guide you through implementing a cross-platform native mobile application using the Xamarin framework and toolset:

- Choosing between Xamarin and Xamarin.Forms
- Organizing Xamarin.Forms application projects
- Selecting the presentation architecture
- Useful architectural patterns

By the end of this chapter, you will be able to set up the initial structure of a Xamarin. Forms application with the presentation model, as well as the main architectural structure.

Technical Requirements

You can find the code that will be used in this chapter in this book's GitHub repository: https://github.com/PacktPublishing/Mobile-Development-with-.NET-Second-Edition/tree/master/chapter04.

Choosing between Xamarin and Xamarin.Forms

Xamarin, as a runtime and framework, provides developers with all the necessary tools to create cross-platform applications. In this quest, one of the key goals is to create a codebase with a minimal number of resources and time; another is to decrease the maintenance costs of the project. This is where Xamarin.Forms comes into the picture.

As we explained previously in *Chapter 2, Defining Xamarin, Mono, and .NET Standard*, by using the Xamarin classic approach, developers can create native applications. With this approach, we aren't really worried about creating a cross-platform application since we are creating an application, since all the target platforms are using the same development tools and language. The shared components between the target platforms would, in this case, be limited to the business logic (that is, view-models) and the data access layer (that is, models). However, if we are dealing with a consumer application, the implementation of the business logic and data access layer would be of the least of our concerns for the mobile application.

In a cloud-connected mobile application, as part of a mainstream consumer-oriented suite, we would generally expect the actual domain implementation to be moved to cloud-based services. These services would then be served through a service façade targeting a specific platform. This way, the mobile application is only responsible for executing simple service calls through a gateway API façade, marked as Client Gateway on the bundle of downstream microservices, as shown in the following diagram:

Figure 4.1 – Cloud-Connected Client Service Backend

In an infrastructure setup similar to this, where each application (that is, multiple mobile applications, as well as web applications) – marked as Client in the preceding diagram – can benefit from a tailored mobile API gateway (that is, Client Gateway), the platform implementations diverge from each other, mostly because of the separate UI layer. In other words, expanding the shared business logic and the data access layer cannot really increase the amount of shared code.

As a general rule of thumb, Xamarin classic applications are advised to be used with applications with key features that are dependent on the platform they are running on (peripheral APIs, intrinsic UI components, performance requirements, and so on). However, for a mainstream mobile application with a cloud-based service backend, it might be a better option to use Xamarin.Forms.

The Xamarin.Forms framework aims to standardize the UI implementation process while preserving the nativity of the application on multiple platforms. In essence, applications that are created with Xamarin.Forms are rendered with native UI elements from the target platform. As a matter of fact, once compiled and linked, a Xamarin application package is not any different than a Xamarin.Forms application for any given target platform.

In short, a Xamarin.Forms application might be better suited for consumer-oriented, cloud-connected applications, since the actual business concerns and related domain is implemented in the service layer, while the mobile application is just responsible for providing access to this layer with the most intuitive and attractive user interface.

Organizing Xamarin.Forms application projects

Even the simplest cloud-connected mobile applications can grow to sizes where they are not possible to manage. To keep the maintainability of the project under control, you would need to organize different tiers of the applications in a proper structure. Let's take a look at different tiers of a Xamarin.Forms application and how we can organize these tiers for better maintainability.

When developing a Xamarin.Forms application, the essentials of the application include the target platform projects. These projects, also know NAS heads, act as a harness to initialize the Xamarin.Forms framework and application, and they also contain the native rendering or API implementations. Additionally, we would have a platform-agnostic project that contains the Xamarin.Forms views. The platform-agnostic project would also contain the platform abstractions so that the custom components can be implemented on platform-specific projects.

As the project grows, developers will need to create a separate project that would only contain the view-model and platform-agnostic service's implementation. In this case, the project would become the main target of the unit testing process, since this layer does not depend on the UI elements or platform services directly. Additionally, a separate project can be used to share **Data Transfer Object (DTO)** models between the services layer and the client applications. In a setup like this, the overall architectural layout will look similar to the following:

Figure 4.2 – Xamarin.Forms Project Structure

The preceding diagram shows how these components can be grouped into separate projects and what their dependency structure would look like. As shown on the left, we have the platform harness projects, which contain the references to the native platform, whereas on the right, we have the .NET standard implementation, which makes up the platform-agnostic part of the application. The highest elements in the dependency hierarchy are the native projects. At the bottom of the hierarchy, we have the common package, which contains various utilities, data contracts, and possible abstractions to application services.

In some implementations where platform-specific APIs need to be tested, platform-specific unit tests are used, which are executed on the target platform rather than on the development platform itself. These tests might as well be platform integration tests. Additionally, you may see automated UI tests being added to the mobile solution that will be executed as part of functional testing.

Taking this structure into account for Xamarin.Forms applications, let's take a look at the following user story:

"As a product owner, I would like to create a mobile solution for our shop-a-cross shopping platform, so that the target consumer group can be extended to iOS and Android mobile users."

In this story, as we mentioned previously, we have a cloud-based service backend implementation that is already in use by an established web application. The product owner is considering exposing the backend to a group of mobile applications.

Let's start implementing this story by creating the initial solution. Follow these steps:

1. Create an empty solution called `ShopAcross.Mobile` that will contain the mobile application projects using the **Blank Solution** project template under the **Miscellaneous** section:

Figure 4.3 – Visual Studio – New Solution

2. Create a solution folder called `Client`.
3. Create the Xamarin.Forms projects using `Blank Forms App`. Use `ShopAcross` as the app name and use `ShopAcross.Mobile.Client` as the project name.
4. Now, create a .NET Standard Library project that will contain the DTO contacts for service communication called `ShopAcross.Service.Data`.

   In bigger projects, this DTO package might be delivered as a NuGet package, but here, let's assume we are creating the data contracts manually.

5. Next, create the application core project using the .NET Standard Library project template called `ShopAcross.Mobile.Core`.

   We will use this project to store our view-models. Since, in this project, we might utilize some primitives that are used in data binding, we should also add a reference to the `Xamarin.Forms` NuGet package.

6. Now, from the `ShopAcross.Mobile.Core` project, add a project reference to the `ShopAcross.Service.Data` project.

7. Add other references from the `ShopAcross.Mobile.Client`, `ShopAcross.Mobile.Client.iOS`, and `ShopAcross.Mobile.Client.Android` projects to `ShopAcross.Mobile.Core`.

The final structure should look similar to the following:

Figure 4.4 – Xamarin.Forms Projects

In this section, we learned about the elements that make up a Xamarin.Forms application. We took a closer look at the functionality of these elements and how they depend on each other. Finally, using this information about different tiers, we created the initial solution structure for our sample mobile application.

Selecting the presentation architecture

Now that we've prepared the project structure and divided the application into contextual tiers, we should set up a structural model for how the application will be presenting the data it retrieves from data sources to the user. Let's take a closer look at the different structural models that we can utilize while working with the presentation layer.

When developing a cross-platform mobile application, it is perhaps one of the most crucial decisions to select the presentation architecture. The view and the business logic implementation should factor in the architectural concepts that the selected pattern entails.

Model-View-Controller (MVC) implementation

Both the iOS and Android platforms are inherently designed to be used with a derivative of the **Model-View-Controller** (**MVC**) pattern. If we were dealing with a native application, it would have been the most logical path to use MVC with a **Mediating Controller** for iOS and **Model-View-Presenter** (**MVP**) or a slightly derived version, and then the **Model-View-Adapter** (**MVA**) pattern for Android. A strict MVC pattern targets a one-way data flow and simplifies the implementation:

Figure 4.5 – Classic MVC Flow

The MVC pattern was born as a reaction to the single responsibility principle. In this pattern, the **View** (UI implementation) component is responsible for presenting the data that's received from the **Model** (service layer). In the preceding diagram, this flow is annotated with the *Updates* label. The view is then responsible for delegating the user input to the **Controller**. In a manner of speaking, the user essentially interacts with the controller (that is, they *use* the controller). The controller then communicates the changes requested by the user by manipulating the **Model**.

While it is being used widely with web applications, generally, a derived version is used for mobile and desktop applications. Derivatives of this pattern include MVA and MVP.

In an MVA architecture (or Mediating Controller), the adapter acts as a mediator between the **View** and **Model**, and is responsible for defining the strategy for one or more view components, as well as acting as the observer for these UI components:

Figure 4.6 – Mediating Controller

In an MVC implementation, while using both the classic and mediator patterns, the **Controller** becomes the heart and soul of the application. It needs to be aware of the **Model**, as well as the **View** (which is tightly coupled), since it implements a strategy for the view events (user input) that are acting as both the strategy implementer and observer.

Let's demonstrate this pattern while implementing a login view for the application we created in the previous section:

1. First, we need to create the view. Create a content page with a XAML design component called `LoginView` within the `ShopAcross.Mobile` project:

    ```xml
    <ContentPage xmlns=http://xamarin.com/schemas/2014/forms
        xmlns:x=http://schemas.microsoft.com/winfx/2009/xaml
        x:Class="ShopAcross.Mobile.Client.LoginView">
        <ContentPage.Content>
            <StackLayout VerticalOptions="CenterAndExpand"
                Padding="20">
                <Label Text="Username" />
                <Entry x:Name="usernameEntry"
    Placeholder="username"/>
    ```

```xml
                    <Label Text="Password" />
                    <Entry x:Name="passwordEntry"
    IsPassword="true"
                        Placeholder="password" />
                    <Button x:Name="loginButton" Text="Login" />
                    <Label x:Name="messageLabel" />
            </StackLayout>
        </ContentPage.Content>
</ContentPage>
```

2. Next, create the two entries (that is, username and password), a button for logging in, and a label field, which we will use to display the result of the login function.

3. In order to support the implementation of a controller for this view, which will handle field validation, as well as the login and signup actions, we must expose the entry and button components to the associated controller:

```csharp
public partial class LoginView : ContentPage
{
    // private LoginViewController _controller;

    public LoginView()
    {
        InitializeComponent();

        // _controller = new LoginViewController(this);
    }

    internal Entry UserName { get { return this.usernameEntry; } }

    internal Entry Password { get { return this.passwordEntry; } }

    internal Label Result { get { return this.messageLabel; } }
```

```
        internal Button Login { get { return this.
  loginButton; }}
    }
```

4. Now, create the controller with a reference to the view class:

   ```
   public class LoginViewController
   {
       private LoginView _loginView;

       public LoginViewController(LoginView view)
       {
           _loginView = view;
       }
   }
   ```

5. The controller should define event handling methods for various events that are raised on the view as a result of user interaction. Add the following event handler methods to the controller class:

   ```
   public class LoginViewController
   {
       // ... cont'd

       void LoginClicked(object sender, EventArgs e)
       {
           // TODO: Login
           _loginView.Result.Text = "Successfully Logged In!";
       }

       void UserNameTextChanged(object sender,
           TextChangedEventArgs e)
       {
           // TODO: Validate
       }
   }
   ```

6. Now that the event handler methods have been created, we can subscribe to the events on the view reference. You can add these subscription calls to the constructor:

```
public LoginViewController(LoginView view)
{
    _loginView = view;

    _loginView.Login.Clicked += LoginClicked;

    _loginView.UserName.TextChanged +=
UserNameTextChanged;
}
```

7. Finally, you can comment out the controller references in the `LoginView` class.

As you can see, even though we can further refactor our code so that we can insert abstraction layer(s) between the controller and the view, there is a strong coupling between the two. In order to remedy this, we can resort to a **Model–View–ViewModel** (**MVVM**) setup.

Model-View-ViewModel (MVVM) implementation

In response to the tight-coupling problem, another derivative of MVC was born with the release of the **Windows Presentation Foundation** (**WPF**). The idea that was coined by Microsoft was the concept of outlets being exposed by a controller (or `ViewModel`, in this case) and the outlets being coupled with the view elements. The concept of these outlets and their coupling is called a **binding**. In the MVVM pattern, bindings replace the two-way communication routes between `View` and `ViewModel`, whereas `ViewModel` is still tightly coupled with `Model`:

Figure 4.7 – MVVM Pattern

Using bindings, we can decrease the amount of knowledge the view-model has about the inner workings of the view elements, and then let the application runtime handle how to synchronize the outlets of `View` and `ViewModel`.

In addition to bindings, the concept of "command" becomes invaluable so that we can delegate the user actions to `ViewModel`. A command is a stateful single execution unit that represents a function and data that's used to execute this function.

Using our previous example, we can create a view-model to demonstrate the benefits of using MVVM:

1. Let's start by creating a class that will represent the user interaction points on our view. Create a new class under the `ShopAcross.Mobile.Core` project called `LoginViewModel`:

    ```csharp
    public class LoginViewModel
    {
        private string _userName;

        private string _password;

        private string _result;
    ```

```csharp
    public LoginViewModel()
    {
    }
}
```

Notice that the class is defining three fields representing the two input fields on the view for username and password, as well as a result field to display the login result.

2. Next, let's expose these fields through some `public` properties:

```csharp
public class LoginViewModel
{
    // ... cont'd
    public string UserName
    {
        get { return _userName; }
        set
        {
            if (_userName != value)
            {
                _userName = value;
            }
        }
    }

    public string Password
    {
        get { return _password; }
        set
        {
            if (_password != value)
            {
                _password = value;
            }
        }
    }

    public string Result
```

```csharp
{
    get { return _result; }
    set
    {
        if (_result != value)
        {
            _result = value;
        }
    }
}
}
```

3. Finally, add the `Login` function:

```csharp
public class LoginViewModel
{
    // ... cont'd
    public void Login()
    {
        //TODO: Login
        Result = "Successfully Logged In!";
    }
}
```

4. At this stage of the implementation, we can bind the `Entry` fields from our view to the view-model. To assign the view-model to the view, we need to use `BindingContext` from our `LoginView`, making sure the `ShopAcross.Mobile.Core` namespace is added with a `using` statement:

```csharp
public partial class LoginView : ContentPage
{
    public LoginView()
    {
        InitializeComponent();
        //_controller = new LoginViewController(this);
        BindingContext = new LoginViewModel();
    }
}
```

Now that we are not using the controller any longer, you can also remove the outlets (the internal properties) that are exposing the controls.

5. Now, let's set up the bindings for the `Entry` fields:

```
<Label Text="Username" />
<Entry x:Name="usernameEntry" Placeholder="username"
  Text="{Binding UserName}" />
<Label Text="Password" />
<Entry x:Name="passwordEntry" IsPassword="true"
  Placeholder="password" Text="{Binding Password}" />
<Button x:Name="loginButton" Text="Login" />
<Label x:Name="messageLabel" Text="{Binding Result}" />
```

When executing this sample, you will notice that the values for the entries containing unidirectional data flow (that is, the `UserName` and `Password` fields are only propagated from `View` to the view-model) are behaving as expected; the values that are entered in the associated fields are pushed to the properties, as expected.

The view to view-model binding context setup can also be done in XAML as well. `<ContentPage.BindingContext>` can be used to set the binding context to the view-model, which is initialized using the correct `clr` namespace (for example, `<core:LoginViewModel />`). For this to work as expected, the view-model class needs to have a parameterless constructor.

To increase the binding's performance and decrease the resources that are used for a certain binding, it is important to define the direction for the binding. There are various `BindingMode` available, as follows:

- **OneWay**: This is used when `ViewModel` updates a value. It should be reflected on the view.
- **OneWayToSource**: This is used when the view changes a value. The value change should be pushed to the view-model.
- **TwoWay**: The data flow is bi-directional.
- **OneTime**: Data synchronization only occurs once once the binding context has been bound, and the data has been propagated from the view-model to the view.

With this information at hand, the username and password fields should be using the `OneWayToSource` binding, whereas the message label should be using a `OneWay` binding mode, since the result is only updated by the view-model.

The next step is to set up the commands for the functions to be executed (that is, login and signup). Semantically, a command is composed of a method (with its enclosed data and/or arguments) and a state (whether it can be executed or not). This structure is described by the ICommand interface:

```
public interface ICommand
{
    void Execute(object arg);
    bool CanExecute(object arg);
    event EventHandler CanExecuteChanged;
}
```

In Xamarin.Forms, there are two implementations of this interface: Command and Command<T>. Using either of these classes, command bindings can be accomplished. For instance, in order to expose the Login method as a command, follow these steps:

1. First, declare our Command property in the LoginViewModel class:

    ```
    private Command _loginCommand;

    public ICommand LoginCommand { get { return _loginCommand; } }
    ```

2. In order to initialize _loginCommand, use the following constructor:

    ```
    public LoginViewModel()
    {
        _loginCommand = new Command(Login, Validate);
    }
    ```

Note that we used two actions to initialize the command. The first parameter, which is of the Action type, is the actual method execution, while the second parameter, which is of the Func<bool> type, is a method reference that returns a Boolean indicating whether the method can be executed.

3. The `Validate` method's implementation should look like this:

```csharp
public bool Validate()
{
    return !string.IsNullOrEmpty(UserName) && !string.IsNullOrEmpty(Password);
}
```

4. Finally, in order to complete the implementation, send the `CanExecuteChanged` event whenever the `UserName` or `Password` fields are changed:

```csharp
public string UserName
{
    get
    {
        return _userName;
    }
    set
    {
        if (_userName != value)
        {
            _userName = value;
            _loginCommand.ChangeCanExecute();
        }
    }
}

public string Password
{
    get
    {
        return _password;
    }
    set
    {
        if (_password != value)
        {
            _password = value;
```

```
            _loginCommand.ChangeCanExecute();
        }
    }
}
```

5. Now, add a command binding to the **Login** button so that the created `LoginCommand` is utilized by the view:

```
<Button x:Name="loginButton" Text="Login"
    Command="{Binding LoginCommand}"/>
```

Now, if you were to run the application, you would see how the disabled and enabled states of the command are reflected on the UI:

Figure 4.8 – MVVM command binding

Now that the command has been set up, we only have the result message binding, which is still not working as expected. At this point, tapping the **Login** button will update the view-model data, but the user interface will not reflect this data change. The reason for this because this field should be bound with a `OneWay` binding (changes in the source should be reflected on the target). The main requirement for this is that the source (view-model) should be implementing the `INotifyPropertyChanged` interface, which is defined in the `System.ComponentModel` namespace. `INotifyPropertyChanged` is the essential mechanism for propagating the changes on the binding context to the view elements:

```
/// <summary>
Notifies clients that a property value has changed.
</summary>
public interface INotifyPropertyChanged
{
    /// <summary>
    Occurs when a property value changes.
    </summary>
    event PropertyChangedEventHandler PropertyChanged;
}
```

A simple implementation would require invoking the `PropertyChanged` event with the property that is currently being changed.

> **Important Note**
>
> If the change you've made to a property is affecting multiple data points (for example, assigning a list data source changes the item count property), then the view-model is responsible for firing the same event for all the properties that the UI needs to invalidate.

6. By introducing the interface implementation and using the event trigger on the setter of the `Result` property, we should be able to see the outcome of the `Login` command:

```
public class LoginViewModel : INotifyPropertyChanged
{
    // ... cont'd
    public event PropertyChangedEventHandler PropertyChanged;
```

```csharp
        public string Result
        {
            get
            {
                return _result;
            }
            set
            {
                if (_result != value)
                {
                    _result = value;
                    PropertyChanged?.Invoke(this, new
                        PropertyChangedEventArgs(nameof(Result)));
                }
            }
        }
    }
```

This finalizes the view-model implementation for our login view. We can now create unit tests for the `LoginViewModel` class and expand the implementation with additional exception handling and other necessary expansions.

Architectural Patterns for Unidirectional Data Flow

In both the Mediating Controller and MVVM patterns, both of which we have implemented, as the view's complexity increases, the data flow paths become unimaginably complicated. This complexity is mostly due to the duplex nature of the view model, which decreases the predictability of the view-model. In a complex view, even though the view-model still preserves the innate finite automata attributes, since the number of states increases exponentially with each two-way binding that's introduced, the maintainability of the code plummets.

As a response to this complexity problem, in data-driven application projects, several other MVC derivatives can be utilized to enforce unidirectional data flow. These patterns aim to achieve unidirectional data flow – in simple terms – by treating the application data as immutable items and renewing the application state as a new state through user input and/or data triggers.

Flux architecture is one of the responses to bi-directional data issues. In the Flux model, the application state is managed in immutable data stores. The application domain can then query these data stores, as well as mutate these stores (that is, by creating new immutable versions), using reducers:

Figure 4.9 – Flux Architecture

In terms of Xamarin.Forms, as shown in the preceding diagram, Flux artifacts such as *Data Stores*, *Actions* (also known as Reducers), and the *Dispatcher* can be introduced to the existing MVVM model. By creating data stores to manage the application data and directing the data from data stores to the view-models, unidirectional data flow can be achieved. To handle user interaction, we can create small action blocks that are triggered by commands to dispatch reducers, which then mutate the data stores.

The other unidirectional architectural models used in Xamarin.Forms are Model-View-Update (popularized by the F# language) and Model-View-Intent (used especially with Android applications).

In this section, we took a closer look at different architectural patterns that are used for the presentation's structure. We also implemented the first view of our application using MVC and MVVM. We created a setup where the view is responsible for creating the view-model; however, by using an implementation of **Inversion of Control** (**IoC**), such as dependency injection or the service locator pattern, the view can be dismissed of this duty. In the next section, we will take a closer look at other architectural patterns that are prominent in the Xamarin.Forms ecosystem.

Useful architectural patterns

Xamarin.Forms, as a framework, contains modules that help developers implement well-known architectural patterns so that they can create maintainable and robust applications. In this section, we will take a closer look at some of the most prominent architectural/design patterns; that is, Inversion of Control, event aggregator, and decorator.

Inversion of Control

IoC is a design principle in which the responsibility of selecting concrete implementations for the dependencies of a class is delegated to an external component or source. This way, the classes are decoupled from their dependencies so that they can be replaced/updated without much hassle.

The most common implementation of this principle is using the service locator pattern, where a container is created to store the concrete implementations. This is often registered via an appropriate abstraction, as shown in the following diagram:

Figure 4.10 – Inversion of Control in Xamarin.Forms

Xamarin.Forms offers **DependencyService**, which can be especially helpful when you're creating platform-specific implementations for platform-agnostic requirements. We must also remember that it should only be used in Xamarin.Forms platform projects; otherwise, we would be creating an unnecessary dependency on Xamarin.Forms libraries.

As you can see, Inversion of Control not only helps decrease the inter-module coupling but also allows us to *abstractize* the platform-specific components.

Event aggregator

An event aggregator (also known as publisher/subscriber or Pub-Sub) is a messaging pattern where senders of messages/events, called publishers, do not program the messages to be sent directly to a single/specific receiver, called subscribers, but, instead, categorize published messages into classes without knowledge of which subscribers, if any, there may be. Messages are then funneled through a so-called aggregator and delivered to the subscribers. This approach provides a complete decoupling between the publishers and subscribers while maintaining an effective messaging channel.

The event aggregator's implementation within the Xamarin.Forms framework is done via `MessagingCenter`. `MessagingCenter` exposes a simple API that is composed of two methods for subscribers (that is, subscribe and unsubscribe) and one method for publishers (send).

We can demonstrate how to apply the event aggregator pattern by creating a simple event sink for service communication or authentication issues in our application. In this event sink (which will be our subscriber), we can subscribe to error messages that are received from various view-models (given that they all implement the same base type) and alert the user with a friendly dialog:

```
MessagingCenter.Subscribe<BaseViewModel> (this, "ServiceError",
 (sender, arg) =>
    {
          // TODO: Handler the error
    });
```

We would have the following in the event of an unhandled exception in our view-model:

```
public void Login()
{
    try
    {
        //TODO: Login
        Result = "Successfully Logged In!";
    }
    catch(Exception ex)
    {
```

```
            MessagingCenter.Send(this, "ServiceError",
 ex.Message);
        }
    }
```

`MessagingCenter` allows us to connect to different tiers, almost creating a messaging bus within the application. As shown here, the infrastructure for this architectural pattern is already provided for you in the Xamarin.Forms framework.

Decorator

The decorator pattern is a design pattern that allows behavior to be added to an individual object dynamically, without it affecting the behavior of other objects from the same class. Xamarin.Forms makes use of this pattern to use platform-agnostic visual elements (the views used in XAML) and attaches renderers to these elements that define the way they are rendered (creating native platform-specific controls) on target platforms. The composition of Xamarin.Forms elements does not change the behavior of the renderers and vice versa, allowing developers to create custom renderers and attach them to views without it affecting other visual elements. The following diagram shows the abstraction of the renderer class's interaction with the decorator pattern:

Figure 4.11 – Decorator Pattern in Xamarin.Forms

As you can see, each Xamarin.Forms *control* is represented by a view definition in the shared/standard domain. The control references a specific abstraction of a *view renderer*, which then uses the platform-specific implementation of the given view render on the target platform. In this setup, a derived *custom control* implementation immediately inherits the base control's view renderer association. *Custom renderers,* however, would need to be exported for a specific shared control definition to be used by the layout engine.

A similar approach is used to create so-called effects, which are simple behavioral modifiers that are attached to existing visual elements, as well as their native counterparts.

Summary

In this chapter, we took a deep dive into the architectural aspects of implementing a Xamarin application and set up the foundation for an MVVM application. To demonstrate the implementation of different presentation architectures, we implemented the login view using both the MVC and MVVM patterns. As you have seen, while both of these patterns can be used with Xamarin.Forms applications, each have a different take on the interaction between the view and the controller, and each have advantages and shortcomings. Additionally, other patterns such as MVU and Flux can provide further improvements to the maintainability of your project. We also briefly browsed through several other patterns that we might need in order to implement Xamarin applications. You should now be able to create a Xamarin.Forms application from scratch, as well as set up the boilerplate solution for your next project with a proper application infrastructure and architecture.

In the next chapter, we will implement the initial views of our application with standard Xamarin.Forms components. In the remainder of this book, we will try to implement the components of the application that were discussed in this chapter.

5
UI Development with Xamarin

Material Design, which is the most prominent UI pattern for Android applications, Apple's human interface guidelines, and UWP's Fluid UI language, can make it overwhelming for UX designers and developers to decide on a unified application design. Factors to consider include, but are not limited to, user expectations of the target platform and branding-related product owners' requirements, regardless of the platform.

In this chapter, we will demonstrate how to set up the application layout while utilizing some of the important decision factors for a consistent UX design. We will then create simple application pages and connect them to create a navigational hierarchy using the standard navigation services. We will also take a step back and have a look at the Xamarin Shell implementation for creating the application page hierarchy. We will also browse through Xamarin.Forms view elements and see how they can be connected to the application data without strongly coupling them with business logic by using MVVM.

The following topics will walk you through creating the skeleton of our sample application:

- Application layout
- Implementing navigation structure
- Implementing Shell navigation

- Using Xamarin.Forms and Native controls
- Creating data-driven views
- Collection views

By the end of this chapter, you will be able to create attractive data-driven Xamarin. Forms pages using out-of-the-box layouts and views, as well as set up various navigation hierarchies between them.

Technical Requirements

You can find the code that will be used in this chapter in this book's GitHub repository: https://github.com/PacktPublishing/Mobile-Development-with-.NET-Second-Edition/tree/master/chapter05.

Application layout

In this section, we will take a look at certain UI patterns that allow developers and UX designers to create a compromise between user expectations and product demands. By doing so, a consistent UX across all platforms can be achieved.

For designers, as well as developers, probably one of the most exciting phases of the application life cycle is the design phase. In this phase, there are multiple factors that need to be carefully considered, thus avoiding any rash decisions. An application's design, in simple terms, should satisfy the following:

- The consumers' expectations
- The platform imperatives
- Development costs

Let's get started!

Consumer expectations

The feature set of an application should really correlate with customers' expectations. Layout options and a navigation hierarchy should serve the purpose of the application while keeping the user interaction demands in mind. According to the requirements, an application can be designed as a single-page application or with a complex hierarchy of navigation pages; the content can be text-only or rich media elements can be used; and context actions can provide access to user actions or the interaction can be laid over multiple application pages.

At the view level, in general terms, an application view contains three different types of elements: content, navigation, and actions. It is the developers' and designers' responsibility to create the optimal blend of these elements. In most modern applications, content elements can take on multiple functionalities, in that the content elements become user interaction points, as well as navigation elements.

For instance, let's assume, as our design requirements, we had a list of items defined with an image, a simple title, and a description (that is, a simple two-column, two-row template). Moveover, we need to implement actions related to these content items. In this case, the design, the flow, and the behavior of the elements would really depend on what those actions are. In order to demonstrate different interactions on content elements, let's use the following user story:

"As a user, I would like to see a list of items and interact with them so that I can execute certain actions on those items."

Interaction models for the list view and the complimenting pages can differ greatly. Let's take a closer look at several models where content items are used as interactive elements:

- **List/Detail View**: This list could be a common item list view that's used for detail navigation, where the item detail page exhibits the actions available for an item. In this case, we are assuming that the user needs to see the details of an item before they can execute the necessary action on an item (for example, if the items are hard to distinguish just using the listing):

Figure 5.1 – Content elements as navigation items

The content items in this list view are behaving as navigation items, and on the details screen, the user can execute the actions that are related to those specific items. However, for a simple action, the user would need to change the view and would lose the context of the list.

- **Item Context Actions**: If an action can be executed on the list view, we do not need to take the user to a secondary view, and can allow them to execute the actions by directly interacting with the list:

Figure 5.2 – Content elements as context action items

In this implementation, the list view acts as the single interaction context and actions are executed on the items directly. In other words, content elements are used as action elements instead of using them for navigation.

- **List Context Actions**: Finally, if there are actions available for execution on multiple content elements, the content items themselves could be used with additional styling (for example, an overlay of a checkmark on the image element). This implementation would replace the possible use of checkboxes or radio buttons for the economical use of design space. This would further improve the user experience since we would, again, be allowing the user to interact with the content itself rather than the user input elements.

> **Important Note**
> Additionally, to decrease the amount of unnecessary control elements and embellishments, the iOS and Windows platforms emphasize the use of calligraphy while creating content elements. When using font variations, the visual priority of certain content elements can be adjusted to provide the correct information. For instance, in the previous examples, the title of the element was created using a smaller font, thus emphasizing the description.

Platform imperatives

When dealing with cross-platform mobile applications, developers need to create applications that will satisfy multiple design surfaces, as well as guidelines for multiple operating systems and **idioms**. Platform imperatives refer to the platform guidelines that developers and designers need to find a compromise between to create a unified UI experience across platforms.

> **Important Note**
> An **idiom** is how the form factor is defined in Xamarin.Forms applications. It can be used to create specific views for various phone form factors, as well as for tablet, desktop, and TV, and even for design surfaces for wearables such as Tizen watches.

When dealing with different idioms, target device capabilities, design surfaces, and input methods should be taken into consideration.

To make the best use of the space available for web applications on desktop and mobile devices, developers often use responsive design techniques that can also be applied to Xamarin applications:

- **Fluid layout**: In a fluid layout, items are stacked in a horizontal list and can take up as many rows as required to list them, depending on the horizontal space available:

Figure 5.3 – Fluid Layout for Idioms

- **Orientation change**: Items listed in a horizontal list on a device with a wider screen can be stacked vertically on devices with smaller screens with a greater height relative to the width.
- **Restructure**: The general layout for the elements can be completely restructured according to the available space. For instance, a view can use three segments in a horizontal setup in landscape mode, whereas in portrait mode, two of these segments can be merged into one:

Figure 5.4 – Restructuring UI Elements for Idioms

- **Resize**: Rich media content elements, as well as text content, can be resized to make the best use of the design space available:

Figure 5.5 – Resizing UI Elements for Idioms

Additionally, as we mentioned previously, device capabilities can play a big role in how an application should react to user input. For instance, the hardware back button is a nice example of this design consideration. If we were designing a mobile application that targeted the Android, iOS, and UWP platforms, we would need to remember that only Android offers a hardware or software back button. This capability, or lack of it on other platforms, makes it crucial to include a back navigation element on a second-tier application view. Similarly, if we were designing an application to be used on mobile devices (let's say, on iOS and Android), but at the same time the application should run on TVs with Tizen or Android operating systems, the input method and how the user navigates through the screens would become a crucial design factor.

Development cost

Finally, technical feasibility is another important aspect of objectively analyzing the design requirements of an application. In some cases, the development costs of creating a custom control to mimic a web application outweighs the business or platform value that's added to the native counterpart of the same application.

Each mobile platform that Xamarin and Xamarin.Forms target offers a different user experience and a different set of controls. Xamarin.Forms creates an abstraction on top of this set of native controls so that the same abstraction is rendered using native views on a specific platform. In this context, trying to introduce new design elements or customize controls that are inherently different in appearance but behave like each other can have costly repercussions.

For instance, if the web counterpart of the application uses a checkbox for a certain preference, the mobile view to use in this case would be a toggle switch. Insisting on a checkbox would mean additional development hours, as well as an undesirable user experience on the target platform. Similarly, using checkboxes for (multi) selection rather than highlighting the selected content can lead to UX degradation for the specific mobile platform and platform users.

As you can see, there are several factors to consider while designing the application layout. These UX factors should all be kept in mind while you're working out a design. In other words, mobile application UX design is not simply shrinking what an application could have on web or desktop platforms. So far, we have looked at the consumer's expectations of the application, the platform imperatives, and the development costs. Finding an optimum compromise between these factors can provide a desirable application to all stakeholders. Nevertheless, the application design decisions do not end here. In the next section, we will demonstrate different navigation strategies in mobile applications.

Implementing navigation structure

One of the main decisions to make before starting development is to decide on the navigation hierarchy of your application. Generally, this decision should have been taken care of during the UX design phase.

According to the requirements and target audience of your application, the navigation hierarchy can be designed in different ways. Some of these navigation strategies can be summarized as follows:

- Single-page view
- Simple navigation
- Multi-page views
- Master/detail view

Let's get started!

Single-page view

In a single-page view, as the name suggests, a single view is used for the content and possible user interaction, and actions are either executed on this view or on action sheets. Depending on the design requirements, this view can be implemented using a single-page implementation such as `ContentPage` or `TemplatedPage`:

Figure 5.6 – Xamarin.Forms Page Types

`ContentPage` is among the most commonly used page definitions. Using this page structure, developers are free to include any layout and view elements within the content definition of a content page.

Now, let's extend the requirements for our sample application with the following user story:

"As a user, I would like to have a list of items that have recently been added to the store, so that I can easily be informed of new products."

To implement this requirement, we will modify the `MainPage` in our application and add our list view to this page using the following steps:

1. Open the `ShopAcross` solution and create a new content page called `HomeView` (use the **Forms ContentPage XAML** template):

2. Open the `App.xaml.cs` file and modify the constructor by setting `MainPage` to a new instance of `HomeView`:

    ```
    public App()
    {
        InitializeComponent();
        MainPage = new HomeView();
    }
    ```

3. Before adding the list view and the related content items, let's designate the content area and the list context-related action items toolbar:

    ```xml
    <?xml version="1.0" encoding="UTF-8"?>
    <ContentPage Title="Home"
        xmlns="http://xamarin.com/schemas/2014/forms"
        xmlns:x="http://schemas.microsoft.com/winfx/2009/xaml"
        x:Class="ShopAcross.Mobile.Client.HomeView">
        <ContentPage.ToolbarItems>
            <!-- Removed for brevity -->
        </ContentPage.ToolbarItems>
        <ContentPage.Content>
            <!-- Removed for brevity -->
        </ContentPage.Content>
    </ContentPage>
    ```

Here, the content containers that are being used are the `Content` and `Toolbar` items. These will be used to create a list view of items and the toolbar action buttons, respectively.

4. Now, let's add our list view with an empty template. Use `ContentPage.Content` to insert our `ListView`:

```xml
<ListView ItemsSource="{Binding RecentProducts}"
    SeparatorVisibility="None">
    <ListView.ItemTemplate>
        <DataTemplate>
            <ViewCell>
                <!-- TODO -->
            </ViewCell>
        </DataTemplate>
    </ListView.ItemTemplate>
</ListView>
```

5. Now, insert the `ViewCell` definition for the list view items:

```xml
<ViewCell>
    <Grid>
        <Grid.RowDefinitions>
            <RowDefinition />
            <RowDefinition />
        </Grid.RowDefinitions>
        <Grid.ColumnDefinitions>
            <ColumnDefinition Width="60" />
            <ColumnDefinition Width="Auto" />
        </Grid.ColumnDefinitions>
        <Image
            Grid.RowSpan="2" Grid.Column="0" Margin="5,5"
            Source="{Binding Image}" />
        <Label
            Grid.Row="0" Grid.Column="1" Font="Small"
            Text="{Binding Title}"
            VerticalTextAlignment="End" />
        <Label
            Grid.Row="1" Grid.Column="1"
            Text="{Binding Description}"
            VerticalTextAlignment="Start" />
    </Grid>
```

```xml
        <ViewCell.ContextActions>
            <ToolbarItem Text="Edit" />
            <ToolbarItem IsDestructive="true" Text="Delete" />
        </ViewCell.ContextActions>
</ViewCell>
```

6. At this stage, the application will not work because of the missing bindings and binding context. In order to remedy this, let's create a base binding data object (that is, `BaseBindableObject`) in the `ShopAcross.Mobile.Core` project:

```csharp
public class BaseBindableObject : INotifyPropertyChanged
{
    public event PropertyChangedEventHandler PropertyChanged;

    protected void SendPropertyChanged([CallerMemberName] string propertyName = null)
    {
        PropertyChanged?.Invoke(this, new PropertyChangedEventArgs(propertyName));
    }
}
```

7. Now, copy and paste the following code into a view model class (that is, `ProductViewModel`) in the core project:

```csharp
public class ProductViewModel : BaseBindableObject
{
    public string Title { get; set; }

    public string Description { get; set; }

    public string Image { get; set; }
}
```

8. We can now add the view model for `HomeView` to the `HomeViewModel` class:

```csharp
public class HomeViewModel: BaseBindableObject
{
    public HomeViewModel()
    {
        RecentProducts = new ObservableCollection<ProductViewModel>(GetRecentProducts());
    }

    public ObservableCollection<ProductViewModel> RecentProducts { get; } = new ObservableCollection<ProductViewModel>();

    public IEnumerable<ProductViewModel> GetRecentProducts()
    {
        yield return new ProductViewModel {
            Title = "First Item",
            Description = "First Item short description",
            Image = "https://picsum.photos/800?image=0"
        };

        //... Removed for brevity
    }
}
```

9. Finally, create a new instance of `HomeViewModel` and assign it to the `BindingContext` class of `HomeView`:

```csharp
public HomeView()
{
    InitializeComponent();
    BindingContext = new HomeViewModel();
}
```

Now, running the application will result in a content page displaying the list view using the defined item template.

ContentPage is a derivative of TemplatedPage, which is another page type that can be used with Xamarin.Forms applications. TemplatedPage allows developers to create a base style for TemplatePage (that is, ContentPage) so that certain global-level customizations can be applied to these pages.

For instance, in order to expand our previous implementation with a footer, we can follow these steps:

1. First, define a style for this page (in App.xaml):

    ```xml
    <Application.Resources>
        <ResourceDictionary>
            <ControlTemplate x:Key="PageTemplate">
                <Grid>
                    <Grid.RowDefinitions>
                        <RowDefinition />
                        <RowDefinition Height="25" />
                    </Grid.RowDefinitions>
                    <Grid.ColumnDefinitions>
                        <ColumnDefinition />
                    </Grid.ColumnDefinitions>
                    <ContentPresenter Grid.Row="0" />
                    <BoxView Grid.Row="1" Color="Navy" />
                    <Label
                        Grid.Row="1"
                        Margin="10,0,0,0"
                        Text="(c) Hands-On Cross Platform 2020"
                        TextColor="White"
                        VerticalOptions="Center" />
                </Grid>
            </ControlTemplate>
        </ResourceDictionary>
    </Application.Resources>
    ```

    In this template, notice that ContentPresenter is used as the placeholder for ContentPage.

2. Now, we can use this template in the `HomeView` page with the following code:

```xml
<ContentPage
    xmlns="http://xamarin.com/schemas/2014/forms"
    xmlns:x="http://schemas.microsoft.com/winfx/2009/xaml"
    ControlTemplate="{StaticResource PageTemplate}"
    x:Class="ShopAcross.Mobile.Client.HomeView">
```

This will result in the footer appearing on our `HomeView`:

Figure 5.7 – HomeView

So far, we have only created the main page of our application as a content page. However, we have already implemented the basic structure to continue introducing additional views and view-models. Now, let's learn how to navigate to and from our views.

Simple navigation

Within the Xamarin ecosystem, each platform has its own intrinsic navigation stack and applications are built around those stacks. Developers are responsible for maintaining these stacks in order to create the desired UX flow for users.

To navigate between pages, Xamarin.Forms exposes a `Navigation` service, which can be used together with the `NavigationPage` abstract page implementation. In other words, `NavigationPage` cannot be categorized as a page type to provide content for users; however, it is a crucial component used to maintain the navigation stack, as well as the navigation bar, within Xamarin.Forms applications.

In the previous section, we created our `HomeView`, which displays a list of recently added products. To demonstrate some simple navigation methods, let's consider the following user story:

"As a user, I would like to be able to open the details of a recently added product from the home page, so that I can get additional information about the selected product."

To display the product's details, we need to introduce our product details view. Follow these steps:

1. Let's start by creating another XAML-based `ContentPage` in the `ShopAccross.Mobile.Client` project called `ProductDetailsView`.

2. Now, add the following content to the **Content** Section:

    ```xml
    <StackLayout Padding="10" Orientation="Vertical" Spacing="10">
        <Label Text="{Binding Title, Mode=OneTime}" FontSize="Large" />
        <Image Source="{Binding Image}" HorizontalOptions="FillAndExpand" />
        <Label Text="{Binding Description}" FontSize="Large" />
    </StackLayout>
    ```

3. Now that we have a basic `ProductDetailsView` ready, we can navigate from `HomeView` to `ProductDetailsView`. To create a navigation element, let's introduce a navigation page as our main page with the root element set to `HomeView`:

    ```csharp
    public App()
    {
        InitializeComponent();
        MainPage = new NavigationPage(new HomeView());
    }
    ```

4. Now, add the following method to `HomeView.xaml.cs`:

   ```
   private void Handle_ItemTapped(object sender,
   ItemTappedEventArgs e)
   {
       var itemView = new ProductDeatilsView();
       itemView.BindingContext = e.Item;
       Navigation.PushAsync(itemView);
   }
   ```

5. Finally, add the event handler to `HomeView.xaml` to navigate to a product's details when the respective item is tapped:

   ```
   <ListView ItemTapped="Handle_ItemTapped"
   ItemsSource="{Binding RecentProducts}"    >
   ```

In this example, we are navigating from `HomeView` to `ProductDetailsView`. After this navigation, on iOS, you will notice that the title of the first page is inserted as back-button text in the navigation bar. Additionally, since the `Title` property is used for `HomeView`, the text is also displayed in the navigation bar.

Prior to Xamarin.Forms 3.2, the only way to customize what and how the navigation bar was displayed was using some form of native customization (for example, a custom renderer for `NavigationPage`). Nevertheless, you can now add custom elements to the navigation bar using the `TitleView` dependency property of a navigation page.

Using the `HomeView` page as an example, we can add the following XAML section to our `ContentPage`:

```
<NavigationPage.TitleView>
    <StackLayout Orientation="Horizontal"
VerticalOptions="Center" Spacing="10">
        <Image Source="xamarin.png"/>
        <Label
            Text="Custom Title View"
            FontSize="16"
            TextColor="Black"
            VerticalTextAlignment="Center" />
    </StackLayout>
</NavigationPage.TitleView>
```

For the `xamarin.png` file to be available for the application you will need to add it to the `Resources` folder on iOS and the `resources/drawable` folder on Android.

The resulting view will have the defined `StackLayout` instead of the `Home` title that was previously displayed:

Figure 5.8 – Custom Navigation Page Title

Even though this customization slightly compromises the native behavior for navigation, in certain scenarios, the compromise could be justified; for instance, having a search box on the title view is a prominent pattern on Android applications.

In this section, we added one more tier to our navigation hierarchy and implemented the navigation functionality between these tiers. So far, we have only used `ContentPage` as the base for our views. There are, however, certain templates that can host multiple pages.

Multi-page views

`CarouselPage` and `TabbedPage` are two Xamarin.Forms page implementations that derive from the `MultiPage` abstraction. These pages can both host multiple pages with unique navigation between them.

To illustrate the usage of `MultiPage` implementations, we can use the following user story:

"As a user, I would like to have a stream of product details for recent products where I can easily browse through them using a swipe gesture, so that I can reach various products, details easily rather than selecting one from the list view."

In this implementation, we will utilize the previously created `HomeView` and `HomeViewModel`. Without further ado, let's start the implementation:

1. We will start the implementation by creating a `CarouselPage`. We can use the XAML-based **Content Page** template as a starting point. Let's name this page `RecentProductsView`.

2. Now that the page has been created, you can use the following XAML content to define different products from the recent products list as binding contexts for multiple children of this page:

   ```xml
   <?xml version="1.0" encoding="UTF-8"?>
   <CarouselPage
           xmlns="http://xamarin.com/schemas/2014/forms"
           xmlns:x="http://schemas.microsoft.com/winfx/2009/xaml"
           xmlns:local="using:ShopAcross.Mobile.Client"
           x:Class="ShopAcross.Mobile.Client.RecentProductsView">
       <CarouselPage.Children>
           <local:ProductDetailsView BindingContext="{Binding RecentProducts[0]}" Title="First" Icon="xamarin.png"/>
           <local:ProductDetailsView BindingContext="{Binding RecentProducts[1]}" Title="Second" Icon="xamarin.png"/>
           <local:ProductDetailsView BindingContext="{Binding RecentProducts[2]}" Title="Third" Icon="xamarin.png"/>
       </CarouselPage.Children>
   </CarouselPage>
   ```

3. We will also need to change the class declaration to derive from `CarouselPage` rather than `ContentPage`:

   ```
   public partial class RecentProductsView : CarouselPage
   {
   }
   ```

4. Then, we need to assign a new instance of `HomeViewModel` to `BindingContext` in the class constructor:

```
public RecentProductsView()
{
    InitializeComponent();
    BindingContext = new HomeViewModel();
}
```

5. Now that we have created `RecentProductsView`, we can add a navigation method to `HomeView`:

```
private void RecentItems_Clicked(object sender, EventArgs e)
{
    var recentProducts = new RecentProductsView();
    Navigation.PushAsync(recentProducts);
}
```

6. Finally, we can add the toolbar menu button to `HomeView`:

```
<ContentPage.ToolbarItems>
    <ToolbarItem Text="Recent" Clicked="RecentItems_Clicked" />
</ContentPage.ToolbarItems>
```

Now that we have the recent items page set, let's consider the following user story:

"As a registered user, I would like to have the option to set favorite categories so that when I am browsing through the recently added products, only the products from the categories I've selected are displayed."

For the user to select certain categories as their favorites, we will need to prepare a settings screen for the user. On this settings screen, we can display any personalization option. If we were implementing a single-page application, we could use a flyout to display this page, but for the sake of demonstrating the peer navigation and multi-page templates, let's use a tabbed page to introduce additional pages to our application.

Follow these steps to create `SettingsView` and add it as a peer to `HomeView`:

1. Before we create `TabbedPage`, we should introduce our `SettingsView`. Use the XAML-based `ContentPage` template to create a page named `SettingsView`.

2. Once the page has been created, add the following content:

   ```xml
   <ContentPage.Content>
       <StackLayout Orientation="Vertical" Padding="10">
           <Label Text="Selected Categories" FontSize="Title" />
           <ListView>
           </ListView>
       </StackLayout>
   </ContentPage.Content>
   ```

3. For the template, we will use a simple `Grid` with two columns:

   ```xml
   <ListView.ItemTemplate>
       <DataTemplate>
           <ViewCell>
               <Grid>
                   <Grid.ColumnDefinitions>
                       <ColumnDefinition Width="75" />
                       <ColumnDefinition />
                   </Grid.ColumnDefinitions>
                   <Switch Grid.Column="0" />
                   <Label Text="{Binding .}" Grid.Column="1"
                       VerticalTextAlignment="Center"
                       FontSize="Subtitle"/>
               </Grid>
           </ViewCell>
       </DataTemplate>
   </ListView.ItemTemplate>
   ```

4. For the content, we can use a set of arbitrary categories:

   ```xml
   <ListView.ItemsSource>
       <x:Array Type="{x:Type x:String}">
           <x:String>computers</x:String>
   ```

```xml
            <x:String>white furniture</x:String>
            <x:String>gadgets</x:String>
            <x:String>car electronics</x:String>
            <x:String>iot</x:String>
        </x:Array>
    </ListView.ItemsSource>
```

5. Now, add `RootTabbedView` using the *Forms* `TabbedPage` *XAML* template.
6. Now, add the following content to our root page:

```xml
<?xml version="1.0" encoding="utf-8"?>
<TabbedPage
    xmlns="http://xamarin.com/schemas/2014/forms"
    xmlns:x="http://schemas.microsoft.com/winfx/2009/xaml"
    xmlns:local="clr-namespace:ShopAcross.Mobile.Client"
    xmlns:core="clr-namespace:ShopAcross.Mobile.Core;assembly=ShopAcross.Mobile.Core"
    x:Class="ShopAcross.Mobile.Client.RootTabbedView">
    <TabbedPage.BindingContext>
        <core:HomeViewModel />
    </TabbedPage.BindingContext>
    <!--Pages can be added as references or inline-->
    <TabbedPage.Children>
        <NavigationPage Title="Home" Icon="xamarin.png">
            <x:Arguments>
                <local:HomeView BindingContext="{Binding .}" />
            </x:Arguments>
        </NavigationPage>
        <NavigationPage Title="Settings" Icon="xamarin.png">
            <x:Arguments>
                <local:SettingsView/>
            </x:Arguments>
        </NavigationPage>
    </TabbedPage.Children>
</TabbedPage>
```

7. Finally, change the `MainPage` assignment to the newly created one in `App.xaml.cs`.

The resulting page will, in fact, host the two children in their respective layout and navigation stacks. If you now click on the **Recent** toolbar action button, you will see how `CarouselPage` and `TabbedPage` are both used in the same application:

Figure 5.9 – Multi-Page Views

> **Important Information**
>
> It is important to note that, on iOS, the title and icon properties of children are used to create tabbed navigation items. For icons to display properly, the image that is used should be *30x30* for normal resolution, *60x60* for high resolution, and *90x90* for iPhone 6 resolution. On Android, the title is used to create tab items.

In particular, `TabbedPage` is one of the fundamental controls used in iOS applications at the top of the navigation hierarchy. The implementation of `TabbedPage` can be extended by creating a navigation stack for each of the tabs separately. This way, navigating between tabs preserves the navigation stack for each tab independently, with support for navigating back and forth.

In this section, we looked at multi-page views, which you can use to create a so-called peer-navigation structure. In particular, `TabbedPage` is the most prominent setup that's used as the top navigation tier in iOS applications. Another multi-page setup that's used as the root of the navigation stack where you need multiple pages to be accessible at the same time to the user is the master/detail setup. In the next section, we will be setting up a navigation flyout menu for our application.

Master/detail view

On Android and UWP, the prominent navigation pattern and the associated page type is master/detail, and is uses a so-called navigation drawer. In this pattern, jumping (across the different tiers of the hierarchy) or cross-navigating (within the same tier) across the navigation structure is maintained with `ContentPage`, which is known as the master page. User interaction with the master page, which is displayed in the navigation drawer, is propagated to the `Detail` view. In this setup, the navigation stack exists for the detail view, while the master view is static.

To replicate the tab structure in the previous example, we can create `MasterDetailPage`, which will host our list of menu items. `MasterDetailPage` will consist of the `Master` content page and the `Detail` page, which will host `NavigationPage` to create the navigation stack. Follow these steps to complete this setup:

1. We will start by creating our `MasterDetailPage` using the *Forms MasterDetailPage XAML* template. Use `RootView` as the name. This template should create three separate pages and me as part of the multi-page setup. For this exercise, we will not be using the `RootViewMaster` and `RootViewDetail` pages, nor the `RootViewMenuItem` class, so you can safely delete them.

2. Now, open the `RootView.xaml` file and add the following content to set up the master section:

```xml
<MasterDetailPage.Master>
    <ContentPage Title="Main" Padding="0,30,0,0"
        Icon="slideout.png">
        <StackLayout>
            <ListView
                x:Name="listView"
                ItemsSource="{Binding .}"
                SeparatorVisibility="None">
                <ListView.ItemTemplate>
```

```xml
            <DataTemplate>
                <ViewCell>
                    <Grid Padding="5,10">
                        <Grid.ColumnDefinitions>
                            <ColumnDefinition Width="30"/>
                            <ColumnDefinition Width="*" />
                        </Grid.ColumnDefinitions>
                        <Image Source="{Binding Icon}" />
                        <Label Grid.Column="1" Text="{Binding
                            Title}" />
                    </Grid>
                </ViewCell>
            </DataTemplate>
          </ListView.ItemTemplate>
        </ListView>
      </StackLayout>
    </ContentPage>
</MasterDetailPage.Master>
```

3. Notice that the `Master` page simply creates a `ListView` containing the menu item entries.

> **Important Note**
>
> It is also important to note that the so-called hamburger menu icon needs to be added as the `Icon` property for the `Master` page (see `slideout.png`); otherwise, the title of the master page will be used instead of the menu icon.

4. Add `slideout.png` to the `Resources` folder on iOS and the Resources/drawable folder on Android.

5. Next, we will create a simple data structure that will store our menu metadata. You can add the following class to a new file or the `RootView.xaml.cs` file:

```csharp
public class NavigationItem
{
    public int Id { get; set; }
    public string Title { get; set; }
```

```
    public string Icon { get; set; }
}
```

6. Now, we should create the list for the navigation. Add the following initialization code to the constructor in `RootView.xaml.cs`:

```
public RootView()
{
    InitializeComponent();
    var list = new List<NavigationItem>();
    list.Add(new NavigationItem { Id = 0, Title = "Home", Icon = "xamarin.png" });
    list.Add(new NavigationItem { Id = 1, Title = "Settings", Icon = "xamarin.png" });
    BindingContext = list;
}
```

7. The `Detail` page assignment will now look as follows:

```xml
<MasterDetailPage.Detail>
    <NavigationPage Title="List">
        <x:Arguments>
            <local:HomeView />
        </x:Arguments>
    </NavigationPage>
</MasterDetailPage.Detail>
```

At this point, running the application will create the navigation drawer and the contained `Master` page:

Figure 5.10 – Master/Detail View

8. To complete the implementation, we also need to handle the `ItemTapped` event from the master list:

```csharp
private void Handle_ItemTapped(object sender, ItemTappedEventArgs e)
{
    if(e.Item is NavigationItem item)
    {
        Page detailPage = null;

        if(item.Id == 1)
        {
            detailPage = new SettingsView();
        }
        else
        {
            detailPage = new HomeView();
        }

        this.Detail = new NavigationPage(detailPage);
```

```
            this.IsPresented = false;
        }
    }
```

Now, the implementation is complete. Every time a menu item is used, the navigation category is changed and a new navigation stack is created; however, within a navigation category, the navigation stack is intact. Also, note that the `IsPresented` property of `MasterDetailPage` is set to `false` to dismiss the master page immediately once a new detail view is created.

In this section, we started our implementation with a single-view application that was expanded by using adding multi-page views, as well as a navigation drawer. In these setups, we extensively used the `NavigationPage` and `NavigationService` implementations of Xamarin.Forms. In addition to this classic implementation, you can use Xamarin Shell in your application to decrease the complexity of setting up the navigation infrastructure. In the next section, we will take a quick look at how to use Xamarin Shell to create a similar application hierarchy.

Implementing Shell Navigation

In this section, we are going to use Xamarin Shell to demonstrate how it can make a developer's life easier. We will be implementing a simple Master/Detail view using Xamarin Shell.

In applications where the navigation hierarchy is more complex than a three-tier vertical and peer navigation, extensively using the navigation service, as well as the recreated views and view models, can cause maintainability and performance issues. Navigational links between pages on different tiers and peers can cause serious headaches for the development team in particular.

Xamarin Shell can help ease this complexity by introducing a layer between the navigational infrastructure and the Xamarin.Forms pages. The premise of `Shell` is to provide almost a web application-like route handling and templating infrastructure so that complex navigational links and multi-page views can be created with ease.

The simplest way to illustrate how Xamarin Shell works would be to recreate the application hierarchy that we created in the previous section. Follow these steps to convert the application so that it can use `Shell`:

1. We will start by adding a so-called `AppShell`. `AppShell` will be used to register the main routes of our application. To do this, create a new XAML-based content page named `AppShell`.

2. Once `AppShell` has been created, change the content of `AppShell.xaml` to the following:

   ```xaml
   <Shell
       xmlns="http://xamarin.com/schemas/2014/forms"
       xmlns:x="http://schemas.microsoft.com/winfx/2009/xaml"
       xmlns:local="clr-namespace:ShopAcross.Mobile.Client"
       x:Class="ShopAcross.Mobile.Client.AppShell">
       <FlyoutItem Title="Home" Icon="xamarin.png">
           <ShellContent ContentTemplate="{DataTemplate local:HomeView}"/>
       </FlyoutItem>
       <FlyoutItem Title="Settings" Icon="xamarin.png">
           <ShellContent ContentTemplate="{DataTemplate local:SettingsView}"/>
       </FlyoutItem>
   </Shell>
   ```

3. Now, let's change the base class definition in `AppShell.xaml.cs`:

   ```
   public partial class AppShell : Shell
   {
       public AppShell()
       {
           InitializeComponent();
       }
   }
   ```

We have now successfully created an `AppShell` with two flyout navigation items defined.

4. Next, let's introduce `AppShell` to our infrastructure by assigning it to `MainPage`:

```
public App()
{
    InitializeComponent();
    //MainPage = new RootView();
    MainPage = new AppShell();
}
```

Now, if you run the application, you will see that the master/detail setup is set up through `Shell`; you do not need to set up a list of items and handle different events to implement a stateful navigation menu.

Another important note is that after changing a setting on `SettingsView` (that is, toggle one of the categories) and navigating away and back to `SettingsView`, you will notice that `SettingsView` preserved its state. This can give you clues about how the stateful navigation is managed on Xamarin Shell.

Taking our implementation even further, let's introduce routes to our navigation menu items and use these routes within a view:

1. First, let's add the following routes to the defined `ShellContent` items in `AppShell.xaml`:

    ```
    <ShellContent Route="home" ContentTemplate="{DataTemplate local:HomeView}"/>
    <ShellContent Route="settings" ContentTemplate="{DataTemplate local:SettingsView}"/>
    ```

    Once these routes have been configured, we can use the Shell navigation to go to a certain navigation state.

2. Now, add a button to `SettingsView.xaml`:

    ```
    <Button Text="Back to Home" Clicked="Button_Clicked" />
    ```

3. Then, add the following method to `SettingsView.xaml.cs`:

    ```
    private async void Button_Clicked(object sender, EventArgs e)
    {
        await Shell.Current.GoToAsync("//home");
    }
    ```

Now, if you run the application, navigate to the settings view, and click on the button, the Shell should take you back to the home page.

The URI-based navigation infrastructure also allows navigation between tiers, as well as relative paths.

In this section, we tried to demonstrate the power of Xamarin Shell, at least for implementing a navigation hierarchy. Xamarin Shell provides other useful layouts, as well as functions such as search. We will look at these in the next section.

Using Xamarin.Forms and native controls

Now that we are more familiar with the different page types and navigation patterns, we can move on to creating the actual UI for our pages. In this section, we will be demonstrating various Xamarin.Forms elements and their usages, as well as how native controls can be used within Xamarin.Forms visual trees.

Creating a UX that is flexible enough for Xamarin target platforms can be dreadfully complicated, especially if the stakeholders involved are not familiar with the aforementioned UX design factors. Nevertheless, Xamarin.Forms offers various layouts and views that help developers find the optimal solution for a project's needs.

> **Important Note**
> In Xamarin.Forms, the visual tree is composed of three layers: pages, layouts, and views. Layouts are used as containers for views, which are the user controls for creating pages. These are the main interactive surfaces for users.

Let's take a closer look at the UI components.

Layouts

Layouts are container elements that are used to allocate user controls across a design surface. To satisfy platform imperatives, layouts can be used to align, stack, and position view elements. The different types of layouts are as follows:

- `StackLayout`: This is one of the most overused layout structures in Xamarin. Forms. It is used to stack various view and other layout elements with prescribed requirements. These requirements are defined through various dependency or instance properties, such as alignment options and dimension requests.

For instance, on the `ProductDetailsView` page, we used `StackLayout` to combine an item's `Image` with its respective title and description:

```xml
<StackLayout Padding="10" Orientation="Vertical">
    <Label Text="{Binding Title}" FontSize="Large" />
    <Image Source="{Binding Image}"
 HorizontalOptions="FillAndExpand"/>
    <Label Text="{Binding Description}" />
</StackLayout>
```

In this setup, the important declarations are `Orientation`, which defines that the stacking should occur vertically; `HorizontalOptions`, which is defined for the `Image` element, which allows `Image` to expand both horizontally and vertically, depending on the available space; and `StackLayout`, which can be employed to create orientation-change-responsive behavior.

- `FlexLayout`: This can be used to create fluid and flexible arrangements of view elements that can adapt to the available surface. `FlexLayout` has many available directives that developers can use to define alignment directions. In order to demonstrate just a few of these, let's assume `ProductDetailsView` requires an implementation of a horizontal layout, where certain features are listed in a floating stack that can be wrapped into as many rows as required:

```xml
 <StackLayout Padding="10" Orientation="Vertical"
 Spacing="10">
    <Label Text="{Binding Title}" FontSize="Large" />
    <Image Source="{Binding Image}"
 HorizontalOptions="FillAndExpand" />
    <FlexLayout Direction="Row" Wrap="Wrap">
        <Label Text="Feature 1" Margin="4"
 VerticalTextAlignment="Center" BackgroundColor="Gray" />
        <Label Text="Feat. 2" Margin="4"
 VerticalTextAlignment="Center" BackgroundColor="Lime"/>
        <!-- Additional Labels -->
    </FlexLayout>
    <Label Text="{Binding Description}" />
 </StackLayout>
```

This would create a design structure similar to the one described in the fluid layout responsive UI pattern:

Figure 5.11 – Flex Layout

- `Grid`: If it is not desired for the views in a layout to expand and trigger layout cycles – in other words, if a certain page requires a more top-down layout structure (that is, with the parent element determining the layout) – then `Grid` would be the most suitable control. Using the `Grid` layout, controls can be laid out in accordance with column and row definitions, which can be adjusted to respond to control size changes or the overall size of `Grid`.

While creating the control template for our page, we used a `Grid` to create a rigid structure so that we could place the footer with an absolute height value, while allowing the rest of the screen to be covered by the content presenter:

```xml
<ControlTemplate x:Key="PageTemplate">
    <Grid>
        <Grid.RowDefinitions>
            <RowDefinition />
            <RowDefinition Height="25" />
        </Grid.RowDefinitions>
        <Grid.ColumnDefinitions>
            <ColumnDefinition />
        </Grid.ColumnDefinitions>
        <ContentPresenter Grid.Row="0" />
        <BoxView Grid.Row="1" Color="Navy" />
        <Label Grid.Row="1" Margin="10,0,0,0" Text="(c) Hands-On
                Cross Platform 2018" TextColor="White"
                VerticalOptions="Center" />
    </Grid>
</ControlTemplate>
```

Note that we used a margin value for the label. To avoid using the margin, we could have created a column definition with a fixed value and, according to the desired outcome, set that margin column so that it applied to the content presenter as well:

```
<Grid>
    <Grid.RowDefinitions>
        <RowDefinition />
        <RowDefinition Height="25" />
    </Grid.RowDefinitions>
    <Grid.ColumnDefinitions>
        <ColumnDefinition Width="10" />
        <ColumnDefinition />
        <ColumnDefinition Width="10" />
    </Grid.ColumnDefinitions>
    <ContentPresenter Grid.Column="1" Grid.Row="0" />
    <BoxView Grid.Row="1" Grid.ColumnSpan="3" Color="Navy" />
    <Label Grid.Row="1" Grid.Column="1" Text="(c) Hands-On Cross
    Platform 2018" TextColor="White" VerticalOptions="Center" />
</Grid>
```

With this set up, `BoxView` will expand on three columns, while the footer text and the actual content will be isolated to the second column, Column-1, with Column-0 and Column-2 acting as the margins.

`Grid` can also be used to structure a certain segment of a view. For instance, if we were to add a specifications section to our `ProductDetailsView` page, it would look similar to the following:

```
<StackLayout Padding="10" Orientation="Vertical"
Spacing="10">
    <!-- Removed for Brevity -->
    <Label Text="{Binding Description}" />
    <Label Text="Specifications" Font="Bold" />
    <Grid>
        <Grid.RowDefinitions>
            <RowDefinition Height="Auto"/>
            <RowDefinition Height="Auto"/>
```

```xml
                <RowDefinition Height="Auto"/>
                <RowDefinition Height="Auto"/>
                <RowDefinition Height="Auto"/>
            </Grid.RowDefinitions>
            <Grid.ColumnDefinitions>
                <ColumnDefinition Width="3*" />
                <ColumnDefinition Width="5*" />
            </Grid.ColumnDefinitions>
            <Label Text="Specification 1"
                Grid.Column="0" Grid.Row="0"/>
            <Label Text="Value for Specification"
                Grid.Column="1" Grid.Row="0"
    TextColor="Gray"/>
            <Label Text="Another Spec."
                Grid.Column="0" Grid.Row="1" />
            <Label Text="Value for Specification that is a little
                longer"
                Grid.Column="1" Grid.Row="1"
    TextColor="Gray"/>
            <!-- Additional Specs go here -->
        </Grid>
    </StackLayout>
```

Notice the columns are set to use 3/8th and 5/8th of the screen to result in the optimal use of the space available. This would create a view similar to the following:

Figure 5.12 – Grid Layout

After adding this last element to the screen, you might notice that the screen space is exhausted vertically, so the final grid element might overflow out of the view port, depending on the screen size.

- `ScrollView`: To get the screen to scroll so that all the content is visible to the user, we can introduce `ScrollView`. `ScrollView` is another prominent layout element and acts as a scrollable container for the contained view elements.

  In order to enable the scrolling of the screen so that all the specifications are visible, we can simply wrap the main layout in `ProductDetailsView.xaml` in a `ScrollView`:

  ```
  <ContentPage.Content>
      <ScrollView>
          <StackLayout Padding="10" Orientation="Vertical"
            Spacing="10">
              <!-- Removed for brevity -->
          </StackLayout>
      </ScrollView>
  </ContentPage.Content>
  ```

  An additional use of `ScrollView` comes into the picture when `Entry` fields are involved. When the user taps on an `Entry` field, the behavior on a mobile device is that the keyboard slides up from the bottom of the screen, creating a vertical offset and decreasing the design space. In the view that `Entry` is contained in, the keyboard might overlap with the `Entry` field that is currently in focus. This would create an undesirable user experience. To remedy this behavior, the form content should be placed in `ScrollView` so that the appearance of the keyboard does not push the `Entry` field in question out of bounds of the screen.

- `AbsoluteLayout` and `RelativeLayout`: These are the other layout options that we have not covered so far. Both these layouts, generally speaking, treat the view almost like a canvas and allow items to be placed on top of each other, using either the current screen (in the case of `AbsoluteLayout`) or the other controls (in the case of `RelativeLayout`) as a reference for positioning.

For instance, if we were to place a **floating action button** (**FAB**) from Material Design on our `HomeView`, we could easily achieve that using an absolute layout by placing the button in the bottom-right corner of the screen (that is, position proportional) and adding a margin to our FAB:

```xml
<AbsoluteLayout>
    <ListView
        ItemsSource="{Binding Items}"
        ItemTapped="Handle_ItemTapped"
        SeparatorVisibility="None" >
        <ListView.ItemTemplate>
            <DataTemplate>
                <!-- Removed for brevity -->
            </DataTemplate>
        </ListView.ItemTemplate>
    </ListView>
    <Image
    Source="AddIcon.png"
    HeightRequest="60"
    WidthRequest="60"
    AbsoluteLayout.LayoutFlags="PositionProportional"
    AbsoluteLayout.LayoutBounds="1.0,1.0"
    Margin="10"/>
</AbsoluteLayout>
```

This would create a view where the FAB (that is, the image used instead of a FAB) is displayed over the list view items:

Figure 5.13 – Relative Layout

Additionally, `RelativeLayout`, in a similar fashion, allows developers to create proportional calculations between elements, as well as for the view itself.

Xamarin.Forms view elements

The main view elements we've used in our application so far have been `Label` and `Image` (while creating the list and details views). Additionally, on the login screen, we used the `Entry` and `Button` views. The main difference between these two sets of controls is the fact that, while `Label` and `Image` are used to display (generally) read-only content, `Entry` and `Button` are elements that are used for user input.

If we take a closer look at `Label`, we'll see that various properties are used to create a customized display for text content to accentuate the calligraphy/typography (referring to the platform imperatives of iOS and UWP) in our design. Developers can not only customize the look and feel of the text content, but also create rich text content using `Span` elements. Spans are analogous to `Run` elements in WPF and web elements that share the same name (that is, `Span`). In later versions of Xamarin.Forms, `Span` can recognize gestures, enabling developers to create interactive regions within a single block of text content. To utilize Spans, we can use the `FormattedText` attribute of the label.

To further customize (and perhaps apply branding to) an application, custom fonts can also be introduced. When it comes to including a custom font, each platform requires a different step to be executed.

As a first step, the developer needs to have access to the TFF file for the font, and this file needs to be copied to the platform-specific projects. On iOS, the file(s) need to be set as `BundleResource`, and on Android as `AndroidAsset`. On iOS only, custom fonts should be declared as part of the fonts provided by the application entry in the `Info.plist` file:

Figure 5.14 – Bundle Resources

At this point, the custom font we've already used can be added to the target label with the `FontFamily` attribute; however, the declarations for the font family differ for Android and iOS:

```xml
<Label Text="{Binding Description}">
    <Label.FontFamily>
        <OnPlatform x:TypeArguments="x:String">
            <On Platform="iOS" Value="Ubuntu-Light" />
            <On Platform="Android" Value="Ubuntu-Light.ttf#Ubuntu-Light" />
            <On Platform="UWP" Value="Assets/Fonts/Ubuntu-Light.ttf#Ubuntu-Light" />
        </OnPlatform>
    </Label.FontFamily>
</Label>
```

To make it easier to use the font or even apply it to all the labels in the application, the `App.xaml` file can be used. This will add it to the application's resources:

```xml
<Application.Resources>
    <ResourceDictionary>
        <!-- Removed for brevity -->
        <OnPlatform x:Key="UbuntuBold" x:TypeArguments="x:String">
            <On Platform="iOS">Ubuntu-Bold</On>
            <On Platform="Android">Ubuntu-Bold.ttf#Ubuntu-Bold</On>
        </OnPlatform>
        <OnPlatform x:Key="UbuntuItalic" x:TypeArguments="x:String">
            <On Platform="iOS">Ubuntu-Italic</On>
            <On Platform="Android">Ubuntu-Italic.ttf#Ubuntu-Italic</On>
        </OnPlatform>

        <!-- Additional Fonts and Styles -->
    </ResourceDictionary>
</Application.Resources>
```

Now, we can define either implicit or explicit styles for certain targets:

```xml
<Style x:Key="BoldLabelStyle" TargetType="Label">
    <Setter Property="FontFamily" Value="{StaticResource UbuntuBold}" />
</Style>
<!-- Or an implicit style for all labels -->
<!--
<Style TargetType="Label">
    <Setter Property="FontFamily" Value="{StaticResource UbuntuRegular}" />
</Style>
-->
```

> **Important Information**
>
> This can be taken one step further to include a font that includes glyphs (for example, `FontAwesome`) so that we can use labels as menu icons. A simple implementation would be to create a custom control that derives from `Label` and set up a global implicit style that targets this custom control.

The interactive counterparts of `Label` are `Entry` and `Editor`, both of which derive from the `InputView` abstraction. These controls can be placed in user forms to handle single-line or multi-line text input, respectively. To improve the user experience, both these controls expose the `Keyboard` property, which can be used to set the appropriate type of software keyboard for user entries (for example, `Chat`, `Default`, `Email`, `Numeric`, `Telephone`, and so on).

The rest of the user input controls are more scenario-specific, such as `BoxView`, `Slider`, `Map`, and `WebView`.

It is also important to mention that there are three additional user input controls, namely `Picker`, `DatePicker`, and `TimePicker`. These pickers represent the combination of the data field that is displayed on the form and the picker dialog that's used once the data field comes into focus.

If customizing these controls does not satisfy the UX requirements, Xamarin.Forms allows developers to reference and use native controls.

Native components

In some cases, developers need to resort to using native user controls – especially when a certain control only exists for a certain platform (that is, no Xamarin.Forms abstraction exists for that specific UI element). In these types of situations, Xamarin enables users to declare native views within Xamarin.Forms XAML and set/bind the properties of these controls.

To include native views, first, the namespaces for the native views must be declared:

```
xmlns:ios="clr-namespace:UIKit;assembly=Xamarin.
iOS;targetPlatform=iOS"
xmlns:androidWidget="clr-namespace:Android.
Widget;assembly=Mono.Android;targetPlatform=Android"
xmlns:formsandroid="clr-namespace:Xamarin.
Forms;assembly=Xamarin.Forms.Platform.
Android;targetPlatform=Android"
```

Once the namespace has been declared, we can, for instance, replace `Label` in our `ItemView.xaml` and use its native counterpart directly:

```
<!-- <Label Text="{Binding Description}" /> -->
<ios:UILabel Text="{Binding Description}" View.
HorizontalOptions="Start"/>
<androidWidget:TextView Text="{Binding Description}"
x:Arguments="{x:Static formsandroid:Forms.Context}" />
```

Now, the view will include a different native control for each platform. Additionally, the `UILabel.Text` and `TextView.Text` properties now carry the binding to the `Description` field.

> **Important Note**
> It is important to note that, for native view references to work, the view in question should not be included in `XamlCompilation`. In other words, the view should carry the `[XamlCompilation(XamlCompilationOptions.Skip)]` attribute.

It is also possible to further customize the native fields using native types and properties. For instance, to add a drop shadow to the `UILabel` item, we can use the `ShadowColor` and `ShadowOffset` values:

```xml
<ios:UILabel
    Text="{Binding Description}"
    View.HorizontalOptions="Start"
    ShadowColor="{x:Static ios:UIColor.Gray}">
        <ios:UILabel.ShadowOffset>
            <iosGraphics:CGSize>
                <x:Arguments>
                    <x:Single>1</x:Single>
                    <x:Single>2</x:Single>
                </x:Arguments>
            </iosGraphics:CGSize>
        </ios:UILabel.ShadowOffset>
</ios:UILabel>
```

The outcome of this declaration is as follows (compare this to the Xamarin.Forms `Label` field we defined earlier):

Figure 5.15 – Native Properties

With that, we have completed this implementation. In this section, we extended our sample application with additional view elements and basic layouts. As you have seen, these out-of-the-box layouts and views provide developers with simple customization options. Now that we have a basic UI, let's take a closer look at how we can introduce domain data to these UI elements. In the next section, we will deal with data-driven views.

Creating data-driven views

The MVVM architecture, as you saw in *Chapter 4, Developing Mobile Applications with Xamarin*, mainly concentrates on data and how to decouple data from views. However, this decoupling does not mean the views and controls that are created should not respond to data content changes, either as a result of user input or state data being updated. In order to facilitate the propagation of data models, from the view model to the view, as well as between views, data bindings, and other data-related Xamarin.Forms mechanisms are crucial tools.

In this section, we are going to demonstrate various features that allow us, as developers, to retrieve, transform, and update the domain data without directly referencing these data points. First, we will revise our knowledge about data binding fundamentals. We will then move on to value converters and how we can use them in conjunction with data bindings. We will also look at data triggers and visual state, as well as how data can drive changes on the UI and impose certain behaviors on view elements.

Data binding essentials

The simplest data binding in Xamarin.Forms comprises the path of the property we want to link to the current view property. In this type of declaration, we assume that the `BindingContext` class of the whole and/or the parent view is set to use the target source view model.

If we look at the navigation implementation from our `HomeView` to `ProductDetailsView`, you will notice that the selected item from the list is set as the binding context for `ProductDetailsView`:

```
private void Handle_ItemTapped(object sender, Xamarin.Forms.ItemTappedEventArgs e)
{
    var itemView = new ProductDetailsView();
    itemView.BindingContext = e.Item;
    Navigation.PushAsync(itemView);
}
```

Once `BindingContext` has been set, we can move on to using the property model of `ProductViewModel`, given that `ProductViewModel` is set to trigger `PropertyChangedEvent` (from `INotifyPropertyChanged`) for the `Title` property:

```
<Label Text="{Binding Title}" FontSize="Large" />
```

Data binding does not always need to be related to a value property (for example, `Text`, `SelectedItem`, and so on); it can also be used to identify the visual properties of a view.

For instance, the chips that we previously added to `ProductDetailsView` define whether certain features are supported for the currently selected item. Let's assume that we have Boolean properties on the view model side to show or hide these values. The bindings would look similar to the following:

```xml
<Label x:Name="Feat1" Text="Feature 1" IsVisible="{Binding HasFeature1}" BackgroundColor="Gray" />
  <Label x:Name="Feat2" Text="Feat. 2" IsVisible="{Binding HasFeature2}" BackgroundColor="Lime"/>
```

In both these binding scenarios, we are binding a value from the view model to a specific view element. Another valid scenario is where the change of view affects another view (that is, View-to-View binding). Let's assume that, on `ProductDetailsView`, the visibility of our specs depends on the visibility of the label, with `x:Name` set to `Feat1`:

```xml
<Grid IsVisible="{Binding Path=IsVisible,Source={x:Reference Feat1}}">
```

It is important to note that, in a real-world project, the View-to-View binding would generally be utilized to reflect the user input in one view on another view. In this example, it would be much more appropriate for the binding to use the same view model property (that is, `HasFeature1`).

The bindings we have outlined so far do not really depend on any change being reflected in the UI once the visual tree has been created. In such a setup, it would be an avoidable performance compromise to listen for any change event on the view model properties. To remedy this overhead, we could have set the binding mode to `OneTime`:

```xml
<Label Text="{Binding Title, Mode=OneTime}" FontSize="Large" />
```

This way, the binding is only executed when `BindingContext` changes. If we wanted the changes in `ViewModel` (generally referred to as the source) to be reflected in `View` (referred to as the target), we could have used `OneWay` binding. If the direction of this unidirectional data flow provided by the `OneWay` binding is the other way round, we could also utilize `OneWayToSource`. `TwoWay` bindings provide an infrastructure that supports the bi-directional flow of data.

Although the runtime tries to convert the source type into the target type while establishing a binding, the outcome might not always be desirable (for example, the `ToString` method of a different type might not provide the correct display value). In these types of situations, developers can resort to using value converters.

Value converters

Value converters can be described as simple translation tools that implement the `IValueConverter` interface. This interface provides two methods, which allow us to translate the source to the target, as well as translate from the target to the source, to support various binding scenarios.

For instance, if we were to display the release date of an item from our inventory, we would need to bind to the respective property on `ProductViewModel`. However, once the page has been rendered, the result is less than satisfactory:

Figure 5.16 – Full Date Format Displayed

To format the date, we can create a value converter, which is responsible for converting the `DateTime` value into a string:

```
public class DateFormatConverter : IValueConverter
{
    public object Convert(object value, Type targetType, object
        parameter, CultureInfo culture)
    {
        if(value is DateTime date)
        {
            return date.ToShortDateString();
        }

        return null;
    }

    public object ConvertBack(object value, Type targetType,
```

```
object
    parameter, CultureInfo culture)
    {
        // No Need to implement ConvertBack for OneTime and
OneWay bindings.
        throw new NotImplementedException();
    }
}
```

It is also responsible for declaring this converter in our `ProductDetailsView` XAML:

```xml
<ContentPage
    ...
    xmlns:converters="using:FirstXamarinFormsApplication.Client.Converters"
    x:Class="FirstXamarinFormsApplication.Client.ItemView">
    <ContentPage.Resources>
        <ResourceDictionary>
            <converters:DateFormatConverter x:Key="DateFormatConverter" />
        </ResourceDictionary>
    </ContentPage.Resources>
    <ContentPage.Content>
        <!-- Removed for brevity -->
        <Label Text="{Binding ReleaseDate, Converter={StaticResource DateFormatConverter}}" />
        <!-- Removed for brevity -->
    </ContentPage.Content>
</ContentPage>
```

Now, the display will use the short date format, which is culture-dependent (for example, `M/d/yyyy` for the EN-US region):

Figure 5.17 – Formatted Date Display

We can take this implementation one step further by using a binding to pass the date format string (for example, `M/d/yyyy`) to use a fixed date format.

Xamarin.Forms also provides the use of formatted strings to handle simple string conversions, so that simple converters such as `DateFormatConverter` can be avoided. The same implementation with a fixed date format could have been set up as follows:

```
<Label Text="{Binding ReleaseDate, StringFormat='Release {0:M/d/yyyy}'}" />
```

The outcome would look like this:

Figure 5.18 – String Format Example

Additionally, we may like to handle scenarios where the release date is set to null (that is, when the `ReleaseDate` property is set to `Nullable<DateTime>` or simply `DateTime`). For this scenario, we can resort to using `TargetNullValue`:

```
<Label Text="{Binding ReleaseDate, StringFormat='Release {0:M/d/yyyy}', TargetNullValue='Release Unknown'}" />
```

`TargetNullValue`, as the name suggests, is a replacement value when the binding target has been resolved but the value that was found is null. Similarly, `FallbackValue` can be used when the runtime cannot resolve the target property on the binding context.

Expanding this implementation, we may want to display `Label` with a different color if the release date is unknown. To achieve this, we could potentially create a converter that returns a certain color, depending on the release value, but we could also use a property trigger to set the font color, depending on the label's `Text` property value. In this situation, the use of a trigger is a better choice, since using the converter would mean hardcoding the color value, whereas the trigger can use dynamic or static resources and can be applied with styles for the target view.

Triggers

Triggers can be defined as declarative actions that need to be executed. The different types of triggers are as follows:

- **Property trigger**: Property changes for a view
- **Data trigger**: Data value changes for a binding
- **Event trigger**: The occurrence of certain events on the target view
- **Multi-trigger**: Used to implement a combination of triggers

To illustrate the use of triggers, we can use our previous example, where `ReleaseDate` for a certain item does not exist. In this scenario, because of the `TargetNullValue` attribute being defined, the text of the label will be set to `Release Unknown`. Here, we can make use of a property trigger, which sets the font color:

```
<Label x:Name="ReleaseDate" Text="{Binding ReleaseDate,
StringFormat='Release {0:M/d/yyyy}', TargetNullValue='Release
Unknown'}">
    <Label.Triggers>
        <Trigger TargetType="Label" Property="Text"
Value="Release
        Unknown">
            <Setter Property="TextColor" Value="Red" />
        </Trigger>
    </Label.Triggers>
</Label>
```

Here, the target type defines the containing element (that is, the target of the trigger action), and the property and value define the cause of the trigger. Multiple setters can then be applied to the target that's modifying the values of the view.

In a similar fashion, we could have created a data trigger to set the color of the title, depending on the release date label's value:

```
<Label Text="{Binding Title, Mode=OneTime}" FontSize="Large">
    <Label.Triggers>
        <DataTrigger TargetType="Label"
            Binding="{Binding Source={x:Reference ReleaseDate},
                              Path=Text}"
            Value="Release Unknown">
```

```xml
            <Setter Property="TextColor" Value="Red" />
        </DataTrigger>
    </Label.Triggers>
</Label>
```

Here, we are setting the binding context of `DataTrigger` to another view (that is, View-to-View) binding. If we were using the view model as the binding context, we could have used `ReleaseDate` as well.

Finally, if we have don't have a release date but we have the data to support that an item is, in fact, already been released to the public, we can use `MultiTrigger`:

```xml
<MultiTrigger TargetType="Label">
    <MultiTrigger.Conditions>
        <PropertyCondition Property="Text" Value="Release Unknown" />
        <BindingCondition Binding="{Binding IsReleased}" Value="false"/>
    </MultiTrigger.Conditions>
    <Setter Property="TextColor" Value="Red" />
</MultiTrigger>
```

Event triggers are odd members of the trigger family, since they rely on events being triggered on the target view instead of `Setters`; they use `Action`.

For instance, to add a little UX enhancement, we can add a fade animation to the image in the item view. To use this animation, we need to implement it as part of an `Action`:

```csharp
public class AppearingAction : TriggerAction<VisualElement>
{
    public AppearingAction() { }

    public int StartsFrom { set; get; }

    protected override void Invoke(VisualElement visual)
    {
        visual.Animate("FadeIn",
            new Animation((opacity) => visual.Opacity = opacity, 0, 1),
            length: 1000, // milliseconds
```

```
            easing: Easing.Linear);
    }
}
```

Now that `TriggerAction` has been created, we can define an event trigger on the image (that is, using the `BindingContextChanged` event):

```
<Image Source="{Binding Image}"
 HorizontalOptions="FillAndExpand">
    <Image.Triggers>
        <EventTrigger Event="BindingContextChanged">
            <actions:AppearingAction />
        </EventTrigger>
    </Image.Triggers>
</Image>
```

This will create a subtle fade-in effect, which should coincide with the image being loaded, thus providing a more pleasant user experience.

Actions can also be used with property and data triggers by using `EnterAction` and `ExitAction`, which define the two states according to the trigger condition(s). However, in the context of property and data triggers, to create more generalized states, as well as to modify the common states for a control, **Visual State Manager** (**VSM**) can be utilized. This way, multiple setters can be unified in a single state, thus decreasing the clutter within the XAML tree and creating a more maintainable structure.

Visual states

Visual states and VSM will be familiar concepts to WPF and UWP developers; however, they were missing from Xamarin.Forms' runtime until recently. Visual states define various conditions that a control must meet to be rendered. For instance, an `Entry` element can be in a `Normal`, `Focused`, or `Disabled` state, and each state defines a different visual setter for the element. Additionally, custom states can also be defined for a visual element and, depending on triggers or explicit calls to `VisualStateManager`, can manage the visual state of elements.

To demonstrate this, we can create three different states for our label (for example, `Released`, `UnReleased`, and `Unknown`) and deal with states using our triggers.

First, we need to define the states for our label control (which can then be moved to a resource dictionary as part of a style):

```xml
<Label x:Name="ReleaseDate" ...>
    <Label.Triggers>
        <!-- Removed for Brevity -->
    </Label.Triggers>
    <VisualStateManager.VisualStateGroups>
        <VisualStateGroup x:Name="CommonStates">
            <VisualState x:Name="Released">
                <VisualState.Setters>
                    <Setter
                        Property="BackgroundColor"
                        Value="Lime" />
                    <Setter
                        Property="TextColor"
                        Value="Black" />
                </VisualState.Setters>
            </VisualState>
            <VisualState x:Name="UnReleased">
                <VisualState.Setters>
                    <Setter Property="TextColor" Value="Black" />
                </VisualState.Setters>
            </VisualState>
            <VisualState x:Name="Unknown">
                <VisualState.Setters>
                    <Setter Property="TextColor" Value="Red" />
                </VisualState.Setters>
            </VisualState>
        </VisualStateGroup>
    </VisualStateManager.VisualStateGroups>
</Label>
```

As you can see, one of the defined states is `Unknown`, and it should set the text color to red. To change the state of the label using a trigger, we can implement a trigger action:

```csharp
public class ChangeStateAction : TriggerAction<VisualElement>
{
    public ChangeStateAction() { }

    public string State { set; get; }

    protected override void Invoke(VisualElement visual)
    {
        if(visual.HasVisualStateGroups())
        {
            VisualStateManager.GoToState(visual, State);
        }
    }
}
```

We can use this action as our `EnterAction` for the previously defined multi-trigger:

```xml
<MultiTrigger TargetType="Label">
    <MultiTrigger.Conditions>
        <!-- Removed for brevity -->
    </MultiTrigger.Conditions>
    <MultiTrigger.EnterActions>
        <actions:ChangeStateAction State="Unknown" />
    </MultiTrigger.EnterActions>
</MultiTrigger>
```

We can achieve the same result by using setters. However, it is important to mention that, without defining an `ExitAction` once the label has been set to the given state, it will not revert to the previous state.

In this section, you learned how to successfully keep the data decoupled from your view elements while creating a declarative visual tree that will respond to different data types and user interaction. Most of the visual elements that were used in this section were targeting a single data item and its properties. In the next section, we will analyze different views that specifically deal with collections of data items.

Collection Views

In the early phases of Xamarin.Forms, `StackLayout` and `ListView` were the two most popular options for displaying a collection of elements. The differentiating factor for these two views was the fact that `StackLayout` was only used for static content (that is, no collection data binding) whereas `ListView` was used to create a collection view where a collection of data items (that is, `ItemsSource`) was displayed in the form of a template definition.

In fact, so far, we have used the `ListView` element while creating our `HomeView`, as well as the `RootView` menu. If you look at how HomeView's uses of `ListView`, you will immediately notice the main elements of the collection binding that allow the data binding in a `ListView`:

```xml
<ListView ItemsSource="{Binding RecentProducts}">
    <ListView.ItemTemplate>
        <DataTemplate>
            <ViewCell>
                <Grid>
                    <!-- Removed for brevity -->
                </Grid>
            </ViewCell>
        </DataTemplate>
    </ListView.ItemTemplate>
</ListView>
```

`ItemsSource` can be described as the collection binding context, which defines what data to be used in the view, whereas `ItemTemplate`, which contains a `DataTemplate`, is used to define how the data should be displayed.

`ItemsSource` is defined as an `IEnumerable`, which means any kind of collection can be assigned as a data source to `ListView`. Nevertheless, using a collection that implements the `INotifyCollectionChanged` interface (such as `ObservableCollection`) can prove to be invaluable when you're dealing with a dynamic set of data. In this setup, any change to the data source collection, such as adding or removing an item, would immediately be reflected on the rendered set of elements.

`DataTemplate` can define a custom template using a `ViewCell`. For instance, in our example, we have used a `Grid` to set up a layout for our product listings. In these types of scenarios, it is a general rule of thumb to avoid relative sizes and positions so that we don't incur performance penalties. Additionally, simple data items can be represented using a specialized cell template such as `EntryCell`, `SwitchCell`, `TextCell`, or `ImageCell`.

DataTemplates can be combined with a `DataTemplateSelector` to display different templates based on a predicate targeting the bound data context.

As we mentioned previously, `StackLayout` and `Grid` were initially only used to display static content. However, these static views can also be bound to a data collection using attached properties such as `BindableLayout`, `ItemsSource`, and `BindableLayout.ItemTemplate`. Just like in our `ListView` example, these properties would then be used while rendering to create child elements within the parent layout. Nevertheless, using `BindableLayout` setup with controls such as `StackLayout` would come with performance penalties if the collection size is large and the data is dynamic.

Another option for displaying collections of data items is using `CollectionView`. `CollectionView` was introduced a little later than `ListView` and provides a much more flexible templating option set, as well as better performance. `CollectionView`, like `ListView`, supports the Pull-to-Refresh functionality out of the box.

Summary

In this chapter, we implemented some simple views using the intrinsic controls of the Xamarin.Forms framework and set up a basic navigation hierarchy. We also looked at the Xamarin Shell navigation infrastructure, which provides an alternative to your navigational infrastructure. In our views, we used various controls and discussed how to create responsive and data-driven UI elements based on simple data items, as well as collections.

With the extensive set of layouts, views, and customization options available, developers can create attractive and intuitive user interfaces. Moreover, the data-driven UI options can help developers separate (decouple) any business domain implementation from these views, which, in turn, will improve the maintainability of any mobile development project.

Nevertheless, at times, standard controls might not be enough to meet project requirements. In the next chapter, we will take a closer look at customizing the existing UI views and implementing custom native elements.

6
Customizing Xamarin.Forms

Xamarin.Forms allows developers to modify UI-rendering infrastructure in various ways. The customizations that are introduced by developers can target a certain platform feature on a certain control element or they can create a completely new view control. These customizations can be made on the Xamarin.Forms tier or on the target native platform.

In this chapter, we will go through the steps and procedures that are involved in customizing Xamarin.Forms without compromising on either performance or **User Experience** (**UX**). We will start our journey by defining the development domains for our customizations. Beginning with platform-agnostic customizations, such as behaviors, styles, and XAML extensions, we will make our way into native domains by implementing platform-specific functionality and customizations. Finally, we will take a look at custom renderers and custom controls.

The following sections will cover different development domains for Xamarin.Forms customizations:

- Xamarin.Forms Development domains
- Xamarin.Forms Shared domains
- Customizing the Native domains
- Creating Custom controls

By the end of this chapter, you will be able to customize the view elements within Xamarin.Forms and the native boundaries. Additionally, you will be able to add behavioral modifications to these elements.

Technical Requirements

You can find the code for this chapter via GitHub at `https://github.com/PacktPublishing/Mobile-Development-with-.NET-Second-Edition/tree/master/chapter06`.

Xamarin.Forms development domains

In this section, we will start by defining the development domains for Xamarin.Forms applications. We will create a quadrant plane that has shared versus native as one axis and business logic versus UI as another. We will then place various customization options in these quadrants according to their implementation and utilization.

So far, in this book, you will have noticed that application development using the Xamarin.Forms framework is executed on multiple domains. While the Xamarin.Forms layer creates a shared development domain that will be used to target native platforms, the target platforms can still be utilized for platform-specific implementations.

If we were to separate a Xamarin.Forms application into four quadrants by development strategy and application domain category, it would look like this:

Figure 6.1 – Xamarin Customization Domains

In this setup, quadrant I (that is, the shared business logic) represents the core logic implementation of the application. This domain will contain the view models, domain data descriptions, and service client implementation. Most importantly, the abstractions for platform-specific APIs (that is, the interfaces that will be implemented on the native platform) should be created in this domain so that each other domain, along with the view models within this domain, can make use of them.

Quadrant II and III represent the UI customizations that we need to implement in order to create the desired UX for the application. Until now, we have been creating our visual trees using only quadrant II. Simple data-driven applications and **Line-of-Business** (**LOB**) applications can solely utilize this domain. However, if we were to create a consumer-facing application, then complying with the branded UX requirements and creating an intuitive UI should be our main goals. In this scenario, we can resort to creating customizations for Xamarin.Forms views using quadrant III.

In this paradigm, quadrant I only connects with quadrant II using data binding and converter implementations. Quadrant II is responsible for propagating the delivered data to quadrant III.

In quadrant II, the customization options for developers are mostly restricted to the extensibility options provided by the out-of-the-box views that are offered by the Xamarin.Forms framework. Compositions of these views and behavioral modifications can provide highly maintainable cross-platform source code. By using styling options, visual states, and data-driven templates, the UX can meet these requirements.

When moving from the shared platform to the native platform (that is, crossing from quadrant II to quadrant III), developers are blessed with platform specifics and Xamarin.Forms effects. Using these extensibility points, we, as developers, can modify the behavior of native controls and modify the rendered native UI, creating a bridge between the Xamarin.Forms view abstractions and the target native controls. A combination of these extensibility features with Xamarin.Forms behaviors can improve the maintainability of the application.

Quadrant-III-specific development comprises custom renderers and native controls. Native controls can be created and combined under Xamarin.Forms compositions, thereby decreasing the complexity of the Xamarin.Forms XAML trees (that is, the composite controls).

Finally, quadrant IV represents platform-specific APIs, such as geolocation, the usage of peripherals, such as Bluetooth or NFC, or SaaS integrations/SDKs that require native implementation.

We have now classified our customization options into specific quadrants. Seeing how all of these options sit on these quadrants could help us to identify the specific customization option for a specific scenario. It should be a general rule of thumb to start weighing your options from quadrant I, and if no other option is available, move on to the next quadrant. As you move to quadrant III and IV, because the amount of cross-platform code decreases, the maintainability of the project also decreases. So, without losing any more time, let's start with the shared domain customization options, namely, quadrant I and II.

Xamarin.Forms shared domains

In *Chapter 5, UI Development with Xamarin*, we used intrinsic Xamarin.Forms controls and their styling attributes to create our UI. By using data binding and data triggers, we created data-driven views. The extensibility options are, of course, not limited to the control attributes that are available on this layer. Both the behavior and the look and feel of rendered controls can be modified using standard customization and extensibility options. Let's take a look at the different customization options in the shared Xamarin.Forms domain.

Using styles

In the previous chapter, in our ShopAcross application, when working on the product details view, we created a simple chips container to display the various features of an item that was currently being offered through the application.

In the previous setup, we were only utilizing the `Margin` property and `VerticalTextAlignment` for the labels:

```
<FlexLayout Direction="Row" Wrap="Wrap">
    <Label Text="Feature 1" Margin="4"
VerticalTextAlignment="Center" BackgroundColor="Gray" />
    <Label Text="Feat. 2" Margin="4"
VerticalTextAlignment="Center" BackgroundColor="Lime"/>
    <!-- Additional Labels -->
</FlexLayout>
```

This fluid layout setup creates small rectangles that contain the feature name. However, the look and feel are slightly different from what a chip would look like in material design (for example, the padding and rounded corners).

Let's now modify these items to make the labels look more like chips in order to improve the user experience:

1. We will start by wrapping the label in a frame and then styling the frame. Open `ProductDetailsView.xaml` and add a frame outside each feature label. Then, move the `BackgroundColor` assignment to the `Frame` element:

   ```
   <Frame
       BackgroundColor="Gray"
       CornerRadius="7"
       Padding="3"
       Margin="4"
       HasShadow="false">
     <Label x:Name="Feat1" Text="Feature 1"
         VerticalTextAlignment="Center"
         HorizontalTextAlignment="Center" />
   </Frame>
   ```

   This certainly creates a more desirable look for our chip:

   Figure 6.2 – Customized Chips

   However, note that adding these properties to each feature will create a completely redundant XAML structure.

   We can extract the common attribute definitions into two separate styles (that is, one for the feature label and one for the frame itself) that will be applied to each element, thereby decreasing the chance of redundancy.

2. In order to do this, open `App.xaml` and add the following style definitions within the existing `ResourceDictionary`:

   ```
   <Style TargetType="Frame">
       <Setter Property="HasShadow" Value="false" />
   </Style>
   <Style TargetType="Frame" x:Key="ChipContainer">
   ```

```xml
        <Setter Property="CornerRadius" Value="7" />
        <Setter Property="Padding" Value="3" />
        <Setter Property="Margin" Value="3" />
    </Style>
    <Style TargetType="Label" x:Key="ChipLabel">
        <Setter Property="VerticalTextAlignment"
Value="Center" />
        <Setter Property="HorizontalTextAlignment"
Value="Center" />
        <Setter Property="TextColor" Value="White" />
    </Style>
```

3. Next, apply these **implicit** (that is, the `HasShadow="false"` setter will be applied to all the frames on the application level) and **explicit styles** (note the `x:Key` declaration on the `ChipContainer` and `ChipLabel` styles) on the `Frame` and `Label` controls:

```xml
<FlexLayout Direction="Row" Wrap="Wrap"
 FlowDirection="LeftToRight" AlignItems="Start">
    <Frame BackgroundColor="Gray" Style="{StaticResource
        ChipContainer}">
        <Label x:Name="Feat1" Text="Feature 1" Style="
        {StaticResource ChipLabel}" />
    </Frame>
    <Frame BackgroundColor="Lime"
     Style="{StaticResource ChipContainer}">
        <Label x:Name="Feat2" Text="Feat. 2"
        Style="{StaticResource ChipLabel}" />
    </Frame>
    <!-- Additional Labels -->
</FlexLayout>
```

By doing so, we will decrease the clutter and redundancy in our XAML tree. Styles can be declared at the application level (as demonstrated in this scenario) as **global styles** using `App.xaml`. Additionally, they can also be declared at page and view levels using local resource dictionaries.

Another approach to styling controls is to use CSS style sheets. While these style sheets currently do not support the full extent of the XAML control styles, they can prove powerful, especially when utilizing the CSS selectors. Let's get started with CSS in Xamarin.Forms by recreating the styles for our chip views:

1. First, start by creating a new folder in the `ShopAcross.Mobile.Client` project, called `Resources`. Then, add a new file, called `Styles.css`. Ensure that the build action for this file is set to `EmbeddedResource`.

2. Next, add the following style declarations to `Styles.css`:

   ```css
   .ChipContainerClass {
       border-radius: 7;
       padding: 3;
       margin: 3;
   }

   .ChipLabelClass {
       text-align: center;
       vertical-align: central;
       color: white;
   }
   ```

   For those of you who are not familiar with CSS, here, we have created two style classes, named `ChipContainerClass` and `ChipLabelClass`.

3. Now, add these style classes to the `Frame` and `Label` controls using the `StyleClass` attribute:

   ```xml
   <Frame IsVisible="{Binding HasFeature1}"
          BackgroundColor="Gray"
          StyleClass="ChipContainerClass">
       <Label x:Name="Feat1" Text="Feature 1"
              StyleClass="ChipLabelClass" />
   </Frame>
   ```

4. In order to decrease the clutter, apply the style directly to the child label within the frame with the `ChipContainerClass` style class (note that we will not need to use an explicit style declaration for the `Label` element):

```
.ChipContainerClass {
    border-radius: 7;
    padding: 3;
    margin: 3;
}

.ChipContainerClass>^label {
    text-align: center;
    vertical-align: central;
    color: white;
}
```

The difference between `.ChipContainerClass>label` and `.ChipContainerClass>^label` is that by using the `^` (base class) notation, we can ensure that even if we modify the view using a custom control deriving from `label`, the styles are applied in the same way.

5. Now, remove the `ChipLabelClass` declaration from the `Label` control.

As you can see, styles can really help to decrease the chance of redundancy within XAML declarations. By doing this, you are creating a more maintainable project. Styles can also be used to create themes that are either bound to the system theme or the user preferences. Styles can also be used in conjunction with Xamarin.Forms behaviors to not only modify the visualization, but also the behavior of elements.

Creating behaviors

Behaviors are an eloquent use of the decorator pattern, allowing developers to modify their Xamarin.Forms controls without having to create derived controls. In this section, we will create a simple behavior to demonstrate how behaviors can help to create a data-driven application UI.

In order to demonstrate the use of behaviors, let's take a look at the following user story:

As a software developer, I would like to delegate the validation behavior in LoginView to the UI elements so that the same behavior can be reused for various controls, without replicating it on different view models.

As you might remember, in `LoginView`, we actually used the `Command.CanExecute` delegate to validate our fields. In this example, we will separate the validators for the email field and the password field. In this way, we can allow the UI to give feedback to the user as a result of an incorrect entry. This is more user-friendly than only disabling the login window. To set this up, follow these steps:

1. First, create a validation rule infrastructure, starting with the validation interface. Create a folder, called `Common`, in the `ShopAcross.Mobile.Core` project, and add a new interface, called `IValidationRule`:

   ```csharp
   public interface IValidationRule<T>
   {
       string ValidationMessage { get; set; }
       bool Validate (T value);
   }
   ```

2. In order to implement the required validation, create a new class, called `RequiredValidationRule`, deriving from `IValidationRule`. We can also add a short validation message stating that this field is a required field:

   ```csharp
   public class RequiredValidationRule : IValidationRule<string>
   {
       public string ValidationMessage { get; set; } = "This field is a required field";

       public bool Validate (string value)
       {
           return !string.IsNullOrEmpty(value);
       }
   }
   ```

   Now, we can create our validation behavior for the `Entry` field, which will make use of any given validation rule (starting with `RequiredValidationRule`, which we just implemented).

3. For this, create a new folder, called `Behaviors`, in the `ShopAcross.Mobile.Client` project, and add a new class, called `ValidationBehavior`:

   ```csharp
   public class ValidationBehavior : Behavior<Entry>
   {
   ```

```csharp
protected override void OnAttachedTo(Entry bindable)
{
    base.OnAttachedTo(bindable);

    bindable.TextChanged += ValidateField;
}

protected override void OnDetachingFrom(Entry bindable)
{
    base.OnDetachingFrom(bindable);

    bindable.TextChanged -= ValidateField;
}

private void ValidateField(object sender,
    TextChangedEventArgs args)
{
    if (sender is Entry entry)
    {
        // TODO:
    }
}
```

In this implementation, the `OnAttachedTo` and `OnDetachingFrom` methods are the crucial entry point and teardown logic implementations. In this scenario, when the behavior is attached to a target control, we are subscribing to the `TextChanged` event, and when the behavior is removed, we are unsubscribing from the event so that any undesired memory leak issues can be avoided. This implementation is important as well since, thinking about our quadrant plane, we are crossing from quadrant I to II by adding this validation behavior to the Xamarin.Forms `Entry` view element.

4. The next order of business is to implement a bindable property for the validation rule so that the validation rules are dictated by the view model (or another business logic module), decoupling it from the view.

To do this, open the `ValidationBehavior` class and add the following properties to it:

```
public static readonly BindableProperty
ValidationRuleProperty =
        BindableProperty.CreateAttached("ValidationRule",
typeof(IValidationRule<string>),
typeof(ValidationBehavior), null);


public static readonly BindableProperty HasErrorProperty
=
        BindableProperty.CreateAttached("HasError",
typeof(bool), typeof(ValidationBehavior), false,
BindingMode.TwoWay);

public IValidationRule<string> ValidationRule
{
    get { return this.GetValue(ValidationRuleProperty) as
IValidationRule<string>; }
    set { this.SetValue(ValidationRuleProperty, value); }
}

public bool HasError
{
    get { return (bool) GetValue(HasErrorProperty); }
    set { SetValue(HasErrorProperty, value); }
}
```

5. Now that we have an outlet for the validation rule along with an output field (so that we can attach additional UX logic to it), add the following implementation for the `ValidateField` method:

```
private void ValidateField(object sender,
TextChangedEventArgs
 args)
 {
     if (sender is Entry entry && ValidationRule != null)
     {
         if (!ValidationRule.Validate(args.NewTextValue))
```

```
                {
                    entry.BackgroundColor = Color.Crimson;
                    HasError = true;
                }
                else
                {
                    entry.BackgroundColor = Color.White;
                    HasError = false;
                }
            }
        }
```

6. Next, extend the `LoginViewModel` class with the appropriate rule property (in this case, `UserNameValidation`):

```
public IValidationRule<string> UserNameValidation { get; set; }
    = new RequiredValidationRule();
```

7. Now, bind the behavior to the validation rule that's exposed from the view model. Then, observe the `Entry` field behavior according to the text input:

```
<Entry x:Name="usernameEntry" Placeholder="username"
Text="{Binding UserName, Mode=OneWayToSource}" >
    <Entry.Behaviors>
        <behaviors:ValidationBehavior
x:Name="UserNameValidation"
            ValidationRule="{Binding
            BindingContext.UserNameValidation,
                Source={x:Reference Root}}" />
    </Entry.Behaviors>
</Entry>
```

While attaching the behavior, you will need to add the `x:Name` attribute to the `ContentPage` declaration in `LoginView.xaml` with the value of `Root` (please view the preceding reference) and introduce the CLR namespace reference for `Behaviors`.

Here, the main benefit is that we do not have to modify the `Entry` field, and the implemented behavior can be maintained as a separate module.

> **Important note**
> The binding context for a behavior is not the same as the page layout or the view, which is why the source of the binding value for the validation rule must reference the page itself and use `BindingContext` as part of the binding path.

8. To extend this implementation, add a validation error message label that will be displayed alongside the `HasError` bindable property (this can be anywhere on the page layout, as long as the `UserNameValidation` element is accessible):

```
<Label Text="UserName is required" FontSize="12"
TextColor="Gray"
    IsVisible="{Binding HasError, Source={x:Reference
UserNameValidation}}"/>
```

9. The outcome will look similar to the following:

Figure 6.3 – Custom behavior in the Username field

Here, we have implemented a validation behavior that can be bound to a validation implementation in the application core layer. In other words, we have created another bridge between quadrants II and I. This way, the implementation can be used whenever we need to implement a similar validation on any entry across the project, and the view model would just be responsible for defining the validation requirements. Nevertheless, with this implementation, the behavior declarations on the controls could, again, cause clutter with larger forms. You can use attached properties to decrease the amount of repeated code to enable and disable a behavior. In the next section, we will walk you through the creation of attached properties.

Attached properties

Another way to alter the default control behavior is to use attached properties by declaring a bindable extension for the existing controls. This approach is generally used for small behavioral adjustments, such as enabling/disabling other behaviors and adding/removing effects.

We can demonstrate this implementation by recreating the previous scenario with an attached property rather than a behavior. Let's get started:

1. In order to implement such a behavior, first, we need to create a bindable property that will be used with the Xamarin.Forms view elements. For this, create a new folder, called `Extensions`, in the `ShopAcross.Mobile.Client` project, and add a new class, called `Validations`:

```csharp
public static class Validations
{
    public static readonly BindableProperty ValidateRequiredProperty =
        BindableProperty.CreateAttached(
            "ValidateRequired",
            typeof(bool),
            typeof(RequiredValidationRule),
            false,
            propertyChanged: OnValidateRequiredChanged);

    public static bool GetValidateRequired(BindableObject view)
    {
        return (bool)view.GetValue(ValidateRequiredProperty);
    }

    public static void SetValidateRequired(BindableObject view,
        bool value)
    {
        view.SetValue(ValidateRequiredProperty, value);
    }
```

```
        private static void OnValidateRequiredChanged(
            BindableObject bindable, object oldValue,
 object
            newValue)
    {
        // TODO:
    }
}
```

With attached behaviors, the static class can be directly accessed so that it sets the attached property to the current control (instead of creating and adding a behavior).

2. Now, remove the behavior declaration and set the attached property to the `usernameEntry` view:

```
<Entry x:Name="usernameEntry" Placeholder="username"
    Text="{Binding UserName, Mode=OneWayToSource}"
    extensions:Validations.ValidateRequired="true" >
```

3. Next, implement the `ValidateRequired` property-changed handler. This is so that we can have the attached property insert and remove the required validation to various `Entry` views:

```
    private static void OnValidateRequiredChanged(
        BindableObject bindable,
        object oldValue,
        object newValue)
    {
        if(bindable is Entry entry)
        {
            if ((bool)newValue)
            {
                entry.Behaviors.Add(new ValidationBehavior()
                {
                    ValidationRule = new
 RequiredValidationRule()
                });
            }
            else
            {
```

```csharp
                var behaviorToRemove = entry.Behaviors
                    .OfType<ValidationBehavior>()
                    .FirstOrDefault(
                        item => item.ValidationRule is
                        RequiredValidationRule);

                if (behaviorToRemove != null)
                {
                    entry.Behaviors.
Remove(behaviorToRemove);
                }
            }
        }
    }
```

Here, we have created an attached property to modify the added behaviors of a Xamarin.Forms element. Remember, attached properties can also be used to modify other properties of view elements.

XAML markup extensions

In this section, you will learn how to use and create yet another very utile customization option: **markup extensions**.

So far, when we have created XAML views, we have resorted to several markup extensions that are supported either by the Xamarin.Forms framework or the XAML namespace itself. Some of these extensions are as follows:

- `x:Reference`: This is used to refer to another view on the same page.
- `Binding`: This is used throughout the view model implementation.
- `StaticResource`: This is used to refer to styles.

These are all markup extensions that are resolved by the associated service implementation within the Xamarin.Forms framework.

To address specific needs in your application, custom markup extensions can be implemented in order to create a more maintainable XAML structure. To create a markup extension, the `IMarkupExtension<T>` class needs to be implemented. This depends on the type that needs to be provided.

For instance, in our previous example, the error label and the field descriptors were hardcoded into the XAML view. This could create issues if the application needs to support multiple localizations.

Let's use the following user story to implement a custom markup extension:

As a user, I would like to have the UI of the application translated to my phone's language setup so that I can easily navigate through a UI that contains content in my native language.

Here, we will implement the localization of the `LoginView`. The following steps will guide you through the process:

1. First, create a markup extension that will translate the associated text values. Then, create a class in the `Extensions` folder, called `TranslateExtension`:

    ```
    [ContentProperty("Text")]
    public class TranslateExtension :
    IMarkupExtension<string>
    {
        public string Text { get; set; }

        public string ProvideValue(IServiceProvider serviceProvider)
        {
            // TODO:
            return Text;
        }

        object IMarkupExtension.ProvideValue(IServiceProvider serviceProvider)
        {
            return (this as
            IMarkupExtension<string>).
    ProvideValue(serviceProvider);
        }
    }
    ```

    Note that the `Text` property is set as `ContentProperty`, which allows developers to provide a value for this extension simply by manually adding a value for the extension.

2. Let's now incorporate the extension into the XAML structure in `LoginView.xaml`:

```xml
<Label Text="{extensions:Translate LblUsername}" />
<Entry x:Name="usernameEntry" Placeholder="username"
    Text="{Binding UserName, Mode=OneWayToSource}" >
    <Entry.Behaviors>
        <behaviors:ValidationBehavior x:Name="UserNameValidation" ValidationRule="{Binding BindingContext.UserNameValidation, Source={x:Reference Root}}" />
    </Entry.Behaviors>
</Entry>
<Label Text="{extensions:Translate LblRequiredError}"
    FontSize="12" TextColor="Gray"
    IsVisible="{Binding HasError, Source={x:Reference UserNameValidation}}"/>
```

3. The `ProvideValue` method will, therefore, need to translate the `LblUsername` and `LblRequiredError` keys. Use the following implementation to achieve this:

```csharp
public string ProvideValue(IServiceProvider serviceProvider)
{
    switch (Text)
    {
        case "LblRequiredError":
            return "This a required field";
        case "LblUsername":
            return "Username";
        default:
            return Text;
    }
}
```

Here, we have used hardcoded values for the translation. However, in a real-life implementation, you would either load the values from a web service or resource file according to the current culture settings of the system.

In this section, we have created various customizations for quadrant II (that is, the shared domain). We have demonstrated the use of styles, behaviors, and attached properties. We even created a markup extension to easily translate string resources. As you might have noticed, so far, we have not touched native projects. Our complete implementation was done on the shared UI and Core projects. In the next section, we will move on to quadrant III and custom native controls.

Customizing native domains

Native customizations of UI controls can vary from simple platform-specific adjustments to creating a completely custom native control to replace the existing platform renderer. In this section, we will implement customizations on quadrant III, departing from the platform-agnostic domain. We will take a closer look at platform specifics and Xamarin effects.

Platform specifics

While the UI controls offered by Xamarin.Forms are customizable enough for most UX requirements, additional native behaviors might be needed. For certain native control behaviors, a platform-specific configuration can be accessed using the `IElementConfiguration` interface implementation of the target control. For instance, in order to change the `UpdateMode` picker (that is, `Immediately` or `WhenFinished`), you can use the `On<iOS>` method to access the platform-specific behavior:

```
var picker = new Xamarin.Forms.Picker();
picker.On<iOS>().SetUpdateMode(UpdateMode.WhenFinished);
```

The same can be implemented in XAML using the `Xamarin.Forms.PlatformConfiguration.iOSSpecific` namespace:

```
<ContentPage
    ...
    xmlns:ios="clr-namespace:Xamarin.Forms.
 PlatformConfiguration.iOSSpecific;assembly=Xamarin.Forms.Core">
    <!-- ... -->
        <Picker ios:Picker.UpdateMode="WhenFinished">
            <!-- Removed for brevity -->
        </Picker>
    <!-- ... -->
</ContentPage>
```

Similar platform configurations are available for other controls and platforms within the same namespace (that is, `Xamarin.Forms.PlatformConfiguration`). These platform-specific attached properties create a bridge between quadrant III and quadrant II by exposing methods that can manipulate native controls on a specific platform. However, what if the native property that we want to modify was not exposed by a specific platform? Well, we would probably need to resort to using **effects**.

Xamarin.Forms effects

Xamarin.Forms effects are an elegant bridge between the cross-platform domain (quadrant II) and the native domain (quadrant III). Effects are generally used to expose a certain platform behavior or implementation of a given native control through the shared domain. This is to ensure that a completely new custom native control is not required for the implementation.

Similarly to the Xamarin.Forms views/controls, effects exist on both the shared domain and the native domain with their abstraction and implementation, respectively. While the shared domain is used to create a routing effect, the native project is responsible for consuming it.

For instance, let's assume that the details we receive for our product items actually contain some HTML data, which we want to present within the application:

As a product owner, I would like to reuse the HTML-based product descriptions from our web application on our native mobile platforms. This is so that the content does not need to be sanitized before being pushed to a mobile platform.

In this scenario, we are aware of the fact that the `Label` element on Xamarin.Forms is rendered with `UILabel` in iOS and `TextView` in Android. While `UILabel` provides the `AttributedString` property (which can be created from HTML), the Android platform offers an intrinsic module for parsing HTML. We can expose these platform-specific features using an effect, and, therefore, enable the Xamarin.Forms abstraction to accept HTML input. Let's get started:

1. Create the routing effect that will provide the data for the platform effects. Then, create a new folder in the `ShopAcross.Mobile.Client` project, called `Effects`, and a class, called `HtmlTextEffect`:

    ```
    public class HtmlTextEffect: RoutingEffect
    {
        public HtmlTextEffect(): base("ShopAcross.HtmlTextEffect")
        {
        }

        public string HtmlText { get; set; }
    }
    ```

2. Now, we can use this effect in our XAML. Open `ProductDetailsView.xaml` and add the following effect to the `Description` label:

    ```
    <Label Text="{Binding Description}">
      <Label.Effects>
        <effects:HtmlTextEffect
          HtmlText="&lt;b&gt;Here&lt;/b&gt; is some &lt;u&gt;HTML&lt;/u&gt;" />
      </Label.Effects>
    </Label>
    ```

    It is important to note that the content within the `HtmlText` attribute should be encoded to avoid XAML compilation issues. Additionally, without the platform implementation of this routing effect, the label will still display the binding data.

    Now, we need to implement the iOS effect that will parse the `HtmlText` property of our effect.

3. Create a new folder, called `Effects`, in the `ShopAcross.Mobile.Client.iOS` project, and create a new class, called `HtmlTextEffect`:

   ```
   [assembly: ResolutionGroupName("ShopAcross")]
   [assembly: ExportEffect(typeof(HtmlTextEffect),
   "HtmlTextEffect")]
   namespace ShopAcross.Mobile.Client.iOS.Effects
   {
       public class HtmlTextEffect: PlatformEffect
       {
           protected override void OnAttached()
           {
           }

           protected override void OnDetached()
           {
           }
       }
   }
   ```

   Platform effects are primarily composed of two main components: registration and implementation. The effect that's registered with `ResolutionGroupName` of the `ExportEffect` attribute will be used in the runtime environment to resolve the routing effect that was implemented in the first step. Also, note that the `ExportEffect` attribute uses the reference to the iOS-specific attribute, so you will need to add the `using` statement for the current namespace (that is, `ShopAcross.Mobile.Client.iOS.Effects`).

   In order to modify the native control, you can now use the `Control` property of `PlatformEffect`. The `Element` property refers to the Xamarin.Forms control that requires this effect.

4. Now, implement the `OnAttached` method (which will be executed when `PlatformEffect` is resolved) to add the `AttributedText` if a `PlatformEffect` exists on the attached control:

   ```
   protected override void OnAttached()
   {
       var htmlTextEffect = Element.Effects
               .OfType<Client.Effects.HtmlTextEffect>
   ```

```
                ().FirstOrDefault();

    if(htmlTextEffect != null && Control is UILabel
label)
    {
        var documentAttributes = new
NSAttributedStringDocumentAttributes();
        documentAttributes.DocumentType =
NSDocumentType.HTML;
        var error = new NSError();

        label.AttributedText = new
NSAttributedString(htmlTextEffect.HtmlText,
documentAttributes, ref error);
    }
}
```

5. A similar implementation for the Android platform will create the HTML rendering of the controls. Use the `OnAttached` property to add the HTML content:

```
protected override void OnAttached()
{
    var htmlTextEffect = Element.Effects
            .OfType<Client.Effects.HtmlTextEffect>
            ().FirstOrDefault();

    if (htmlTextEffect != null && Control is TextView
label)
    {
        label.SetText(
            Html.FromHtml(htmlTextEffect.HtmlText,
            FromHtmlOptions.ModeLegacy),
            TextView.BufferType.Spannable);
    }
}
```

The resulting screen should display the hardcoded text rather than the view model data provided:

Figure 6.4 – Fixed HTML content using effects

While we have managed to display HTML content on our Xamarin.Forms view, the value we have used is still not bindable. With a little restructuring, and by using attached properties (that is, an attached behavior), we can use data binding and effects together.

Composite customizations

Behaviors and effects, when used together, can create eloquent solutions to common native element requirements without having to resort to custom controls and renderers.

Let's now extend our effect to use data that has been provided by the view model:

1. Before we begin, let's first extend our `ProductViewModel` class with an `IsHtml` property and add some sample data to `HomeViewModel`:

   ```
   yield return new ProductViewModel {
       Title = "First Item",
       IsHtml = true,
       Description = "<b/>Here</b> is some <u>HTML</u>;",
       Image = "https://picsum.photos/800?image=0" };
   ```

   And, picking up from where we left off with the `HtmlText` effect, let's create an attached behavior that will allow us to switch the HTML rendering on or off.

Customizing native domains 165

2. Create a class, called `HtmlText`, in the `Extensions` folder in the `ShopAcross.Mobile.Client` project:

```
public static class HtmlText
{
    public static readonly BindableProperty IsHtmlProperty =
        BindableProperty.CreateAttached("IsHtml",
            typeof(bool), typeof(HtmlText), false,
            propertyChanged: OnHtmlPropertyChanged);
    public static bool GetIsHtml(BindableObject view)
        => (bool)view.GetValue(IsHtmlProperty);

    public static void SetIsHtml(BindableObject view,
        bool value) => view.SetValue(IsHtmlProperty, value);

    private static void OnHtmlPropertyChanged(
        BindableObject bindable, object oldValue, object newValue)
    {
        var view = bindable as View;
        if (view == null) { return; }

        // TODO: Implement the behavior
    }
}
```

3. The behavior of this attached property will result in the addition or removal of the HTML effect, depending on the `IsHtml` property declaration. Add the following code to `OnHtmlPropertyChanged`:

```
if (newValue is bool isHtml && isHtml)
{
    view.Effects.Add(new HtmlTextEffect());
}
else
{
    var htmlEffect = view.Effects
```

```
            .FirstOrDefault(e => e is HtmlTextEffect);

        if (htmlEffect != null)
        {
            view.Effects.Remove(htmlEffect);
        }
    }
```

Now, we can modify our HTML effect so that it uses the existing text assignment on the forms view to create `NSAttributedText` and `ISpannable` for the iOS and Android platforms, respectively.

4. Copy and replace the existing effects for both iOS and Android with the following code:

```
public class HtmlTextEffect: PlatformEffect
{
    protected override void OnAttached()
    {
        SetHtmlText();
    }

    protected override void OnDetached()
    {
        // TODO: Remove formatted text
    }

    protected override void OnElementPropertyChanged(PropertyChangedEventArgs args)
    {
        base.OnElementPropertyChanged(args);

        if (args.PropertyName == Label.TextProperty.PropertyName)
        {
            SetHtmlText();
        }
    }
```

```
            private void SetHtmlText()
            {
                // Removed for brevity
            }
        }
```

Notice that we have also used the OnElementPropertyChanged method to listen for any Text property value changes. This will be the main access point for binding data.

5. For the SetHtmlText method, use the following for iOS and, similarly, modify the Android effect so that it uses the Label element's Text property rather than resolving the attached effects:

```
private void SetHtmlText()
{
    if (Control is UILabel label && Element is Label formLabel)
    {
        var documentAttributes = new NSAttributedStringDocumentAttributes();
        documentAttributes.DocumentType = NSDocumentType.HTML;
        var error = new NSError();
        label.AttributedText = new NSAttributedString(formLabel.Text, documentAttributes, ref error);
    }
}
```

6. Now, we will add the behavior to our XAML:

```
<Label Text="{Binding Description}" effects:HtmlText.IsHtml="{Binding IsHtml}" />
```

We can now control the displayed text attributes on both platforms using the `IsHtml` attached property on the view model.

With the implementation of this composite customization, we come to the end of this section. So far, we have focused on customizations in the third quadrant and have tried to create a bridge to quadrant II. We have used platform specifics, implemented native control modifications using effects, and, finally, we have created composite customizations that utilize effects and attached properties. If none of these customization options provide what is really required by the desired UI, a complete custom control implementation can be considered as an alternative option. In the next section, we will take a look at various different options when it comes to creating custom controls.

Creating Custom Controls

Just like any other development platform, it is also possible to create custom views/controls that look, behave, and render differently compared to out-of-the-box Xamarin.Forms controls. However, creating a custom control doesn't mean that the complete Xamarin.Forms render infrastructure needs to be implemented for target platforms along with the shared domain. Depending on the UX and platform requirements, the following can occur:

- Custom controls can be created solely as a composition of other Xamarin.Forms controls.
- Existing Xamarin.Forms controls can be modified with custom renderers on different platforms.
- Custom Xamarin.Forms controls can be created with custom renderers.

Creating a Xamarin.Forms control

A Xamarin.Forms control can be created for various reasons, one of which is to decrease the clutter in your XAML tree and create reusable view blocks. Let's begin.

First, we will take a step back and look at the validatable entries that we previously created for the login screen:

```
<Label x:Name="lblUserName" Text="..." />
<Entry x:Name="txtUserName" Placeholder=".." Text="..." >
    <Entry.Behaviors>
        <behaviors:ValidationBehavior 
x:Name="UserNameValidation"
            ValidationRule="..." />
```

```
        </Entry.Behaviors>
    </Entry>
    <Label x:Name="errUserName" Text="..." IsVisible="..."/>
```

The control block is composed of a label that is associated with the entry and the error label, which is only visible if there is a validation error within the label. A similar structure is used with the password field. By simply exposing a couple of the binding data points, this block can easily be converted into a custom control. The following steps will guide you through the process of extracting a custom control out of this entry block:

1. In order to create the base control, we will use `ContentView`. Add a new folder in the `ShopAcross.Mobile.Client` project named `Controls`, and add a `ContentView`, called `ValidatableEntry`, using the **Forms ContentView XAML** template:

    ```
    <ContentView
        xmlns="http://xamarin.com/schemas/2014/forms"
        xmlns:x=http://schemas.microsoft.com/winfx/2009/xaml
        xmlns:behaviors="clr-namespace:ShopAcross.Mobile.Client.Behaviors"
        x:Class=" ShopAcross.Mobile.Client.Controls.ValidatableEntry"
        x:Name="RootView">
        <ContentView.Content>
            <StackLayout>
                <!-- TODO: // Insert Controls -->
            </StackLayout>
        </ContentView.Content>
    </ContentView>
    ```

    Here, notice that a name declaration is used to create a reference to the control itself. This is because we will create bindable properties on the control and bind them to the children values that we previously identified.

2. Now, create our bindable properties within the `ValidatableEntry.xaml.cs` file:

    ```
    public static readonly BindableProperty LabelProperty =
        BindableProperty.CreateAttached("Label",
        typeof(string),
    ```

```csharp
        typeof(ValidatableEntry), string.Empty);

public static readonly BindableProperty
PlaceholderProperty =
    BindableProperty.CreateAttached("Placeholder",
typeof(string),
    typeof(ValidatableEntry), string.Empty);

public static readonly BindableProperty ValueProperty =
    BindableProperty.CreateAttached("Value",
typeof(string),
    typeof(ValidatableEntry), string.Empty, BindingMode.
TwoWay);

public static readonly BindableProperty
ValidationRuleProperty =
    BindableProperty.CreateAttached("ValidationRule",
typeof(IValidationRule<string>),
    typeof(ValidationBehavior), null);
```

3. We should also create accessors for these properties using the bindable properties as a backing field:

```csharp
public string Label
{
    get
    {
        return (string)GetValue(LabelProperty);
    }
    set
    {
        SetValue(LabelProperty, value);
    }
}
```

Repeat these same steps for the `Placeholder`, `Value`, and `ValidationRule` properties.

4. Next, wire up these properties to the children attributes of the view elements that we will add into the `ContentView.Content` node in `ValidatableEntry.xaml`:

```xml
<StackLayout>
    <Label Text="{Binding Label, Source={x:Reference RootView}}" />
    <Entry Placeholder="{Binding Placeholder, Source={x:Reference RootView}}" Text="{Binding Value, Mode=OneWayToSource, Source={x:Reference RootView}}" >
        <Entry.Behaviors>
            <behaviors:ValidationBehavior x:Name="ValidationBehavior"
                ValidationRule="{Binding ValidationRule, Source={x:Reference RootView}}" />
        </Entry.Behaviors>
    </Entry>
    <Label Text="{Binding ValidationRule.ValidationMessage, Source={x:Reference RootView}}"
        FontSize="12" TextColor="Gray" IsVisible="{Binding HasError, Source={x:Reference ValidationBehavior}}"/>
</StackLayout>
```

5. Finally, replace the original entry block in the `LoginView.xaml` file with our custom control:

```xml
<controls:ValidatableEntry
    Label="{extensions:Translate LblUsername}"
    Placeholder="{behaviors:Translate LblUsername}"
    ValidationRule="{Binding UserNameValidation}"
    Value="{Binding UserName, Mode=OneWayToSource}"/>
```

Here, we have created our custom `ContentView`, which will bundle a node of the visual tree into a single control. This control can also be used for other entry fields that require validation.

In this section, we specifically dealt with an implementation that was done in quadrant II. We used the existing Xamarin.Forms infrastructure to create a custom control that can be rendered on a native platform with multiple native elements. Next, we will take a look at how to create a custom renderer for Android so that we can make use of the built-in validation displays along with the floating label design concept.

Creating a custom renderer

At times, a target platform can offer out-of-the-box functionality that exceeds our expected requirements via the use of customized controls from Xamarin.Forms. In these types of situations, it might be a good idea to replace the Xamarin.Forms implementation on a specific platform with a custom implementation.

For instance, the form entry fields that we were trying to achieve with our custom implementation, in the previous section, would look far more platform appropriate if they were implemented with a `TextInputLayout` that followed material design guidelines:

Figure 6.5 – Material Design Floating Label Entry

In this layout, we can bind the label to the floating label and the error text to the helper text area of the floating label edit text. However, by default, Xamarin.Forms uses `FormsEditText` (a derivative of `EditText`) rather than `TextInputLayout` for Android. In order to remedy this, we can implement our own custom renderer that will use the desired control. Let's see how we can do this:

1. The first step in creating a renderer is to decide whether to create a renderer deriving from `ViewRenderer<TView, TNativeView>` or the actual render implementation. For `EntryRenderer`, the Xamarin.Forms base class is `ViewRenderer<Entry, FormsEditText>`. Unfortunately, this means that we won't be able to make use of the base class implementation since our renderer will need to return `TextInputLayout` to the native platform. Therefore, we will need to create a renderer from scratch. To do this, create a new folder, called `Renderers`, in the `ShopAcross.Mobile.Client.Android` project, and add a new class, called `FloatingLabelEntryRenderer`. The renderer declaration should look like this:

    ```
    public class FloatingLabelEntryRenderer :
    ViewRenderer<Entry, TextInputLayout>
    {
        public FloatingLabelEntryRenderer(Context context) :
            base(context)
        {
    ```

```
        }

        private EditText EditText => Control.EditText;

        protected override TextInputLayout
CreateNativeControl()
        {
            // TODO:
            return null;
        }

        protected override void
OnElementPropertyChanged(object sender,
PropertyChangedEventArgs e)
        {
            // TODO:
        }

        protected override void
OnElementChanged(ElementChangedEventArgs<Entry> e)
        {
            base.OnElementChanged(e);

            // TODO:
        }
    }
```

In this declaration, we should initially be dealing with several override methods, as follows:

- `CreateNativeControl`: This is responsible for creating the native control using the `Element` properties.
- `OnElementChanged`: This is similar to the `OnAttached` method in behaviors and effects.
- `OnElementPropertyChanged`: This is used to synchronize changes from the Xamarin.Forms element to the native element.

2. For `CreateNativeControl`, we need to create an `EditText` control, just like the standard renderer, but we also want to wrap it in `TextInputLayout`:

```
protected override TextInputLayout CreateNativeControl()
{
    var textInputLayout = new TextInputLayout(Context);
    var editText = new EditText(Context);
    editText.SetTextSize(ComplexUnitType.Sp, (float)Element.FontSize);
    textInputLayout.AddView(editText);
    return textInputLayout;
}
```

3. For `OnElementPropertyChanged`, we are interested in the `Placeholder` property and the associated `OneWay` binding (that is, from `Element` to `Native`). Therefore, we will be using the `Placeholder` value as the hint text for the `EditText` field:

```
protected override void OnElementPropertyChanged(object sender, PropertyChangedEventArgs e)
{
    if (e.PropertyName == Entry.PlaceholderProperty.PropertyName)
    {
        Control.Hint = Element.Placeholder;
    }
}
```

4. In addition to the property, we want to update the placeholder when `Element` is attached to the renderer (that is, the initial synchronization):

```
protected override void OnElementChanged(ElementChangedEventArgs<Entry> e)
{
    base.OnElementChanged(e);

    if (e.OldElement == null)
    {
        var textView = CreateNativeControl();
        SetNativeControl(textView);
```

```
            }
```

```
            Control.Hint = Element.Placeholder;
            EditText.Text = Element.Text;
        }
```

5. Another value we would like to keep in sync is the actual Text value. However, here, the synchronization should be able to support TwoWay binding.

   In order to listen for input text changes, we will implement the ITextWatcher interface with our renderer:

   ```
   public FloatingLabelEntryRenderer : ViewRenderer<Entry,
   TextInputLayout>, ITextWatcher
   {
       // ... removed for brevity
       void ITextWatcher.AfterTextChanged(IEditable @string)
       {
       }

       void ITextWatcher.BeforeTextChanged(ICharSequence s,
   int start, int count, int after)
       {
       }

       void ITextWatcher.OnTextChanged(ICharSequence s, int
   start, int before, int count)
       {
           if (string.IsNullOrEmpty(Element.Text) &&
   s.Length() == 0)
           {
               return;
           }

           ((IElementController)Element)
               .SetValueFromRenderer(Entry.TextProperty,
   s.ToString());
       }
   }
   ```

6. Now we can introduce our text watcher when the element is changed:

```
if (e.OldElement == null)
{
    var textView = CreateNativeControl();
    textView.EditText.AddTextChangedListener(this);
    SetNativeControl(textView);
}
```

7. Once the renderer is complete, we will also need to register the renderer so that the Xamarin.Forms runtime is aware of the association between the `Entry` control and this new renderer:

```
[assembly: ExportRenderer(typeof(Entry),
typeof(FloatingLabelEntryRenderer))]
namespace ShopAcross.Mobile.Client.Droid.Renderers
```

8. Now that the renderer is going to be handling both the label and the placeholder, we won't need the additional label within `ValidatableEntry`, so we will only be using them for iOS:

```
<ContentView>
    <OnPlatform x:TypeArguments="View">
        <On Platform="iOS">
            <Label Text="{Binding Label, Source={x:Reference RootView}}" />
        </On>
    </OnPlatform>
</ContentView>
<Entry Placeholder="{Binding Placeholder, Source={x:Reference RootView}}" Text="{Binding Value, Mode=OneWayToSource, Source={x:Reference RootView}}" >
    <Entry.Behaviors>
        <behaviors:ValidationBehavior x:Name="ValidationBehavior"
            ValidationRule="{Binding ValidationRule, Source={x:Reference RootView}}" />
    </Entry.Behaviors>
</Entry>
```

> **Important note**
> The reason why we have wrapped the `OnPlatform` declaration is that even though it's syntactically correct, adding a view to a parent with multiple children cannot be rendered because of the way reflection is implemented. In order to remedy this issue, the platform-specific declaration needs to be wrapped into a benign view with a single child.

The final outcome will look like this:

Figure 6.6 – Custom Renderer for a Floating Label

Notice that the floating label is displayed for the Android platform in the username field, whereas, on iOS, the `Label` view is rendered over the `Entry` field for the username.

In this section, we have implemented a custom renderer that replaces the out-of-the- box implementation for the Android platform, in return for the native controls that are rendered. It is also important to mention that the `ITextWatcher` interface we used to handle the text changes is a Java interface. This truly demonstrates how we have now moved completely to quadrant III and are getting closer to quadrant IV. We can further expand this implementation to include the error indicator within the custom control. Though, this would mean that we need to create a custom control and attach a custom renderer to it. In the following section, we will implement a complete custom control with a custom renderer.

Creating a custom Xamarin.Forms control

To create a complete custom control, the implementation needs to start with the Xamarin. Forms view abstraction. This abstraction provides the integration with XAML along with the view models (that is, the business logic) that are associated with that specific view.

For the floating label entry, we would, therefore, need to create a control with the required bindable properties exposed. For our use case, in addition to the `Entry` control attributes, we would need the validation error description and a flag identifying whether there is such an error. Let's begin the implementation of our custom control:

1. We will start by deriving our custom control from `Entry` itself and adding the additional properties. For this implementation, create a new class in the `Controls` folder of the `ShopAcross.Mobile.Client` project, and use the following class definition:

    ```
    public class FloatingLabelEntry : Entry
    {
        public static readonly BindableProperty ErrorMessageProperty =
            BindableProperty.CreateAttached("ErrorMessage", typeof(string), typeof(FloatingLabelEntry), string.Empty);

        public static readonly BindableProperty HasErrorProperty =
            BindableProperty.CreateAttached("HasError", typeof(bool), typeof(FloatingLabelEntry), false);

        public string ErrorMessage
        {
            get
            {
                return (string)GetValue(ErrorMessageProperty);
            }
            set
            {
                SetValue(ErrorMessageProperty, value);
            }
        }
    ```

```
        }

        public bool HasError
        {
            get
            {
                return (bool)GetValue(HasErrorProperty);
            }
            set
            {
                SetValue(HasErrorProperty, value);
            }
        }
    }
```

2. Now, modify your `FloatingLabelRenderer` to use the new control as the `TElement` type parameter:

```
[assembly: ExportRenderer(typeof(FloatingLabelEntry),
 typeof(FloatingLabelEntryRenderer))]
 namespace ShopAcross.Mobile.Client.Droid.Renderers
 {
     public class FloatingLabelEntryRenderer :
 ViewRenderer<FloatingLabelEntry, TextInputLayout>,
 ITextWatcher
```

3. In the renderer, we need to listen for any `HasErrorProperty` changes and set the error description and error indicator accordingly. So, let's expand `OnElementPropertyChanged` as follows:

```
protected override void OnElementPropertyChanged(object
 sender, PropertyChangedEventArgs e)
 {
     ....
     else if (e.PropertyName == FloatingLabelEntry.
 HasErrorProperty.PropertyName)
     {
         if (!Element.HasError || string.
 IsNullOrEmpty(Element.ErrorMessage))
```

```
            {
                EditText.Error = null;
                Control.ErrorEnabled = false;
            }
            else
            {
                Control.ErrorEnabled = true;
                EditText.Error = Element.ErrorMessage;
            }
        }
    ....
}
```

4. Using this control within `ValidatableEntry` instead of the `Entry` control will create a pleasant material design layout:

```
<controls:FloatingLabelEntry
    Placeholder="{Binding Placeholder, Source={x:Reference RootView}}"
    Text="{Binding Value, Mode=OneWayToSource, Source={x:Reference RootView}}"
    ErrorMessage="{Binding ValidationRule.ValidationMessage, Source={x:Reference RootView}}"
    HasError="{Binding HasError, Source={x:Reference ValidationBehavior}}">
    <Entry.Behaviors>
        <behaviors:ValidationBehavior x:Name="ValidationBehavior"
            ValidationRule="{Binding ValidationRule, Source={x:Reference RootView}}" />
    </Entry.Behaviors>
</controls:FloatingLabelEntry>
```

The resulting page should now display the validation error message as a so-called tip within the `TextInputLayout`:

Figure 6.7 – Custom Floating Label Control

> **Important Note**
> Even though we have created and used this custom control for both Android and iOS, because the iOS renderer is not implemented, iOS will still display the next best thing from the inheritance tree (that is, `EntryRenderer`).

In this section, we started our implementation in quadrant II by implementing a custom control within the Xamarin.Forms shared domain. Then, we moved on to create a custom renderer and a custom control.

Summary

Overall, Xamarin.Forms has many extensibility points for various scenarios. Nevertheless, we, as developers, should be careful about using these extensibility points sensibly in order to create robust, simple, and yet sophisticated UIs. In this chapter, to understand the customization options that were available, we identified the implementation domains/quadrants of our Xamarin.Forms application and went over different customization options for each quadrant. Finally, we created a custom control to demonstrate the complete implementation of a user control in both shared and native domains.

This chapter finalizes the Xamarin side of the development effort of our project. In the next few chapters, we will continue developing a cloud infrastructure using .NET Core for our mobile application.

Section 3: Azure Cloud Services

Creating a modern mobile application generally requires a robust service backend and infrastructure. The Azure cloud infrastructure provides a wide spectrum of services and development platforms for developers to create .NET Core components that can be used with mobile applications. These services vary from simple **Platform as a Service** (**PaaS**) hosting components to sophisticated multi-model persistence stores.

The following chapters will be covered in this section:

- *Chapter 7, Azure Services for Mobile Applications*
- *Chapter 8, Creating a Datastore with Cosmos DB*
- *Chapter 9, Creating Microservices Azure App Services*
- *Chapter 10, Using .NET Core for Azure Serverless*

7
Azure Services for Mobile Applications

Whether you are dealing with a small start up application or handling a large amount of data for an enterprise application, Microsoft Azure is always a convenient choice because of its cost-effective subscription model and the scalability that it offers. There are a number of services available in different managed service models, such as **Software as a Service (SaaS)**, **Platform as a Service (PaaS)**, and **Infrastructure as a Service (IaaS)**. These include Notification Hubs, Cognitive Services, and Azure Functions, which can change the impression of the user regarding your application with few or no additional development hours. This chapter will provide you with a quick overview in terms of how to use some of these services while developing .NET Core applications.

In this chapter, we will be designing our service backend using the service offerings available on the Azure platform. We will first browse through the services available on the Azure platform and continue by taking a deeper look at data stores, Azure Serverless PaaS offerings, and finally development services. The following topics will guide you through this chapter:

- An overview of Azure services
- Data stores
- Azure Serverless
- Development services

By the end of this chapter, you will be acquainted with various architectural models that utilize Azure services and you will have a better understanding of how to incorporate these models into your mobile application projects. We will take a closer look at persistence services as well as Azure Serverless offers. Finally, Azure DevOps and Visual Studio App Center will be discussed.

An overview of Azure services

We are living in the age of cloud computing. Many of the software paradigms that we learned and applied to our applications 10 years ago are now completely obsolete. The good old n-tier applications and development team simplicity have been replaced by distributed modules for the sake of maintainability and performance.

Without further ado, let's start preparing the scope of our application by setting up the architecture and exploring the concepts of the Azure platform.

An introduction to distributed systems

In this section, we will discuss different hosting models for a distributed backend system and what the pros and cons are of these setups.

In the previous chapters of this book, we started the development of our client application; this will require some additional views and modifications. In order to continue with the development, we first need to set up our backend. For our application, we will need a service backend that will do the following:

- Provide static metadata about products
- Manage user profiles and maintain user-specific information
- Allow users to upload and publicly share data
- Index and search user uploads and shares
- Notify a set of users with real-time updates

Now, putting these requirements and our goal of creating a cloud infrastructure aside, let's try to imagine how we could implement a distributed system with an on-premises n-tier application setup:

Figure 7.1 – N-tier on-premises backend

In the setup shown in the preceding screenshot, we have a web tier that exposes the closed logical n-tier structure to the client. Notice that the system is divided into logical tiers and that there is no over-the-wire communication involved. We will maintain this structure with an on-premises server. Multiple servers with a load-balanced implementation could still work if there is a need for scaling. In most cases, synchronization and normalization will occur in the data tier. From a deployment and management perspective, each deployment will result in a complete update (on multiple servers). Additionally, each logical module's requirements will have to be maintained separately even if it was a monolith implementation, and applying updates to the on-premises server should not be taken lightly because of these requirements. Deployments to distinct servers will also have to be handled with care.

> **Important note**
> Knight Capital Group was an American global financial services firm specializing in the electronic execution of sales and trading. In August 2012, the company went from $400 million in assets to bankruptcy overnight because of a new deployment that was only released on seven of the eight servers that the company operated. The 45-minute nightmare, where the correct deployments were competing with the old code on a single server, resulted in a $460 million loss.

We can easily move the complete web application to a cloud IaaS **virtual machine** (**VM**). However, this migration will only help with maintenance, and scaling would still have to be on a system level rather than a component level. The bottleneck, in this case, would most likely be the data tier since the application components being scaled would only put more pressure on the data repository.

In order to understand this n-tier setup, let's take a closer look at the possible components that would be involved. We would use a SQL database for data storage, a message queue such as Rabbit MQ or MSMQ, and an ASP.NET web API implementation for the web tier. Identity management would probably be an integrated solution, such as ASP.NET Identity. Notifications could be a polling implementation from the client side or, alternatively, a SignalR implementation can be considered within the ASP.NET web application. Search functionality would probably have to be on the SQL Server level for improved performance. All of this is based on the assumption that we are using the Microsoft .NET stack and that the target hosting platform is a Microsoft IIS server on a Windows host.

Next, let's break down our logical modules into smaller services that can communicate with each other within a **Service-Oriented Architecture (SOA)** ecosystem:

Figure 7.2 – Microservice Setup

The setup in the preceding screenshot is a bit lighter as compared to the one in *Figure 7.1*, where each component can be independently developed and deployed (that is, decoupled from the other elements in the system). From a maintenance perspective, each service can be deployed onto separate servers or VMs. In return, they can be scaled independently from one another. Moreover, each of these services can now be containerized so that we can completely decouple our services from the operating system. After all, we only need to have a web server in which our set of services can be hosted and served to the client. At this point, .NET Core will turn our application into a cross-platform web module, allowing us to use both Windows and Unix containers. This whole endeavor could be labeled as migrating from an IaaS strategy to a PaaS approach. Additionally, the application can now implement an **Infrastructure as Code (IaC)** structure, where we don't need to worry about the current state of the servers that the application is running on.

Well, this sounds great, but how does it relate to cloud architecture and Azure? The main purpose of creating a cloud-ready application is to create an application with functionally independent modules that can be hosted by appropriate, maintainable, and scalable cloud resources. At this point, we are no longer talking about a single application, but a group of resources working hand-in-hand for various application requirements:

Figure 7.3 – Azure PaaS Setup

In the preceding diagram of a distributed model, each component is made up of simple PaaS services where there is no direct dependency among them. The components are completely scalable and are replaceable as long as the system requirements are satisfied. For instance, if we begin with a small web API application service, it will probably reside within an application service plan. However, if the requirements are satisfied, then we can replace this microservice with an Azure function implementation that would change the deployment model and the execution runtime, but still keep the system intact. Overall, in a cloud model, the replaceable nature of individual components (as long as the overall system is in check) minimizes risks and the effort of maintenance.

Going back to our requirements, we are free to choose between a relational database such as a SQL Server PaaS or a NoSQL setup with Cosmos DB. Additionally, we can improve performance by using a Redis Cache between the data stores and the web gateway. Search functions could be executed using Azure Search indices, and App Services and Azure Functions can be employed for the API layer. Additionally, a simple ESB implementation or Azure Durable Functions can help with the long-running asynchronous operations. Finally, notifications can be executed by using Azure SignalR or Notification Hubs.

Of course, the choice of resources will largely depend on the architectural approach that is chosen.

Cloud architecture

In this section, we will be analyzing several architectural patterns for cloud-hosted distributed applications and the relevant Azure service offerings.

In the cloud platform, the design of the system consists of individual components. While each component should be designed and developed separately, the way in which these components are composed should follow certain architectural patterns that will allow the system to provide resilience, maintainability, scalability, and security.

Particularly for mobile applications, some of the following compositional models can help to contribute to the success of the application.

In order to correlate these patterns, we will be discussing our ShopAcross application, so let's define a new user story for a new feature we will be working on in the upcoming sections:

As a product owner, I would like to introduce an auctioning feature, where users can create posts for their goods, such as vehicles to be auctioned, so that I can increase the target group of my application.

This feature increases the data input/output to our application persistence store and increases the complexity of our backend service. Let's now take a look at several models that could help us in this quest.

Gateway aggregation

In a microservices setup, the application is made up of multiple domains, and each domain implements its own microservice counterpart. Since the domain is segregated, the data that is required for the client application view can be constructed by executing multiple calls for the backend services. In an evolving application ecosystem, this will, in time, push all the complexities of the business tier into the client application. While this could still be acceptable for a web application, a mobile application's performance will degrade in time as the complexity of the system grows. In order to avoid this problem, a gateway service façade can be placed in between the client application and the microservices:

Figure 7.4 – Gateway Aggregation Setup

Let's consider applying the same logic within our application. Let's assume that an auctioned vehicle's data is handled by one API (business item), the vehicle's metadata is handled by another API (static data), the user information is served through yet another API, and, finally, we have a bidding API. While this setup provides the necessary segregation for a microservice setup, it requires the client application to execute multiple service calls to view and/or create a single posting. In such a scenario, the gateway can be used to orchestrate the microservices so that the client application can be relieved of this responsibility.

If, in fact, we are planning to support a web application as a client, then the data models and service orchestration might differ from the mobile application. In this case, we would need to consider creating separate gateways for each client app, thereby decreasing the maintainability costs of a single super gateway.

Backends for frontends

In a multi-client system, each client might require the data to be aggregated in a certain way. This will depend on the target platform resources, technical feasibility, and use cases. In this type of scenario, the gateway API would be required to expose multiple service endpoints for different microservice and data compositions. Instead, each client app can be served data through a separate gateway, thereby reducing the complexities of supporting multiple client applications through a single façade:

Figure 7.5 – Backends for frontends

In the preceding example, we have three separate gateways (in other words, Gate-A, Gate-B, and Gate-C) set up to support three different client applications. Each gateway implements its own aggregation model rather than creating a single complex façade full of client-specific adjustments.

For instance, let's assume that our application development team implements a UWP application on top of an original mobile application that is targeting iOS and Android platforms. In this case, UWP views would be viewed on a larger design real estate and the data requirements would be different to the mobile applications. For a simple solution, gateway API endpoints can now be extended with parameters to limit or extend the object tree that is returned in the response (that is, info, normal, or extended), or additional `Get{Entity}Extended` endpoints can be introduced. Nevertheless, in this way, while minimizing the complexity of the client applications, we are causing the gateway to grow and are decreasing the maintainability of this tier. If we introduce separate gateways, we will be separating the life cycle of these APIs for clients that already have separate application life cycles. This could help in creating a more maintainable system.

However, what if we have certain compositions or aggregations that repeat throughout the execution of client applications? These repeating patterns can be construed as data design problems, where the segregation of data results in a degradation of performance. If the microservice setup, in fact, requires these domain separations, we will need to come up with a data composition on the data store level.

A materialized view

The aggregation of certain data dimensions can be done on a data store level. In fact, as developers with a SQL background, we are familiar with SQL views that can be composed of multiple relational tables and can be indexed on the data store level. While this provides a different perspective on the available data, it can even create an aggregate of multiple domain-specific data models. Nevertheless, these views are still nothing beyond a runtime abstraction. Moreover, if the persistence stores are dispersed over multiple servers, we would need an independent process to synchronize the data between the domain stores with another aggregation store and persist the denormalized data. In other words, materialize the view. Similar strategies can be applied to NoSQL databases such as Cosmos.

For instance, this data denormalization process can be executed on Cosmos DB using the Azure Cosmos DB change feed. Changes on one document collection can be synchronized across multiple collections, which are optimized for executing various searches or aggregating data operations:

Figure 7.6 – Denormalized data with Azure Functions

For instance, going back to our auction functionality, when we are dealing with the search function, we will be executing a search on multiple document collections; that is, the user will need to search by vehicle, auction data, bids, and profile data. In other words, the data points on different dimensions should all be available through an inner join for the search execution. This can be achieved using a summary table for the vehicle posts, allowing searchable fields to be synchronized across collections.

The cache-aside pattern

Caching is yet another factor that can help improve the performance of the application, that is, the type of data we are caching and the application layers that we are caching this information on. The cache-aside pattern is the implementation of a multiplexer that will handle data consistency between the cache store and the data store depending on the incoming requests and the data lifespan:

Figure 7.7 – Cache-aside Implementation

In this setup, an incoming request, branded with a certain unique identifier (for example, `{EntityName}_{EntityId}`), is first searched for within the cache store and, if not there, is retrieved from the data store and inserted into the cache. In this way, the next request will be able to retrieve the data from the cache.

In a to-cache or not-to-cache dilemma, data entropy can be a fundamental decision factor. For instance, caching data for static reference items can be beneficial; however, caching the auction information, where the data is impure and the recurrence of requests for the same data points is less likely than static references, will not provide added value to the system.

The cache-aside strategy can also be implemented on the client side using local storage such as SQLite. At times, a certain document collection that it would not make sense to cache on the server side can beneficially be cached on the client side. For instance, the vehicle metadata for a certain make and model for the current user might be a repeating request pattern; however, considering the entropy of this data and the access frequency of other users to the same item, it would not be a server cache dimension.

Queue-based load leveling

Message queues are neither a new concept nor exclusive to the cloud architecture. However, in a distributed system with microservices, they can help with the decoupling of services and allow you to throttle resource utilization. Serverless components that are designed for scalability and performance, such as Azure Functions, can provide excellent consumers for work queues within the cloud infrastructure.

For instance, let's consider an application use case where the registered user is creating an auction item. They have selected the make and model, added additional information, and have even added several photos for the vehicle. At this point, if we allow the posting of this auction item to be a synchronous request, we will be locking certain modules in the pipeline to a single request. Primarily, the request would need to create a document in the data store; however, additional functions would also be triggered within the system to process images, notify subscribed users, and even start an approval process for the content administrator. Now, imagine this request is executed by multiple users of the application (for example, multiple registered users creating multiple posts). This would result in resource utilization peaks, which, in turn, would put the resilience and availability of the application at risk.

As a solution to this problem, we can create a message queue that will be consumed by an Azure function, which will orchestrate the creation of the auction data. The message queue can either be an enterprise service bus or an Azure storage queue:

Figure 7.8 – Queue-based request processing

This sounds great, but how does this implementation affect the client implementation? Well, the client application will need to implement either a polling strategy to retrieve the status of the asynchronous job, or it can be notified using a push-pull mechanism, where the server would first send the auction ID before the process is even queued. Then, when it is finalized, the server can notify the client with the same ID, allowing it to pull the completed server data. At this point, the local version of the data can be stored and served to the user until the actual server data is available. For this type of notification, notification mechanisms such as Azure SignalR or Notifications Hub can be employed.

Competing consumers

In the previous example, we used Azure functions as the consumers of a message queue. This approach could already be accepted as an implementation of competing consumers where the message queue provided is handled by multiple worker modules.

While this would provide scaling requirements and allow for performant execution, as a product owner, we would not have any control over the function instances created to consume the events from the message queue. In order to be able to throttle and manage the queue, a message broker mechanism can be introduced, which will control the flow of messages into the queue. Once the messages are pushed into the queue, multiple consumers can retrieve, process, and complete the messages.

The publisher/subscriber pattern

Let's assume that we have completed our brokered queue implementation and dispatched a consumer to finalize a long-running operation. At this point, as previously mentioned, our application is expecting a done signal so that it can get rid of any transient data.

In an open system, like the one we are in the process of implementing, where each service can communicate with each other (rather than a closed system where execution is handled sequentially downstream), we are no longer dealing with a deterministic synchronous model, and yet the consumers of the system still expect results. In order to allow the source system (that is, the publisher) to propagate the output of an operation to the interested parties (that is, the subscribers), an output channel can be established. This implementation pattern can be attributed to the publisher/subscriber pattern (which is also known as the pub/sub pattern).

Going back to our asynchronous web request, the output channel would then deliver the result to the notification module and deliver the results to the client application.

The same pattern implementation can be established with another message queue using Service Bus or the actual implementation of the pub/sub pattern on the Azure infrastructure, EventGrid. Either of these services can allow the output from a long-running process to be fanned out to interested parties, such as an Azure function, which will push the notification message or trigger a message on Azure SignalR.

The circuit breaker and retry patterns

In a cloud system, where there are multiple moving pieces involved, it is hard to avoid failure. In this context, the resilience of a system is determined by how fast and how often it can recover from a failure. The circuit breaker and retry patterns are complementary patterns that are generally introduced in a microservice ecosystem. The circuit break pattern can be used to decrease the time and resources of a system if a failure is imminent. In these types of situations, it is better to allow the system to fail sooner rather than later so that the failure can be handled by a secondary process or a failover mechanism can be initiated.

For instance, if we have a service that is prone to timeouts (for example, under heavy load or due to an external service failure), a circuit breaker can be implemented to continuously monitor the incoming requests in the closed-circuit state. Failures can be retried seamlessly with regard to the client application. When consequent failures occur, the circuit can be put into a half-open or open state temporarily, so that the following requests are immediately dropped without trying the execution (knowing that it will probably fail until the issue is fixed). In this state, the client app can disable the feature or, if there is a failover/workaround implemented, then this implementation can be used. Once the circuit open state expires, the system can reintroduce this endpoint, first, in a half-open state and, finally, in a closed state, and the system is said to be healed.

Built-in Azure monitoring functions accompanied by application telemetry can provide alerts and notifications, which can help with the maintenance of Azure applications.

Azure service providers and resource types

In the previous sections, we have analyzed various models and mentioned several Azure offerings. In this part, you will learn how these service offerings in the Azure ecosystem are organized.

The Azure ecosystem, along with the ever-growing set of services it provides, allows developers to create various distributed cloud applications with ease. As we have seen in the *Cloud architecture* section, many PaaS and SaaS offerings create a catalog of solutions for everyday problems by designing scalable and resilient applications.

By quickly looking at the (incomplete) catalog of services, you will notice that each service is provided as part of a provider category:

Figure 7.9 – Azure service offerings

The services in each category are provided by one or multiple service providers. Each service in these catalogs is versioned so that the provisioning of these services can be handled by Azure Resource Manager.

In order to visualize the number of providers available under the same roof, you can use the Azure PowerShell module:

```
Get-AzResourceProvider -ListAvailable | Select-Object
ProviderNamespace, RegistrationState
```

This will return a set of providers that are available for your subscription. These providers can be Microsoft-provided modules or third-party offers:

Figure 7.10 – Microsoft Azure providers

> **Important note**
>
> Microsoft Azure Documentation provides helpful Azure PowerShell commands, which can be directly executed in the Cloud Shell without having to use PowerShell (on Windows) or Bash (on Linux or macOS). Additionally, a cross-platform version, PowerShell (Core), which utilizes .NET Core, is available on non-Windows operating systems.

If you dive into a specific namespace, for instance, the `Microsoft.Compute` provider namespace, you can get a better overview of the services offered, and the geographical regions where these resources are available can be seen in the following screenshot:

```
Azure:/
PS Azure:\> Get-AzResourceProvider -ProviderNamespace Microsoft.Compute
>> | Select-Object ResourceTypes, Locations

ResourceTypes                                                              Locations
-------------                                                              ---------
{availabilitySets}                                                         {East US, East US 2, ...
{virtualMachines}                                                          {East US, East US 2, ...
{virtualMachines/extensions}                                               {East US, East US 2, ...
{virtualMachineScaleSets}                                                  {East US, East US 2, ...
{virtualMachineScaleSets/extensions}                                       {East US, East US 2, ...
{virtualMachineScaleSets/virtualMachines}                                  {East US, East US 2, ...
{virtualMachineScaleSets/networkInterfaces}                                {East US, East US 2, ...
{virtualMachineScaleSets/virtualMachines/networkInterfaces}                {East US, East US 2, ...
{virtualMachineScaleSets/publicIPAddresses}                                {East US, East US 2, ...
{locations}                                                                {}
{locations/operations}                                                     {East US, East US 2, ...
{locations/vmSizes}                                                        {East US, East US 2, ...
{locations/runCommands}                                                    {East US, East US 2, ...
{locations/usages}                                                         {East US, East US 2, ...
{locations/virtualMachines}                                                {East US, East US 2, ...
{locations/publishers}                                                     {East US, East US 2, ...
{operations}                                                               {East US, East US 2, ...
{restorePointCollections}                                                  {Southeast Asia, East...
{restorePointCollections/restorePoints}                                    {Southeast Asia, East...
{virtualMachines/diagnosticSettings}                                       {East US, East US 2, ...
```

Figure 7.11 – Microsoft.Compute provider services

In an Azure resource group, the `Resource` type defines which resource we are really after as well as the version of this resource. These resource definitions, if prepared as part of a resource group **Azure Resource Manager** (**ARM**) template, make up our declarative IaC.

ARM is the platform service that allows the provisioning of resources within a subscription. It exposes a web API that can be consumed using PowerShell, Azure CLI, and CloudShell, as well as the Azure portal itself. The declarative syntax used in resource manager templates provides a consistent, idempotent deployment experience, which allows developers and automation engineers to manage the infrastructure life cycle with confidence.

In this section, several distributed application models as well as architectural patterns were discussed. We also briefly took a look at the resource groups and providers in an extensive Azure catalog of offers. In the next section, we will focus on persistence store services available on Azure.

Data stores

Defining domains and creating the architecture that our distributed system is going to be built upon inherently starts with deciding on the persistence store. In return, data domains can be defined, and access models can be designated. In most cases, this decision does not need to be limited to a single data store, but the system can make use of multiple data types and different data stores. The Azure platform offers various resources with different data management concepts and feature sets. It is important to choose a data store model that is best suited to the application requirements and take account of cost and management. Let's now take a look at these different models and when to use them.

Relational database resources

Relational databases are probably the most prominent applications of a data store. Transactional consistency that implements the **Atomic**, **Consistent**, **Isolated**, **Durable** (**ACID**) principles offers developers a strong consistency guarantee. Nevertheless, from a scalability and performance perspective, common SQL implementations such as MSSQL or MySQL are, in most scenarios, outperformed by NoSQL databases such as Mongo and Cosmos DB. Azure SQL Database, Azure Database for MySQL, and PostgreSQL are available both as IaaS and PaaS offerings on the Azure platform.

In the PaaS resource model, the operational costs and scalability of the databases are handled through a unit called the **Database Transaction Unit** (**DTU**). This unit is an abstract benchmark that is calculated using CPU, memory, and data I/O measures. In other words, DTU is not an exact measure, but a normalized value depending on the aforementioned measures. Microsoft offers a DTU calculator, which can provide estimates on DTU usage based on performance counters collected on a live database.

From a security perspective, several advanced features are available for Azure SQL databases. These security features are available on various levels of data accessibility:

- Network security is maintained by firewalls and access is granted explicitly by using IP and Virtual Network firewall rules.

- Access management implementation consists of SQL authentication and Azure Active Directory authentication. The security permissions can be as granulized as data tables and rows.

- Threat protection is available through log analytics and data auditing as well as threat detection services.

- Information protection through data masking and encryption on various levels protects the data itself.

Being one of the most conservative data models, as you can see, it is still very popular on the Azure platform and available as both IaaS and PaaS offerings. Now that we have covered relational databases, let's move on to more "liberal" NoSQL data storage models.

Azure storage

The Azure storage model is one of the oldest services in the cloud ecosystem. It is a NoSQL store and provides developers with a durable and scalable persistence layer. Azure storage is made up of four different data services, and each of these services is accessed over HTTP/HTTPS with a well-established REST API.

Let's take a closer look at these data services available within Azure storage.

Azure blobs

Azure Blob storage is the cloud storage offering for unstructured data. Blobs can be used to store any kind of data chunks, such as text or binary data. Azure Blob storage can be accessed through the URL provided for the storage account created:

`http://{storageaccountname}.blob.core.windows.net`

Each storage account contains at least one container, which is used to organize the blobs that are created. Three types of blobs are used for different types of data chunks to be uploaded:

1. **Block blobs**: These are designed for large binary data. The size of a block blob can go up to 4.7 TB. Each block blob is made up of smaller blocks of data, which can be individually managed. Each block can hold up to 100 MB of data. Each block should define a block ID, which should conform to a specific length within the blob. Block blobs can be regarded as discrete storage objects, such as files in a local operating system. They are generally used for storing individual files such as media content.

2. **Page blobs**: These are used when there is a need for random read/write operations. These blobs are made up of pages of 512 bytes. A page blob can store up to 8 TB of data. In order to create a page blob, a maximum size should be designated. Then, the content can be added in pages by specifying an offset and a range that aligns with the 512-byte page boundaries. VHDs stored in the cloud are a perfect fit for page blob usage scenarios. In fact, the durable disks provided for Azure VM are page blob-based (that is, they are Azure IaaS disks).

3. **Append blobs**: As the name suggests, these are append-only blobs. They cannot be updated or deleted, and the management of individual blocks is not supported. They are frequently used for logging information. An append blob can grow up to 195 GB.

As you can see, blob storage, especially block blobs, are ideal for storing image content for our application. Azure Storage Client library methods provide access to CRUD operations for blobs and can be directly used in the client application. However, it is generally a security-aware approach to use a backend service to execute the actual upload to blob storage so that the Azure security keys can be kept within the server rather than the client.

Azure files

Azure files can be considered a cloud-hosted, file-sharing system. It is accessible through the **Server Message Block** (**SMB**), also known as Samba, and allows storage resources to be used on hybrid (that is, on-premises and cloud) scenarios. Legacy applications that are using network shared folders (or even local files) can be easily pointed to the Azure files network storage. Azure files, just like any other Azure storage data service, are accessible through the REST API and Azure storage client libraries.

Azure queues

In order to implement asynchronous processing patterns, if you are not after advanced functionalities and queue consistency, Azure queues can be a cost-effective alternative to Service Bus. Azure queues can be larger and easier to implement and manage for simpler use cases. Similar to Service Bus, Azure queue messages can also be used with Azure Functions, where each message triggers an Azure function that handles the processing. If triggers are not used, then only a polling mechanism can handle the message queue. This is because, unlike Service Bus, they don't provide blocking access or an event trigger mechanism such as `OnMessage` on Service Bus.

Azure tables

Azure tables are a NoSQL-structured cloud data store solution. The implementation of Azure Table storage follows a **key-value pair** (**KVP**) approach, where structured data without a common schema can be stored in a table store. Azure Table storage data can be easily visualized on the Azure portal and data operations are supported through Azure Storage client libraries such as other Azure storage services. Nevertheless, Azure Table storage is now part of Azure Cosmos DB and can be accessed using the Cosmos DB table API and SDK.

Cosmos DB

Cosmos DB is the multi-façade, globally distributed database service offering of Microsoft on the Azure cloud. With its key benefits being scalability and availability, Azure Cosmos DB is a strong candidate for any cloud-based undertaking. Being a write-optimized database engine, it guarantees less than 10 ms latency on read/write queries at the 99th percentile globally.

Cosmos DB provides developers with five different consistency models to allow for an optimal compromise between performance and availability, depending on requirements. The so-called consistency spectrum defines various levels between strong consistency and eventual consistency or, in other words, higher availability and higher throughput.

In spite of the fact that it was designed as NoSQL storage, it does support various storage model protocols, including SQL. These storage protocols support the use of existing client drivers and SDKs, and can replace existing NoSQL data stores seamlessly. Each API model can also be accessed through the use of the available REST API:

API	Model	Containers	Items
SQL API	Document	Collections	Documents
MongoDB	Document	Collections	Documents
Gremlin	Graph	Graphs	Nodes and Edges
Cassandra	Column Family	Table	Rows
Azure Table Storage	KVP Store	Table	Items

Figure 7.12 – CosmosDB Access Models

With the variety of access models it offers, CosmosDB is on its way to becoming the go-to service on Azure platform for data persistence. But what if the data we want to handle is more volatile than the type of data that we store in a long-term persistence store? Azure Cache for Redis can be a great solution for temporary data that is used in these types of scenario.

Azure Cache for Redis

The Azure Cache for Redis resource is a provider that implements an in-memory data structure store that is similar to Redis. It helps improve the performance and scalability of distributed systems by decreasing the load on the actual persistence store. With Redis, data is stored as KVPs, and because of its replicated nature, it can also be used as a distributed queue. Redis supports the execution of transactions in an atomic manner.

We will be using the cache-aside pattern with the help of Azure Cache for Redis to implement in our application backend.

In this section, we browsed through the PaaS offerings on Azure for data storage. In the next section, we will take a look at another PaaS service that can help greatly with the maintainability and costs of distributed systems: Azure Serverless.

Azure Serverless

As you may have noticed, in modern cloud applications, PaaS components are more abundant than IaaS resources. Here, application VMs are replaced with smaller application containers, and the database as a platform replaces the clustered database servers. Azure Serverless takes infrastructure and platform management one step further. In a serverless resource model, such as Azure Functions, event-driven application logic is executed on-demand on a platform that is provisioned, scaled, and managed by the platform itself. In the Azure Serverless platform, event triggers can vary from message queues to webhooks, with intrinsic integration into various resources within the ecosystem.

Azure functions

Azure functions are managed, event-driven logic implementations that can provide lightweight ad hoc solutions for the cloud architecture. In Azure functions, the engineering team is not only oblivious to the execution infrastructure, but also to the platform, since Azure functions are implemented cross-platform with .NET Core, Java, and Python.

The execution of an Azure function starts with the trigger. Various execution models are supported for Azure functions, including the following:

1. **Data triggers**: `CosmosDBTrigger` and `BlobTrigger`
2. **Periodic triggers**: `TimerTrigger`

3. **Queue triggers**: `QueueTrigger`, `ServicesBusQueueTrigger`, and `ServiceBusTopicTrigger`
4. **Event triggers**: `EventGridTrigger` and `EventHubTrigger`

The trigger for an Azure function is defined within the function manifest/configuration: `function.json`.

Once the trigger is realized, the function runtime executes the run block of an Azure function. The request parameters (that is, the input bindings) that are passed to the run block are determined by the trigger that was used.

For instance, the following function implementation is triggered by a message entry in an Azure storage queue:

```
public static class MyQueueSample
{
    [FunctionName("LogQueueMessage")]
    public static void Run(
        [QueueTrigger("%queueappsetting%")] string
        queueItem, ILogger log)
    {
        log.LogInformation($"Function was called with:
        {queueItem}");
    }
}
```

The output parameters (that is, the output binding) can also be defined as an `out` parameter within the function declaration:

```
public static class MyQueueSample
{
    [FunctionName("LogQueueMessage")]
    public static void Run(
        [QueueTrigger("%queueappsetting%")] string
         queueItem,
        [Queue("%queueappsetting%-out")] string outputItem
        ILogger log)
    {
        log.LogInformation($"Function was called with:
        {queueItem}");
```

```
    }
}
```

Note that the `[Queue]` attribute is used from the queue storage bindings for Azure functions as an output binding, which will create a new message entry in another queue. Further similar binding types are available out of the box for Azure functions.

> **Important note**
> We have used C# and .NET Standard in these examples to create compiled Azure functions. Script-based C#, Node.js, and Python are also options for creating functions using a similar methodology.

Conceptually, Azure functions can be treated as per-call web services. Nevertheless, Durable Functions, an extension of Azure Functions, allows developers to create durable (that is, stateful) functions. These functions allow you to write stateful functions with checkpoints, where the orchestrator function can dispatch stateless functions and execute a workflow.

Azure functions can be used either as individual modules executing business logic on certain triggers or as a bundle of imperative workflows (using durable functions); alternatively, they can be used as processing units of **Azure Logic Apps**.

Azure Logic apps

Azure Logic apps are declarative workflow definitions that are used to orchestrate tasks, processes, and workflows. Similar to functions, they can be integrated with many other Azure resources as well as external resources. Logic apps are created, versioned, and provisioned using a JSON app definition schema. Designers are available both on the Azure portal as well as Visual Studio:

Figure 7.13 – Logic app designer

Logic apps' tasks are not only limited to Azure functions, but also include so-called commercial and/or third-party connectors (for example, sending an SMS with Twilio, using SendGrid to send an email, or posting a Tweet). In addition to this, the **Enterprise Integration Pack** (**EIP**) provides industry-standard messaging protocols.

Just like with Azure functions, the execution of a logic app starts with the trigger, and each output step is stored within the execution context. Processing blocks such as conditionals, switches, and `foreach` loops are available within the app flow. Additionally, logic app workflows can be dispatched by **Azure Event Grid** events.

Azure Event Grid

Azure Event Grid is a cloud-based event aggregate implementation that supports the pub/sub event routing strategy. An event grid consists of event sources (that is, the publishers) and event subscriptions (that is, the consumers):

Figure 7.14 – Event Grid actors

Similar to Azure function triggers, various event sources are available for developers and Azure Event Grid can be used to route or multicast certain events from one Azure resource to another. Events do not need to be triggered by a system resource, but can also be created using an HTTP request, allowing custom modules to send events to consumers.

With event grid, we are finishing this section. In this section, we have discussed Azure Functions and Logic apps and finally the event grid that can be used as the mediator between the other Azure components used in the application. Now that we have browsed through the services that we can utilize in our application, let's move on to the services that can help us manage the life cycle of our project.

Development services

Azure resources are not just limited to application requirements that are provisioned and maintained with the application life cycle. They also include certain platform services that are used to implement the application life cycle and development pipeline, such as Azure DevOps and Visual Studio App Center. In this section, we will take a look at these freemium offers that we will be using to manage our application development and deployments throughout the remainder of the book.

Azure DevOps

Azure DevOps (previously known as TFS Online or Visual Studio Team Services), which started as the Microsoft **Application Lifecycle Management (ALM)** suite for on-premises product TFS, is now the most widely utilized freemium management portal. Azure DevOps instances can be created from the Azure Portal as well as through the Azure DevOps portal. This process of procurement starts with creating a DevOps organization.

Once the organization is created, a new project can be created that includes the source control repositories and the backlog. Both the ALM process and the version control options are available under the **Advanced** section of the project settings:

Figure 7.15 – Azure DevOps project setup

It is important to mention that the TFVC and Git repositories are available at the same time. A single Azure DevOps project may contain multiple repositories. Because of cross-platform support and integration with IDEs (such as Visual Studio Code and Visual Studio for Mac), as well as native IDEs (such as Android Studio), Git is generally the repository type of choice for Xamarin and native mobile developers.

An extensive feature set is available for DevOps implementations on Azure DevOps. The Azure portal (apart from the overview) is divided into five main sections, as follows:

- Boards (project management)
- Repos (source control)
- Pipelines (CI/CD)
- Test plans (test management)
- Artifacts (package management)

According to the freemium subscription model, up to five contributors can be included in a project for free. Additional team members will need to have either a valid Visual Studio or **Microsoft Developer Network (MSDN)** license, or they will be assigned to a read-only stakeholder role.

Visual Studio App Center

Visual Studio App Center is a suite of tools that bundles various development services used by mobile developers (such as Xamarin, Native, and Hybrid) into a single management portal. App Center has tight integration with Azure DevOps, and they can be used in conjunction with one another. Multiple application platforms are supported by App Center and various features are available for these platforms:

Figure 7.16 – App Center platforms

From a CI/CD perspective, App Center allows mobile application builds to be executed with source artifacts from various repository systems such as Azure DevOps and GitHub. Applications can be compiled using out-of-the-box build templates and application packages can be distributed to designated groups, without having to use any other store.

The prepared application packages can also be put through automated acceptance tests by means of UI tests. Multiple testing runtimes are supported for automated UI tests, such as Xamarin.UITest and Appium.

Finally, application telemetry and diagnostic data can be collected both from beta and production versions of mobile applications, and valuable application feedback can be reintroduced into the backlog. Push notifications are another valuable feature that can be used to engage application users.

App Center also uses a freemium subscription model, where the build and test hours are limited by the subscription; however, limited usage of the CI/CD features and unlimited distribution features are available for free.

Summary

Overall, developing a distributed application development is now much easier with tightly integrated Azure modules. Both cloud and hybrid applications can be created using the available resources and modules implemented with the .NET Core stack. It is also important to remember that resources should not define application requirements; rather, an optimal solution should be devised, bearing in mind the available modules, requirements, and costs.

In this chapter, we have discussed various application models and architectural models in the cloud context. We have also browsed through available Azure resources that will be used in the following chapters to create our application backend. In the next chapter, we will start by creating our data store using Cosmos DB.

8
Creating a Datastore with Cosmos DB

Creating a data store is an essential part of both mobile and web application projects. Scalability, cost-effectiveness, and performance are three key factors that determine which database is appropriate for your application. Cosmos DB, with its wide range of scalability options and subscription models, can provide an ideal solution for mobile applications. Cosmos DB offers a multi-model and multi-API paradigm that allows applications to use multiple data models while storing application data with the most suited API and model for the application, such as SQL, Cassandra, Gremlin, or MongoDB.

In this chapter, we will talk about the basic concepts of Cosmos DB, analyze and experiment with data access models, and finally, we will start creating the data model and datastore for our application and implement the data access modules.

In this chapter, we will cover the following topics:

- The basics of Cosmos DB
- Data access models
- Modeling data
- Learning about Cosmos DB in depth

By the end of this chapter, you will be comfortable with implementing and accessing data models on either the SQL API or Mongo access models provided by Cosmos DB.

Technical Requirements

You can find the code used in this chapter at the following GitHub link: `https://github.com/PacktPublishing/Mobile-Development-with-.NET-Second-Edition/tree/master/chapter08`.

The basics of Cosmos DB

From a cloud-based application perspective, **Cosmos DB** is yet another persistence store that's available that you can include in your resource group. As we discussed previously, the biggest advantages of Cosmos DB also make up the unique feature set of Cosmos DB, namely global distribution, the multi-model, and high availability.

In our example app, we will be using Cosmos DB and creating our data model around the available persistence models. Let's start by adding a Cosmos DB instance to our resource group:

The basics of Cosmos DB   215

Create Azure Cosmos DB Account

Basics Network Tags Review + create

Azure Cosmos DB is a fully managed globally distributed, multi-model database service, transparently replicating your data across any number of Azure regions. You can elastically scale throughput and storage, and take advantage of fast, single-digit-millisecond data access using the API of your choice backed by 99.999 SLA. learn more

PROJECT DETAILS

Select the subscription to manage deployed resources and costs. Use resource groups like folders to organize and manage all your resources.

* Subscription: Visual Studio Enterprise with MSDN
* Resource Group: HandsOnCrossPlatform-MSDN
  Create new

INSTANCE DETAILS

* Account Name: autoauction
  documents.azure.com
* API: Core (SQL)
* Location: West Europe
* Geo-Redundancy: Enable | **Disable**
* Multi-region Writes: Enable | **Disable**

Figure 8.1 – Creating a Cosmos DB Account

On this screen, we are going to set up the resource group, the account name (which also defines the access URL), and additional parameters related to the data access model, as well as global distribution. Before deciding on any Cosmos resource attribute, let's take a look at these basic concepts. In the following subsections, we will learn about how Cosmos DB employs global distribution, what the consistency spectrum looks like and different consistency requirements, and finally, how the pricing model can be adjusted to your needs.

Global distribution

Global distribution is an available option that deals with the global reach of your application. If you are planning to make your application globally available and you expect to have the same latency in each market, it is possible to select Geo-Redundancy to allow distribution in multiple regions. Once the Cosmos DB resource is created, this can be done using the **Replicate data globally** blade:

Figure 8.2 – Cosmos DB gGlobal Replication

Great! Now, we have the application present on five different data centers across four continents. In other words, we have enabled multi-homing for our persistence store.

In addition to Geo-Redundancy, you can enable multiple write regions. Multiple write regions allow you to set multiple masters for your distributed datastore. This data will not only be replicated across different regions but will also provide the same write throughput.

When the global distribution regions are configured, you can set one of the read regions, that is, its failover region.

Consistency spectrum

Once data persistence becomes a globally distributed, multi-homed operation, the consistency concept becomes a fundamental subject. In Cosmos DB, there are five well-defined consistency levels that allow developers to optimize, in simple terms, the trade-off between consistency and performance:

| Strong | Bounded Staleness | Session | Consistent Prefix | Eventual |

Stronger Consistency → **Weaker Consistency**

Higher availability, lower latency, higher throughput

Figure 8.3 – Consistency Spectrum

The default consistency level can be set on the database level, as well as within the client session that's consuming the data. However, the client set's consistency cannot be set to a stronger consistency than the default consistency level.

In order to understand this consistency, we will be using the baseball analogy that's used by the Microsoft research paper. In this example, we are considering the various stakeholders in a baseball game and how they read and write the score.

Without a doubt, the person who needs the strongest consistency is the official scorekeeper. They would read the current score and increment the score when any of the teams score. Then, they would like to have the assurance that the data they are reading is the latest version. However, since the scorekeeper is the only person who will be executing a write operation, we might be able to get away with a less consistent read level, such as **session consistency**, which provides the monotonic reads, monotonic writes, read-your-writes, and write-follows-reads guarantees given that there is a single writer session.

Following the official scorekeeper, another stakeholder with a **strong consistency** requirement is the umpire, the person who officiates the baseball game behind the home plate. The umpire's decision to end the game in the second half of the ninth inning depends on whether the home team is ahead (that is, if the visiting team has no way of equalizing the score, there is no need for the home team to bat). In this decision, they would require a linearizability guarantee (that is, they will be reading the latest version of any given data point). From their perspective, each operation should be happening atomically, and there is a single global state (that is, the source of truth). In this setup, the performance (that is, low latency) is compromised in exchange for a quorum state in a distributed cluster.

Unlike the umpire, a periodic reporter (for example, for 30 minutes) would just like assurance of a *consistent prefix*; in other words, they just rely on the consistent state of the data up until the returned write operation. For them, the data state consistency is more important than the latency of the result since the operation is executed periodically to give an overall update.

Another stakeholder that doesn't care much about the latency but cares about the consistent state would be the sportswriter. The writer can receive the final result of the game and provide their commentary the next day, as long as the result they received is the correct one. In a scenario similar to this, **eventual consistency** would probably return the correct final result, but when you want to limit the eventual consistency promise with a delay period, *bounded staleness* can be a solution. In fact, the umpire could have used a similar strategy for their read operations with a shorter delay.

By applying these concepts to our application model, we can decide for ourselves which modules would require which type of consistency.

Let's assume that our users receive a review or rating from the participants once the transaction is completed. In this scenario, the rating system does not really require an ordered set of writes, nor is the consistency of much importance. We would be able to get away with each review for the same user if we had written and read with the promise of *eventual consistency*.

Next up is the notification system, which sends out the highest bids for an auction item in certain intervals to only interested parties. Here, the read operation only needs to be performed with the promise so that the order in which the bids have been written to our data store is preserved, in other words, with a *consistent prefix*. This becomes especially crucial if we are sending statistics similar to *the value of the item has raised by 30% in the last hour*. Similarly, the period for this consistency can be defined by the read system, making it *bounded staleness* consistency.

Now, let's assume, that the user would like to keep a set of auctions in a watch list. This watch list would only be written by the user themselves, and the important read assurance would be to read-your-writes. This can be handled by *session consistency*. Additionally, the creation of a new auction item or updates would again be only session consistent.

Finally, probably the most consistent process in the setup would be the actual bidding (that is, *strong consistency*). Here, in order to bid for an auction item, as well as to announce the results of an auction, we rely on strong consistency since bidding on the items is a multi-actor operation and we would like to make sure that the incoming bids are executed in a consistent manner.

This, of course, is just a presumptuous setup where the costs and implementation are completely left out of the equation. In a real-world implementation, session consistency would provide the best trade-off between consistency and performance while decreasing costs.

Pricing

The pricing model for Cosmos DB is rather complicated. This calculation involves many factors, such as global availability, consistency, and another abstract unit called the **Request Unit** (**RU**). Similar to the **Data Transaction Unit** (**DTU**), it is a measure of the system resources that are used (for example, CPU, memory, and IO) to read a 1 KB item. A number of factors can affect the RU's usage, such as item size, complexity, indexing, consistency level, and executed queries. It is possible to keep track of the RU consumption by using the request charge headers that are returned by the DB.

Let's take a look at the following document DB client execution:

```
var query = client.CreateDocumentQuery<Item>(
UriFactory.CreateDocumentCollectionUri(DatabaseId,
CollectionId),
        new FeedOptions { MaxItemCount = -1 })
            .Where(item => !item.IsCompleted)
            .AsDocumentQuery();
```

This would translate into a SQL query as follows:

```
select * from Items where Items.isCompleted = false
```

We can retrieve the request charge by using the **Query Stats** tab on the **Data Explorer** blade:

Figure 8.4 – Cosmos DB Query Stats

According to the datasets and application execution, request charges become more and more important. The Cosmos DB costs can be optimized for your application's needs by analyzing the provided telemetry.

In this section, we went over fundamental concepts of Cosmos DB including global distribution and consistency. Finally, one of the key decision factors of a cloud-based data store – pricing model – was discussed and request units were analyzed.

Data access models

Probably the most important option to select before creating the Cosmos DB instance is the access model (that is, the API). In our application, we will be using the SQL API since it is inherently the only native access model and allows the usage of additional features such as triggers. This is why the SQL API will be the first access model that we will dive into in this section. Nevertheless, we will also go over the Mongo API, which can provide a viable alternative with its strong community support as well as the mitigated risk of vendor-lock. Other options that will be discussed in this section include Gremlin, Cassandra, and Azure Table Storage.

The SQL API

Previously a standalone offer known as Azure Document DB, the SQL API allows developers to query a JSON-based NoSQL data structure with a SQL dialect. Similar to actual SQL implementations, the SQL API supports the use of stored procedures, triggers (that is, change feeds), and user-defined functions. Support for SQL queries allows for the (partial) use of LINQ and existing client SDKs, such as the Entity Framework.

The MongoDB API

The MongoDB API that's provided by Cosmos DB provides a wide range of support for the MongoDB query language (at the time of writing, the MongoDB 3.4 wire protocol is in preview). Cosmos DB instances that are created with the MongoDB API type can be accessed using existing data managers, such as Compass, Studio 3T, RoboMongo, and Mongoose. This level of comprehensive support for MongoDB provides developers with the option of seamless migration from existing MongoDB stores. Azure portal data provides both shell and query access to MongoDB resources in order to visualize and analyze the data. In order to demonstrate this, let's execute several MongoDB queries from the MongoDB documentation library.

Given that we have a collection called `survey`, we will start by inserting the collection of survey results:

```
db.survey.insert([
{ "_id": 1, "results": [{ "product": "abc", "score": 10 }, { "product": "xyz", "score": 5 }]},
{ "_id": 2, "results": [{ "product": "abc", "score": 8 }, { "product": "xyz", "score": 7 }]},
{ "_id": 3, "results": [{ "product": "abc", "score": 7 }, { "product": "xyz", "score": 8 }]}
])
```

This will result in an error message similar to the following:

```
ERROR: Cannot deserialize a 'BsonDocument' from BsonType 'Array'.
```

This is because the `insert` command is not fully supported on the web shell. In order to have proper command execution, we need to move on to a local terminal (given that the Mongo toolset is installed):

```
$ mongo handsoncrossplatformmongo.documents.azure.com:10255 -u handsoncrossplatformmongo -p {PrimaryKey} --ssl --sslAllowInvalidCertificates
MongoDB shell version v4.0.3
connecting to: mongodb://handsoncrossplatformmongo.documents.azure.com:10255/test
WARNING: No implicit session: Logical Sessions are only supported on server versions 3.6 and greater.
Implicit session: dummy session
MongoDB server version: 3.2.0
WARNING: shell and server versions do not match
globaldb:PRIMARY>show databases
sample   0.000GB
globaldb:PRIMARY>use sample
switched to db sample
globaldb:PRIMARY>db.survey.find()
globaldb:PRIMARY>db.survey.insert([{"_id":1, "results":[{"product":"abc", "score":10}, { "product":"xyz", "score":5}]}, { "_id":2, "results":[{"product":"abc", "score":8}, { "product":"xyz", "score":7}]}, { "_id":3,
```

```
"results":[{"product":"abc", "score":7}, { "product":"xyz",
"score":8}]} ])
BulkWriteResult({
  "writeErrors" : [ ],
  "writeConcernErrors" : [ ],
  "nInserted" : 3,
  "nUpserted" : 0,
  "nMatched" : 0,
  "nModified" : 0,
  "nRemoved" : 0,
  "upserted" : [ ]
})
globaldb:PRIMARY>db.survey.find()
{"_id":1, "results":[{"product":"abc", "score":10},
{"product":"xyz", "score":5}]}
{"_id":2, "results":[{"product":"abc", "score" : 8},
{"product":"xyz", "score":7}]}
{"_id":3, "results":[{ "product":"abc", "score" : 7},
{"product":"xyz", "score":8}]}
```

> **Important Note**
>
> The Mongo server and the client, `Mongo.exe`, can be downloaded from the MongoDB website. On macOS, the `brew install mongo` command will install Mongo. The personalized connection string or the complete shell connect command can be copied from the Quick Start section on the Cosmos DB resource.

Next, we can continue our execution back on the cloud shell or local `mongo` shell. We will now execute a `find` query where the product should be `"xyz"` and the score should be greater than or equal to 8:

```
db.survey.find(
    { results: { $elemMatch: { product: "xyz", score: { $gte: 8
} } } }
)
```

Next, we will find all the survey results that contain the product `"xyz"`:

```
db.survey.find(
    { "results.product": "xyz" }
)
```

Finally, we will increment the first score where the product is `"abc"`:

```
db.survey.update({
    "results.product" : "abc"
},
{
    $inc : {'results.0.score' : 1}
});
```

You can visualize the results on the shell window of the data explorer:

Figure 8.5 – Data explorer shell

As we have illustrated here, Mongo databases and documents are fully supported by Cosmos DB. Applications implemented with Mongo data stores can easily be developed and tested on simple mongo daemons and can be deployed to cloud environments using Cosmos DB. This makes Mongo one of the most attractive general-purpose NoSQL access models on Cosmos DB.

Others

Gremlin, which is a graph data model, and Cassandra, which is a column-family model, both have wire protocol support. These APIs allow integration with cluster computing and big data analysis platforms such as Spark (GraphX). Apache Spark clusters can be created within Azure HDInsight to analyze streaming and historical data.

The final member of Cosmos DB, as we mentioned previously, is Azure Table storage, which provides access to a key/value pair store that supports the automatic sharding of data, as well as indexing.

Each access model supported within Cosmos DB can be used for specific cases, the SQL API and Mongo being the two most common access models. It is also important to remember a single Cosmos DB subscription should be set up with a specific model. Once we decide on an access model, we can start modeling the data.

Modeling data

The best way to get accustomed to various data models offered by Cosmos DB would be to implement inherently relational domain models using the provided NoSQL data access APIs. This way, it is easier to grasp the benefits of different data models. In this section, we will be creating the main aggregate roots of our domain on Cosmos DB using the SQL API access model and we will implement the repository classes that we will use in our web applications to access these document collections. Finally, we will also talk about denormalized and referenced data.

For this exercise, let's create a relational data model for our auction applications.

In this setup, we have three big clusters of data:

1. **Vehicles**, which includes the manufacturer, model, year, engine specifications, and some additional attributes describing the car
2. **Users**, which consists of the sellers and buyers of the cars sold through auctions
3. **Auctions**, which consists of some metadata about the sale that's provided by the selling user, as well as the vehicles and bids provided by the users

We will describe this data using the SQL API.

Creating and accessing documents

The most trivial way of considering the data model design, when dealing with a NoSQL database, would be to imagine the **Data Transformation Object** (**DTO**) models required for the application. In the case of a non-RBMS data platform, it is important to remember that we are not bound by references, unique keys, or many-to-many relationships.

For instance, let's take a look at the simplest model, namely *User*. User will have basic profile information, which can be used in the remainder of the application. Now, let's imagine what the DTO for the user object would look like:

```
{
    "id": "efd68a2f-7309-41c0-af52-696ebe820199",
    "firstName": "John",
    "lastName": "Smith",
    "address": {
        "addressTypeId": 4000,
        "city": "Seattle",
        "countryCode": "USA",
        "stateOrProvince": "Washington",
        "street1": "159 S. Jackson St.",
        "street2": "Suite 400",
        "zipCode": "98101"
    },
    "email": {
        "emailTypeId": 1000,
        "emailAddress": "john.smith@test.com"
    },
    "isActive": true,
    "phone": {
        "phoneTypeId": 1000,
        "number": "+1 121-212-3333"
    },
    "otherPhones": [{
        "phoneTypeId": 3000,
        "number": "+1 111-222-3333"
```

226   Creating a Datastore with Cosmos DB

```
    }],
    "signUpDate": "2001-11-02T00:00:00Z"
}
```

Let's create our collection with the name `UsersCollection` and with the partition key set to `/address/countryCode`.

Next, import this data into our database:

Figure 8.6 – Cosmos DB Documents View

OK; now, we have our first document created. But what are these additional fields that were added by the system? These are references to the container and item that holds the document data for our collection:

_rid	System generated	Unique identifier of container
_etag	System generated	Entity tag used for optimistic concurrency control
_ts	System generated	Last updated timestamp of the container
_self	System generated	Addressable URI of the container

Figure 8.7 – System Generated Properties

Out of these fields, the most important ones are `_etag` and `_ts`, both of which define the state of an entity at a given point in time. Notice that the descriptions do not refer to the document, but rather the item and entity. The main reason for this is that on Cosmos DB, storage buckets are referred to as containers, and the entities stored within these containers are referred to as items. Collections, tables, or graphs are the realization of these containers, depending on the API type that is being used.

Now, we can start creating our data access layer, which will be part of the User API, to provide the required data to our mobile application. Let's begin:

1. First, let's create a new solution file in a new folder of your choice using the following command:

```
dotnet new sln -n ShopAcross.Web
```

2. We can now create our core repository project, which we will use to store our repository interfaces:

```
dotnet new classlib -o ShopAcross.Web.Repository
```

3. Create a generic interface in this newly created project that will allow us to retrieve the user feed, as well as a single user:

```
public interface IRepository<T> where T : class
{
    Task<T> GetItemAsync(string id);
    Task<IEnumerable<T>> GetItemsAsync();
    //Task<Document> AddItemAsync(T item);
    //Task DeleteItemAsync(string id);
    //Task<Document> UpdateItemAsync(string id, T item);
}
```

4. Create a new project that will implement the repository access model using the SQL API on Cosmos DB as follows:

```
dotnet new classlib -o ShopAcross.Web.Repository.Cosmos
```

5. Create our implementation for Cosmos DB:

```csharp
public class CosmosCollection<T> : IRepository<T> where T : class
{
    private Container _cosmosContainer;

    public CosmosCollection(string collectionName)
    {
        CollectionId = collectionName;
        var client = new CosmosClient(Endpoint, Key);
        var client = new CosmosClient(Endpoint, Key);
        var database = client.GetDatabase(DatabaseId);
        _cosmosContainer = database.GetContainer(CollectionId);
    }

    // ... Removed for brevity
}
```

6. Implement our repository method for getting all items:

```csharp
public class CosmosCollection<T> : IRepository<T> where T : class
{
    // ...Removed for brevity
    public async Task<IEnumerable<T>>GetItemsAsync()
    {
        using FeedIterator<T> resultSet =
            _cosmosContainer.GetItemLinqQueryable<T>(
                requestOptions: new QueryRequestOptions
                {MaxItemCount = -1}).ToFeedIterator();

        List<T> results = new List<T>();
```

```
                while (resultSet.HasMoreResults)
                {
                    FeedResponse<T> response =
                            await resultSet.ReadNextAsync();
                    results.AddRange(response);
                }

            return results;
        }
    }
```

7. Let's do the same for retrieving a single item:

```
    public async Task<T>GetItemAsync(string id)
    {
        // Query for items by a property other than Id
        var queryDefinition = new QueryDefinition
            ($"select * from {CollectionId} c where c.Id = @EntityId")
            .WithParameter("@EntityId", id);

        using FeedIterator<T> resultSet = _cosmosContainer.GetItemQueryIterator<T>(queryDefinition);
        var response = await resultSet.ReadNextAsync();
        return response.FirstOrDefault();
    }
```

8. Now, we are ready to load the document(s) we have imported into our document collection:

```
    var cosmosCollection = new
        CosmosCollection<User>("UsersCollection");

    var collection = await cosmosCollection.GetItemsAsync()
```

9. You can additionally pass the partition key (that is, `countryCode`) to decrease the query costs, considering that otherwise it would be a cross-partition call:

```
using FeedIterator<T> resultSet = _cosmosContainer.
GetItemQueryIterator<T>(
queryDefinition: null,
requestOptions: new QueryRequestOptions
    {
        MaxItemCount = -1,
        PartitionKey = new PartitionKey("USA")
    });
```

10. Now, load the complete set of entries for the given collection. However, in most scenarios, we would use a predicate to load the set that is needed. So, add a `Where` clause to our query:

```
public async Task<IEnumerable<T>> GetItemsAsync(
Expression<Func<T, bool>> predicate)
{
    using FeedIterator<T> resultSet =
        _cosmosContainer.GetItemLinqQueryable<T>(
requestOptions: new QueryRequestOptions
        {
MaxItemCount = -1,
PartitionKey = new PartitionKey("USA")
        })
.Where(predicate)
            .ToFeedIterator();

    // ...
}
```

11. Now, create the add, update, and remove methods accordingly, which will provide the complete set of CRUD operations for the collections:

    ```csharp
    public async Task<T> AddItemAsync(T item)
    {
        var resp = await _cosmosContainer.CreateItemAsync(item);
        return resp.Resource;
    }

    public async Task<T> UpdateItemAsync(string id, T item)
    {
        var resp = await _cosmosContainer.ReplaceItemAsync(item, id);
        return resp.Resource;
    }

    public async Task DeleteItemAsync(string id)
    {
        _ = await _cosmosContainer.DeleteItemAsync<T>(id, PartitionKey.None);
    }
    ```

12. Finally, following the code-first approach, in order to avoid having the document collection created manually every time, you can use the initialization function to create the database and collection if they do not exist when the client is first created.

We have now created a complete document collection and basic CRUD functions. Now, we will continue and further extend our domain model via data denormalization.

Denormalized data

Data normalization is the process of structuring a database model by decomposing existing structures and creating replacement references to decrease redundancy and improve data integrity. However, data normalization inherently applies to relational databases. In the case of a document collection, embedded data is preferred over referential integrity. In addition, data views that cross the boundaries of a single collection should also be replicated on different pivots according to the design requirements.

Let's continue with our data model design with vehicles and auctions. These two data domains are going to be handled with separate APIs and will have separate collections. However, in a general feed (for example, latest auctions), we would need to retrieve data about the auctions, as well as the cars in the auction and bids provided by users for that specific auction. Let's see how we can do this:

1. For the vehicle's declaration, we will need the main product information:

```
{
    "id" : "f5574e12-01dc-4639-abeb-722e8e53e64f",
    "make" : "Volvo",
    "model": "S60",
    "year": 2018,
    "engine": {
        "displacement" : "2.0",
        "power" : 150,
        "torque" : 320,
        "fuelType": { "id": "11", "name": "Diesel" }
    },
    "doors": 4,
    "driveType": { "id" : "20", "name" : "FWD" },
    "primaryPicture" : "",
    "pictures" : [],
    "color": "black",
    "features": [ "Heated Seats", "Automatic Mirrors", "Windscreen Defrost", "Dimmed Mirrors", "Blind Spot Detection" ]
```

Notice that the features array contains a list of features that have been selected from a list of reference values, but instead of creating a many-to-many relational table, we chose to embed the data here, which is a compromise of the normal form. A similar approach could have been used for the `fuelType` and `driveType` references, but conceptually speaking, we have a many-to-one relationship on these data points, so they are embedded as reference data objects themselves.

2. Moving forward, create the auction data:

```
{
    "id" : "7ad0d2d4-e19c-4715-921b-950387abbe50",
    "title" : "Volvo S60 for Sale",
```

```
        "description" : "..."
        "vehicle": {
            "id" : "f5574e12-01dc-4639-abeb-722e8e53e64f",
            "make" : "Volvo",
            "model": "S60",
            "year": 2018,
            "engine": {
                "displacement" : "2.0",
                "power" : 150,
                "torque" : 320,
                "fuel": { "id": "11", "name": "Diesel" }
            },
            "primaryPicture" : "",
            "color": "black"
        },
        "startingPrice": {
            "value" : 25000,
            "currency" : {
                "id" : "32",
                "name" : "USD",
                "symbol" : "$"
            }
        },
        "created": "2019-03-01T10:00Z",
        "countryCode": "USA"
        "user": {
            "id" : "efd68a2f-7309-41c0-af52-696ebe820199",
            "firstName": "John",
            "lastName": "Smith"
        }
    }
```

3. If this was a relational model, this data would have been enough for identifying an auction. Nevertheless, it would decrease the number of round trips to load additional data if we embedded the highest bid (or even the most recent or highest bids) within the same structure:

```
"highestBids": [
    {
        "id" : "5d669390-2ba4-467a-b7f9-26fea2d6a129",
        "offer" : {
            "value" : 26000,
        },
        "user": {
            "id" : "f50e4bd2-6beb-4345-9c30-18b3436e7766",
            "firstName": "Jack",
            "lastName": "Lemon",
        },
        "created" : "2019-03-12T11:00Z"
    }
],
```

> **Important note**
> In this scenario, we could have also embedded the complete bid structure within the auction model. While this would decrease the redundancy and dispersion of data across collections, bids are not a finite collection like the feature set we saw in the vehicle object, and each new bid would have required a complete document replacement on the auction collection.

We can say that the `Auction` table is acting as a Materialized View for the listing, while vehicle and bids provide easy access to the required data points for the application views. Here, the responsibility of data integrity falls on the client application rather than the database itself.

Referenced data

In the previous examples, we used embedding extensively to create an optimized data structure. This, of course, does not mean we haven't used any references. Most of the embedded objects that are used are actually reference descriptions.

In order to visualize the referential data points, let's normalize our Auction data:

```
{
    "id" : "7ad0d2d4-e19c-4715-921b-950387abbe50",
    "description" : "Volvo S60 for Sale",
    "vehicleId": "f5574e12-01dc-4639-abeb-722e8e53e64f",
    "startingPrice": {
        "value" : 25000,
        "currencyId" : "32"
    },
    "highestBids":[
        "5d669390-2ba4-467a-b7f9-26fea2d6a129"
    ],
    "created": "2019-03-01T10:00Z",
    "countryCode": "USA",
    "userId": "efd68a2f-7309-41c0-af52-696ebe820199"
}
```

Here, we have a 1-* relation between the `Vehicle` and the `Auction`, a 1-* relation between the currency and the starting price value, a 1-* relation between the Auction and Bids, and a 1-* relation between User and Auctions. All of these references are embedded into the `auction` object, but what about the reciprocal references? For instance, if we were implementing a user profile view, we might want to show how many bids they were involved in and possibly a feedback value from the winning buyer or the seller:

```
{
    "id": "efd68a2f-7309-41c0-af52-696ebe820199",
    "firstName": "John",
    "lastName": "Smith",
    "numberOfAuctions" : 1,
    "auctions" : [
        {
            "auctionId": "7ad0d2d4-e19c-4715-921b-950387abbe50",
            "role" : { "roledId" : "20", "roleName": "seller"
},
            "auctionReview" : 1,
            "auctionState" : { "stateId" : "10", "stateName" :
```

```
            "Closed" }
                    }
            ]
            ...
}
```

These types of situations completely depend on the application use cases. As we have mentioned previously, we are not bound to foreign keys and constraints in the NoSQL setup, and the design should not necessarily dictate embedding or referencing. Cosmos DB provides features such as stored procedures and triggers to assign the responsibility of data integrity back into the database. Additionally, indexing and partitioning strategies can improve the overall performance of the application.

Cosmos DB in depth

Cosmos DB as a platform is much more than a simple database. The design of your data model, as well as the implementation of the data access layer, depends greatly on the feature being utilized. **Partitioning** and **indexing** setup can help improve performance, while also providing the roadmap for query strategies. **Data triggers**, **stored procedures**, and the **change feed** are extensibility points that allow developers to implement language-integrated transactional JavaScript blocks, which can greatly decrease the system's overall complexity and also compensate for the write transaction compromise in favor of denormalized data.

Partitioning

Cosmos makes use of two types of partitions – namely physical and logical partitions – in order to scale individual containers (that is, collections) in a database. The partition key that's defined at the time of the creation of a container defines the logical partitions. These logical partitions are then distributed into groups to physical partitions with a set of replicas to be able to horizontally scale the database.

In this scheme, the selection of the partition key becomes an important decision that will determine the performance of your queries. With a properly selected partition key, the data would be sharded (that is, data sharding) uniformly so that the distributed system will not show so-called hot partitions (that is, request peaks on certain partitions, while the rest of the partitions are idle). Hot partitions would ultimately result in performance degradation.

In the `UsersCollection`, we have used `/address/countryCode` as the partition key. This means that we are expecting a set of users with a normal distribution across the countries. However, in a real-life implementation, the number of users from a certain market really depends on the size of that market. To put it in layman's terms, the number of users from Turkey or Germany could not be the same as Bosnia and Herzegovina, if we were to think about the population count and demand.

> **Important note**
> Once a container is created in Cosmos DB, changing other properties of a collection such as the ID or the partition key are not supported. Only the indexing policy can be updated.

The partition key does not necessarily need to be a semantic dissection of data. For instance, in the `UsersCollection` scenario, the partition key could easily be defined according to the first letter of the name of the month that they signed up, as well as a synthetic partition key, such as a generated value from a range (for example, 1-100) that is assigned at the time of creation. Nevertheless, since the ID of an item within a container is only unique in that container, the container and ID combination defines the index of that item. In order to achieve higher throughputs, the queries should be executed within a specific container. In other words, if the partition key can be calculated before a query on the client side, the application would perform better than executing cross-partition queries:

```
FeedIterator<T>resultSet = _cosmosContainer
        .GetItemLinqQueryable<T>(
requestOptions: new QueryRequestOptions
                {
                        MaxItemCount = -1,
                        PartitionKey = new PartitionKey("USA")
                })
        .Where(predicate)
        .ToFeedIterator();
```

For instance, let's take a look at the following execution on this collection:

```
var cosmosCollection = new
CosmosCollection<User>("UsersCollection");

await cosmosCollection.GetItemsAsync(
```

```
        (item) =>item.FirstName.StartsWith("J"));

// Calling with the partition key
await cosmosCollection.GetItemsAsync(
        (item) =>item.FirstName.StartsWith("J"), "USA");
```

The results from this query (on a collection with only two entries per partition), when using the previous expression, are as follows:

```
Executing Query without PartitionKey
Query: {"query":"SELECT VALUE root FROM root WHERE
STARTSWITH(root[\"firstName\"], \"J\") "}
Request Charge : 2.96 RUs
Partition Execution Duration: 218.08ms
Scheduling Response Time: 26.67ms
Scheduling Run Time: 217.45ms
Scheduling Turnaround Time: 244.65ms

Executing Query with PartitionKey
Query: {"query":"SELECT VALUE root FROM root WHERE
STARTSWITH(root[\"firstName\"], \"J\") "}
Request Charge : 3.13 RUs
Partition Execution Duration: 136.37ms
Scheduling Response Time: 0.03ms
Scheduling Run Time: 136.37ms
Scheduling Turnaround Time: 136.41ms
```

Even with the smallest dataset, the execution results show quite an improvement in the total time required to execute.

> **Important note**
> In order to retrieve metrics for a Cosmos query, you can use the `FeedResponse<T>.Diagnostics` property. Unlike the previous SDK, the diagnostic data collection is enabled by default.

In a similar fashion, we can expand our data models for vehicle and auction, and we can create the collections with the car make or color so that we have evenly distributed partitions.

Indexing

Azure Cosmos DB, by default, assumes that each property in an item should be indexed. When a complex object is pushed into the collection, the object is treated as a tree with properties that make up the nodes and values, as well as the leaves. This way, each property on each branch of the tree is queryable. Each consequent object either uses the same index tree or expands it with additional properties.

This indexing behavior can be changed at any time for any collection. This can help with the costs and performance of the dataset. Index definition uses wildcard values to define which paths should be included and/or excluded.

For instance, let's take a look at the indexing policy of our `AuctionsCollection`:

```
Partition key
/vehicle.color

Indexing Policy
1  {
2      "indexingMode": "consistent",
3      "automatic": true,
4      "includedPaths": [
5          {
6              "path": "/*",
7              "indexes": [
8                  {
9                      "kind": "Range",
10                     "dataType": "Number",
11                     "precision": -1
12                 },
13                 {
14                     "kind": "Range",
15                     "dataType": "String",
16                     "precision": -1
17                 },
18                 {
19                     "kind": "Spatial",
20                     "dataType": "Point"
21                 }
22             ]
23         }
24     ],
25     "excludedPaths": [
26         {
27             "path": "/\"_etag\"/?"
28         }
29     ]
30 }
```

Figure 8.8 – Indexing Policy

The /* declaration includes the complete object tree, except for the excluded _etag field. These indexes can be optimized using more specialized index types and paths.

For instance, let's exclude all paths and introduce an index of our own:

```
"includedPaths": [
    {
        "path": "/description/?",
        "indexes": [
            {
                "kind": "Hash",
                "dataType": "String",
                "precision": -1
            }
        ]
    },
    {
        "path": "/vehicle/*",
        "indexes": [
            {
                "kind": "Hash",
                "dataType": "String",
                "precision": -1
            },
            {
                "kind": "Range",
                "dataType": "Number",
                "precision": -1
            }
        ]
    }
],
"excludedPaths": [
    {
        "path": "/*"
    }
]
```

Here, we have added two indexes: one hash index for the scalar value of the description field (that is, `/?`), and one range and/or hash index to the vehicle path and all the nodes under it (that is, `/*`). The hash index type is the index that's used for equality queries, while the range index type is used for comparison or sorting.

By using the correct index paths and types, query costs can be decreased and scan queries can be avoided. If the indexing mode is set to `None` instead of `Consistent`, the database returns an error on the given collection. The queries can still be executed using the `EnableScanInQuery` flag.

Programmability

One of the most helpful features of Cosmos is its server-side programmability, which allows developers to create stored procedures, functions, and database triggers. These concepts are not too foreign for developers that have created applications on SQL databases, and yet the ability to create stored procedures on NoSQL databases, and what's more, on a client-side scripting language such as JavaScript, is quite unprecedented.

As a quick example, let's implement a trigger to calculate the aggregate value(s) on a user's profile:

1. As you may remember, we added the following reference values to `UserProfile` for the cross-collection partition:

```
public class User
{
    [JsonProperty("id")]
    public string Id { get; set; }

    [JsonProperty("firstName")]
    public string FirstName { get; set; }

    //...

    [JsonProperty("numberOfAuctions")]
    public int NumberOfAuctions { get; set; }

    [JsonProperty("auctions")]
```

```
        public List<BasicAuction> Auctions { get; set; }

    //...
}
```

Now, let's create an aggregate update function that will update the number of auctions whenever there is an update on the user profile. We will use this function to intercept the update requests to the collection (that is, a pre-execution trigger) and modify the object's content.

2. The function should first retrieve the current collection and the document from the execution context:

```
function updateAggregates(){
    // HTTP error codes sent to our callback function by server.
    var ErrorCode = {
        RETRY_WITH: 449,
    }

    var collection = getContext().getCollection();
    var collectionLink = collection.getSelfLink();

    // Get the document from request (the script runs as trigger,
    // thus the input comes in request).
    var document = getContext().getRequest().getBody();
```

3. Now, let our function count the auctions that the update is pushing:

```
if (document.auctions != null) {
    document.numberOfAuctions = document.auctions.length;
}

getContext().getRequest().setBody(document);
```

4. We can now add this trigger to the `UsersCollection` as a **Pre** trigger on **Replace** calls:

Cosmos DB in depth   243

> Trigger Id
> [updateAggregates]
>
> Trigger Type
> [Pre ▼]
>
> Trigger Operation
> [Replace ▼]

Figure 8.9 – Cosmos DB trigger

5. However, the `trigger` function will still not execute until we explicitly add the trigger to the client request:

```
var requestOption = new ItemRequestOptions();
requestOption.PreTriggers= new []{ "updateAggregates"};
await _client.ReplaceDocumentAsync(item, id,
requestOption);
```

Great! The number of auctions the user has participated in is being calculated every time the user's profile is updated. However, in order to insert a new auction (for example, when the user is actually creating an auction or bidding on one), we would need to update the whole user profile (that is, partial updates are currently not supported on the SQL API).

6. Let's create a stored procedure that will insert an auction item on a specific user profile to push *partial* updates:

```
function insertAuction(id, auction) {
    var collection = getContext().getCollection();
    var collectionLink = collection.getSelfLink();

    var response = getContext().getResponse();
```

7. Next, retrieve the user profile object that we have to insert the auction into:

```
var documentFilter = 'Select * FROM r where r.id = \'' +
id + '\'';
var isAccepted = collection.queryDocuments(
collectionLink,
documentFilter,
    function (err, docs, options) {
```

```
        if (err) throw err;

        var userProfile = docs[0];

        // TODO: Insert Auction
    });
```

8. Now, we can update the document with the new auction:

```
userProfile.auctions[userProfile.auctions.length] = auction;
collection.replaceDocument(userProfile._self, userProfile, function (err) {
    if (err) throw err;
});
```

9. Finally, we will create an additional function for the `UserProfileRepository`:

```
public async Task InsertAuction(string userId, Auction auction)
{
    try
    {
        
        _ = await _cosmosContainer.Scripts
                    .ExecuteStoredProcedureAsync<T>(
                        "insertAuction",
                        new PartitionKey("USA"),
                        (dynamic)userId,
                        (dynamic)auction);
    }
    catch (DocumentClientException e)
    {
        throw;
    }
}
```

Now, the auctions are inserted into the user profile and the aggregate column is updated when the stored procedure is called.

Triggers, functions, and stored procedures are all limited to the collection they are created in. In other words, one collection trigger cannot execute any changes on another collection. In order to execute such an update, we would need to use an external process such as the caller application itself or an Azure function that's triggered with the change feed on Cosmos DB.

The change feed

Azure Cosmos DB continuously monitors changes in collections, and these changes can be pushed to various services through the change feed. The events that are pushed through the change feed can be consumed by Azure Functions and App Services, as well as stream processing and data management processes.

Insert, update, and soft-delete operations can be monitored through the change feed, with each change appearing exactly once in the change feed. If there are multiple updates being made to a certain item, only the latest change is included in the change feed, thus making it a robust and easy-to-manage event processing pipeline.

Summary

Cosmos DB provides a new perspective to the NoSQL database concept, with a wide range of services for various scenarios. Additionally, with Cosmos DB access models, in comparison to relational data models, consumer applications have more responsibility for the referential data integrity. The weak links between the data containers can be used as an advantage by a microservice architecture.

In this chapter, you have created a completely new Cosmos DB resource using the SQL API as our access model. However, other access models were discussed, and we have also executed sample queries on Mongo. Once the Cosmos DB resource was created, you created sample document collections, modeled your data, and implemented simple repository classes to access this data. You now understand the fundamental concepts of Cosmos DB and are ready to use it as your persistence store.

In the next chapter, we will be creating the service layer for our application suite.

9
Creating Microservices Azure App Services

Azure App Service is a **Platform as a Service (PaaS)** offering for both mobile and app developers that can host a number of different application models and services. While developers can create a simple mobile app service to act as a datastore access layer within minutes without writing a single line of code, intricate and robust .NET Core applications can also be implemented with intrinsic integration to other Azure services.

In this chapter, we will go through the basics of Azure App Service and create a simple, data-oriented backend for our application using ASP.NET 5, with authentication provided by **Azure Active Directory (Azure AD)**. We will also improve the performance of our web API endpoint with Redis cache. The following sections will guide you through the process of creating our service backend:

- Choosing the right app model
- Creating our first microservice
- Integrating with Redis cache
- Hosting the services
- Securing the application

By the end of this chapter, you will be fully capable of designing and creating web services from scratch as well as integrating them into cloud infrastructure with additional non-functional requirements for performance and authentication.

Technical requirements

You can find the code used in this chapter through the following GitHub link: https://github.com/PacktPublishing/Mobile-Development-with-.NET-Second-Edition/tree/master/chapter09.

Choosing the right app model

The Azure stack offers multiple ways to host web applications, varying from simple **Infrastructure as a Service (IaaS)** offerings such as **Virtual Machines (VMs)** to completely managed PaaS hosting services such as App Service. Because of the platform-agnostic nature of .NET Core and ASP.NET Core, even Linux containers and container orchestration services such as Kubernetes are available options.

Azure compute offers can be organized according to the separation of responsibilities into three main categories, namely IaaS, PaaS, and **Containers as a Service (CaaS)**, as shown in the following diagram:

Figure 9.1 – Managed Hosting Models

Besides IaaS and PaaS, there are various hosting options, each with its own advantages and use cases. We will now take a closer look at these offerings.

The following sections will walk you through different application hosting models in the Azure ecosystem.

Azure virtual machines

Virtual machines (**VMs**), are one of the oldest IaaS offerings on the Microsoft Azure Cloud. In simple terms, this offering provides a hosting server on the cloud with complete control. The Azure Automation service provides you with the much-required tools to manage these servers with **Infrastructure as Code** (**IaC**) principles using PowerShell **Desired State Configuration** (**DSC**) and scheduled runbooks. You can scale and monitor them with ease according to your application requirements.

With both Windows and Linux variants available, Azure VMs can be an easy, shallow cloud migration path for already-existing applications.

The scaling of VMs is done by adjusting the system configuration (for example, CPU, virtual disk, RAM, and so on) at the VM level or by introducing additional VMs to the infrastructure.

VM hosting takes place on the leftmost side of the managed model spectrum; in other words, it provides an almost fully self-managed hosting model. Moving toward the managed area, we have containers as a service.

Containers in Azure

If VMs are the virtualization of hardware, containers virtualize the operating system. Containers create isolated sandboxes for applications that share the same operating system kernel. This way, application containers that are composed of the application, as well as its dependencies, can be easily hosted on any environment that meets the container demands. Container images can be executed as multiple application containers, and these container instances can be orchestrated with orchestration tools such as Docker Swarm, Kubernetes, and Service Fabric.

Azure currently has two managed container orchestration offerings: **Azure Kubernetes Service** (**AKS**) and Service Fabric Mesh.

Azure Container Service with Kubernetes

Azure Container Service (**ACS**) is a managed container orchestration environment where developers can deploy containers without much hassle and enjoy the automatic recovery and scaling experience.

Kubernetes is an open source container orchestration system that was originally designed and developed by Google. Azure Kubernetes is a managed implementation of this service where most of the configuration and management responsibilities are delegated to the platform itself. In this setup, as a consumer of this PaaS offering, you are only responsible for managing and maintaining the agent nodes.

AKS provides support for Linux containers as well as Windows operating system virtual containers. Windows container support is currently in private preview.

Service Fabric Mesh

Azure Service Fabric Mesh is a fully managed container orchestration platform where consumers do not have any direct interaction with the configuration or maintenance of the underlying cluster. So-called polyglot services (that is, any language and any operating system) are run in containers. In this setup, developers are just responsible for specifying the resources that the application requires, such as the number of containers and their sizes, networking requirements, and autoscale rules.

Once the application container is deployed, Service Fabric Mesh hosts the container in a mesh consisting of clusters of thousands of machines, and cluster operations are completely hidden from the developers. Intelligent message routing through **Software-Defined Networking (SDN)** enables service discovery and routing between microservices.

Service Fabric Mesh, even though it shares the same underlying platform, differs significantly from Azure Service Fabric. While Service Fabric Mesh is a managed hosting solution, Azure Service Fabric is a complete microservice platform that allows developers to create containerized or otherwise cloud-native applications.

Microservices with Azure Service Fabric

Azure Service Fabric is a hosting and development platform that allows developers to create enterprise-grade applications composed of microservices. Service Fabric provides comprehensive runtime and life cycle management capabilities, as well as a durable programming model that makes use of mutable state containers, such as reliable dictionaries and queues.

Service Fabric applications can be made up of three different hosted service models: containers, services/actors, and guest executables.

Similar to its managed counterpart (that is, Service Fabric Mesh) and Azure Kubernetes, Service Fabric is capable of running containerized applications that target both Linux and Windows containers. Containers can easily be included in a Service Fabric application that is bundled together with other components and scaled across high-density shared compute pools, called clusters, with predefined nodes.

Reliable services and reliable actors are truly cloud-native services that make use of the Service Fabric programming model. Ease of development on local development clusters and available SDKs for .NET Core, as well as Java, allow developers to create both stateful and stateless microservices in a platform-agnostic manner.

> **Important Note**
>
> Development environments are available for Windows, Linux, and Mac OS X. The Linux and OS X development setups rely on running Service Fabric itself in a container. .NET Core is the preferred language for creating applications that target each of these platforms. The available Visual Studio Code extensions make it easy to develop .NET Core Service Fabric applications on each operating system.

Finally, guest executables can be an application that's been developed on a variety of languages/frameworks, such as Node.js, Java, or C++. Guest executables are managed and treated as stateless services and can be placed on cluster nodes, side by side with other Service Fabric services.

Azure container-based resources can provide the agility for developing highly sophisticated microservice ecosystems; however, any model you choose for containers and container hosting would require configuration and infrastructure management, and would generally come with a steep learning curve. If you are looking for an alternative with less burden for configuration and infrastructure management, we can move forward in our managed hosting model spectrum and choose Azure App Service as our hosting model.

Azure App Service

Azure App Service is a fully managed web application hosting service. App Service can be used to host applications regardless of the development platform or operating system. App Service provides first-class support for ASP.NET (Core), Java, Ruby, Node.js, PHP, and Python. It has out-of-the-box continuous integration and deployment with DevOps platforms such as Azure DevOps, GitHub, and BitBucket. Most of the management functionality of a usual hosting environment is integrated into the Azure portal on the App Service blade, such as scaling, CORS, application settings, SSL, and so on. Additionally, WebJobs can be used to create background processes that can be executed periodically as part of your application bundle.

Web App for Containers is another Azure App Service feature that allows containerized applications to be deployed as an app service and orchestrated with Kubernetes.

Mobile App Service is/was an easy way to integrate all the necessary functionality for a simple mobile application, such as authentication, push notifications, and offline synchronization. However, Mobile App Service is currently being transitioned to App Center and does not support ASP.NET Core.

Finally, Azure Functions provides a platform to create code snippets or stateless on-demand functions and host them without having to explicitly provision or manage infrastructure.

In this section, we have learned about different hosting models and their pros and cons. We started our investigation with Azure VMs, took a short detour for containers, and finally, arrived at PaaS models for Azure App Service and Functions. Now that we have covered the basics in regard to choosing a model, we will next look at how to create our first microservice.

Creating our first microservice

For our mobile application, in *Chapter 8*, *Creating a Datastore with Cosmos DB*, we created a simple data access proxy that retrieves data from Cosmos DB. In this exercise, we will be creating small web API components that will expose various methods for CRUD operations on our collections.

Initial setup

Let's begin our implementation:

1. First, create an ASP.NET Core project:

Figure 9.2 – Creating an ASP.NET Project

2. Once the project is created, do a quick test to check whether the `dotnet` core components are properly set up.

3. Open a console window and navigate to the project folder. The following commands will restore the referenced packages and compile the application:

```
dotnet restore
dotnet build
```

4. Once the application is built, we can use the `run` command and execute a GET call to the `api/values` endpoint:

Figure 9.3 – First Run for the ASP.NET Core App

This should result in the output of the values from the `WeatherForecastController` controller's GET method.

> **Important Note**
> In the previous example, we used `curl` to execute a quick HTTP request. **Client URL (curl)** is a utility program that is available on Unix-based systems, macOS, and Windows 10.

5. Next, we will set up the *Swagger* endpoint so that we have a metadata endpoint, as well as a UI to execute test requests. For this purpose, we will be using the Swashbuckle NuGet packages to generate the API endpoint metadata. A basic setup of *Swashbuckle* requires three packages, and we can reference them together by adding the `Swashbuckle.AspNetCore` meta-package:

Creating our first microservice 255

Figure 9.4 – Swashbuckle NuGet

6. After adding the meta-package and the dependencies, modify the `Startup` class to declare the services:

```
public class Startup
{
    //... <Removed>

    public void ConfigureServices(IServiceCollection services)
    {
        //... <Removed>
        services.AddSwaggerGen(c =>
            {
                c.SwaggerDoc("v1", new OpenApiInfo { Title = "Auctions Api", Version = "v1"});
            });
    }

    public void Configure(IApplicationBuilder app, IHostingEnvironment env)
    {
        //... <Removed>
        app.UseSwagger();
        app.UseSwaggerUI(c =>
            {
```

```
                    c.SwaggerEndpoint("/swagger/v1/swagger.
    json", "Auctions Api");
                });
        }
    }
```

7. Now, run the application and navigate to the `{dev host}/swagger` endpoint. We will see the generated Swagger UI and method declarations:

Figure 9.5 – Swagger UI

We now have our boilerplate API project ready, which means that we can move on to implementing our services.

Implementing retrieval actions

Considering the auctions dataset, since we have created our MVC application, we should include two `GET` methods in our controller: one for retrieving the complete collection of auctions and one that will retrieve a specific auction.

Let's see how we can do this:

1. Before starting the implementation, let's rename `WeatherForecastController` to `AuctionsController`.

2. We can simply initialize our repository and return the results for the first GET method:

```
[HttpGet]
public async Task<IEnumerable<Auction>> Get()
{
    var result = Enumerable.Empty<Auction>();

    try
    {
        result = await _cosmosCollection.GetItemsAsync(item =>
        true);
    }
    catch (Exception ex)
    {
        // Log the error or throw depending on the requirements
    }

    return result;
}
```

Notice that the predicate we are using here is targeting the complete set of auctions. We can expand this implementation with query parameters that filter the set with additional predicates.

3. The GET method for retrieving a specific item would not be much different:

```
[HttpGet("{id}")]
public async Task<User> Get(string id)
{
    User result = null;

    try
```

```csharp
{
    result = await _cosmosCollection.
GetItemAsync(id);
}
catch (Exception ex)
{
    // Log or throw error depending on the 
requirements
}

return result;
}
```

This would suffice for the requirements, but to improve the interaction between our mobile application and the Cosmos collection, we can also enable **OData** queries and create a transparent query pipeline to the datastore. To do this, we can implement an OData controller using the available .NET Core packages, or we can enable the queries on our current MVC controller.

> **Important Note**
> It is important to note that the Swashbuckle package that we used to generate the Swagger UI currently does not support OData controllers, so these APIs would not be available on the Swagger interface.

4. For OData implementation, we begin by setting up our infrastructure in our startup class:

```csharp
public void ConfigureServices(IServiceCollection 
services)
{
    services.AddOData();
    services.AddODataQueryFilter();
    // ... Removed
}
```

5. Now, set up the routes for the MVC controller:

```csharp
public void Configure(IApplicationBuilder app, 
IHostingEnvironment env)
{
```

```csharp
        if (env.IsDevelopment())
        {
            app.UseDeveloperExceptionPage();
        }
        app.UseMvc(builder =>
            {
                builder.Count().Filter().OrderBy().Expand().Select().MaxTop(null);
                builder.EnableDependencyInjection();
            });

        // ... Removed
}
```

6. Create a new method on the Cosmos repository client, which will be returning a queryable set rather than a result set:

```csharp
public IQueryable<T> GetItemsAsync()
{
    var feedOptions = new FeedOptions {
        MaxItemCount = -1, PopulateQueryMetrics = true, EnableCrossPartitionQuery = true };

    IOrderedQueryable<T> query = _client.CreateDocumentQuery<T>(
        UriFactory.CreateDocumentCollectionUri(DatabaseId, CollectionId), feedOptions);

    return query;
}
```

7. Finally, we need to implement our query action:

```csharp
[HttpGet]
[EnableQuery(AllowedQueryOptions = AllowedQueryOptions.All)]
public ActionResult<IQueryable<Auction>> Get(ODataQueryOptions<Auction> queryOptions)
{
```

```csharp
    var items = _cosmosCollection.GetItemsAsync();
    return Ok(queryOptions.ApplyTo(items.AsQueryable()));
}
```

Now, simple OData queries can be executed on our collection (for example, first-tier OData filter queries). For instance, if we were executing a query on the `Users` endpoint, a simple filter query to retrieve users with one or more auctions would look like this:

```
http://localhost:20337/api/users?$filter=NumberOfAuctions ge 1
```

In order to be able to expand the query options and execute queries on related entities, we would need to create an **Entity Data Model (EDM)** and register respective OData controllers.

> **Important Note**
>
> Another, more appropriate option to enable an advanced search would be to create an Azure search index and expose the Azure search functionality on top of this index.

For an in-memory EDM and data context, we will be using `Microsoft.EntityFrameworkCore`'s features and functionality. Let's begin with the implementation:

1. Create a `DbContext` that will define our main data model and the relationships between the entities:

```csharp
public class AuctionsStoreContext : DbContext
{
    public AuctionsStoreContext(DbContextOptions<AuctionsStoreContext> options)
        : base(options)
    {
    }

    public DbSet<Auction> Auctions { get; set; }

    public DbSet<User> Users { get; set; }
```

```
       protected override void OnModelCreating(ModelBuilder
       modelBuilder)
       {
           modelBuilder.Entity<User>().OwnsOne(c =>
    c.Address);
           modelBuilder.Entity<User>().HasMany<Auction>(c =>
           c.Auctions);
       }
   }
   ```

2. Now, let's register this context within the ConfigureServices method:

   ```
   public void ConfigureServices(IServiceCollection
   services)
   {
       services.AddDbContext<AuctionsStoreContext>(option =>
           option.UseInMemoryData("AuctionsContext"));
       services.AddOData();
       services.AddODataQueryFilter();
       // ... Removed
   }
   ```

3. Now, create a method that will be returning the EDM:

   ```
   private static IEdmModel GetEdmModel()
   {
       ODataConventionModelBuilder builder = new
       ODataConventionModelBuilder();
       var auctionsSet = builder.
   EntitySet<Auction>("Auctions");
       var usersSet = builder.EntitySet<User>("Users");
       builder.ComplexType<Vehicle>();
       builder.ComplexType<Engine>();
       return builder.GetEdmModel();
   }
   ```

4. Finally, register an OData route so that entity controllers can be served through this route:

```
app.UseMvc(builder =>
{
        builder.Count().Filter().OrderBy().Expand().Select().MaxTop(null);
        builder.EnableDependencyInjection();
        builder.MapODataServiceRoute("odata", "odata", GetEdmModel());
});
```

5. Now that the infrastructure is ready, you can navigate to the $metadata endpoint to take a look at the EDM that was generated:

```xml
<?xml version="1.0" encoding="ISO-8859-1"?>
<edmx:Edmx xmlns:edmx="http://docs.oasis-open.org/odata/ns/edmx" Version="4.0">
  <edmx:DataServices>
    <Schema xmlns="http://docs.oasis-open.org/odata/ns/edm" Namespace="HandsOnCoreWeb.Data">
      <EntityType Name="Auction">
        <Key>
          <PropertyRef Name="Id"/>
        </Key>
        <Property Name="Id" Nullable="false" Type="Edm.String"/>
        <Property Name="Description" Type="Edm.String"/>
        <Property Name="Vehicle" Type="HandsOnCoreWeb.Data.Vehicle"/>
        <Property Name="StartingPrice" Type="HandsOnCoreWeb.Data.Price"/>
        <Property Name="CountryCode" Type="Edm.String"/>
        <NavigationProperty Name="HighestBids" Type="Collection(HandsOnCoreWeb.Data.Bid)"/>
        <NavigationProperty Name="User" Type="HandsOnCoreWeb.Data.User"/>
      </EntityType>
      <EntityType Name="User">
        <Key>
          <PropertyRef Name="Id"/>
        </Key>
        <Property Name="Id" Nullable="false" Type="Edm.String"/>
        <Property Name="FirstName" Type="Edm.String"/>
        <Property Name="LastName" Type="Edm.String"/>
        <Property Name="NumberOfAuctions" Nullable="false" Type="Edm.Int32"/>
        <Property Name="Auctions" Type="Collection(HandsOnCoreWeb.Data.AuctionInfo)"/>
        <Property Name="Address" Type="HandsOnCoreWeb.Data.Address"/>
      </EntityType>
```

Figure 9.6 – OData EDM

6. Now, by implementing a quick `ODataController`, we can expose the complete set to OData queries:

```csharp
public class AuctionsController : ODataController
{
```

```csharp
        private readonly CosmosCollection<Auction> _
cosmosCollection;

        public AuctionsController()
        {
            _cosmosCollection = new
CosmosCollection<Auction>("AuctionsCollection");
        }

        // GET: api/Users
        [EnableQuery]
        public IActionResult Get()
        {
            var items = _cosmosCollection.GetItemsAsync();
            return Ok(items.AsQueryable());
        }

        [EnableQuery]
        public async Task<IActionResult> Get(string key)
        {
            var auction = await _cosmosCollection.
GetItemsAsync(item => item.Id == key);
            return Ok(auction.FirstOrDefault());
        }
    }
```

With the given `ODataController` in place and the additional implementation for the users collection, various entity filter expressions can be executed, such as the following:

- `http://localhost:20337/odata/auctions?$filter=Vehicle/Engine/Power%20gt%20120`
- `http://localhost:20337/odata/users?$filter=Address/City%20eq%20'London'`
- `http://localhost:20337/odata/users?$filter=startswith(FirstName,%20'J')`
- `http://localhost:20337/odata/auctions('7ad0d2d4-e19c-4715-921b-950387abbe50')`

With this, we have successfully exposed an OData endpoint for a Cosmos Document DB, using ASP.NET Core and Entity Framework Core. Now that we have the retrieval methods in place, we need to implement methods that will deal with the creation and manipulation of data.

Implementing update methods

Implementing the update endpoint would in fact be different, to say the least, when we are dealing with a NoSQL datastore that doesn't support partial updates. According to the application requirements, we can choose two distinct patterns.

In the classic concurrency model, we would be receiving a PUT request with the complete object body and checking whether the update is being executed on the latest version of the object. This concurrency check can be done on the _ts property collection items. The timestamp property is also used by the Cosmos DB containers themselves for handling concurrency issues. Let's begin.

In this model, the incoming object body would be verified to check whether it carries the latest timestamp, and if not, a 409 response signifying a conflict will be sent back as a response. If the timestamp matches the one in the repository, then we are free to upsert the entity:

```
[EnableQuery]
[HttpPut]
public async Task<IActionResult> Put([FromODataUri]string key,
[FromBody] Auction auctionUpdate)
{
    var cosmosCollection = new
CosmosCollection<Auction>("AuctionsCollection");
    var auction = (await cosmosCollection.GetItemsAsync(item =>
item.Id == key)).FirstOrDefault();

    if (auction == null)
    {
        return NotFound();
    }

    if (auction.TimeStamp != auctionUpdate.TimeStamp)
    {
        return Conflict();
```

```
    }

        await cosmosCollection.UpdateItemAsync(key, auctionUpdate);

        return Accepted(auction);
}
```

However, with this approach, as the object tree grows in size, and the complexity increases on our container items, the update's requests would get bigger and harder to execute (for example, higher probability of conflicts, unintentional removal of properties, and so on). The following screenshot shows a request that's been sent to update only the description field of an auction document:

Figure 9.7 – ASP.NET Update Request/Response

In order to decrease the impact of an update call, at least for the client, we can utilize `PATCH` methods. In a `PATCH` method, only a part of the object tree is delivered as a delta, or only the partial update operations are delivered as patch operations.

Let's implement a `PATCH` action for the same auction service and check out the request:

```
[EnableQuery]
[HttpPatch]
public async Task<IActionResult> Patch(
    string key,
    [FromBody] JsonPatchDocument<Auction> auctionPatch)
{
    var cosmosCollection = new
CosmosCollection<Auction>("AuctionsCollection");
    var auction = (await cosmosCollection.GetItemsAsync(item =>
item.Id == key)).FirstOrDefault();

    if (auction == null)
    {
        return NotFound();
    }

    auctionPatch.ApplyTo(auction);
    await cosmosCollection.UpdateItemAsync(key, auction);
    return Accepted(auction);
}
```

The request for the given endpoint would look similar to the following:

```
PATCH /odata/auctions('3634031a-1f45-4aa0-9385-5e2c86795c49')

[
    {"op" : "replace", "path" : "description", "value" :
"Updated Description"}
]
```

The same optimistic concurrency control mechanism we have implemented with the timestamp value can be implemented with the `Test` operation:

```
PATCH /odata/auctions('3634031a-1f45-4aa0-9385-5e2c86795c49')

[
    { "op": "test", "path": "_ts", "value": 1552741629 },
    { "op" : "replace", "path" : "vehicle/year", "value" : 2017},
    { "op" : "replace", "path" : "vehicle/engine/displacement", "value" : "2.4"}
]
```

In this example, if the timestamp value does not match the value in the request, the consequent update operations would not be executed.

We have now completed the `UPDATE` and `PATCH` methods, so let's move on to the `DELETE` action.

Implementing a soft delete

If you're planning on integrating the storage-level operations with triggers and/or a change feed, a soft delete implementation can be used instead of implementing the complete removal of objects. In the soft delete approach, we can extend our entity model with a specific property (for example, `isDeleted`) that will define that the document is deleted by the consuming application.

In this setup, the consuming application can make use of the `PATCH` method that was implemented or an explicit `DELETE` method, which can be implemented for our entity services.

Let's take a look at the following `PATCH` request:

```
PATCH /odata/auctions('3634031a-1f45-4aa0-9385-5e2c86795c49')

[
    { "op": "test", "path": "_ts", "value": 1552741629 },
    { "op" : "replace", "path" : "isDeleted", "value" : true},
    { "op" : "replace", "path" : "ttl", "value" : "30"}
]
```

With this request, we are indicating that the auction entity with the given ID should be marked for deletion. Additionally, by setting the **Time To Live (TTL)** property, we are triggering an expiry on that given entity. This way, both the triggers and the change feed will be notified about this update and, within the given TTL, the entity will be removed from the datastore.

> **Important Note**
> TTL is an intrinsic feature of Cosmos DB. The TTL can be set at the container level, as well as at the item level. If no value has been set at the container level, the value set of the items will be ignored by the platform. However, the container can have a -1 default expiry and the items that we want to expire after a certain period can declare a value greater than 0. TTL does not consume resources and is not calculated as part of the consumed RUs.

With the delete implementation, we have the complete set of functions to create the basic CRUD structure for a microservice in accordance with the Cosmos collections. We started the implementation with a simple .NET Core-style request pipeline, we created UPDATE and PATCH methods, and finally, we finished the implementation with the soft delete implementation. We can now start dealing with the retouches for our API. We will start with performance improvements using Redis.

Integrating with Redis cache

In a distributed cloud application with a fine-grained microservice architecture, distributed caching can provide much-desired data coherence, as well as performance improvements. Generally speaking, the distribution of the infrastructure, the data model, and costs are deciding factors regarding whether to use a distributed cache implementation.

ASP.NET Core offers various caching options, one of which is distributed caching. The available distributed cache options are as follows:

1. Distributed memory cache
2. Distributed SQL server cache
3. Distributed Redis cache

While the memory cache is not a production-ready strategy, SQL and Redis can be viable options for a cloud application that's been developed with .NET Core. However, in the case of a NoSQL database and semi-structured data, Redis would be an ideal choice. Let's see how we can introduce a distributed cache and make it ready for use:

1. In order to introduce a distributed cache that can be used across controllers, we would need to use the available extensions so that we can inject an appropriate implementation of the `IDistributedCache` interface. `IDistributedCache` would be our main tool for implementing the cache, aside from the pattern we mentioned previously:

```csharp
public interface IDistributedCache
{
    byte[] Get(string key);

    Task<byte[]> GetAsync(string key, CancellationToken token = default(CancellationToken));

    void Set(string key, byte[] value, DistributedCacheEntryOptions options);

    Task SetAsync(string key, byte[] value, DistributedCacheEntryOptions options, CancellationToken token = default(CancellationToken));

    void Refresh(string key);

    Task RefreshAsync(string key, CancellationToken token = default(CancellationToken));

    void Remove(string key);

    Task RemoveAsync(string key, CancellationToken token = default(CancellationToken));
}
```

270   Creating Microservices Azure App Services

As you can see, using the injected instance, we would be able to set and get data structures as byte arrays. The application would first reach out to the distributed cache to retrieve the data. If the data we require does not exist, we would retrieve it from the actual datastore (or service) and store the result in our cache.

2. Before we can implement the Redis cache in our application, we can head over to the Azure portal and create a Microsoft Azure Redis Cache resource within the same resource group we have been using up until now.

3. Once the Redis cache instance is created, make a note of one of the available connection strings. The connection strings can be found under the **Manage Keys** blade, which is accessed by using the **Show access keys** option on the **Overview** screen. We can now continue with our implementation.

4. Start the implementation by installing the required Redis extension:

Figure 9.8 – Redis Extension

5. After the extension and its dependencies have been installed, configure our distributed cache service using the extension method:

```
services.AddDistributedRedisCache(
    option =>
    {
        option.Configuration = Configuration.GetConnectionString("AzureRedisConnection");
        option.InstanceName = "master";
    });
```

6. Now insert the connection string we retrieved from the Azure portal in the `appsettings.json` file, and head over to our controller to set up the constructor injection for the `IDistributedCache` instance:

```
private readonly IDistributedCache _distributedCache;

public UsersController(IDistributedCache
distributedCacheInstance)
{
    _distributedCache = distributedCacheInstance;
}
```

And that's about it – the distributed cache is ready to use. We can now insert serialized data items as a key/value (where the value is a serialized byte array) into our cache without having to communicate with the actual data source.

Combined with the backend for the frontend pattern, the Redis cache can deliver the cached data to the application gateway service without having to contact multiple microservices, providing a simple cost-cutting solution, as well as the promised performance enhancements.

Hosting the services

Since our web implementation makes use of ASP.NET Core, we are blessed with multiple deployment and hosting options that span across Windows and Linux platforms. The first option we will be looking at is the Azure Web App setup, which can be set up on a Windows or Linux service plan. We will then move our ASP.NET application into a Docker container, which can be hosted on any of the container orchestration platforms that we have previously mentioned or simply also within an Azure web app running on a Linux server farm.

Azure Web App for App Service

At this point, without any additional implementation or configuration, our microservices are ready for deployment and they can already be hosted on the Azure cloud as a fully managed app service. In order to deploy the service as an app service, you can use Visual Studio Azure extensions, which allow you to create a publish profile, as well as the target hosting environment.

Let's see how we can do this:

1. Right-click on the project to be deployed. You will see the **Pick a publish target** selection window:

Figure 9.9 – Publish Target

For a complete managed hosting option, we can choose the **App Service** or **App Service Linux** options and continue to create a new app service.

2. If we were to choose the **App Service** option, the application would be hosted on the Windows platform with a full .NET Framework profile, whereas the Linux option would use Linux operating systems with the .NET Core runtime. Selecting the **Create New** option allows us to select/create the resource group we want the App Service instance to be added to:

Figure 9.10 – Azure App Service

3. Once published, copy the URL from the site URL field and execute a query using `curl`:

```
Microsoft Windows [Version 10.0.17134.590] (c) 2018
Microsoft Corporation. All rights reserved.

C:\Users\can.bilgin>curl https://netcoreuserapi-dev.
azurewebsites.net/odata/users?$filter=FirstName%20eq%20
%27Jane%27

{"@odata.context":"https://
netcoreuserapi-dev.azurewebsites .net/
odata/$metadata#Users","value":[{"Id":"7aa0c870- cb90-
4f02-bf7e-867914383190","FirstName":"Jane","LastName":
"Doe","NumberOfAuctions":1,"Auctions":[],"Address":
{"AddressTypeId":4000,"City":"Seattle","Street1":"23
Pike St.","CountryCode":"USA"}}]}

C:\Users\can.bilgin>
```

Containerizing services

Another option for hosting would be to containerize our application(s), which would come with the added benefit of configuration as code principles. In a container setup, each service would be isolated within its own sandbox and easily migrated from one environment to the next with a high level of flexibility and performance. Containers can also provide cost savings compared to web apps if they are deployed to the previously mentioned container registries and platforms, such as ACS, AKS, Service Fabric, and Service Fabric Mesh.

> **Important Note**
> Containers are isolated, managed, and portable operating environments. They provide a location where an application can run without affecting the rest of the system, and without the system affecting the application. Compared to VMs, they provide much higher server density since, instead of sharing the hardware, they share the operating system kernel.

Docker is a container technology that has become almost synonymous with containers themselves in recent years. The Docker container hosting environment can be created on Windows and macOS using the provided free software. Let's get started:

1. In order to prepare a Windows development machine for Docker containerization, we would need to make sure that we have installed the following:

2. Docker for Windows (for hosting Windows and Linux containers)

3. Docker tools for Visual Studio (opt-in installation for Visual Studio 2017 v15.8+)

4. Now that we have the prerequisites, we can add a Docker container image definition to each microservice project using the **Add | Docker Support** menu item:

Figure 9.11 – Docker Support

5. This will create a multistage Docker file that will, in simple terms, do the following:
6. Copy the source code for the application into the container image.
7. Restore the required .NET Core runtime components, depending on the type of the container (Windows or Linux).
8. Compile the application.
9. Create a final container image with the compiled application components.
10. Here, the Docker file we have created for `UsersApi` looks like this:

```
FROM microsoft/dotnet:2.2-aspnetcore-runtime AS base
WORKDIR /app
EXPOSE 80
EXPOSE 443


FROM microsoft/dotnet:2.2-sdk AS build
WORKDIR /src
COPY ["NetCore.Web.UsersApi/NetCore.Web.UsersApi.csproj", "NetCore.Web.UsersApi/"]
COPY ["NetCore.Data.Cosmos/NetCore.Data.Cosmos.csproj", "NetCore.Data.Cosmos/"]
COPY ["NetCore.Data/NetCore.Data.csproj", "NetCore.Data/"]
RUN dotnet restore "NetCore.Web.UsersApi/NetCore.Web.
```

```
UsersApi.csproj"
COPY . .
WORKDIR "/src/NetCore.Web.UsersApi"
RUN dotnet build "NetCore.Web.UsersApi.csproj" -c Release -o /app

FROM build AS publish
RUN dotnet publish "NetCore.Web.UsersApi.csproj" -c Release -o /app

FROM base AS final
WORKDIR /app
COPY --from=publish /app .
ENTRYPOINT ["dotnet", "NetCore.Web.UsersApi.dll"]
```

As you can see, the first stage that defines the base is a reference to Microsoft-managed container images in the public Docker registry. The build image is where we have the source code for our ASP.NET Core application. Finally, the build and final images are the last stages where the application is compiled (that is, `dotnet publish`) set up as an entry point on our container.

In other words, the created container image has the final application code, as well as the required components, regardless of the host operating system and other containers running on that host.

Now, if you navigate to the parent directory of the `UsersApi` project on a console or terminal (depending on the operating system that Docker is installed on) and execute the following command, Docker will build the container image:

```
docker build -f ./NetCore.Web.UsersApi/Dockerfile -t netcore-usersapi .
```

Once the container image is built by the Docker daemon, you can check whether the image is available to start as a container using the following command:

```
docker image ls
```

If the image is on the list of available container images, you can now run the container, using either the exposed port of 80 or 443 (the following command maps the container port 80 to host port 8000):

```
docker run -p 8000:80 netcore-usersapi
```

The container development is, naturally, more integrated with Visual Studio on the Windows platform. In fact, ASP.NET Core applications, once containerized, contain a run/debug profile for Docker that can be directly started from the Visual Studio UI:

Figure 9.12 – Docker Launch Settings

At this stage, our container configuration is ready to be used, and it can already be deployed to Azure Web App for Containers. Container orchestration support can be added using the available tools in Visual Studio.

In this section, we have tested both the PaaS and CaaS models, first using an app service to host our application, then moving on to containerize the .NET application using Docker. Both the ASP.NET application package and containers can be hosted on App Service. Now that our app is ready to be hosted on the cloud, let's take a look at the available options for securing it.

Securing the application

In a microservice setup with a client-specific backend, multiple authentication strategies can be used to secure web applications. ASP.NET Core provides the required OWIN middleware components to support most of these scenarios.

278   Creating Microservices Azure App Services

Depending on the gateway and downstream services architecture, authentication/authorization can be implemented on the gateway and the user identity can be carried over to the backend services:

Figure 9.13 – Gateway Identity

Another approach would be where each service can utilize the same identity provider in a federated setup. In this setup, a dedicated **Security Token Service (STS)** would be used by client applications, and a trust relationship would need to be established between the STS and the app services:

Figure 9.14 – Microservice Identity

While choosing the authentication and authorization strategy, it is important to keep in mind that the identity consumer in this setup will be a native mobile client. When mobile applications are involved, the authentication flow of choice is generally the OAuth 2 authorization code flow:

Figure 9.15 – OAuth Stages

Again, depending on the application you are building, multiple **OpenID Identity Connect** (**OIDC**) providers, such as Microsoft Live, Facebook, and Google, can be introduced to allow users to choose their preferred identity.

ASP.NET Core Identity

ASP.NET Core Identity is the default membership system that can provide a relatively trivial yet extensive implementation of an STS, as well as login, registration, and management UIs. Compared to its predecessor, ASP.NET Core Identity provides developers with a wider range of authentication scenarios, such as OAuth, two-factor authentication, a QR code for **Time-Based One-Time Password** (**TOTP**), and so on.

ASP.NET Core Identity uses a SQL database as a persistence store by default and can be replaced with other repository implementations. Entity Framework Core is used to implement the standard repository functionality.

External OIDC providers that are supported by ASP.NET Core Identity are Facebook, Twitter, Google, and Microsoft. Additional provider implementations can be found on third-party or community-provided packages.

Using ASP.NET Core Identity, the created STS can then be consumed by the Xamarin application through a simple set of HTTP requests to register, authenticate, and authorize users. Additionally, Xamarin applications can utilize available identity provider SDKs, as well as cross-provider packages.

While this identity management should suffice, since the requirements are for a solely ASP.NET Core-based solution, once additional Azure resources are included in a distributed application, such as Azure serverless components, cloud-based identity management could prove to be a better choice.

Azure AD

Azure AD is a cloud-based **Identity as a Service (IDaaS)** offering and, hitherto, the only authentication and identity management process that's integrated with the resource manager for distributed applications developed on the Azure infrastructure. Azure AD is used to manage access to any SaaS/PaaS resources in resource groups. It supports protocols such as OpenID Connect, OAuth, and SAML to provide SSO and access control to resources within a directory.

The authorization for access to and between resources can be set up using the identity principles defined within the directory. The principle can represent a user with a single organization (possibly with an associated on-premises Active Directory), an application (a resource that's set up within the directory or external application, such as a native mobile app), or an external identity from a different Azure directory or an external identity provider.

Generally speaking, this setup where user identities are defined within an organization unit and users from other directories are introduced as guests is referred to as Azure AD **Business to Business (B2B)**.

In order to set up an application-wide authentication scheme using Azure AD B2B, follow these steps:

1. Create a directory that will define the organization that will be using the application suite (that is, the mobile application and associated services).

   > **Important Note**
   > Any Azure subscription is accompanied with, at a minimum, free-tier Azure AD (depending on the subscription type) and, in most cases, the creation of a new directory is not necessary.

   You can create a new directory by using the **Create a Resource** interface on the Azure portal. Once you have selected Azure AD, you will need to declare an organization name and initial domain name (for example, `netcorecrossplatform.onmicrosoft.com`).

2. Additional custom domains can be added to this declaration at a later time:

Figure 9.16 – Creating Azure Active Directory

3. Once the directory is created, you'll see that the organization should be available as a domain option so that you can set up the authentication for an ASP.NET Core web application using Visual Studio:

Figure 9.17 – Adding Authentication

Once the application project is created or updated with the selected authentication option, it will automatically add an application registry to Azure AD and add/configure the required middleware for application authentication. The configuration for Azure AD at application startup would look similar to the following:

```
services.AddAuthentication(AzureADDefaults.
BearerAuthenticationScheme)
    .AddAzureADBearer(options => Configuration.
Bind("AzureAd", options));
```

The configuration that was created (matching the Azure AD application registration) is as follows:

```
"AzureAd": {
    "Instance": "https://login.microsoftonline.com/",
    "Domain": "netcorecrossplatform.onmicrosoft.com",
```

```
        "TenantId": "f381eb86-1781-4732-9543-9729eef9f843",
        "ClientId": "ababb076-abb9-4426-b7df-6b9d3922f797"
    },
```

For Azure AD, authentication on the client application (considering we are using Xamarin and Xamarin.Forms as the development platforms) can be implemented using the **Microsoft Authentication Library** (**MSAL**). Follow these steps:

4. In order for the client application to be able to use the identity federation within this organization, register (yet) another application on Azure AD. However, this registration should be declared for a native application:

Figure 9.18 – Registering an Application to Azure AD

5. After the application registration is created, use the current directory (that is, the tenant) and the client application (that is, application registration) to set up the authentication library. In this setup, the identity flow can be defined simply as follows:

- The native application retrieving an access token using the authorization code flow
- The native application executing an HTTP request to the gateway service (that is, our ASP.NET Core service exposing mobile app-specific endpoints)
- The gateway service verifying the token and retrieving an on-behalf-of token to call the downstream stream services

  This way, the user identity can be propagated to each layer and the required authorization procedures can be implemented using the claim principle.

6. In order to allow identity propagation, the gateway service application registration (that is, the service principal) should be given the required identity delegation permissions to the downstream service registrations:

Figure 9.19 – Adding API Permissions

7. Now, the user identity can access the resources, given that their identity exists within the target organization and that it has the required permissions.

For a business-facing application (that is, a **Line of Business** (**LOB**) application), Azure AD B2B can provide a secure identity management solution with ease, and no additional custom implementation. However, if the application needs to be client-facing, we would need a more flexible solution with additional support for registration. Azure B2C can provide the required support for individual user accounts.

Azure AD B2C

Azure AD B2C is an identity management service for consumer-facing scenarios with the option to customize and control how customers sign up, sign in, and manage their profiles when using your applications. This targets various platforms.

B2C is a modern federated identity management service where the consumer applications (that is, the relying parties) can consume multiple identity providers and verification methods.

In the B2C realm, the user flows for sign-up and sign-in are referred to as user journeys. User journeys can be customized with policies if required. The Identity Experience Framework consumes these policies to achieve the desired user flows. The Identity Experience Framework is the underlying platform that establishes multi-party trust and completes the steps in a user journey.

Similar to Azure AD itself, a tenant describes a user domain where certain relations between the users and applications can be defined. However, in B2C, the domain is customer-specific, not organization-specific. In other words, a tenant defines an access group that is governed by the policy descriptions and the linked identity providers.

In this setup, multiple applications can be given access to multiple tenants, making B2C a perfect fit for development companies with a suite of applications that they want to publish to consumers. Consumers, once they sign up using one of the linked OIDC identity providers, can get access to multiple consumer-facing applications.

In this section, we started our security model investigation with .NET Core Identity. While it provides the most mainstream requirements for smaller consumer applications, it could quickly get overcomplicated if the number of requirements for identity management grows. As you have seen, Azure AD can also be very easily integrated into ASP.NET applications and can provide the infrastructure for complex LOB scenarios. And finally, we have briefly looked at Azure AD B2C, which provides a complete federated identity management platform with flexible extensibility options.

Summary

In this chapter, we have browsed through the PaaS platforms, as well as the architectural approaches that are available for hosting and implementing ASP.NET Core web services. Using the flexible infrastructure offered by ASP.NET Core, it is a relief for developers to implement microservices that consume data from Cosmos DB collections. The services that contain CRUD operations on domain objects can be optimized and improved with Redis, as well as containerization, and hosted on multiple platforms and operating systems. Security, being one of our main concerns in a distributed cloud architecture, can be ensured using the available identity infrastructure and IDaaS offerings such as Azure AD and Azure AD B2C on an Azure cloud stack.

In the next chapter, we will move on to Azure serverless, which is yet another service platform on which .NET Core can prove to be vital.

10
Using .NET Core for Azure Serverless

Azure functions are serverless compute modules that take advantage of various triggers, including HTTP requests. Using Azure functions, developers can create business logic containers, completely isolated from the problems brought by monolithic web application paradigms and infrastructure. They can be used as simple HTTP request processing units and so-called microservices, as well as for orchestrating complex workflows. Azure functions come in two flavors (compiled or script-based) and can be written in different languages, including C# with .NET Core modules.

In this chapter, you will get a chance to use different runtimes available for Azure functions and get a glimpse of the available configuration, trigger, and hosting options for Azure serverless. We will then incorporate Azure functions into our infrastructure so that we can process data on different triggers. We will then integrate Azure functions with a logic app, which will be used as a processing unit in our setup.

The following topics will be covered in this chapter:

- Understanding Azure Serverless
- Implementing Azure Functions
- Creating logic applications
- Integrating Azure services with functions

By the end of this chapter, you will know more about the foundational concepts of Azure functions and logic apps. You will be able to integrate Azure serverless components into your cloud infrastructure and implement functions according to your needs. In other words, you will be able to confidently set up Azure functions and logic apps for your ad hoc requirements in your next cloud-based project.

Understanding Azure Serverless

Developing a distributed system on a cloud platform has its perks as well as its disadvantages, such as growing complexity as the data you are managing spreads across multiple processes. It is extremely common to find yourself in a deadlock situation where you have to compromise on architectural requirements in favor of decreasing the cost of introducing a new feature. Azure serverless components can provide flexible solutions to ad hoc requirements with their simplistic event-driven computing experience.

In *Chapter 8, Creating a Datastore with Cosmos DB*, we created a document structure as a repository, and later, in *Chapter 9, Creating Microservices Azure App Services*, we implemented ASP.NET Core services as containerized microservices so that we could cover our main application use cases. These use cases can be considered the primary data flow through the application, and our main concern for performance is concentrated on these data paths. Nevertheless, the secondary use cases, such as keeping track of the statuses of auctions for a user that they have previously gotten involved in, or creating a feed to inform users about new vehicles up for auction, are the features that could increase the return rate of the users and maintain the user base. Therefore, we will need a steadfast, event-driven strategy that will not interfere with the primary functionality and should be able to scale without having to interfere with the infrastructure.

In short, Azure functions and other Azure serverless components are tailor-made Azure offerings for these types of event-driven scenarios where one or more Azure infrastructure services would need to be orchestrated.

Developing Azure Functions

Azure functions, as one of the earliest members of the Azure serverless ecosystem, provide a wide variety of options for development languages and SDKs, welcoming developers from different platforms. In this section, we will learn about the development options and function integration options. We will finally implement a sample Azure function to create a materialized view using data from different document stores in our Cosmos DB database.

The available options for development environments to develop Azure functions include, but are not limited to, the following:

- Using the Azure portal
- Using the Azure CLI with Azure functions Core Tools
- Using Visual Studio or Visual Studio Code
- Using other IDEs such as Eclipse or IntelliJ IDEA

As for the language and runtime, we can create our functions with the following:

- Java/Maven
- Python
- C# (.NET Core and Scripts)
- JavaScript/Node
- F# (.NET Core)

As you can see, multiple platform and development environment combinations can be used to create Azure functions. This means that any operating system, including Windows, macOS, and Linux, can be used as a development station. In the following sections, we will try to demonstrate the versatile nature of Azure functions using some of these platforms and tools for developing Azure functions.

Using Azure Function Runtimes

We will start our journey across Azure function options with available runtimes. For this demonstration, we will first create an Azure function with Python using nothing but a simple text processor and will continue to do the same on .NET and C#.

Without further ado, let's start with the cross-platform development toolset using macOS by creating our example functions using Azure Functions Core Tools:

1. In order to install the platform runtime, we will first register the `azure/functions` repository:

    ```
    brew tap azure/functions
    ```

2. Once the `azure/functions` repository has been registered, continue with the installation of Azure Functions Core Tools:

    ```
    brew install azure-functions-core-tools
    ```

The installation should not take long, and you should see an output similar to this:

```
Tapping azure/functions
Cloning into '/usr/local/Homebrew/Library/Taps/azure/homebrew-functions'...
remote: Enumerating objects: 7, done.
remote: Counting objects: 100% (7/7), done.
remote: Compressing objects: 100% (7/7), done.
remote: Total 7 (delta 0), reused 5 (delta 0), pack-reused 0
Unpacking objects: 100% (7/7), done.
Tapped 1 formula (34 files, 30.7KB).
Cans-MacBook-Pro:python can.bilgin$ brew install azure-functions-core-tools
Installing azure-functions-core-tools from azure/functions
Downloading https://functionscdn.azureedge.net/public/2.5.553/Azure.Functions.Cli.osx-x64.2.5.553.zip
######################################################################## 100.0%
🍺  /usr/local/Cellar/azure-functions-core-tools/2.5.553: 1,151 files, 466.9MB, built in 2 minutes 5 seconds
```

Figure 10.1 – Installing Azure Functions Core Tools

Once the installation is complete, we can continue with the development of our sample functions. To demonstrate functions, we will create a simple calculator function (that is, $x + y = z$).

3. Next, initialize a virtual work environment to start with Python development:

```
$ python3 -V
Python 3.6.4
$ python3 -m venv .env
$ ls
.env
$ source .env/bin/activate
(.env) $
```

4. Once the environment is created and activated, initialize the function project using the following command. When prompted, choose python as the runtime:

```
(.env) $ func init myazurefunctions
Select a worker runtime:
1. dotnet
2. node
3. python
Choose option: 3
python
```

5. Once the project is created, create a new function called `add`. When prompted, choose `HTTP trigger` as the template:

```
(.env) $ cd myazurefunctions/
(.env) $ func new
Select a template:
1. Azure Blob Storage trigger
...
9. Timer trigger
Choose option: 5
HTTP trigger
Function name: [HttpTrigger] add
```

6. Now that the function has been created, you can use any editor to edit the __init__.py file in order to implement the function, as follows:

```python
import logging

import azure.functions as func


def main(req: func.HttpRequest) -> func.HttpResponse:
    logging.info('Python HTTP trigger function processed a request.')

    reqX = req.params.get('x')
    reqY = req.params.get('y')

    logging.info(f"Received Parameters: {reqX} and {reqY}")

    if reqX and reqY:
        x = int(reqX)
        y = int(reqY)

        result = x + y
        logging.info(f"Result is {result}")

        return func.HttpResponse(f"Addition result is {result}")
    else:
        return func.HttpResponse(
            "Please pass query parameters for 'x' and 'y'",
            status_code=400
        )
```

Figure 10.2 – Azure Function in Python

7. In order to test our function, within the project directory, execute the following command, which will start the local function server:

```
func host start
```

8. Once the function server is running, execute a `get` query on the given port that is displayed on the terminal window. This will trigger the HTTP request and return the result:

```
curl 'http://localhost:7071/api/add?x=5&y=8'
Addition result is 13
```

We have now successfully created an Azure function using Python and an HTTP trigger template.

If, in the creation step, we had chosen the first option, that is, `dotnet`, the project would have been created with a compiled C# function template:

```
$ func init myazurefunctions
Select a worker runtime:
1. dotnet
2. node
3. python
Choose option: 1
dotnet

$ cd myazurefunctions
$ func new
Select a template:
1. QueueTrigger
2. HttpTrigger
...
12. IotHubTrigger
Choose option: 2
Function name: add

$ nano add.cs
$ func host start
```

Our source code for the add function would look similar to the following:

```csharp
using System;
using System.IO;
using System.Threading.Tasks;
using Microsoft.AspNetCore.Mvc;
using Microsoft.Azure.WebJobs;
using Microsoft.Azure.WebJobs.Extensions.Http;
using Microsoft.AspNetCore.Http;
using Microsoft.Extensions.Logging;
using Newtonsoft.Json;

namespace myazurefunctions
{
    public static class add
    {
        [FunctionName("add")]
        public static async Task<IActionResult> Run(
            [HttpTrigger(AuthorizationLevel.Function, "get", "post", Route = null)] HttpRequest req,
            ILogger log)
        {
            log.LogInformation("C# HTTP trigger function processed a request.");

            string reqX = req.Query["x"];
            string reqY = req.Query["y"];

            log.LogInformation($"Received Parameters: {reqX} and {reqY}");

            if(!string.IsNullOrEmpty(reqX) && !string.IsNullOrEmpty(reqY))
            {
                var x = int.Parse(reqX);
                var y = int.Parse(reqY);

                var result = x + y;

                log.LogInformation($"Result is {result}");

                return (ActionResult)new OkObjectResult($"Addition result is {result}");
            }
        }
    }
}
```

Figure 10.3 – Azure Function in C#

Of course, while this works for demonstration purposes, development with Visual Studio (for both macOS and Windows) as well as Visual Studio Code would provide the comfort of an actual .NET development environment.

In this part, we have successfully created an HTTP-triggered function both on Python and .NET. While doing this, as a development environment, we used a simple text editor and the Azure CLI to demonstrate the simplicity of Azure function development. In the next section, we will take a deeper look at other triggers that can be used for functions and learn how bindings work.

Function triggers and bindings

The function projects and the functions that we created in the previous section, in spite of the fact that they are implemented and executed on completely separate runtimes, carry function manifests that adhere to the same schema (that is, `function.json`). While the manifest for Python implementation can be found in the folder carrying the same name as the function, the dotnet version is only generated at compile time from the attributes used within the implementation (this can be found in the `bin/output/<function>` folder). Comparing the two manifests, we can immediately identify the respective sections where the input, output, and triggering mechanisms are defined for these functions:

Figure 10.4 – Azure Function bindings

As we mentioned earlier, Azure functions are event-driven Azure resources. The trigger mechanisms define not only when the function is going to be executed but also the input and output data types and/or connected services. For instance, a blob storage entry can be used as a trigger, as well as input and output.

Similarly, `HttpTrigger` can define the execution method, as well as the input and output mechanisms (like in the previous examples). This way, additional service integrations can be included within the function as declarative attributes rather than functional implementations.

Some of these binding types are as follows:

	Trigger	Input	Output
Blob storage	✓	✓	✓
Cosmos DB	✓	✓	✓
Event Grid	✓		✓
Event Hubs	✓		✓
Http and Webhooks	✓		✓
IoT Hub	✓		✓
Queue Storage	✓		✓
SendGrid			✓
Service Bus	✓		✓
SignalR		✓	✓
Table storage		✓	✓
Timer	✓		
Twilio			✓

Figure 10.5 – Available Azure Binding Options

In addition to the listed items, there are other extensions available via Azure Functions Core Tools or NuGet packages and, by default, only timer and HTTP extensions are registered in a function runtime.

As you can see, Azure Function bindings provide a very trivial manifest approach to integrate functions with various events from different resources. Nevertheless, the manifest will probably not be enough to configure our event-driven functions; we will need a proper configuration facility.

Configuring functions

Azure Functions use the same configuration infrastructure as ASP.NET Core applications, hence utilizing the `Microsoft.Extensions.Configuration` module.

While the application is running on the local runtime during development, in order to read the configuration values from the `local.settings.json` file, a configuration builder needs to be created and the `AddJsonFile` extension method needs to be used. After the configuration instance is created, the configuration values, as well as the connection strings, can be accessed through the indexer property of the configuration instance.

During deployment to the Azure infrastructure, the settings file is used as a template to create the app settings that will be governed through the Azure portal, as well as the resource manager. These values can also be accessed with the same principle, but they are added as environment variables.

In order to support both scenarios, we can use the extension methods that are available during the creation of the configuration instance:

```
var config = new ConfigurationBuilder()
                .SetBasePath(context.FunctionAppDirectory)
                .AddJsonFile("local.settings.json", optional: true,
                reloadOnChange: true)
                .AddEnvironmentVariables()
                .Build();
```

Now that we are familiar with how to set up a function manifest and configure it, let's take a look at the options that are at our disposal for hosting it.

Hosting functions

Azure Functions, once deployed, are hosted on the App Service infrastructure. In App Service, as you saw in the previous examples, only the compute and possibly other integrated resources are accumulated toward your bill. In addition, Azure Functions, in a consumption plan, are active only when they are triggered by one of the events that has been configured; hence, Azure Functions can be extremely cost-effective in mission-critical integration scenarios. Function resources can also be scaled out and down, depending on the load they are handling.

The second plan that's available for functions is the premium plan. In the premium plan, you have the option to set up always-running functions to avoid cold starts, as well as to configure unlimited execution duration. Unlimited duration can come in handy with longer-running processes since, by default, Azure Functions have a hard limit of 5 minutes, which can be extended to 10 minutes with additional configuration.

This section summed up the available hosting options for Azure functions and finished our coverage of the fundamental concepts of Azure functions. Now, let's use these concepts to implement an Azure function for our `ShopAcross` application.

Creating our first Azure function

One of the patterns mentioned previously in the context of Azure was the materialized view. For instance, in our initial structure, we have basic information about the auctions that are embedded within user documents. This way, auctions can be included as part of the user profile and users can be rated based on their involvement in successful auctions. In this setup, since the auction data on the user profile is just denormalized data chunks from the main auction table, the services would not need to directly interact with the auctions table.

Let's take a look at the following user story and see how we can implement this solution:

"As a solution architect, I would like to implement an Azure function that will update the Cosmos DB Users collection with modified auctions data so that the Auctions API can be decoupled from the Users API."

Our task here would be to implement an Azure function that will be triggered when an auction document is modified. The changes on this document should be propagated to the Users collection:

Figure 10.6 – SynchronizingDocument Data on Cosmos DB

In this setup, we will start by doing the following:

1. First, we will create our **Azure Functions** project, which will be hosted as a function app in our resource group:

Figure 10.7 – Cosmos DB Triggered Function Template

This will create our first function with the following declaration:

```
[FunctionName("Function1")]
public static void Run(
    [CosmosDBTrigger(
        databaseName: "ProductsDb",
        collectionName: "AuctionsCollection",
        ConnectionStringSetting = "DbConnection",
        LeaseCollectionName = "leases")]
    IReadOnlyList<Document> input, ILogger log)
```

By using `CosmosDBTrigger` here, we are instructing the Azure Functions runtime to create a lease so that we can connect to the Cosmos DB change feed on the given database (that is, `ProductsDb`) and collection (that is, `AuctionsCollection`) using the set connection string setting (that is, `DbConnection`).

2. Now, let's expand our configuration to include the given connection string setting:

```
{
    "ConnectionStrings": {
        "DbConnection":
"AccountEndpoint=https://handsoncrossplatform.documents.
azure.com:443/;AccountKey=...;"
    }
}
```

3. Let's now add the additional lease settings. After this step, our trigger declaration will look like this:

```
[CosmosDBTrigger(
        databaseName: "ProductsDb",
        collectionName: "AuctionsCollection",
        ConnectionStringSetting = "DbConnection",
        LeaseCollectionPrefix = "AuctionsTrigger",
        LeaseCollectionName = "LeasesCollection")]
```

By defining a lease collection, you can record the triggers that are consumed by Azure functions. In order to use a single lease collection, on top of the `LeaseCollectionName` option, we can also add the `LeasePrefix` property to our declaration. This way, each lease entry will receive a prefix value, depending on the function declaration.

4. After this, we can run our function in debug mode and see whether our trigger is working as expected. After updating a document on the `AuctionsCollection` collection, you will receive the updated data almost immediately:

Figure 10.8 – Executing the Azure Function

5. We are now receiving the modified document. If the modifications are based on the incoming data alone, we could have added an output binding with a single document or an `async` collector to modify or insert documents into a specific collection. However, we would like to update a list of auctions that the user is involved in. Therefore, we will get a Cosmos client instance using the attribute declaration:

```
[CosmosDBTrigger(
    databaseName: "ProductsDb",
    collectionName: "AuctionsCollection",
    ConnectionStringSetting = "DbConnection",
    LeaseCollectionPrefix = "AuctionsTrigger",
    LeaseCollectionName = "LeasesCollection")]
IReadOnlyList<Document> input,
[CosmosDB(
    databaseName: "ProductsDb",
    collectionName: "UsersCollection",
    ConnectionStringSetting = "DbConnection")]
DocumentClient client,
```

Now, using the client, we can execute the necessary updates on the Users document collection.

In this section, we have successfully implemented functions using Python and C#, using HTTP and Cosmos DB triggers. Now we have a wider knowledge about the available development and integration options for Azure functions. Next, we will be looking into another Azure serverless member, logic apps.

Developing a Logic App

Logic apps are simple, event-driven workflow declarations that can utilize a number of intrinsic actions as well as other Azure serverless resources. They also work on a similar trigger-based execution strategy to Azure functions. In this section, we will learn how to create simple workflows using logic apps and how to integrate them with other Azure resources.

When tasked with implementing a logic app, in theory, a developer will not necessarily need anything else other than a text editor, since logic apps are an extension of ARM resource templates. The manifest for a logic app consists of four main ingredients:

- Parameters
- Triggers

- Actions
- Outputs

Parameters, triggers, and outputs, similar to the binding concept from Azure functions, define when and how the application is going to be executed. Actions define what the application should do.

Logic apps can be created using an IDE with an additional schema and/or visual support, such as Visual Studio, or can be developed solely on the Azure portal using the web portal.

The following sections will take you through the steps of creating and designing logic apps, using the Logic App Designer, connectors, Azure functions, and in-built flow control mechanisms.

Implementing Logic Apps

In order to create a Logic App with Visual Studio, we need to do the following:

1. We need to use the Azure Resource Group project template and select the **Logic App** template from the screen that follows:

Figure 10.9 – Azure Logic App

This will create a resource group manifest that contains the logic app definition. The logic app can now be modified using the logic app designer within Visual Studio, given that the Azure Logic Apps Tools extension is installed (right-click on the resource group JSON file and choose **Open with Logic App Designer**).

2. The first step to implementing a Logic App is to select the trigger, which will be the initial step in our workflow. For this example, let's select **When a HTTP request is received**.

3. Now that the logic app flow has been created, let's expand the HTTP request and paste a sample JSON payload as the body of a request we are expecting for this application trigger:

Figure 10.10 – HTTP Trigger Schema

This will generate `Request Body JSON Schema`. Now, we can send our requests, just like in the sample JSON payload.

4. Next, we will add an action to send an email (there are many email solutions; for this example, we will be using the **Send an email** action using Outlook):

Figure 10.11 – Send an Email Action

As you can see, we are in fact using the email, subject, and message parameters defined in our trigger to populate the email action.

5. Finally, we can add a **Response** action and define the response header and body. Now, our application is ready to execute:

Figure 10.12 – HTTP Response Action

After the logic app is deployed, you can retrieve the request URL, as well as the integrated security token, from the Azure portal designer. Executing a simple POST call with the required parameters would trigger the logic application and trigger actions:

```
curl -H "Content-Type:application/json" -X POST -d
'{"email":"can.bilgin@authoritypartners.com", "title":"Test",
"subject":"Test", "message" : "Test Message"}' "https://prod-
00.northcentralus.logic.azure.com:443/workflows/5bb---------/
triggers/manual/paths/invoke?api-version=2016-10-01&sp=%2Ftrigg
ers%2Fmanual%2Frun&sv=1.0&sig=eOB---------------"
```

```
Successfully sent the email to can.bilgin@authoritypartners.com
```

As you can see, using logic apps, these types of simple or even more intricate business workflows can be declaratively converted into web services and executed on triggers such as queues, feeds, and webhooks. Connectors are the key components in this setup that serve these actions and the triggers that are available for logic apps.

Using connectors

In the previous example, we used the HTTP trigger and response actions, as well as the Outlook email action. These actions and triggers are packaged in so-called connectors for the logic app infrastructure. Connectors are essentially part of a bigger SaaS ecosystem that also involves Microsoft Flow and Power Apps, as well as logic apps. Connectors can be described as encapsulated connectivity components for various SaaS offerings (for example, email, social media, release management, HTTP requests, file transfer, and so on).

On top of the standard free set of connectors (including third-party connectors), the **Enterprise Integration Pack** (**EIP**), which is a premium offering, provides building blocks for B2B enterprise integration services. These integration scenarios generally revolve around the supported industry standards, that is, **Electronic Data Interchange** (**EDI**) and **Enterprise Application Integration** (**EAI**).

It is also possible to create custom logic apps connectors in order to implement additional custom use cases that cannot be realized with the available set of connectors.

If/when the actions provided through the available connectors do not satisfy the requirements, Azure functions can be integrated as tasks into logic apps. This way, any custom logic can be embedded into the workflow using .NET Core and simple HTTP communication between logic apps and functions.

Creating our first Logic App

The main service application, so far, is built to accommodate the main application use cases and provide data for users so that they can create auctions and user profiles, as well as bidding on auctions. Nevertheless, we need to find more ways to engage users by using their interests. For this type of engagement model, we can utilize various notification channels. The most prominent of these channels is a periodic notification email setup.

The user story we will use for this example is as follows:

"As a product owner, I would like to send out periodic emails to registered users if there are new auctions available, depending on their previous interests, so that I can engage the users and increase the return rate."

Before we start implementing our logic app, in spite of the fact that it is possible to use the Cosmos DB connector to load data, let's create two more Azure functions to load the users and latest auctions for email targets and content, respectively. Both of these functions should use `HttpTrigger` and should return JSON data as a response. For this exercise, you can use the same Azure function project that was created in the previous section. Let's get started:

1. The function that will return the list of users that we will send the notifications to is as follows:

```
[FunctionName("RetrieveUsersList")]
public static async Task<IActionResult> Run(
    [HttpTrigger(AuthorizationLevel.Function, "get",
"post", Route = null)] HttpRequest req,
    ILogger log)
{
    // TODO: Retrieve users from UsersCollection
    var users = new List<User>();
    users.Add(new User{ Email = "can.bilgin@authoritypartners.com", FirstName = "Can"});

    return (ActionResult)new OkObjectResult(users);
}
```

2. Next, we will need the data for the latest auctions:

   ```
   [FunctionName("RetrieveLatestAuctionsList")]
   public static async Task<IActionResult> Run(
       [HttpTrigger(AuthorizationLevel.Function, "get",
   "post", Route = null)] HttpRequest req,
       ILogger log)
   {
       // TODO: Retrieve latest auctions from
   AuctionsCollection
       var auctions = new List<Auction>();
       auctions.Add(new Auction
       {
           Brand = "Volvo",
           Model = "S60",
           Year = 2017,
           CurrentHighestBid = 26000,
           StartingPrice = 25000
       });

       return (ActionResult)new OkObjectResult(auctions);
   }
   ```

   Now that we have our data feeds ready, we can start implementing our logic app.

   > **Important Note**
   > In this example, we have used Azure functions to retrieve a set of DTOs in order to be cost-efficient. It is also possible to create a change feed function that will prepare the daily notification feed as soon as the data store is updated with a new user or auction/bid. This way, the logic app can directly load the data from the daily feed document collection or table storage.

3. In our previous example, we created a logic app using an HTTP trigger. For this example, let's start with a recurrence trigger so that we can process our data and prepare a periodic feed:

Figure 10.13 – Recurrence Trigger Setup

4. Next, let's retrieve the set of users using our Azure function. In order to select a function from the available actions, you should locate the **Azure Functions** action in the **Choose an action** dialog, then select the target function app that contains your functions, and finally, select the desired function:

Figure 10.14 – Azure Functions with the Logic App

5. Once we have retrieved the results from the Azure function, it will be in JSON format. In order to ease the design and access properties of the contained data items, it would be good to include a data parse action with a predefined schema. At this point, you can have a simple run and copy the results:

Figure 10.15 – Calling the Azure Function

6. Now, repeat the same actions for the auctions list data, so that we can start building out email content. Our current workflow should look similar to the following:

Figure 10.16 – Sequential Azure Function Calls

7. Before we continue with preparing the email content and sending it to each user on the list, let's structure the flow a little bit so that the data retrieval actions for users and auctions are not executed sequentially:

Figure 10.17 – Parallel Azure Function Calls

So far, we have created a logic app that retrieves the list of users and available auctions from Cosmos DB using two separate Azure functions. The logic app then parses the JSON data so that the object data can be utilized by the following actions. We can now continue with additional control statements and the preparation of the email content.

Workflow execution control

By definition, being an orchestration tool, Logic Apps uses control statements such as `foreach`, `switch`, and `conditionals` in order to compose a controlled workflow using available actions. These control statements can be used as actions within the workflow using the input and output values of other actions within the logic app context. The available set of control statements is as follows:

- **Condition**: Used to evaluate a condition and define two separate paths, depending on the result
- **Foreach**: Used to execute a path of dependent actions for each item in a sequence
- **Scope**: Used to encapsulate a block of actions
- **Switch**: Used to execute multiple separate action blocks, depending on the switch input
- **Terminate**: Terminates the current execution of the logic app
- **Until**: Used as a `while` loop, where a block of actions is executed until a defined condition evaluates to `true`

These statements can be accessed using the **Control** action within **Logic App Designer**:

Figure 10.18 – Control Actions

In our example, we are supposed to send an email to each user with the latest auctions list. We can achieve this with a **For each** action on the list of users:

Figure 10.19 – Using variables from a For each loop

As you can see, we are using the body of the `UsersList` action (that is, `body(UsersList)`, using logic app notation), and for each item in the list, we are retrieving the email (that is, `items('For_each')['email']`) and `firstName`. In a similar manner, we can prepare the auction's email body and assign the result as the body of the subject. In addition to this simple setup, the content can be filtered according to the interest of the user using the data operations that are available:

Figure 10.20 – Complete Azure Logic App View

Now, we will be periodically sending auction updates to users without having to compromise or add additional complexity to our current service infrastructure.

In this section, we have learned about the basic logic app concepts and implemented a fully functional Azure Logic app using several control statements, connectors, and custom Azure functions. As you can see, the declarative and event-driven nature of Azure logic app design makes them a good choice for orchestrating secondary event-driven processes.

Integration with Azure services

So far, we have only utilized Cosmos DB in the context of logic apps and Azure functions among the many Azure services that we can integrate with Azure serverless components. In this section, we will analyze the other available integration options for Azure serverless components with other Azure resources.

As you have seen, these integrations are available through bindings for Azure functions and through connectors for logic apps. Using this integrated business model, multiple architectural patterns can be composed, and event-driven scenarios can be accomplished.

The following sections will take you through repository-, queue-, and event-based Azure resources that can be integrated with Azure serverless components. Let's take a deeper look at some of these integrated services.

Repository

In the Azure Serverless context, it is fair to say that almost all Azure repository models are tightly integrated with the infrastructure. Let's take a look at the following models:

- **Cosmos DB**: This has an available binding for Azure functions. This is a connector with various actions to execute mainstream CRUD actions, as well as advanced scenarios to create, retrieve, and execute stored procedures. Cosmos DB can also be used to trigger Azure functions.

- **SQL Server**: This is another repository service that can be integrated into logic apps with the available connector, hence allowing triggers such as an item being created or modified. Logic apps can also use the SQL and **Azure SQL Data Warehouse** connectors to execute both raw and structured queries on SQL instances. Additionally, SQL connections can be initialized within Azure functions using nothing but the native SQL client that's available as part of .NET Core.

- **Azure Table Storage**: This is another repository model that can be integrated with Azure serverless components. Table Storage tables can be used as input parameters and can be the receivers of new entities as part of an output configuration within the Azure function infrastructure. The connector for logic apps can be utilized to execute various actions on Table Storage:

Figure 10.21 – Azure Table Storage Actions

- **Azure Blob Storage**: This can be used as a trigger for both functions and logic apps. The available function binding and app connector provide a variety of tasks and binding elements that can be utilized within the serverless app model.

Queue-based processing

In order to implement the aforementioned queue-based load-leveling pattern, Azure distributed systems can utilize Azure queues, as well as **Azure Service Bus**. In this way, various asynchronous processing patterns can be implemented.

Azure queues can be configured to trigger functions and logic apps. Both the binding and the connector have available actions so that they can listen to a specific queue. The connector contains actions for executing basic operations, including but not limited to the creation of message queues, the insertion of messages, and the retrieval of messages. An Azure message queue can also be used as an output target of an Azure function to create a message in the configured queue.

The connector and binding for Azure Service Bus have an extended set of available actions and various triggers. Queues and topics are both available for listening for new messages as part of the trigger setup. Logic apps can also execute almost all possible actions that a managed client can achieve through operations related to managing basic messages, dead-letter queues, locks, topics, and subscriptions.

Event aggregation

Another citizen of the Azure serverless ecosystem, **Event Grid** is the most appropriate candidate for implementing the classic publisher/subscriber model between distributed service components, especially when Azure functions and logic apps are involved. In addition to Event Grid, Event Hubs is the best choice for big data pipelines that involve event streaming rather than discreet event distribution.

Event Grid aggregates the events that are collected from various so-called event sources, such as container registries, resource groups, service bus, and storage. Event Grid can also consume and deliver custom topics that are posted by capable components. Aggregated events are then dispersed to the registered consumers or so-called event handlers. Event handlers for Event Grid include, but are not limited to, the following:

- Azure Automation
- Azure Functions
- Event Hubs
- Hybrid connections
- Logic Apps
- Microsoft Flow
- Queue Storage
- Webhooks

This infrastructure means that developers aren't limited by the available triggers for functions and logic apps as the initial point of a certain mission-critical scenario. They can also create a complete event-driven subscription model.

Event Hubs can be integrated as a consumer for Event Grid events and used as triggers and output for Azure functions. A connector is available for logic apps with triggers and actions. An event hub, when used together with Azure functions, can create an extremely agile scaling model for processing big data streams.

We now have a complete picture of integration options for Azure serverless components and in which types of scenarios they can be utilized.

Summary

Overall, Azure Functions and Logic Apps, as part of the Azure Serverless platform, provide ad hoc, event-driven solutions to fill in the gaps in any distributed cloud application. In this chapter, we have analyzed the available development options for Azure Functions. We have implemented simple Azure Functions to denormalize data on a Cosmos DB setup. Finally, we created Logic Apps by utilizing out-of-the-box connector tasks, as well as Azure Functions with HTTP and periodic triggers.

This chapter completes our coverage of the Azure cloud services-related topics. In the following chapters, we will take a look at more advanced topics to improve the integration between Xamarin applications and the cloud-based service backend.

Section 4: Advanced Mobile Development

For developers who are not satisfied with the bare minimum, terms such as responsive, engaging, and asynchronous become the differentiating factors for a mobile application. Providing the patterns and tools to create an application that will provide a fast and fluid user interface and engage the user with a personalized approach is one of the goals of the upcoming chapters.

The following chapters will be covered in this section:

- *Chapter 11, Fluid Applications with Asynchronous Patterns*
- *Chapter 12, Managing Application Data*
- *Chapter 13, Engaging Users with Notifications and the Graph API*

11
Fluid Applications with Asynchronous Patterns

One of the key attributes of an attractive mobile application is its responsiveness. Applications that do not interfere with the interaction of the user and, instead, maintain the ability to render and execute user gestures in a smooth manner are more desirable by users. In order to achieve fast and fluid application norms, together with performance, asynchronous execution patterns come to the rescue. When developing Xamarin applications, as well as ASP.NET Core, both the task's framework and reactive modules can help distribute the execution threads and create a smooth and uninterrupted execution flow.

In this chapter, we will learn about what really makes up the task framework and the foundational concepts related to it. We will also go over some of the most prominent patterns associated with asynchronous execution models with awaitables and observables, and then apply them to various sections of the application. Finally, we will also take a look at native asynchronous execution models.

The following sections will walk you through some key implementation scenarios for asynchronous execution:

- Utilizing tasks and awaitables
- Asynchronous execution patterns
- Native asynchronous execution

By the end of this chapter, you will be able to introduce the TPL and native asynchronous features into your mobile and web applications. These will be written in Xamarin and .NET 5 to help you create more responsive and agile applications.

Utilizing tasks and awaitables

In this section, we will be looking at the basics of tasks and asynchronous execution patterns, as well as identifying the main factors that make them a fundamental part of any modern application.

User experience (**UX**) is a term that is used to describe the composition of UI components and how the user interacts with them. In other words, UX is not only how the application is designed, but also the impression the user has about the application. In this context, the responsiveness of the application is one of the key factors that defines the quality of the application.

In general terms, a simple interaction use case starts with user interaction. This interaction can be a tap on a certain area of the screen, a certain gesture on a canvas, or an actual user input in an editable field on the screen. Once the user interaction triggers the execution flow, the application business logic is responsible for updating the UI to notify the user about the result of their input.

As you can see, in the asynchronous version of the simple interaction model, the application starts executing the designated business flow and doesn't wait for it to complete. In the meantime, the user is free to interact with other sections of the UI. Once the result is available, the application's UI is notified about its completion.

This interaction model defines and satisfies simple execution scenarios, such as validating an email field with a regular expression or displaying a flyout to show the desired details on an item. Nevertheless, as the interaction model and the business logic become more complex and additional dependencies come into the picture, such as web services, we should keep the user appraised about the work the application is doing (for example, a progress bar while downloading a remote resource). For this purpose, we can extend our interaction model so that it provides continuous updates to the user:

Figure 11.1 – Thread Pool Concept

Now, the UI is continuously receiving updates from the background process. These updates can be as simple as a busy signal for a loader ring or data updates for sophisticated completion percentage components. However, this pattern raises another question as to how the application UI is going to handle multiple updates coming in from background processing. Before we can answer this question, let's take a closer look at the application's UI infrastructure and task-based execution.

Task-based execution

An application UI, regardless of the platform it is implemented on, always follows a single-threaded model. Even if the underlying platform or the hardware supports multithreading, the runtime is responsible for providing a single dispatcher to render the UI. This helps us avoid multiple threads trying to update the same section of the screen at the same time.

In this single-threaded model, it is the application's responsibility to lay off the background processing to child threads and synchronize back to the UI thread.

.NET Framework introduced the task-based threading model, also referred to as the **Task Asynchronous Programming (TAP)** model, in .NET 4.0, and since then it has become the norm for asynchronous execution – especially on mobile platforms such as Xamarin.

In simple terms, TAP provides an abstraction over the classic threading model. In this approach, the developer and, implicitly, the application, are not directly responsible for handling the thread's creation, execution, and synchronization, but simply for creating asynchronous work blocks (that is, tasks), thus allowing the underlying runtime to handle all the heavy lifting. Especially considering the fact that .NET Standard is a complete abstraction for various runtimes, such as .NET Core and Mono, this abstraction allows each platform to implement the most platform-appropriate way to handle multithreading. This is one of the main reasons why the `Thread` class is not available in cross-platform modules. Instead, platform-specific framework modules (for example, Xamarin.iOS and Xamarin.Android) provide access to the classic threading model.

A simple asynchronous block can be created using the static helper methods that are available in the `Task` class:

```
Task.Run(() =>
{
    // Run code here
})
```

In this example, we are wrapping a synchronous block of code inside a task. Now, the declaring method can return the created task block. Alternatively, if there are other asynchronous blocks, it should execute this block with an `await` keyword, thus creating an `async` method:

```
public Task SimpleyAsyncChain()
{
    return Task.Run(...);
}

public async Task MyAsyncMethod()
{
    var result = await Task.Run(...);
    await OtherAsyncMethod(result);

    // example async method
    await Task.Delay(300);
}
```

Both implementations in this example create an asynchronous chain of methods that can be awaited at the top level. Exception handling can also be introduced using simple `try`/`catch` blocks, which is no different than using synchronous code:

```csharp
public async Task<MyEntity>
MyAsyncMethodWithExceptionHandling()
{
    MyEntity result = null;

    try
    {
        result = await Task.Run(...);
    }
    catch(Exception ex)
    {
        // TODO: Log the exception
    }

    return result;
}
```

While tasks can be executed sequentially, which is done in the `MyAsyncMethod` method, if there are no dependencies between the asynchronous blocks, they can also be executed in parallel, allowing the runtime to utilize multithreading as much as possible:

```csharp
public async Task MyParallelAsyncMethod()
{
    var result = await Task.Run(...);
    await Task.WhenAll(OtherAsyncMethod(result), Task.Delay(300));
}
```

Using this foundation provided by the TAP model, let's take a look at the following user story:

"As a registered user, I would like to have a view dedicated to my profile so that I can see and verify my public information within the application."

Perhaps the most prominent use of task-based methods is when the application needs to interact with a remote backend (for example, a RESTful web service). However, tasks are deeply integrated, and .NET Framework is the de facto way of handing multithreading. For instance, the starting point of a service proxy client would be to create a simple REST client that would execute various HTTP methods against the target API endpoint.

Before we implement our rest client, we need to define the client interface:

```
public interface IRestClient
{
    Task<TResult> GetAsync<TResult>(string resourceEndpoint, string id)
        where TResult : class;

    Task<TEntity> PostAsync<TEntity>(string resourceEndpoint, TEntity entity) where TEntity : class;

    Task<TEntity> PutAsync<TEntity>(string resourceEndpoint, string id,
        TEntity entity) where TEntity : class;

    Task<TResult> DeleteAsync<TResult>(string resourceEndpoint, string id) where TResult : class; }
```

We can extend this interface with more specialized methods, such as the `GetListAsync` method, which can be helpful for serializing a list of items:

```
Task<IEnumerable<TResult>> GetListAsync<TResult>(string resourceEndpoint) where TResult : class;
```

Now, the implementation of these methods can use the simple `HttpClient` method to execute the remote call and some type of serialization/deserialization:

```
public async Task<TResult> GetAsync<TResult>(string resourceEndpoint, string id)
    where TResult : class
{
    var request = new HttpRequestMessage(HttpMethod.Get, $"{resourceEndpoint}/{id}");
```

```csharp
        var response = await _client.SendAsync(request);

        if (response.IsSuccessStatusCode)
        {
            var content = await response.Content.ReadAsStringAsync();
            return JsonConvert.DeserializeObject<TResult>(content);
        }

        // TODO: Throw Exception?
        return null;
    }
```

Here, the client member field is initialized in the constructor of RestClient, possibly with a base URL declaration, as well as with additional HTTP handlers:

```csharp
public RestClient(string baseUrl)
{
    // TODO: Insert the authorization handler?
    _client = new HttpClient();
    _client.BaseAddress = new Uri(baseUrl);
}
```

Using RestClient, we can then create another level of abstraction to implement the API-specific method calls that will convert the data transformation objects into domain entities:

```csharp
public async Task<User> GetUser(string userId)
{
    User result = null;

    // Should we initialize the client here? Is UserApi client going to
    //be singleton?
    var client = new RestClient(_configuration["serviceUrl"]);

    try
    {
        var dtoUser = await client.GetAsync<User>
```

```
            (_configuration["usersApi"], userId);
        result = User.FromDto(dtoUser);
    }
    catch (Exception ex)
    {
        // TODO:
    }

    return result;
}
```

Here, we have a chain of asynchronous methods finally executing a remote call. On top of this, we now have to connect the user API retrieval call to our view model, which should immediately load the associated user data so that it can be displayed on the target view. In this use case, the user interaction that triggers the business flow is possibly the user tapping on the user profile link. The application responds by navigating to the target view, which initializes the view model. The view model, in turn, requests the remote data for the user profile:

```
public async Task RetrieveUserProfile()
{
    if (string.IsNullOrEmpty(NavigationParameter))
    {
        // TODO: Error/Exception
    }

    var userId = NavigationParameter;

    var userResult = await _usersApi.GetUser(userId);

    CurrentUser = userResult;
}
```

Once the `CurrentUser` property has been set, the view will be notified and updated to display the retrieved information.

This implementation would work in a simple asynchronous chain since the `async/await` construct provided by the language is converted into a state machine during the compilation process. This ensures that the asynchronous threads yield back into the UI thread so that the view model's updates can be propagated back to the UI.

If we want to make sure that the user data assignment is executed on the UI thread, we can use the `InvokeOnMainThread` method, instructing the runtime to execute a block of asynchronous code on the main UI thread:

```
Device.BeginInvokeOnMainThread (() => {
    CurrentUser = userResult;
});
```

The main thread's invocation becomes an essential part of the asynchronous chain when we're dealing with multiple synchronization contexts. But what is the synchronization context and how can we manage it in multi-threaded mobile applications? The next section holds the answer to this!

Synchronization context

When dealing with asynchronous method calls using TAP, it is important to understand that `async` and `await` are language constructs provided by C#, and that the actual multithreaded execution is the injected compiler-generated code that's used to replace the async/await blocks. If the compiler-generated asynchronous state machine is closely observed and the `async` method builder is analyzed, you will notice that, at the start of any asynchronous await call, the current synchronization context is captured and, later on, when the asynchronous operation is completed, it is used again to execute the continuation action.

In a Xamarin application, the **synchronization context** – which is similar to the execution context – refers to the thread that the current asynchronous block is being called from, as well as the target thread that the current asynchronous block should yield to. If an ASP.NET core application is under the magnifying glass, the synchronization context would be referring to the current `HttpRequest` object. In certain cases, the thread pool might be acting in the synchronization context.

As we have mentioned previously, the previous asynchronous example for `UserProfile` would, in fact, be used in the UI thread, since the captured context at the beginning of the execution would probably be for the main UI thread. Once the retrieve operation is completed, the continuation actions (that is, assigning the result to the view-model) would be executed on the main thread. Nevertheless, yielding the asynchronous methods back to the UI could cause performance penalties and even deadlocks if the await chains are not handled properly. In a catastrophic scenario, the UI thread might end up waiting for an asynchronous block, which, in turn, waits for the UI thread to yield back to. In order to avoid such occurrences, it is highly advised to utilize explicit control of the captured context and yield the target context using the `ConfigureAwait` method. Moreover, especially in native mobile applications, you should free the UI thread from any long-running task synchronization using `ConfigureAwait(false)` (that is, do not yield to the captured context). This ensures that the asynchronous methods are not merged back to the UI thread and that the asynchronous compositions are handled within a separate thread pool. For instance, let's say we were to add an additional asynchronous method to the `async` chain from the previous example:

```
var userResult = await _usersApi.GetUser(userId).
ConfigureAwait(false);
var additionalUserData = _usersApi.GetUserDetails(userId).
ConfigureAwait(false);

CurrentUser = userResult;
```

Unlike the previous example, the last statement in this method (the continuation action) would be executed on a different thread than the UI thread. The first asynchronous call would not yield back to the UI thread because of `ConfigureAwait` creating a secondary synchronization context. This secondary context would then be used as the captured context for the second asynchronous call, to which it would yield. Finally, the statement to assign the result would be executed on this secondary context. This would mean that without the `BeginInvokeOnMainThread` helper's execution, the UI would likely not be updated with the incoming data. However, we must, of course, use multiple synchronization contexts and the main thread with caution. While creating a responsive application, we don't want these event-driven asynchronous tasks to wreak havoc on our views and view-models. The easiest way to keep them in check would be to use other the control mechanisms that are available, such as locks, semaphores, and mutexes.

Single execution guarantee

Another popular area of implementation for asynchronous tasks is the commands that are exposed through the view models throughout the mobile application. If the business flow that is to be executed as a response to a user input (for example, a submit button executing an update call on the user profile) depends on an asynchronous code block, then the command should be implemented in such a way that you can invoke the asynchronous function properly.

Let's demonstrate this with our existing view model. First, we need to implement our internal execution method:

```
public async Task ExecuteUpdateUserProfile()
{
    try
    {
        await _usersApi.UpdateUser(CurrentUser);
    }
    catch (Exception ex)
    {
        // TODO:
    }
}
```

Now, let's declare our command:

```
public ICommand UpdateUserCommand
{
    get
    {
        if (_updateUserCommand == null)
        {
            _updateUserCommand = new Command(async () => await
                ExecuteUpdateUserProfile());
        }

        return _updateUserCommand;
    }
}
```

At this point, if the command is bound to a user control such as a button, multiple taps on that button would result in multiple executions of the same command. While this might not cause any issues on the business flow (that is, the user will be updated with the current data multiple times), it could cause performance degradation and unnecessary resource consumption on the service side.

Locks and monitors, as well as mutex implementations, which we are familiar with from classical threading, can also be implemented in task-based asynchronous code blocks using `SemaphoreSlim`. The main usage of `SemaphoreSlim` can be summarized as throttling one or more asynchronous blocks.

For this scenario, we can initialize a semaphore with only one available slot:

```
private static readonly SemaphoreSlim Semaphore = new SemaphoreSlim(1);
```

In the execution block of the command method, we can check whether there is any lease on the current semaphore. If there isn't, we put a lease on one slot, and release it once the command's execution is complete:

```
public async Task ExecuteUpdateUserProfile()
{
    if (Semaphore.CurrentCount == 0)
    {
        return;
    }

    await Semaphore.WaitAsync().ConfigureAwait(false);

    try { ... } catch { ... }

    Semaphore.Release();
}
```

This way, the command cannot be executed more than once at the same time, thus preventing any data conflicts. It is important to note here that since the semaphore count is released after the command's execution, it is a must to use a `try/catch` block in order to prevent the semaphore from being locked after an error occurs.

Logical tasks

In the retrieve example, we executed the view-model data assignment block within a `BeginInvokeOnMainThread` block. While this actually guaranteed that the view-model change will be propagated to the UI thread, with this type of execution, we cannot really say that once the asynchronous method that's awaiting the execution is complete, and when the view-model has been updated. Moreover, the UI execution block could have used another asynchronous code block (for example, to show a popup once the data is retrieved). In this type of situation, we can utilize a task completion source so that we have stricter control over when the asynchronous code block is truly completed:

```
public async Task RetrieveUserProfile()
{
    // Removed for brevity

    TaskCompletionSource<int> tcs = new
TaskCompletionSource<int>();

    var userResult = await _usersApi.GetUser(userId);

    Device.BeginInvokeOnMainThread(async () => {
        CurrentUser = userResult;
        await ShowPopupAsync(); // async method
        tcs.SetResult(0);
    });

    await tcs.Task.ConfigureAwait(false);
}
```

In this example, we are using `TaskCompletionSource`, which represents the asynchronous state machine and accepts a result or an exception. This state machine only gets a result when the UI block's execution is completed and the `RetrieveUserProfile` method is finalized.

`TaskCompletionSource` can also prove useful for describing native UI flows in terms of asynchronous blocks. For instance, the complete UI flow for a user to pick a media file from available content providers can be described as an asynchronous block. In this case, the completion source would be initialized once the user opens the file picker dialog, and the result would be set once the user picks a certain file from the selected content source. The implementation can be extended to throw an exception if the user taps on the cancel button on a certain dialog. This way, user flows that are composed of multiple screens and interactions can be abstracted into asynchronous methods, which means they can be easily used by the view or the view model of the application.

The command pattern

The **command pattern** is a derivation of the flux pattern for reactive mobile applications. In the Android world, this pattern is implemented in a similar way under the name **Model View Intent** (**MVI**), whose sole purpose is creating a unidirectional flow of data and decreasing the complexities that stem from the duplex nature of **Model-View-ViewMode** (**MVVM**).

In this pattern, each view is equipped with multiple commands that are self-contained execution blocks with references to the underlying application infrastructure (similar to a unit of work). In this case, the user interaction is routed to the respective command, and the command's result is propagated to the concerned controls through broadcasts (for example, using the `BroadcastReceiver` implementation).

The task infrastructure in .NET Standard and its implemented runtimes, such as .NET Core, allow developers to implement awaitable context elements, which can easily represent commands and can be awaited using the `Task` syntax.

For a class instance to be awaitable, it should implement the `GetAwaiter` method, which, in turn, is used by the .NET task infrastructure. In a command pattern implementation, we can start by creating a base abstract class that we will use for dependency injection, and also implement the `awaitable` method:

```
public abstract class BaseCommand
{
    protected BaseCommand(IConfiguration configurationInstance, 
IUserApi userApi)
    {
        ConfigurationService = configurationInstance;
        UserApi = userApi;
    }
```

```
    protected IConfiguration ConfigurationService { get;
private set; }

    protected IUserApi UserApi { get; private set;}

    public virtual TaskAwaiter GetAwaiter()
    {
        return InternalExecute().GetAwaiter();
    }

    protected virtual async Task InternalExecute()
    {
    }
}
```

We can also extend the command implementation to actually return a result:

```
public abstract class BaseCommand<TResult> : BaseCommand
{
    protected TResult Result { get; set; }

    public new TaskAwaiter<TResult> GetAwaiter()
    {
        return ProcessCommand().GetAwaiter();
    }

    protected override async Task InternalExecute()
    {
        Result = await ProcessCommand().ConfigureAwait(true);
        await base.InternalExecute().ConfigureAwait(true);
    }

    protected virtual async Task<TResult> ProcessCommand()
    {
        // To be implemented by the deriving classes
        return default(TResult);
```

```
        }
}
```

Now, the implementation of an actual command – for instance, to update a user profile – would look similar to the following:

```
public class UpdateUserCommand : BaseServiceCommand<User>
{
    User _userDetails;

    public UpdateProfileCommand(IConfiguration configuration, IUsersApi
        usersApi, User user) :
        base(configuration, usersApi)
    {
        _userDetails = user;
    }

    protected async override Task<string> ProcessCommand()
    {
        try
        {
            Result = await _usersApi.UpdateUser(CurrentUser);
            return Result;
        }
        catch (Exception ex)
        {
            // TODO:
        }
    }
}
```

Finally, the implemented command can be initialized and executed like so:

```
var result = await new UpdateUserCommand(configuration,
usersApi, user);
```

Here, the base command can also utilize a service locator or some type of property injection, so that the set of services doesn't need to be injected together with the command parameters. Additionally, the messenger service can be utilized to broadcast that it successfully executed the command for multiple user controls.

Creating producers/consumers

Thread-safe collections are an invaluable member of the asynchronous toolset in .NET Core, just like they were in the full .NET Framework. Using blocking collections, concurrent models can be implemented to provide a common ground for asynchronous tasks on multiple threads. The most prominent of these models is, without a doubt, the producer/consumer pattern implementation. In this paradigm, a method executing on a parallel thread/task will produce the data items that will be consumed by another parallel operation, called the consumer, until a bounding limit is reached or production is completed. The two methods will be sharing the same blocking collection, where the blocking collection would act as a broker between the two asynchronous blocks.

Let's illustrate this pattern with a small implementation:

1. We will start by creating the blocking collection that will be used as storage for, let's say, `Auction` items:

   ```
   BlockingCollection<Auction> auctions = new
   BlockingCollection(100);
   ```

2. We can now add the `Auction` items to the blocking collection using a background task. Here, the `GetNewAuction` method will be retrieving/creating auction instances and pushing them down to the pipeline:

   ```
   Task.Run(() =>
   {
       while(hasMoreAuctions)
       {
           auctions.Add(GetNewAuction);
       }

       auctions.CompleteAdding();
   });
   ```

3. Similar to the producer, we can start a separate consumer thread that will be processing the items that are delivered:

   ```
   Task.Run(() =>
   {
       while (!auctions.IsCompleted)
       {
           Process(auctions.Take());
       }
   }
   ```

4. Taking this implementation one step further, we can use the `GetConsumingEnumerable` method to create a blocking enumerable:

   ```
   Task.Run(() =>
   {
       foreach(var auction in auctions.GetConsumingEnumerable())
       {
           Process(auction);
       }
   }
   ```

5. Finally, by utilizing `Parallel.ForEach`, we can add even more consumers without having to go through non-trivial synchronization implementations:

   ```
   Parallel.Foreach(auctions.GetConsumingEnumerable(),
       Process);
   ```

Now, the data that's produced by the producer will be consumed by multiple consumers until the auction's collection sends the `IsCompleted` signal, which will cause the consuming enumerable to break and continue with the rest of the code's execution. In this setup, each consumer would be receiving a different data item. But what if we had multiple consumers expecting the same set of data to execute a different action? This type of setup could have been achieved with an observable/observer implementation.

Using observables and data streams

The `IObserver` and `IObservable` interfaces, which make up the basis for observables and so-called reactive patterns, were introduced in .NET 4, together with TPL. The most prominent implementation of `IObservable` is within the Rx Extensions NuGet library. This is currently an open source project and is managed by .NET Foundation.

Before we jump into reactive data, let's take a step back and try to demonstrate different types of data streams. We will start this demonstration with some simple synchronous code, which we can then use as our base requirement for the other implementations. Before we start, you should create a new .NET 5 console project and modify the `Main` method so that it's `async`:

```
class Program
{
    static async Task Main(string[] args)
    {
    }
}
```

Now that the console application project has been created, let's add a new method called `GetNumbers`:

```
public static IEnumerable<int> GetNumbers()
{
    var count = 0;

    while (count < 10)
    {
        yield return count++;
    }
}
```

This method will be creating a synchronous data pipeline that will be printed on the screen using a simple `for/each` loop:

```
Console.WriteLine("Synchronous Data");

foreach (var item in GetNumbers())
{
```

```
            Console.WriteLine($"Sync: {item}");
}
```

What's happening here is that each time the for/each loop requests a new item from the enumerable, the GetNumbers method yields a number until the numbers reach 10.

Now, imagine that we were to retrieve and push this data into the pipeline asynchronously. We wouldn't be able to use Task<IEnumerable<int>> since this would mean we would need to wait for the complete set of data to finish loading, and we could enumerate through it. We could, however, use a "stream" of asynchronous tasks:

```
public static IEnumerable<Task<int>> GetAsyncNumbers()
{
    var count = 0;

    while (count < 10)
    {
        yield return Task.Run(async () =>
            {
                await Task.Delay(200);
                return count++;
            });
    }
}
```

Here, we are using a Task.Delay call to simulate an asynchronous action. Now, let's use this new producer to print out the data:

```
Console.WriteLine("Asynchronous Data");

foreach (var itemTask in GetAsyncNumbers())
{
    await itemTask
        .ContinueWith(_ => Console.WriteLine($"Async: {_.Result}"));
}
```

At this stage, the evolution of this implementation can go in multiple different directions. The first direction would be to create a blocking collection and iterate through the consumable enumerable. Now, let's rewrite our data source to produce a blocking collection:

```
private static BlockingCollection<int> StartGetNumbers()
{
    var blockingCollection = new BlockingCollection<int>();

    Task.Run(
        async () =>
        {
            var count = 0;
            while (count < 10)
            {
                await Task.Delay(200);
                blockingCollection.Add(count++);
            }
            blockingCollection.CompleteAdding();
        });

    return blockingCollection;
}
```

Following the previous examples, the consumer would look similar to the following:

```
Console.WriteLine("ConsumerProducer");

foreach (var item in StartGetNumbers().
GetConsumingEnumerable())
{
    Console.WriteLine($"Consumer: {item}");
}
```

Another direction we could have taken would be to create an `async` enumerable:

```
private static async IAsyncEnumerable<int> GetNumbersAsync()
{
```

```csharp
    var count = 0;

    while (count < 10)
    {
        await Task.Delay(1000);
        yield return count++;
    }
}
```

Now, we can consume the enumerable asynchronously:

```csharp
Console.WriteLine("Async Stream");

await foreach (int number in GetNumbersAsync())
{
    Console.WriteLine($"Async Stream: {number}");
}
```

So far, we have asynchronously consumed a data source with a blocking collection and asynchronous enumerable. Now, let's take a look at what this would look like using observables.

Observables can be created using Rx extensions, which can be found under the `System.Reactive` namespace in the NuGet package with the same name. If were to rewrite the previous implementation using an observable, it would look like this:

```csharp
private static IObservable<int> GetNumbersObservable()
{
    return Observable.Create<int>(
        async _ =>
        {
            var count = 0;
            while (count < 20)
            {
                await Task.Delay(200);
                _.OnNext(count++);
            }
            _.OnCompleted();
        });
}
```

The important sections in this implementation are the `OnNext` and `OnCompleted` methods, which control the flow of data. This implementation would produce a cold observable, which would start producing data as soon as the first observer is attached to it. If it was a hot observable, the data source would be pushing new items, regardless of the current observer subscription count. Another specificity regarding hot observables is that they would behave as multi-cast producers, whereas with cold observables, we would either reiterate the events or have a set of competing consumers, depending on the observable function's setup.

Now that we have created our observable, let's create a subscription for it:

```
Console.Write("Observables");

var observable = GetNumbersObservable();

var subscriber = observable
    .Subscribe(_ => Console.WriteLine($"Observer: {_}"));
```

Observables are very flexible when it comes to notifying collections and using the `System.Reactive.Linq` implementation. With this, filtering and data transformation can be introduced to help you modify the data that reaches the observer. For instance, using the previous example, we can introduce a filter that only pushes even numbers:

```
var evenSubscriber = observable
    .Where(_ => _ % 2 == 0)
    .Subscribe(_ => Console.WriteLine($"Even Observer: {_}"));
```

There are various additional control methods and conversion strategies from other asynchronous patterns available in the Rx project. Here, we just demonstrated a simple example of a data pipeline and filtered it. Additionally, there's another open source project for Xamarin that exists that was built on the foundation provided by Rx Extensions.

In this section, we provided a brief overview of the available asynchronous facilities on .NET and how we can utilize them in both the application UI and the domain implementation. In the next section, we will look at more specialized execution patterns for views and their associated view-model or controller in a mobile application.

Asynchronous execution patterns

Tasks are generally used to create an easy sequential execution for asynchronous blocks. Nevertheless, in certain scenarios, waiting for a task to complete might be unnecessary or not possible. We can enumerate a couple of scenarios where awaiting a task is not possible or required:

- If we are executing the asynchronous block, similar to the update user command, we would simply bind the command to the control and execute it in a throw-and-forget manner.
- If our asynchronous block needs to be executed in a constructor, we will have no easy way to await the task.
- If the asynchronous code needs to be executed as part of an event handler.

Multiple examples can be listed here regarding common concerns, such as the following:

- Method declaration should not exhibit the `async` and `void` return types.
- Methods should not be forced to execute synchronously with the `Wait` method or the `Result` property.
- Methods that are dependent on the result of an asynchronous block; race conditions should be avoided.

These not-to-be-awaited scenarios can be circumvented with various patterns. In the following sections, we will take a closer look at how we can initialize a view-model that depends on an asynchronous process to be completed. Then, we will apply our TPL knowledge to asynchronous event handling. Finally, we will learn how to deal with asynchronous methods in commands.

Service initialization pattern

In the constructor scenario we described previously, let's assume that the constructor of a view-model should retrieve a certain amount of data. This will then be used by the methods or commands of the same view-model. If we execute the method without awaiting the result, there is no guarantee that, when the command is executed, the `async` constructor's execution would have completed.

Let's demonstrate this with an abstract example:

```
public class MyViewModel
{
    public MyViewModel()
```

```
    {
        // Can't await the method;
        MyAsyncMethod();
    }

    private async Task MyAsyncMethod()
    {
        // Load data from service to the ViewModel
    }

    public async Task ExecuteMyCommand()
    {
        // Data from the MyAsyncMethod is required
    }
}
```

When the `ExecuteMyCommand` method is called immediately after the view-model has been initialized, there is a big chance that we will have a race condition and a possible bug that would elude development for a while.

In a so-called service initialization pattern, to verify that `MyAsyncMethod` is successfully executed, we can assign the resultant task to a field and use this field to await the previously started task:

```
public class MyViewModel
{
    private Task _myAsyncMethodExecution = null;

    public MyViewModel()
    {
        _myAsyncMethodExecution = MyAsyncMethod();
    }

    // ...

    public async Task ExecuteMyCommand()
    {
        await _myAsyncMethodExecution;
```

```
            // Data from the MyAsyncMethod is required
        }
    }
```

This way, the asynchronous race condition is avoided, and the command's execution will need to ensure the task reference is completed.

Asynchronous event handling

As we mentioned earlier, if the chain of calls demands asynchronous execution, the `async` chain should be propagated all the way to the top of the call hierarchy. Deviating from this setup may cause threading issues, race conditions, and possibly deadlocks. Nevertheless, it is also important that the methods don't deviate from the `async Task` declaration, ensuring that the `async` stack and any generated results and errors are preserved.

Event handlers with asynchronous code are a good example of where we would not have much to say about the signature of a method. For instance, let's take a look at the button click handler, which should execute an `awaitable` method:

```
public async void OnSubmitButtonTapped(object sender, EventArgs e)
{
    var result = await ExecuteMyCommand();
    // do additional work
}
```

Once this event handler is subscribed to the button's clicked event, the asynchronous code would be executed properly, and we would not notice any issues with it. However, the method declaration that's using void as the return type would bypass the error handling infrastructure of the runtime and, in the case of an error, regardless of the exception source, the application would crash without leaving any trace as to what has gone wrong. We should also mention that the compiler warnings associated with this type of declaration would be added to the technical debt of the project.

Here, we can create a TAP to **Asynchronous Programming Model** (**APM**) conversion, which can convert the asynchronous chain into a callback method, as well as introduce an error handler. This way, the `OnSubmitButtonTapped` method would not need to be declared with an asynchronous signature. We can easily introduce an extension method that will execute the asynchronous task with callback functions:

```
public static class TaskExtensions
{
    public static async void WithCallback<TResult>(
        this Task<TResult> asyncMethod,
        Action<TResult> onResult = null,
        Action<Exception> onError = null)
    {
        try
        {
            var result = await asyncMethod;
            onResult?.Invoke(result);
        }
        catch (Exception ex)
        {
            onError?.Invoke(ex);
        }
    }
}
```

Another extension method can be introduced to convert tasks without any returned data:

```
public static async void WithCallback(
    this Task asyncMethod,
    Action onResult = null,
    Action<Exception> onError = null)
{
    try
    {
        await asyncMethod;
        onResult?.Invoke();
    }
    catch (Exception ex)
```

```
        {
            onError?.Invoke(ex);
        }
}
```

Now, our asynchronous event handler can be rewritten to utilize the extension method:

```
public void OnSubmitButtonTapped(object sender, EventArgs e)
{
    ExecuteMyCommand()
        .WithCallback((result) => {
            //do additional work
        });
}
```

This way, we will break the asynchronous chain gracefully without jeopardizing the task's infrastructure.

The asynchronous command

In an asynchronous UI implementation, it is almost impossible to avoid command declarations and bindings that handle asynchronous tasks. The general approach here would be to create an `async` delegate and pass it as an action to the command. However, this type of promise-based execution diminishes our capacity to see through the complete life cycle of the asynchronous block. This makes it harder to create unit test for these blocks and avoid scenarios where a terminal event, such as navigating to a different view or closing the application, can interrupt the execution.

Let's look at `UpdateUserCommand`, which we implemented previously:

```
_updateUserCommand = new Command(async () => await
 ExecuteUpdateUserProfile());
```

Here, the command is simply responsible for initiating the user profile update. However, once the command has been executed, there is absolutely no guarantee that the complete execution of the `ExecuteUpdateUserProfile` method took place.

To remedy asynchronous execution monitoring, or lack thereof, we can implement an asynchronous command that follows the task's execution within the command itself. Let's start by declaring our asynchronous command interface:

```
public interface IAsyncCommand : ICommand
{
    Task ExecuteAsync(object parameter);
}
```

Here, we have declared the asynchronous version of the main execute method, which will be used by the actual command method. Let's implement the `AsyncCommand` class:

```
public class AsyncCommand : IAsyncCommand
{
    // ...

    public AsyncCommand(
        Func<object, Task> execute,
        Func<object, bool> canExecute = null,
        Action<Exception> onError = null)
    {
        // ...
    }

    // ...
}
```

This command will be receiving an asynchronous task and an error callback function. `async` will then use the asynchronous delegate, as follows:

```
public async Task ExecuteAsync(object parameter)
{
    if (CanExecute(parameter))
    {
        try
        {
            await _semaphore.WaitAsync();
```

```
            RaiseCanExecuteChanged();

        await _execute(parameter);
    }
    finally
    {
        _semaphore.Release();
    }

    RaiseCanExecuteChanged();
}
```

Notice that we have now successfully integrated the one-time-execute fix that we implemented previously in the asynchronous command block. Each time the semaphore is leased, we will be raising an event, thus propagating the `CanExecute` change event to the bound user control.

Finally, the actual `ICommand` interface will use the `ExecuteAsync` method by using the callback conversion's extension method:

```
void ICommand.Execute(object parameter)
{
    ExecuteAsync(parameter).WithCallback(null, _onError);
}
```

Now, the application unit tests can directly use the `ExecuteAsync` method, whereas the bindings would still use the `Execute` method. We can even extend this implementation further by exposing a Task-typed property, like we did in the service initialization pattern, thus allowing consecutive methods to check for method completion.

This example finalizes this section, which focused on the asynchronous execution patterns that can help us implement not only Xamarin applications but also ASP.NET web services. Of course, these patterns utilize the .NET Core or mono runtime and are applicable when the mobile application is actually in active use. If we have a scenario that requires the backend process to survive the backgrounding of the application, we might need to resort to using the native features of target platforms.

Native asynchronous execution

Other than the asynchronous infrastructure provided by .NET Core, Xamarin target platforms also offer some background execution procedures that might assist developers who are implementing modules that do work when the app is not actually working. In turn, various business processes are executed separately from the main application UI, creating a lightweight and responsive UX.

Android services

On the Android platform, the background process can be implemented as services. Services are execution modules that can be initiated on demand or with a schedule. For instance, a started service can be initiated with an intent. This would run until it is requested to be terminated (or self-terminates). Here, it is important to note that there is no direct communication between the process that initiated the service and the service itself, once the intent is actualized.

In order to implement a simple started service, you would need to implement the `Service` class and decorate the started service's `ServiceAttribute` attribute so that it can be included in the application manifest:

```
[Service]
public class MyStartedService : Service
{
    public override IBinder OnBind(Intent intent)
    {
        return null;
    }

    public override StartCommandResult OnStartCommand(
        Intent intent, StartCommandFlags flags, int startId)
    {
        // DO Work, can reference common core modules
        return StartCommandResult.NotSticky;
    }
}
```

Once the service has been created, you can initiate the service with an `Intent`, as follows:

```
var intent = new Intent (this, typeof(MyStartedService));
StartService(intent);
```

You can also use `AlarmManager` to initiate the service periodically.

Another option for service implementations is using bound services. Unlike started services, they keep an open channel of communication through the usage of a binder. The binder service methods can be called by the initiating process, such as an activity.

iOS backgrounding

The iOS platform also provides background mechanisms for fetching additional data from remote servers, even though the application or even the device is inactive. While it is not as reliable as the alarm manager on Android, these background tasks are highly optimized for preserving the battery. These background tasks can be executed as a response to certain system events, such as geolocation updates or on certain nominal intervals. We have used the word *nominal* here since the periods a background task is executed in are not deterministic and could change over time, according to the execution performance of the background task, as well as the system resources that are available.

For instance, in order to perform a background fetch, you would need to enable **Background fetch** from the **Background Modes** section:

Figure 11.2 – iOS Background Modes

Once `Background fetch` has been enabled, we can introduce our fetch mechanism, which will be executed periodically. This fetch mechanism will generally make a remote service call to update the data to be displayed so that once the application foregrounds, it will not need to repeat these refresh data calls. A perform fetch can be set up in `AppDelegate`:

```
public override bool FinishedLaunching(UIApplication app,
NSDictionary options)
{
    global::Xamarin.Forms.Forms.Init();
    LoadApplication(new App());

    UIApplication.SharedApplication
.SetMinimumBackgroundFetchInterval(UIApplication.
BackgroundFetchIntervalMinimum);

    return base.FinishedLaunching(app, options);
}
```

Now, the iOS runtime will be calling the `PerformFetch` method on regular intervals, so we can inject our retrieval code here:

```
public override void PerformFetch(
    UIApplication application, Action<UIBackgroundFetchResult>
    completionHandler)
{
    // TODO: Perform fetch

    // Return the correct status according to the fetch execution
    completionHandler(UIBackgroundFetchResult.NewData);
}
```

The returned result status is important since the runtime utilizes the result to optimize the fetch interval. The result status can be one of the following three statuses:

- `UIBackgroundFetchResult.NewData`: Called when new content has been fetched, and the application has been updated.
- `UIBackgroundFetchResult.NoData`: Called when the fetch for new content went through, but no content is available.
- `UIBackgroundFetchResult.Failed`: Useful for error handling; this is called when the fetch was unable to go through.

In addition to the background fetch, `NSUrlSession`, coupled with the background transfer infrastructure, can provide background retrieval mechanisms that can be incorporated into the background fetch operations. This way, the application content can be kept up to date, even though it is in an active state.

As we tried to demonstrate here, both the Android and iOS platforms offer their own asynchronous flow mechanisms, and these features are all available on the Xamarin platform. Depending on the use case, developers are free to choose whether to handle asynchronous execution with either a certain TPL pattern implementation or native sub-procedures.

Summary

In short, mobile applications should not be designed to undertake long-running tasks on the user interaction tier, but rather use asynchronous mechanisms to execute these workflows. The UI, in this case, would just be responsible for keeping the user informed about the background execution status. While in the past, background tasks were handled through the classic .NET threading model, nowadays, the TAP model provides a rich set of functionalities, which releases developers from the burden of creating, managing, and synchronizing threads and thread pools. In this chapter, we have seen that there are various patterns that can help us create background tasks. These would then yield back to the UI thread so that the asynchronous process results can be propagated to the UI. We also discussed different strategies for synchronous mechanisms, together with Tasks, thus avoiding deadlocks and race conditions. Additionally, we looked into the native background procedures on iOS and Android.

Overall, asynchronous tasks, as well as background techniques, are mostly used for one common goal: to keep the data up to date within the application domain. In the next chapter, we will take a closer look at different techniques for managing application data effectively.

12
Managing Application Data

Most mobile applications are coupled with certain datasets that are either downloaded through a service backend or bundled into the application. These datasets can vary from simple static text content to real-time updates of a transactional set related to a certain context. In this context, the developers are tasked with creating the optimal balance between remote interaction and data caching. Moreover, offline support is becoming the norm in the mobile application development world. In order to avoid data conflicts and synchronization issues, developers must be diligent about the procedures that are implemented according to the type of data at hand. In this chapter, we will discuss possible data synchronization and offline storage scenarios using SQLite and Akavache, as well as the new .NET Core modules, such as Entity Framework Core.

The following sections will give you insights into how to manage application data:

- Improving HTTP performance with transient caching
- Persistent data cache using SQLite
- Data access patterns

By the end of this chapter, you will understand how investing a small amount of effort in local caching and storage mechanisms can improve the user experience. You will be able to implement local storage on multiple platforms using different schemas and platforms. You will also get familiar with various data access patterns and their application on the Xamarin platform.

Improving HTTP performance with transient caching

In this section, we will take a look at the fundamentals of client-side caching and learn about ways to improve the communication line between the client application and web APIs on the server infrastructure. We will expand on the topic of transient caching using client cache aside and ETags, as well as request-specific caching using key/value stores.

In *Chapter 11*, *Fluid Applications with Asynchronous Patterns*, the client application held a direct asynchronous service communication line with the service infrastructure. This way, the mobile application would load fresh data that was required to display a certain view on every view-model creation. While this provides an up-to-date context for the application, it might not be the most desirable experience for the user since, when we're dealing with mobile applications, we would need to account for bandwidth and network speed issues.

When developing a mobile application, it is a common mistake to assume that the application running on the simulator would behave the same once deployed to a physical device. In other words, it is quite naive to assume that the high-speed internet connection that is used on the development machine would be the same as the possible 3G network connection that you would have on the mobile device.

Fortunately, developers can emulate various network scenarios on device simulators/emulators for iOS and Android. On Android, the emulator features a valuable emulation option for the network type. The **Network type** option allows you to select various network types, from **Global System for Mobile Communications (GSM)** to **Long Term Evolution (LTE)**, as well as the **signal strength** (that is, poor, moderate, good, great). On iOS, the easiest way to emulate various network connections is to install the **Network Link Conditioner tool**, which can be found within the **Additional Tools for Xcode** developer download package. Once the package has been installed, the network connection of the host computer, and implicitly the connectivity of the iOS simulated device, can be adjusted.

Now that we can emulate network connectivity issues, let's take a look at ways we can improve the responsiveness of our application, even under subpar network conditions.

Client cache aside

In *Chapter 9, Creating Microservices Azure App Services*, we utilized server-side caching by implementing a simple cache-aside pattern using the Redis cache. However, this cache only helps us to improve the service infrastructure's performance. In order to be able to create and display view-model data with cached data, we would need to implement a caching store on the mobile application side.

The easiest way to implement this pattern would be to create simple caching store(s) for different entities that we are retrieving from the server. For instance, if we were to retrieve the details of a certain auction, we could first check that the data exists in our caching store. If the data item does not exist, we could retrieve it from the remote server and update our local store with the entity.

In order to demonstrate this scenario, let's start by creating a simple cache store interface that will exhibit only the methods for setting and retrieving a certain entity type:

```csharp
public interface ICacheStore<TEntity>
{
    Task<TEntity> GetAsync(string id);
    Task SetAsync(TEntity entity);
}
```

This implementation assumes that the entities that it will be handling will all have a string-type identifier.

Next, we will implement the constructor for our Auctions API:

```csharp
public class AuctionsApi : IAuctionsApi
{
    private readonly IConfiguration _configuration;
    private readonly ICacheStore<Auction> _cacheStore;

    public AuctionsApi(IConfiguration configurationInstance,
ICacheStore<Auction> cacheStore)
    {
        _configuration = configurationInstance;
        _cacheStore = cacheStore;
    }
}
```

It is important to note that we are intentionally skipping the implementation of the cache store. A simple in-memory cache or a sophisticated local storage cache would both satisfy the interface requirements in this case.

Now that we have created our `IAuctionsApi` implementation, we can go ahead and implement the `get` method using the cache store as the first address to check for the target auction:

```
public async Task<Auction> GetAuction(string auctionId)
{
    // Try retrieve the auction from cache store
    Auction result = await _cacheStore.GetAsync(auctionId);

    // If the auction exists in our cache store we short-circuit
    if (result != null) { return result; }

    // ...
}
```

We have the data entity that was returned from the cache store. Now, we will implement the remote retrieval procedure in case the data item does not exist in the local store:

```
var client = new RestClient(_configuration["serviceUrl"]);

try
{
    result = await client.GetAsync<Auction>(_configuration["auctionsApi"], auctionId);
    await _cacheStore.SetAsync(result);
}
catch (Exception ex)
{
    // TODO:
}

return result;
```

This finalizes a simple cache-aside pattern implementation. Nevertheless, our work is not finished with the caching store since this implementation assumes that, once the entity is cached in our local store, we won't need to retrieve the same entity from the remote server.

Entity tag (ETag) validation

Naturally, in most cases, our previous assumption about static data would fail us, especially when dealing with an entity like `Auction`, where the data entropy is relatively high. When the view-model is created, we would need to make sure that the application presents the latest version of the entity. This would not only avoid incorrect data being displayed on our view but also avoid conflict errors (that is, referring to timestamp integrity checks on Cosmos DB).

In order to achieve this, we would need a validation procedure to verify that the entity at hand is the latest one and that we don't need to retrieve a newer version. The **Entity tag** (**ETag**) is part of the HTTP protocol definition. It is used as part of the available web cache validation mechanisms. Using ETag, the client application can make conditional requests that return the complete dataset if there is a more recent version of the entity that is being retrieved. Otherwise, the web server should respond with the 304 (not modified) status code. One of the ways for the client to execute the conditional requests is by using the `If-None-Match` header, accompanied by the existing ETag value.

Now, let's take a step back and take a look at the auctions controller that we implemented in our RESTful facade:

```
public async Task<IActionResult> Get(string key)
{
    var cosmosCollection = new 
CosmosCollection<Auction>("AuctionsCollection");
    var resultantSet = await cosmosCollection.
GetItemsAsync(item => item.Id == key);
    var auction = resultantSet.FirstOrDefault();

    if(auction == null)
    {
        return NotFound();
    }

    return Ok(auction);
}
```

Since we have used the `Timestamp` field that is retrieved from Cosmos DB to validate whether the entity we are trying to push to the document collection is the latest version, it is fair to use the same field to identify the current version of a specific entity. In other words, the timestamp field, in addition to the ID of that specific entity, would define a specific version of an entity. Let's utilize the `If-None-Match` header to check whether there were any changes made on the given entity since it was loaded by the client application. First, we will check whether the client has sent the conditional header:

```
// Get the version stamp of the entity
var entityTag = string.Empty;

if (Request.Headers.ContainsKey("If-None-Match"))
{
    entityTag = Request.Headers["If-None-Match"].First();
}
```

Regardless of the entity tag value, we will retrieve the latest version of the entity from the document collection. Nevertheless, once the entity is retrieved, we will be comparing the ETag header value to the timestamp that's retrieved from the Cosmos DB collection:

```
if (int.TryParse(entityTag, out int timeStamp) && auction.TimeStamp == timeStamp)
{
    // There were no changes with the entity
    return StatusCode((int)HttpStatusCode.NotModified);
}
```

This completes the server-side setup. Now, we will modify our client application so that it sends the conditional retrieval header:

```
// Try retrieve the auction from cache store
Auction result = await _cacheStore.GetAsync(auctionId);

Dictionary<string, string> headers = null;

// If the auction exists we will add the If-None-Match header
if (result != null)
{
    headers = new Dictionary<string, string>();
    headers.Add(HttpRequestHeader.IfNoneMatch.ToString(),
```

```
result.Timestamp.ToString());
}
```

```
var client = new RestClient(_configuration["serviceUrl"],
headers);
```

At this point, every time we are retrieving an auction entity, we would try to load it from the local cache. However, instead of short-circuiting the method call, we will be just adding the conditional retrieval header to our `RestClient`. We can, of course, further refactor this to create an `HttpHandler` that we can pass as a behavior to the `HttpClient`, or even introduce a behavior on the `RestClient` to handle the caching in a generic manner.

Additionally, we will also need to modify `RestClient` so that it can handle the `NotModified` response that will be returned by the server. Open source implementations of a caching strategy using the standard web caching control mechanisms can be another solution for these modifications.

Key/value store

In the context of transient caching, even a simple key value store can improve the HTTP performance. Akavache, being an asynchronous persistent key/value store, is another one of the available caching solutions on the open source scene. Technically, Akavache is a .NET Standard implementation for various caching stores. Having been implemented on the .NET Standard framework, it can be utilized on both Xamarin and .NET Core applications.

In Akavache, cache stores are implemented as blob storage on various mediums, such as in-memory, a local machine, or a user account. While these stores do not refer to a specific system location across platforms, each has a respective translation, depending on the target platform. For instance, the user account and secure stores refer to shared preferences on iOS, and they would be backed up to the iTunes cloud, whereas on the UWP platform, these two would refer to user settings and/or roaming user data and they would be stored on the cloud associated with the user's Microsoft account. Because of this, each platform imposes its own restrictions on this local blob storage.

Making use of these stores is also quite easy using the extension methods available for the blob cache storage abstraction. The extension method that pertains to the retrieval of data using the cache-aside pattern is outlined as follows:

```
// Immediately return a cached version of an object if
available, but *always*
// also execute fetchFunc to retrieve the latest version of an
object.
IObservable<T> GetAndFetchLatest<T>(this IBlobCache This,
    string key,
    Func<IObservable<T>> fetchFunc,
    Func<DateTimeOffset, bool> fetchPredicate = null,
    DateTimeOffset? absoluteExpiration = null,
    bool shouldInvalidateOnError = false,
    Func<T, bool> cacheValidationPredicate = null)
```

As you can see, the data is retrieved using `fetchFunc` and is put into the current `IBlobCache` object. Generally, the key that's used for local caching is the resource URL itself. Additionally, a cache validation predicate can be included to verify that the retrieved cache data is still valid (for example, not expired).

It is also important to note that Akavache makes heavy use of reactive extensions and that the return types are generally observables rather than simple tasks. Therefore, the returned data should be handled mostly with event subscriptions. The completion might be fired multiple times, depending on the status of the cached data (that is, once for the cached version of the data and once for the remote retrieval).

The transient cache can be a life-saver in low bandwidth connectivity scenarios. Up until now, we have focused on exactly this aspect of data caching. We have looked at samples that use the local cache for storing data elements, entity tags to control the cache expiration, and finally, a key value store to create a generic entity store. Nevertheless, none of these solutions would provide comprehensive offline functionality. For a fully functional offline app, you might need to store the data in a relational model, especially if the data you are retrieving does not have too much entropy. In these types of situations, you would need a little more than a key/value store.

Persistent relational data cache

In the examples in the previous section, we didn't use a relational data store for local data. In most cases, especially if we are dealing with a NoSQL database, the relational data paradigm loses its appeal and data denormalization replaces the data consistency concerns in favor of performance. Nevertheless, in certain scenarios, in order to find the optimal compromise between the two, we might need to resort to relational data mappings. In this section, we will take a look at SQLite and how we can use it to have a locally available relational data store on mobile applications. We will implement data caching with SQLite.NET as well as Entity Framework Core.

In the relational data management world, the most popular data management system for mobile applications is without a doubt SQLite. SQLite is, at its core, a relational database management system contained in a C programming library. What differentiates SQLite from other relational data management systems is the fact that the SQLite engine does not use or require a standalone process that the consuming application communicates with. The SQLite data store and the engine are, in any application scenario, integral parts of the application itself. In simple terms, SQLite is not a client-server engine, but rather an embedded data store.

SQLite has various implementations that span a wide set of platforms, such as native mobile platforms and web and desktop applications, as well as embedded systems. Even though certain browsers still do not and will probably never support SQLite, it still remains the norm as the local store for Xamarin applications and targeted mobile platforms.

SQLite.NET

SQLite.NET was one of the earliest implementations of SQLite on the **Portable Class Library** (**PCL**) platform, and it still remains one of the most popular cross-platform implementations (now targeting .NET Standard).

The implementation patterns with SQLite.NET are based on domain model entity attributes that define the entity indexes and other data columns:

```
public class Vehicle
{
    [PrimaryKey, AutoIncrement]
    public int Id { get; set; }
    [Indexed]
    public string RemoteId { get; set; }
    public string Color { get; set; }
```

```csharp
    public string Model { get; set; }

    public int Year { get; set; }

    public string AuctionId { get; set; }
}
```

Relationships between entities can be introduced using the attributes (for example, `ForeignKey`, `OneToMany`, and `ManyToOne`) that are included in the `SQLite.NET Extensions` module, which allows developers to create the ORM model and helps with data retrieval and update processes.

After the entity model is prepared, the `db` connection can be created using various file path combinations:

```csharp
// Path to the db file
var dbPath = Path.Combine(Environment.
GetFolderPath(Environment.SpecialFolder.MyDocuments),
"Auctions.db");

var db = new SQLiteAsyncConnection(dbPath);
```

With the `db` connection, various actions can be executed using the LINQ syntax and familiar table interaction context:

```csharp
await db.CreateTableAsync<Vehicle>();

var query = db.Table<Vehicle>().Where(_ => _.Year == 2018);

var auctionsFor2018 = await query.ToListAsync();
```

`Sqlite.NET` also supports text-based queries without resorting to LINQ-2-Entity syntax.

`SQLCipher` is another extension that can be used to create encrypted database stores for sensitive data scenarios.

Entity Framework Core

Entity Framework Core combines the years of accumulated ORM structure with SQLite support, making it a strong candidate for local storage implementations. Similar to the classic .NET version of Entity Framework, data contexts can be created and queried using the `UseSqlite` extension with a file path for `DbContextOptionsBuilder`:

```
public class AuctionsDatabaseContext : DbContext
{
    public DbSet<Auction> Auctions { get; set; }

    protected override void
OnConfiguring(DbContextOptionsBuilder optionsBuilder)
    {
        var dbPath = string.Empty;

        switch (Device.RuntimePlatform)
        {
            case Device.Android:
                dbPath = Path.Combine(
                            Environment.GetFolderPath(
                                Environment.SpecialFolder.MyDocuments),
                            "Auctions.db");

            // removed for brevity
        }

        optionsBuilder.UserSqlite($"Filename={dbPath}");
    }
}
```

Now, the `DbSet<TEntity>` declarations can be used to construct LINQ queries, which are used to retrieve data, while the context itself can be used to push updates.

In addition to the extensive relational functionality, Entity Framework Core also offers `InMemory` database support. By using an `InMemory` database instead of application storage, developers can easily mock the local cache implementation to create unit and integration tests.

As you have seen so far in this chapter, in mobile application development, we can either implement transient data caching mechanisms that focus on improving the HTTP communication performance, or we can go with a more complex structured data store that helps us introduce offline features in our consumer apps. The choice between the two depends highly on the type of data and the use cases the application we are dealing with employs. Depending on the type of data in question, there are various data access patterns that we can utilize.

Data access patterns

So far, we have defined various data stores that will be used within the client boundaries as a secondary source of data to help with offline scenarios, as well as when network connectivity is problematic. This way, the user interface does not appear blank—or worse, go into an infinite loading loop. Instead, a previous version of the dataset is displayed to the user immediately while remote retrieval takes place. In this section, we will take a closer look at the patterns that we can implement utilizing the previously mentioned methods and technologies.

Before we can dive into the different architectural patterns to coordinate the local and remote data, let's try to describe the meaning of coordination by means of identifying the types of data that we have in our application. According to the life cycle and entropy of the specific data element, we can categorize the data types into the following groups:

- **Transient data**: These data elements will constantly be changing and the local storage should be continuously invalidated. When dealing with this data type, the application should first load the local cache to respond to user input as fast as possible, but each time, we should execute a remote call to update the local cache and the view-model data. Examples of this would be auction information and bidding entries.

- **Reference data**: These data elements will change from time to time, but it is acceptable to use cache storage as a source of truth (if it exists) with a reasonable time-to-live period. User profiles and vehicle data might be good examples of this data type. When dealing with reference data, the view-model should try to load the entities from the cache. If it does not exist or the data has expired, the application should reach out to the remote server and update the local cache with the remote data.

- **Static data**: There are certain data elements in an application that will probably never change. These static data elements, such as the list of countries or internal enumerator descriptions, would, under normal circumstances, be loaded only once and served from local storage.

Other than these data types, we should also mention volatile entity types, which should not be cached by the application at all unless there is a clear indication for it. For instance, imagine a search query with an arbitrary set of query parameters on vehicles or auction sets returning a paginated list of entries. It is quite unreasonable to even try to cache this data and server through the view-model. On the other hand, the most recent entries list that we might want to display on the main dashboard can, in fact, be categorized as transient data.

Now, let's take a look at some simple implementation patterns that might help with implementing a fluid data flow and user experience.

Implementing the repository pattern

Naturally, while talking about data stores, the foremost abundant pattern in development work is the repository pattern. In the context of local and remote data, we could create small repositories that implement the same exact repository interface and create a manager class to coordinate the repositories.

Let's start with a transient data repository, such as `Auctions`. For the Auctions API, let's assume that we have three methods to retrieve:

- A list of auctions
- The details of a specific auction
- A method to update a specific auction

Let's define our interface for these methods:

```
public interface IAuctionsApi
{
    Task<IEnumerable<Auction>> GetAuctions();

    Task<Auction> GetAuction(string auctionId);

    Task UpdateAuction(Auction auction);
}
```

We will now have two competing repositories that implement the same interface:

```
public class RemoteAuctionsApi : IAuctionsApi
{
    // ...
```

```
}

public class LocalAuctionsApi : IAuctionsApi
{
    // ...
}
```

Here, the simplest way to handle the data would be to implement a wrapper that will keep the local cache up to date and pass the wrapper instance, as well as the local repository instance, to the view-model so that the view-model can handle the initial cache load scenario, thus utilizing the local repository and then calling the wrapper instance.

Let's go ahead and implement the wrapper class, which we will call the manager:

```
public class ManagerAuctionsApi : IAuctionsApi
{
    private readonly IAuctionsApi _localApi;
    private readonly IAuctionsApi _remoteApi;

    // ...

    public async Task<Auction> GetAuction(string auctionId)
    {
        var auction = await _remoteApi.GetAuction(auctionId);

        await _localApi.UpdateAuction(auction);

        return auction;
    }
}
```

The view-model load strategy will make the local API call, update the view model data, and call the remote API with a `ContinueWith` action to update the model:

```
Action<Auction> updateViewModel = (auction) => {
    Device.BeginInvokeOnMainTread(() => this.Auction = auction)
};
```

```
var localResult = await _localApi.GetAuction(auctionId);

updateViewModel(localResult);

// Not awaited
_managerApi.GetAuction(auctionId).ContinueWith(task =>
updateViewModel(task.Result));
```

The implementation for a reference repository would utilize a different strategy:

```
public async Task<User> GetUser(string userId)
{
    var user = await _localApi.GetUser(userId);

    if (user != null) { return user; }

    user = await _remoteApi.GetUser(userId);
    await _localApi.UpdateUser(user);

    return user;
}
```

In this implementation, it is the responsibility of the view-model to finalize the data load by merging the results from the local and remote repositories and propagate the results to the view. What if the repository was conscious enough about the delta between the results from the local and remote store.

Observable repository

By using reactive extensions, we could implement a notifying observable and subscribe to various events on the view-model:

- `OnNext`: We would update the data within the view model, which would be fired twice.
- `OnCompleted`: We would hide any progress indicator we have been showing up until this point.

Before we can implement the view-model subscriptions, let's implement the `GetAuction` method in a reactive manner:

```
public IObservable<Auction> GetAuction(string auctionId)
{
    var localAuction = _localApi.GetAuction(auctionId).ToObservable();
    var remoteAuction = _remoteApi.GetAuction(auctionId).ToObservable();

    // Don't forget to update the local cache
    remoteAuction.Subscribe(auction => _localApi.UpdateAuction(auction));

    return localAuction.Merge(remoteAuction);
}
```

Now that we have our observable result, we can implement the subscription model in our view model:

```
var auctionsObservable = _managerAuctionsApi.GetAuction(auctionId);
auctionsObservable.Subscribe(auction => updateViewModel(localResult));

await auctionsObservable();

IsBusy = false;
```

With the conversions from observable results to the task or vice versa, it is important to be careful with cross-thread issues. As a general rule of thumb, all of the code that updates elements on the UI thread should be executed with `Device.BeginInvokeOnMainTread`.

A static data load would adhere to the same strategy as the reference repository, but it is also possible to initialize the static cache when the application is first run using a background task or embed the static data with a JSON file or with a seeded SQLite database file into the application package. At certain times, this data can still be synchronized with the remote server. Data resolver

The aforementioned static data elements—especially the data points that are attached to the main collections with an ID reference—would probably never change, and yet they would be carried over the wire together with the main data elements. In order to decrease the payload size, we can in fact dismiss these data objects on the DTO models and represent them only by ID. However, in such an implementation, we would need to find a way to resolve these ID references into real data elements.

For instance, let's take a look at the engine entity that we are transferring as part of a vehicle description:

```
public class Engine
{
    [JsonProperty("displacement")]
    public string Displacement { get; set; }

    [JsonProperty("fuel")]
    public FuelType Fuel { get; set; }

    // ...
}
```

The same DTO object is used on the client side. Here, the Fuel type is returned as a complex object rather than a single identifier (the available options are diesel or gas). Assuming that the static data for the fuel type is initialized on the client application, we do not really need to retrieve it from the server. Let's replace the property with an identifier (that is, of the string type).

On the client side, let's extend our model so that it has a reference ID, as well as an entity:

```
public class Engine
{
    [JsonProperty("displacement")]
    public string Displacement { get; set; }

    [JsonProperty("fuelId")]
    public string FuelId { get; set; }

    [JsonIgnore]
    public KeyIdentifier Fuel { get; set; }
}
```

With the ignore attribute, the reference ID will not be omitted during the serialization phase. We will, however, still need to resolve this entry every time an `Engine` instance is retrieved from the server.

Additionally, we have represented similar key/value pairs, such as the `FuelType` complex object, with a generic entity:

```
public class KeyIdentifier
{
    public string KeyGroup { get; set; } // for example, "FuelType"

    public string Key { get; set; } // for example, "1"

    public string Value { get; set; } // for example, "Diesel"
}
```

The easiest way for the runtime to identify the properties that will need to be resolved and the `Target` property that the data will be assigned to is to create a custom data annotation attribute:

```
[AttributeUsage(AttributeTargets.Property)]
public class ReferenceAttribute : Attribute
{
    public ReferenceAttribute(string keyType, string field)
    {
        KeyType = keyType;
        Field = field;
    }

    public string KeyType { get; set; }

    public string Field { get; set; }
}
```

Now, using the annotation we have just created, the engine DTO class would look like this:

```
public class Engine
{
    [JsonProperty("displacement")]
```

```
    public string Displacement { get; set; }

    [Reference("FuelType", nameof(Fuel))]
    [JsonProperty("fuelId")]
    public string FuelId { get; set; }

    [JsonIgnore]
    public KeyIdentifier Fuel { get; set; }
}
```

We are now declaring that the `FuelId` field is a reference to a `KeyIdentifier` object of the `FuelType` type and that the resolved data should be assigned to a property called `Fuel`.

Assuming that the static data about `FuelType` is stored in local storage and can be retrieved as a `KeyIdentifier` object, we can now implement a generic translator for the static data:

```
public async Task TranslateStaticKeys<TEntity>(TEntity entity)
{
    var entityType = typeof(Entity);

    var properties = entityType.GetRuntimeProperties();

    foreach(var property in properties)
    {
        var refAttribute =
        property.CustomAttributes.FirstOrDefault(item =>
        item.AttributeType == typeof(ReferenceAttribute));

        if(customAttribute == null) { continue; }

        var keyParameters = refAttribute.ConstructorArguments;

        // e.g FuelType => Fuel
        var keyType = keyParameters.Value.ToString();
        var propertyName = keyParameters.Value.ToString();
        targetProperty = properties.FirstOrDefault(item =>
```

```
            item.Name ==
                propertyName);

            try
            {
                await TranslateKeyProperty(property, targetProperty,
                    entity, keyType);
            }
            catch(Exception ex)
            {
                // TODO:
            }
        }
    }
}
```

The `TranslateStaticKeys` method iterates through the properties of an entity and if it identifies a property with `ReferenceAttribute`, it invokes the `TranslateKeyProperty` method.

The actual translation method would follow a similar implementation path, hence retrieving the set of key/value pairs for the given type, resolving the key ID into `KeyIdentifier`, and finally assigning the data to the target property:

```
public async Task TranslateKeyProperty<TEntity>(
    PropertyInfo sourceProperty,
    PropertyInfo targetProperty,
    TEntity entity,
    string keyType)
{
    IEnumerable<KeyIdentifier> keyIdentifiers = await _api.GetStaticValues(keyType);

    if(targetProperty != null)
    {
        var sourceValue = sourceProperty.GetValue(entity)?.ToString();

        if(!string.IsNullOrEmpty(sourceValue))
```

```
            {
                var keyIdentifier = keyIdentifiers.
 FirstOrDefault(item =>
                item.Id == sourceValue);

                targetProperty.SetValue(entity, keyIdentifier);
            }
        }
 }
```

Now, after retrieving an entity, we can simply invoke the `translate` method to resolve all outstanding data points:

```
var auction = await _managerAuctionsApi.Get(auctionId);
await Translator.TranslateReferences(auction.Vehicle.Engine);
```

The implementation can be extended to collections and to walk the complete object tree.

This section was a conceptual look at data types and various related architectural patterns. In short, depending on the situation and use cases, you can opt to use any of these patterns in combination with a transient or persistent data cache store.

Summary

In this chapter, we implemented and employed different patterns and technologies to create offline-capable and responsive applications. Throughout this chapter, our main goal was to create an infrastructure that will synchronize and coordinate the data flow between the local and remote storage so that a pleasant user experience can be achieved. Initially, we used the cache-aside pattern and utilized standard HTTP protocol definitions to cache and validate the cached data. We also analyzed technologies such as SQLite, Entity Framework Core, and Akavache. Finally, we briefly looked at the Realm components and how they can be used to manage cross-device and platform data. Overall, there are so many technologies available for developers that have been conceived within the community, and it is important to choose the correct patterns and technology stack for your specific use cases to achieve the best user experience and satisfaction.

In the next chapter, we will take a look at the Graph API, push notifications, and additional ways to engage the customer.

13
Engaging Users with Notifications and the Graph API

Push notifications are the primary tools for an application infrastructure to deliver a message to the user. They are used to broadcast updates to users, send notifications based on certain actions, and engage them for customer satisfaction or according to metrics. On the other hand, the Microsoft Graph API is a service that provides a unified gateway to data that's accumulated through Office 365, Windows 10, and other Microsoft services.

This chapter will explain, in short, how notifications and the Graph API can be used to improve user engagement by taking advantage of push notifications and Graph API data. We will start by learning the fundamentals of notification services on the mobile platform. We will then set off to create a notification service implementation for our cross-platform application using Azure Notification Hubs and iterate over the topic using advanced scenarios. We will also take a look at the feature set of the Graph API for Xamarin applications.

The following sections will drive the discussion about user engagement:

- Understanding Native Notification Services
- Configuring Azure Notification Hubs
- Creating a Notification Service
- The Graph API and Project Rome

By the end of this chapter, you will have a better understanding of what user engagement means for mobile platforms. You will be able to set up your own notification hubs on Azure and identify the right tooling for your application from the wide spectrum of APIs available for you on Graph API.

Understanding Native Notification Services

Push notifications, as it can be deduced from the name, are the generalized name for the messages that are pushed from backend server applications to the target application user interface. Push notifications can target a specific device, or they can target a group of users. They can vary from a simple notification message to a user-invisible call to the application backend on the target platform.

Before moving onto the advanced notification scenarios, we will first focus on the fundamental concepts of notification providers and how they can be utilized on mobile platforms.

Notification providers

Push notifications are, in general terms, sent from the application backend service to the target devices. The notification delivery is handled by platform-specific notification providers, which are referred to as **Platform Notification Systems (PNSes)**. In order to be able to send push notifications to iOS, Android, and UWP applications, as a developer, you would need to create notification management suites/infrastructure for the following:

1. **Apple Push Notification Service (APNS)**
2. **Firebase Cloud Messaging (FCM)**
3. **Windows Notification Service (WNS)**

Each of these notification providers implements different protocols and data schemas to send notifications to users. The main issues with this model for a cross-platform application are as follows:

1. **Cross-Platform Push Notifications**: Each push service (APNS for iOS, FCM for Android, and WNS for Windows) has different protocols.

2. **Different Content Templates**: Notification templates, as well as the data structure, are completely different on all major platforms.

3. **Segmentation**: This is based on interest and location for outing only the most relevant content to each segment.

4. **Maintaining Accurate Device Registry**: Dynamic user base, done by adding registration upon startup, updating tags, and pruning.

5. **High Volume with Low Latency**: Application requirements of high volume with low latency are hard to meet with cross-platform implementations.

These shortcomings, generally speaking, stem from the fact that each PNS is designed and operated with a specific platform in mind, hence the requirements for a cross-platform target group are ignored. Nevertheless, however different the implementations are, the basic flow for sending notifications in each PNS is more or less the same.

Sending notifications with PNS

Using the native notification providers, the application backend can send notifications to target devices if the target device has already opened a notification channel. While the implementation of this process highly depends on the platform at hand, at a high level, the registration and notification flow are very similar on all of the PNSes.

The device should start this flow by registering itself with the PNS and retrieving a so-called PNS handle. This handle can be a token (for example, APNS) or a simple URI (for example, WNS). Once the PNS is retrieved, it should be delivered to the backend service as a calling card, as shown in *step 2* of the following diagram:

Figure 13.1 – Push Notification Service Flow

When the backend service wants to send a notification to this specific device, it contacts the PNS with the saved PNS handle for the device so that the PNS can deliver the notification.

General constraints

The **Apple Push Notification Service (APNS)** and **Firebase Cloud Messaging (FCM)** infrastructure both make use of certain manifest declarations that are very specific to the application that's installed on the target device.

APNS mandates that the application ID (and certificate) used to sign the application package have a non-wildcard bundle declaration (that is, the `com.mycompany.*` type of certificates cannot be used for this implementation).

The device handle (an alphanumeric token or a URL, depending on the platform) is the only piece of device information that is required and used in the notification process. In contrast, the notification service should support multiple applications and platforms.

Azure Notification Hubs

In an environment where multiple platforms and multiple service providers exist, Azure Notification Hubs acts as a mediator between backend services that creates the notification requests and the provider services that deliver these notification requests to target devices.

Notification Hubs infrastructure

Considering the release environments for an application (that is, alpha, beta, and prod) and the notification hubs, each environment should be set up as a separate hub on the Azure infrastructure. Nevertheless, notification hubs can be united with a so-called namespace so that application environments for each platform can be managed in one place.

Notification hub

Semantically, a notification hub refers to the smallest resource in the Azure Notification Hubs infrastructure. It maps directly to the application running on a specific environment and holds one certificate for each **Platform Notification System** (**PNS**). The application can be hybrid, native, or cross-platform. Each notification hub has configuration parameters for different notification platforms to support the cross-platform messaging infrastructure:

Figure 13.2 – Apple PNS Setup

Notification namespace

A namespace, on the other hand, is a collection of hubs. Notification namespaces can be used to manage different environments and to create clusters of notification hubs for bigger target audiences. Using the namespace, developers or the configuration management team can track the notification hub status and use it as the main hub for dispatching notifications, as shown in the following screenshot:

Figure 13.3 – Notification Hub Configuration

In an ideal setup, an application-specific notification service would communicate with the specific hubs, while a namespace would be used to configure and manage these hubs:

Figure 13.4 – Push Notification Hubs Topology

In this configuration, the application-specific notification service never directly communicates with the platform-specific notification services; instead, notifications deliver the messages to the target platforms. In a similar approach, multiple applications that share a common target user group can also be unified under a namespace and use the same notification namespace.

In order to understand the application registration process, we should take a closer look at the notification hub registration and notification process.

Notifications using Azure Notification Hubs

Azure Notification Hubs follows a very similar strategy for providing push notifications to registered user devices. After all, it's providing the basic configuration management for native PNSes. Similar to the PNS process, the Azure Notification Hubs flow can be defined in two parts: registration and notification. These parts also define the life cycle for a user engagement session through push notifications. Let's take a closer look at the registration and notification processes.

Registration

Azure Notification Hubs supports two types of device registration – client and backend registration:

- In the client registration scenario, the application calls the Azure notification hub with the device handle that's received on the native platform. In this scenario, only the device handle can be used to identify the user. In order for the backend services to send notification messages to the target device, the device should pass on the notification information to the backend service.

- In a backend registration scenario, the backend service handles registration with the Azure notification hub. This scenario allows the backend service to insert additional information to the registration data, such as user information (for example, user ID, email, role, and group), application platform information (for example, application runtime, release version, and release stage), and other identifiers for the application and/or user. This type of registration process is more suited for implementations where multiple applications might be receiving notifications from multiple sources so that the notification service can act as an event aggregator.

The registration of the target device with a notification provider using the notification hub is done either using data packages, called registrations, or with extended device information sets, called installations. While the registration package contains the notification handle or the notification URI for a device, the installation contains additional device-specific information.

During the registration process, the client application (or the backend notification service) can also register notification templates associated with tags to personalize the notifications and create notification targets. The tags can be used later to broadcast notifications to groups of devices that belong to a single user, or groups of users with multiple devices, hence enabling a broadcast-ready infrastructure.

Notification

Once the device is registered with the backend service and the notification hub, the backend service can send notifications using the PNS handle of the device that's targeting a specific platform. With this type of notification, the backend server should identify what the target platform is, prepare a notification message using the target platform's schema, and finally send the notification message to the given handle.

Another approach for sending notifications to users is to use notification tags. A specific user tag can be used with an associated template to target multiple platforms. In this case, during registration, the device would be registered with a specific template (depending on the platform) and a user tag identifying the user (for example, `username: can.bilgin`). This way, any notification message that is sent to the notification hub with the given tag will be routed to the target devices that have this registration.

Finally, broadcast messages using various tags that define a certain interest of a user can be employed with notifications. In this notification scenario, the application interface would expose certain notification settings, and these notification settings would then be translated into registration tags. Each time the user updates these settings, the device registration with the backend service would need to be updated with the updated set of tags. For instance, in our application, if we were to include a notification setting that allows the user to receive notifications when a new auction is created for a specific make or model of car, we could use this tag to send notifications to similar users as soon as a new entry is created in the application data store.

As we have seen in this section, Azure Notification Hubs is really a façade that provides a unified management and development toolset for multiple service providers that eases the cumbersome native notification integration for cross-platform applications. Now that we have learned about the native push notifications and Azure Notification Hubs, let's move on to implement a simple notification service.

Creating a notification service

Depending on the granularity of the notification target group, the application design can include a notification service; otherwise, another option would be to have a setup where the notification infrastructure can be integrated into either one of the existing services. For instance, if the application does not require a user-specific messaging scenario, there is no need to track device registrations. In this case, the client-side registration mechanism can be implemented to use notification categories and the backend services can send the notifications to target tags.

As part of our auctions application, let's use the following user story to start the implementation of our notification service:

"As a product owner, I would like to have a notification service created so that I can have an open channel to my user group through which I can engage them individually or as a group to increase the return rate."

In the light of this request, we can start analyzing different use cases and implementation patterns.

Defining the requirements

Since the notification service will be supporting incoming notifications from various modules, the architectural design and implementation would need to adhere to certain guidelines, as well as satisfying registration and notification requirements:

- The notification service should be designed to support multiple notification hubs for different application versions (for example, alpha, beta, and prod).
- The notification service should be designed to receive notification requests for a specific device, specific user, or a group of users (for example, interest groups, certain roles, and people involved in a certain activity).
- Different notification events should be assignable with different notification templates.
- Users should be registered with different templates according to their language preferences.
- Users should be able to opt in or out of certain notifications.

Overall, the notification service implementation should implement an event aggregator pattern, where the publishers are the source of the notification and are responsible for determining the notification specifications, as well as a definition for the target, while the subscribers are the native mobile applications that submit registration requests defining their addressing parameters. Once a notification that meets the criteria for a target comes down the pipeline, the notification is routed to the associated target.

Device registration

Device registration is the first use case to be implemented and tested by the development team. In this scenario, the user would open (or install) the auctions application and authenticate through one of the available identity providers. At this stage, we have the device information as well as the user identity, which we can use for registration. Let's see how this is done:

1. The notification channel will need to be opened as soon as the user opens the application (in the case of a returning user—that is, an existing identity), or once registration/authentication is completed. On iOS, we can use the `UserNotificationCenter` module to authorize for notifications:

```
UNUserNotificationCenter.Current.RequestAuthorization(
    UNAuthorizationOptions.Alert |
    UNAuthorizationOptions.Sound |
    UNAuthorizationOptions.Sound,
    (granted, error) =>
{
    if (granted)
    {
        InvokeOnMainThread(UIApplication.SharedApplication
            .RegisterForRemoteNotifications);
    }
});
```

2. Once the registration is invoked, the `override` method in the `AppDelegate.cs` file can be used to retrieve the device token:

```
public override void RegisteredForRemoteNotifications(
    UIApplication application,
    NSData deviceToken)
```

3. We can now send this token using the authorization token for identifying the user to the notification service device registration controller using a registration data object:

```
public class DeviceRegistration
{
    public string RegistrationId { get; set; } // Registration Id
    public string Platform { get; set; } // wns, apns, fcm
    public string Handle { get; set; } // token or uri
    public string[] Tags { get; set; } // any additional tags
}
```

4. Before we begin interacting with the notification hub, we would need to install the `Microsoft.Azure.NotificationHubs` NuGet package, which will provide the integration methods and data objects. The same package can, in fact, be installed on the client side to easily create the notification channel and retrieve the required information to be sent to the backend service.

5. Once the device registration is received on our service, depending on whether it is a new registration or an update of a previous registration, we can formulate the process to clean up previous registrations and create a notification hub registration ID for the device:

```
public async Task<IActionResult> Post(DeviceRegistration device)
{
    // New registration, execute cleanup
    if (device.RegistrationId == null && device.Handle != null)
    {
        var registrations = await
            _hub.GetRegistrationsByChannelAsync(device.Handle, 100);

        foreach (var registration in registrations)
        {
            await _hub.
```

```
            DeleteRegistrationAsync(registration);
        }

        device.RegistrationId = await _hub.
CreateRegistrationIdAsync();          }

        // ready for registration
        // ...
    }
```

6. We can now create our registration description with the appropriate (that is, platform-specific) channel information, as well as the registration ID we have just created:

```
RegistrationDescription deviceRegistration = null;

switch(device.Platform)
{
    // ...
    case "apns":
        deviceRegistration = new
        AppleRegistrationDescription(device.Handle);
        break;
    //...
}

deviceRegistration.RegistrationId = device.RegistrationId;
```

7. We will also need the current user identity as a tag during the registration. Let's add this tag, as well as the other ones that are sent by the user:

```
deviceRegistration.Tags = new HashSet<string>(device.Tags);

// Get the user email depending on the current identity provider
deviceRegistration.Tags.Add($"username:{GetCurrentUser()}");
```

8. Finally, we can complete the registration by passing the registration data to our hub:

```
await _hub.
CreateOrUpdateRegistrationAsync(deviceRegistration);
```

Here, if we were using installation-based registration rather than device registration, we would have a lot more control over the registration process. One of the biggest advantages is the fact that device installation registration offers customized template associations:

```
var deviceInstallation = new Installation();
// ... populate fields
deviceInstallation.Templates = new Dictionary<string,
InstallationTemplate>();

deviceInstallation.Templates.Add(
    "type:Welcome",
    new InstallationTemplate
    {
        Body = "{\"aps\": {\"alert\" : \"Hi ${FullName} welcome to Auctions!\" }}"
    });
```

To take this one step further, during the registration process, the template can be loaded according to the preferred language of the user:

```
var template = new InstallationTemplate()
template.Body = "{\"aps\": {\"alert\": \"
            + GetMessage("Welcome", user.PreferredLanguage) +
"\" }}";
```

This is how a user registers the device. Now, we will move on to transmitting notifications.

Transmitting notifications

Now that the user has registered a device, we can implement a send notification method on the server. We would like to support free text notifications, as well as templated messages with data. Let's begin:

1. Let's start by creating a base notification method that will define the destination and the message:

    ```csharp
    public class NotificationRequest
    {
        public BaseNotificationMessage Message { get; set; }

        public string Destination { get; set; }
    }
    ```

2. For the simple message scenario, the calling service module is not really aware of the target platform—it just defines a user and a message item. Therefore, we need to generate a message for all three platforms, hence covering all possible devices the user might have:

    ```csharp
    public class SimpleNotificationMessage : BaseNotificationMessage
    {
        public string Message { get; set; }

        public IEnumerable<(string, string)> GetPlatformMessages()
        {
            yield return ("wns", @"<toast><visual><binding template=""ToastText01""><text id=""1"">"
                + Message + "</text></binding></visual></toast>");
            yield return ("apns", "{\"aps\":{\"alert\":\"" + Message +
                "\"}}");
            yield return ("fcm", "{\"data\":{\"message\":\"" + Message +
                "\"}}");
        }
    ```

```
        }
    }
```

3. For the templated version, the message looks a little simpler since we assume that the device already registered a template for the given tag and so we don't need to worry about the target platform. Now, we just need to provide the parameters that are required for the template:

```
public class TemplateNotificationMessage :
BaseNotificationMessage
{
    public string TemplateTag { get; set; }

    public Dictionary<string, string> Parameters { get; set; }
}
```

> **Important note**
> It is generally a good idea to create a generic message template that will be used to send simple text messages and register this template as a simple message template so that we don't need to create a separate message for each platform and push it through all of the available device channels.

4. Now, we can process our notification request on the notification service and deliver it to the target user:

```
if (request.Message is SimpleNotificationMessage
simpleMessage)
{
    foreach (var message in simpleMessage.
GetPlatformMessages())
    {
        switch (message.Item1)
        {
            case "wns":
                await _hub.
SendWindowsNativeNotificationAsync(
                    message.Item2,
                    $"username:{request.Destination}");
```

```
                    break;
                case "aps":
                    await _hub.SendAppleNativeNotificationAsync(
                        message.Item2,
                        $"username:{request.Destination}");
                    break;
                case "fcm":
                    await _hub.SendFcmNativeNotificationAsync(
                        message.Item2,
                        $"username:{request.Destination}");
                    break;
            }
        }
    }
    else if(request.Message is TemplateNotificationMessage templateMessage)
    {
        await _hub.SendTemplateNotificationAsync(
            templateMessage.Parameters,
            $"username:{request.Destination}");
    }
```

We have successfully sent our message to the target user using the `username:<email>` tag. This way, the user will be receiving the push notification on their device. It is up to the platform-specific implementation to handle the message.

Broadcasting to multiple devices

In the previous example, we used the `username` tag to define a specific user as the target of the notification message. In addition to single tags, tag expressions can also be used to define a larger group of users that subscribed to a specific notification category. For instance, in order to send the notification to all of the users that accepted auction updates on new auctions and who are also interested in a specific auto manufacturer, the tag may look as follows:

```
notification:NewAuction && interested:Manufacturer:Volvo
```

Another scenario would be to send a notification about a new highest bid on an auction:

```
notification:HighestBid && auction:afabc239-a5ee-45da-9236-
37abc3ca1375 && !username:john.smith@test.com
```

Here, we have combined three tags, the last of which is the tag that ensures that the user with the highest bid does not get the message that was sent to the rest of the users who are involved in the auction so that they can receive a more personalized *Congratulations* type of message.

Advanced scenarios

The notification messages demonstrated here are only simple models of notifications and do not require extensive implementation, neither on the client application nor on the server side.

Now, we will take a look at some more advanced usage scenarios.

Push to pull

Notification hubs customers in banking, healthcare, and government sectors cannot pass sensitive data via public cloud services such as APNS, FCM, or WNS. In order to support these types of scenarios, we can utilize a scheme where the notification server is only responsible for sending a message ID and the client application only retrieves the target message using the given message ID. This pattern is generally referred to as the Push-2-Pull pattern, and it is a great way to migrate the communication channel from the notification hubs and PNSes to the common web service channel.

Rich media for push messages

Notification messages sent by the native notifications provider (PNS) can also be intercepted and processed before they are presented to the user. On the iOS platform, the Notification Extension framework allows us to create extensions that can modify mutable notification messages.

In order to create a notification extension, you can add a new project and select the notification extension that suits your requirements the most:

Figure 13.5 – Xamarin Notification Content Extension

With the content extension, it is possible to create interactive notification views that can display rich media content, while the service extension can be used to intercept and process the notification payload (for example, to decrypt a secure payload).

Android has similar mechanisms that allow you to modify the notification content before it reaches the user. The toast messages can also exhibit a reply control, which accepts in-place user interaction. While this engagement model increases the usability of the application, it does not contribute to the return rate.

So far in this chapter, we have illustrated various ways to use push notifications as well as scenarios where these methods would be used. Overall, push notifications are powerful developer tools that attract users back to the application and keep them engaged, even when the application is not running. However, if this engagement is not on a personal level, it is nothing better than spam. The Graph API can be a great asset to improve the personalization and continuity across devices.

The Graph API and Project Rome

Since we're discussing cross-platform engagement, this is a great time to talk about the Graph API and Project Rome. These interwoven infrastructure services that are available in the Microsoft Cloud infrastructure allow developers to create application experiences that span across platform and device boundaries.

The Graph API

The Graph API is a collection of Microsoft cloud services that are used to interact with the data that is collected through various platforms, including Microsoft Office 365 and Microsoft Live. The data elements in this web of data are structured around the currently signed-in user. Interactions with certain applications (for example, a meeting that's been created, an email that's been sent, or a new contact being added to the company director) or devices (for example, a sign-in on a new device) are created as new nodes in the relationship graph.

These nodes can then be used to create a more immersive experience for the user, who is interacting with the application data from various sources.

For instance, simply by using the Microsoft Identity within the application, after the user authorizes to access the resources, the application downloads documents, creates thumbnails, retrieves destination users, and creates a complete email before sending it to a group of users. Other than Microsoft-based applications, third-party applications can also create graph data to increase engagement with the user.

Project Rome

Project Rome, which is built upon the premises of the Graph API, can be defined as a device runtime for connecting and integrating Windows-based and cross-platform devices to the Project Rome infrastructure services. This runtime is the bridge between the infrastructure services in the Microsoft cloud and the APIs that are delivered as a programming model for Windows, Android, iOS, and Microsoft Graph, hence enabling client and cloud apps to build experiences using Project Rome's capabilities.

Project Rome exposes several key APIs, most of which can be used in cross-platform application implementations. The current API set is composed of the following:

- Device relay
- User activities
- Notifications

- Remote Sessions
- Nearby sharing

Some of these features are available only for the Windows platform, but all of them require a Microsoft identity to be present within the application domain. One important note is that all of these features can be consumed through the Graph API using the REST interface.

Let's take a closer look at these features and work out different use cases.

Device relay

The device relay is a set of modules that allows device-to-device communication and handover functionality. Semantically, the feature set resembles the previously available application services and URI launch functionalities on the UWP platform. However, with the device relay, an application can essentially communicate with another application on another device or even on another platform (for example, using the SDK, it is possible to launch an application on a Windows device from an Android phone).

User activities

User activities is one of the closest integrations with the Graph API. Using user activities and activity feeds, it is possible for an application to create a history feed with relevant actions when the application was last used. These feeds are fed into the Graph API and synchronized across devices. For instance, using activity feeds, we can create a history of the auctions/vehicles that a user viewed in a certain session. Then, once these items are synchronized through the same live ID over to a Windows device, the user can easily click on an item from the feed and get back to their previous session. If the Windows device does not have the application installed, the operating system will advise the user to install the application on the Windows platform. This way, the penetration of your application will increase on multiple platforms. In simple terms, this feature is solely dedicated to the continuity of user experience across devices and platforms.

A user activity might contain deep links, visualizations, and metadata about the activity that is created as an entry in activity history.

Notifications

Project Rome notifications, also known as Microsoft Graph Notifications, are another way of notifying users. What differentiates Graph Notifications from other platform-specific notification providers is the fact that Graph Notifications target users that are specifically agnostic about the platform they are using. In other words, the destination of the Graph Notifications is not devices, but users. In addition to the user-based notification model, the notification state within Graph notification infrastructure is synchronized across devices so that the application itself does not need to anything more to set a certain message as dismissed or similar to reflect the user interaction on multiple devices.

Remote Sessions

The Remote Sessions API is a Windows-only API, and it allows devices to create shared sessions, join the sessions, and create an interactive messaging platform between different users. The created sessions can be used to send messages across devices as well as keep shared session data within the joint session.

Nearby sharing

Nearby sharing allows apps to send files or websites to nearby devices using Bluetooth or Wi-Fi. This API can be used on Windows as well as native Android runtimes. During a share operation, nearby sharing functionality is also intelligent enough to pick up on the quickest path between the two devices by selecting either a Bluetooth or network connection. The discovery function that is part of the sharing module allows the application to discover the possible targets for the share operation via Bluetooth.

In this section, we have browsed through some of the facilities of the Graph API and its cross-platform consumer SDK. Now, you understand that the Graph API provides access to data and integration into other productivity platforms such as Office 365. By using this data and available extension mechanisms, your consumer apps can personalize the user experience and extend the user interaction not only across user sessions but devices. Moreover, using Project Rome SDKs, you can enhance the user interactivity and experience on mobile platforms.

Summary

In this chapter, we have taken a look at ways to improve user engagement using push notifications and Microsoft Graph API implementations. Keeping user engagement alive is the key factor to maintaining the return rate of your application. Push notifications are an excellent tool that you can use to engage your users, even when your application is not active. Azure notification namespaces and hubs make this engagement a lot easier to implement by creating an abstraction layer between the PNSes and the target device runtimes. On top of the push notifications, we analyzed various APIs that are available on the Graph API through Project Rome and RESTful APIs that are readily available.

In this part of the book, comprising the previous three chapters, we have enhanced our application with asynchronous implementation, local data management, and notifications. In the remainder of the book, we will be focusing on how we can manage the application life cycle effectively and create a fully automated development and delivery pipeline to shorten our time-to-market while increasing the release cadence. In the next chapter, we will be learning about the foundational concepts of application life cyle management.

Section 5: Application Life Cycle Management

Azure DevOps and Visual Studio App Center are the two pillars of application life cycle management when we talk about .NET Core and Xamarin. Azure DevOps, previously known as Visual Studio Online or Team Services, provides a complete suite for implementing DevOps principles, whereas App Center acts as a command center for mobile application development, testing, and deployment. Using these tools, developers and operations teams can implement robust and productive delivery pipelines that can take the application source from the repository to production environments.

The following chapters will be covered in this section:

- *Chapter 14, Azure DevOps and Visual Studio App Center*
- *Chapter 15, Application Telemetry with Application Insights*
- *Chapter 16, Automated Testing*
- *Chapter 17, Deploying Azure Modules*
- *Chapter 18, CI/CD with Azure DevOps*

14
Azure DevOps and Visual Studio App Center

Visual Studio App Center is an all-in-one service provided by Microsoft and is mainly used by mobile application developers. Both Xamarin platforms as well as UWP applications are among the supported platforms. The primary goal of App Center is to create an automated Build-Test-Distribute pipeline for mobile projects. App Center is also invaluable for iOS and Android developers since it is the only platform that offers a unified beta distribution for both target runtimes, which supports telemetry collection and crash analytics. Using Azure DevOps (previously known as Visual Studio Team Service) and App Center, developers can set up a completely automated pipeline for Xamarin applications that will connect the source repository to the final store submission.

This chapter will demonstrate the fundamental features of Azure DevOps and App Center and how to create an efficient application development pipeline suited to individual developers, as well as development teams.

The following topics will be covered in this chapter:

- Using Azure DevOps and Git
- Creating Xamarin application packages
- App Center for Xamarin
- Distribution with App Center
- App Center telemetry and diagnostics

By the end of this chapter, you will have learned how to effectively use Git to create manageable histories for your projects that will be stored on Git. Using these Git repositories, you will be able to create continuous integration and delivery pipelines to provide Android and iOS packages to App Center. These will then be used for distribution and telemetry collection.

Using Azure DevOps and Git

We will start our Azure DevOps journey with an introduction to Git and how to utilize Git on Azure DevOps. We will also discuss different techniques for Git branching and managing these branches.

The first and foremost crucial module of Azure DevOps that is utilized by developers is its available source control options. Developers can choose to use either **Team Foundation Version Control** (**TFVC**) or Git to manage the source code (or even both at the same time). Nevertheless, with the increasing popularity of decentralized source control management, because of the flexibility and integration that the development toolset offers, Git is the more favorable choice to many. Git is natively integrated with both Visual Studio and Visual Studio for Mac.

Creating a Git repository with Azure DevOps

Multiple Git repositories can be hosted under the same project collection in Azure DevOps, depending on the project structure that is required. Each of these repositories can be managed with different security and branch policies.

To create a Git repository, we will use the Repos section of Azure DevOps. Once a DevOps project has been created, an empty Git repository is created for you that needs to be initialized. The other options here would be to import an existing Git repository (not necessarily from another Azure DevOps project or organization) or push an existing local repository from your workstation:

Using Azure DevOps and Git   401

MyFirstXamarinForms is empty. Add some code!

Figure 14.1 – Initializing an Azure DevOps Repository

> **Important Note**
>
> Choosing a repository type used to be an initial decision while creating a Visual Studio Team Services project that couldn't be changed. However, with Azure DevOps, it is possible to create Git repositories even after the initial project's creation, side by side with a TFVC repository.

It's important to note that the clone option allows us to generate Git credentials in order to authenticate with this Git instance. The main reason for this is that Azure DevOps utilizes federated live identity authentication (possibility two-factor authentication), which Git doesn't support by itself. Thus, the users of this repository would need to generate a **Personal Access Token** (**PAT**) and use it as a password. The Git for Windows plugin automatically handles this authentication issue by creating the PAT automatically (and renewing it once it has expired). PAT is currently the only solution if you wish to use Git with Visual Studio for Mac.

In the initialize option, we can also select the `.gitignore` file (similar to TFVC's `.tfignore` file) to be created so that undesired user data from the project folders isn't uploaded to the source repository.

Branching strategy

Using Git and the Git flow methodology/pattern, a development team can base their local and remote branches on two main branches: development and master.

The development branch is used as the default branch (also known as the trunk) and represents the next release source code until the set of features (branches) are completed and signed off by the development team. At this point, a release branch is created, and the final stabilization phase on the next release package uses the release branch as the base for all hotfix branches for development. Each pull request from a hotfix branch that changes the release version will need to be merged back into the development branch.

The general flow of the feature, development, and release branches is shown in the following diagram:

Figure 14.2 – Git flow Branching Strategy

This general flow is as follows:

1. To safeguard the development branch as well as the release branches, developers, whether they're working on local or feature branches, will need to create a pull request that will be verified per the branch's policies.

   > **Important Note**
   > Pull requests promote the peer review process, as well as additional static analysis that needs to be executed in order to contribute to the development or release branches.

2. In this setup, the development branch will have a continuous integration build and deployment to the fast ring of the App Center distribution. This allows the dev and QA team to verify the features that have been merged into the branch immediately.

3. Once the current release branch is ready for regression, it can be merged into the master branch. This merge is generally verified with automated UI tests (that is, automated regression). The master branch is used as the source repository for Visual Studio App Center slow ring deployments (that is, the staging environment).

4. Feature branches that go stale (see the outer feature branch) span across multiple releases and need to be rebased so that the development branch's history is added to the feature branch. This allows the development team to have cleaner metadata about the commits.

5. The hotfix branch is used to rectify either failed store submissions or regression bugs that are reported on release branches. Hotfix branches can be tested with automated UI tests (fully automated regression) and manually using slow ring releases.

6. Once the master branch is ready for release, a new tag is created as part of a code freeze, and a manually triggered build will prepare the submission package for iOS and Android versions of the application.

This methodology can also be modified to use the release branches for staging and store deployments, rather than using the master branch. This approach provides a little more flexibility for the development team and is a little easier than managing a single release branch (that is, the master branch).

Managing development branches

During the development phase, it is important – especially if you are working with a bigger team – to keep a clean history of the development and feature branches.

In an agile-managed project life cycle, the commits on a branch (either local or remote) state that tasks belong to a user story or a bug, while the branch itself may correlate with the user story or bug. Bigger, shared branches among team members can also represent a full feature. In this context, to decrease the amount of commits while still keeping the source code safe, instead of creating a new commit each time a change set push occurs, you can make use of the **Amend Previous Commit** feature:

Figure 14.3 – Amending a Commit

Once the commit has been amended with these changes, the local commit will need to be merged with the remote version. Here, the key to avoiding the merge commit between the remote and local branch (since the remote branch has the older version of the commit, hence a different commit) would be to use the `--force` or `--force-with-lease` options with the `push` command. This way, the local commit (the amended one) will overwrite the remote version:

Figure 14.4 – Enabling Push --Force

It is important to note that it is highly discouraged to amend commits and overwrite remote branches when multiple developers are working on the same branch. This can create inconsistent history for a branch on local repositories of involved parties. To avoid such scenarios, the feature branch should be branched out and rebased onto the latest version of the feature branch once it's ready to be merged.

Let's assume that you have created a local branch from the remote feature branch and have pushed several commits. Meanwhile, your teammates pushed several updates to the feature branch:

Source: (https://www.atlassian.com/git/tutorials/merging-vs-rebasing / CC BY 2.5 AU)

Figure 14.5 – Git Feature Branches

With a conventional sync (pull and push), a merge commit will be created, and the history for the feature branch will look similar to the following:

* Merge Commit

Source: (https://www.atlassian.com/git/tutorials/merging-vs-rebasing / CC BY 2.5 AU)

Figure 14.6 – Git Merge Commit

However, if the local branch is rebased onto the latest version of the remote branch prior to the push, the history will look like this:

* Brand New Commits

Source: (https://www.atlassian.com/git/tutorials/merging-vs-rebasing / CC BY 2.5 AU)

Figure 14.7 – Git Rebase

A rebase strategy should be employed before you create a pull request to the development or release branches so that the clean history of the branch can be preserved, thus avoiding complex merge conflicts.

In this section, we focused on Git repositories on Azure DevOps, how we can create and initialize them, and how to execute well-known Git branching strategies using Visual Studio while using best practices.

Creating Xamarin application packages

Once our application is ready to be tested on real devices, we can start preparing the pipeline so that we can compile and package the application to be deployed to our alpha and beta environments on App Center. Azure DevOps provides out-of-the-box templates for both the Xamarin.Android and Xamarin.iOS applications. These pipelines can be extended to include additional testing and static analysis.

Using Xamarin build templates

Creating a build and release template for Xamarin applications is as trivial as using the Xamarin template for iOS and Android. Additionally, the UWP (if your application supports this platform) template can also be used to create a UWP build:

Figure 14.8 – Xamarin Build Tasks

Once the pipeline has been created, we will need to make several small adjustments to both platforms in order to prepare the application so that we can put it on real devices.

Xamarin.Android build

Let's have a look at the steps for building the Android project:

1. First, identify the correct Android project to be built using the wildcard designation and the target configuration:

Figure 14.9 – Xamarin.Android Build Setup

> **Important Note**
> Note that the configuration and output directory are using pipeline variables. These parameters can be defined in the **Variables** section of the **Pipeline configuration** page.

2. Select a keystore file so that you can sign the application package.

   Unsigned application packages cannot be run on real Android devices. A keystore is a store that contains certificate(s) that will be used for signing the application package. If you are using Visual Studio for development (on Mac or Windows), the easiest way to generate an ad hoc distribution certificate would be to use the Archive Manager:

   Figure 14.10 – Creating a distribution certificate

3. Once the store has been created, the `keystore` file can be found in the following folder on Mac:

   ```
   ~/Library/Developer/Xamarin/Keystore/{alias}/{alias}.
   keystore
   ```

   It can be found in the following folder on Windows:

   ```
   C:\Users\{Username}\AppData\Local\Xamarin\Mono for
   Android\Keystore\{alias}\{alias}.keystore
   ```

4. Now, use the `.keystore` file to complete the signing step of our Android build pipeline:

Android Signing ⓘ   🔗 Link settings   📋 View YAML   ✕ Remove

Version | 3.*

Display name *

Signing and aligning APK file(s) $(build.binariesdirectory)/$(BuildConfiguration)/*.apk

APK files *

$(build.binariesdirectory)/$(BuildConfiguration)/*.apk

Signing Options ∧

☑ Sign the APK ⓘ

Keystore file * ⓘ

NetCoreSample.keystore

Keystore password ⓘ

Password!

Alias ⓘ

netcoresample

Key password ⓘ

Password1!

apksigner arguments ⓘ

-verbose -sigalg MD5withRSA -digestalg SHA1

Figure 14.11 – Signing the Xamarin.Android Package

Note that the `.keystore` file is used by the pipeline as a secure file. In a similar fashion, the keystore password can (should) be stored as a secure variable string.

5. The pipeline is now ready. Compile the Android version of the application to create an APK package.

Next, we will need to prepare a similar pipeline for the iOS platform.

Xamarin.iOS pipeline

Similar to its Android counterpart, the Xamarin.iOS template creates the full pipeline for compiling the iOS project. We will need to modify the parameters for the created tasks so that we can successfully prepare the application package. Let's get started:

1. Before we start the pipeline configuration, head over to the Apple Developer site to generate a distribution certificate, Application ID, and an ad hoc provisioning profile:

Figure 14.12 – Creating a Distribution Certificate

2. Select the distribution certificate option and let the developer site guide you through the steps of generating a CSR and generating the signing certificate.

3. Once the certificate has been created, download and install the certificate so that you can export it as a public/private key pair (.p12). You will need to follow these steps to do this:

4. Open the Keychain Access tool.

5. Identify the distribution certificate that we have downloaded and installed.

6. Expand the certificate, thus revealing the private key.
7. Select both the public certificate and private key so that you can use the **Export** option.

   Once we have the distribution certificate, we will need an app ID in order to generate a provisioning profile. When generating the app ID, the important decision is to decide whether to use a wildcard certificate (this might be a good option to use with multiple applications in their prerelease versions) or a full resource identifier.

8. Finally, create the application provisioning profile for ad hoc distribution. The ad hoc distribution is the most appropriate distribution option for prerelease distribution through App Center.

9. With the **P12** certificate we've exported and the mobile provisioning profile that we have generated and downloaded from the Apple Developer site, head over to Azure DevOps and modify the **Install an Apple certificate** and **Install an Apple provisioning profile** tasks:

Figure 14.13 – Installing our Provisioning Profile and Certificate

Finally, it is important to make sure that the application package is created for real devices, and not a simulator.

10. Select the following settings in the Xamarin.iOS build tasks:

Figure 14.14 – Xamarin iOS Build Setup

Here, the **Signing identity** and **Provisioning profile UUID** boxes can be left blank as these elements will be installed by the pipeline. If multiple profiles or certificates exist in the pipeline, you will need to define a specific one to use.

> **Important Note**
>
> The Apple ad hoc distribution profile requires the UUID of the devices that are allowed to use the distributed version of the application. In simple terms, any device involved in using and testing this version of the application should be registered in this provisioning profile, and the application should be signed with it.

This finalizes the setup for the Xamarin Android and Xamarin iOS build pipelines. Now, we can produce the application packages so that they're ready to be distributed. Nevertheless, we have not considered the environment-specific configurations in these setups. Let's take a look at some possible solutions for environment-specific configurations.

Environment-specific configurations

Native applications differ from web applications from a configuration perspective since the application CI pipeline should embed the configuration parameters into the application package. While the configuration parameters for different environments can be managed with various techniques, such as separate JSON files, compile constants, and so on, the common denominator in these implementations is that each of them uses conditional compilation or compilation constants to determine which configuration parameters are to be included in the application package. In other words, without recompiling the application, it isn't possible to change the environment-specific configurations for an application.

To create multiple distribution rings that are pointing to different service endpoints, the application will need to have different single pipelines with multiple configurations to build, or we would need to create multiple pipelines to build the application for a specific platform and configuration.

Creating and utilizing artifacts

To increase cross-project reusability, we can use the package management extension for Azure DevOps. UI components across Xamarin projects, as well as DTO models shared between Azure projects and the client application, can be merged into NuGet packages with their own life cycle: develop-merge-compile-deploy.

Storing these modules in a separate project/solution in a separate Git repository within the same Azure DevOps project would make integrating into previously created builds easier.

Once the NuGet project is ready to be compiled and packaged with a defined `.nuspec` file, a separate DevOps pipeline can be set up to create this package and push it into an internal feed within the same team project.

A sample NuGet build pipeline would look similar to the following:

Figure 14.15 – NuGet pipeline

To include this feed in the Xamarin iOS and Android pipelines, the NuGet Restore step would need to be configured to include the internal feed, as well as the `Nuget.org` source. Additionally, `Nuget.org` can be set as an upstream source for the internal feed so that the public packages can be cached in the internal feed.

In this section, we have analyzed various pipeline options for multiple platforms, including Xamarin.Android and Xamarin.iOS, as well as NuGet packages. These pipelines are the cornerstones of the continuous integration and delivery pipeline since they provide the artifacts to be distributed.

App Center for Xamarin

Visual Studio App Center, which expands on its predecessor, HockeyApp, and its feature set, is a mobile application life cycle management platform that's used to easily build, test, distribute, and collect telemetry data from iOS, Android, Windows, and macOS applications. Its intrinsic integration with various repository options and build capabilities can even be used to migrate the development and release pipeline from Azure DevOps. Visual Studio App Center, just like Azure DevOps, follows a freemium subscription model, where the developers can access most of its functionality with a free subscription; they would need to have a paid subscription for quota enhancements on certain features.

Integrating with the source repository and builds

Even though we have already set up our source repository on Azure DevOps and its associated build pipelines, App Center can be used for the same purpose.

For instance, if we were to set up the iOS build pipeline, we would follow these steps:

1. Start by creating an application within our organization. An application on App Center also represents a distribution ring:

Figure 14.16 – Creating a New App on App Center

2. Once the application has been created, in order to create a build, connect the App Center application to the target repository. Just like Azure DevOps pipelines, you are free to choose between **Azure DevOps**, **GitHub**, and **Bitbucket**:

Figure 14.17 – Selecting the Source Repository

3. Now that the repository is connected, start creating a build that will retrieve the branch content from the source repository and compile our iOS package:

Figure 14.18 – Setting up our App Center Build

4. Once the build has been set up, it can be built either manually or configured to be a CI build that will be triggered every time there is a push to the source branch (in this case, the master branch).

In this section, we created an app registration and associated our source repository from Azure DevOps with it so that App Center builds can be utilized. Next, we will be creating distribution rings on our App registrations so that our CI pipelines on Azure DevOps can provide packages to App Center for distribution.

Setting up distribution rings

We have been mentioning distribution rings in regard to App Center since we started setting up the ALM pipeline for our applications. As we have already seen, a distribution ring refers to an app that's created on your personal or organization account. This ring represents an environment-specific (for example, Dev) compilation or a certain platform (for example, iOS) on our application.

An App Center application is represented through what is called an application slug. An application slug can be extracted from the URL of the App Center page. The URL syntax is as follows:

1. `https://appcenter.ms/users/{username}/apps/{application}`:

   `App Slug: {username}/{application}`

2. `https://appcenter.ms/orgs/{orgname}/apps/{application}`:

   `App Slug: {orgname}/{application}`

If we go back to our Azure DevOps pipeline, we can use this value to set up the deployment to App Center. However, before we can do this, we will need to create an App Center service connection with an API token that you can retrieve from App Center. This will allow Azure DevOps to authorize with App Center and push application packages:

Figure 14.19 – App Center Integration on Azure DevOps

Let's complete the rest of the configuration parameters:

App Center for Xamarin 421

Figure 14.20 – App Center Distribution Task

Repeating the same steps for the Android version using another App Center application would complete the initial CI setup for our application. This build can be, similar to the App Center build, set up to be triggered with each merge to the develop or master branches.

> **Important Note**
>
> It is extremely convenient to store a markdown sheet (for example, `ReleaseNotes.md`) within the solution folder (that is, in the repository) to record the changes to the application. In each pull request, when developers enter the updates into this file, the release notes about the changes being deployed can easily be pushed to the alpha and beta distribution channels.

In this section, we successfully created application registrations in App Center and created simple build pipelines for demonstrating its capabilities. Finally, we integrated the previously prepared Azure DevOps pipelines into App Center application registrations so that they can be used as distribution rings. In the next section, we will focus on the App Center releases.

Distributing with App Center

Aside from the build, test, and telemetry collection features of App Center, the main feature of App Center is that you can manage the distribution of prerelease applications, as well as automating submissions to public and private App Stores.

App Center releases

Once the application package has been pushed from the build pipeline to App Center, an application release is created. This release represents a version of the application package. This package can be distributed to a distribution group within the current distribution ring or an external distribution target:

Figure 14.21 – App Center Release

When a release is created, it can be accessed by the collaborators group (that is, developers who have management access to App Center).

AppCenter distribution groups

Distribution groups are groups of developers and testers that an application release (environment- and platform-specific versions of the app) can be distributed to:

Figure 14.22 – App Center Distribution Groups

Distribution groups are extremely valuable since they provide additional staging for different distribution rings. For instance, once a release version has been pushed to App Center from Azure DevOps, the first distribution group can verify the application before allowing the second distribution group access to this new release. This way, the automated releases from various pipelines can be delivered to certain target groups on both alpha and beta channels.

Additionally, if you navigate to the collaborators group details on an iOS application ring, you can identify which devices are currently included in the provisioning profile:

Devices   Export UDIDs

Model	Tester	OS
Apple iPhone X	Can Bilgin can_bilgin@hotmail.com	iOS 12.0.1

Figure 14.23 – App Center Device Registration

For registering devices, App Center allows you to automatically provision devices for iOS releases. In this setup, each time a new device is registered within a distribution group (given that automatic provisioning is configured), App Center will update the provisioning profile on the Apple Developer Portal and resign the release package with the new provisioning profile.

App Center distribution to production

Once the application has been certified on lower rings (that is, alpha and beta), the App Center release can be pushed to the production stage. The production stage can be the target public App Store (for example, iTunes Store, Google Play Store, and so on), or the application can be published to users using Mobile Device Management or Mobile Application Management (for example, Microsoft Intune).

To set up iTunes Store as the target store, you will need to add an Apple Developer account to App Center. Similarly, if your target is going to be InTune, an administrator account should be added to your App Center integration:

Figure 14.24 – App Center Distribution to Stores

It is important to note that App Store Connect submissions will not bypass the Apple store verification for the application package – it is simply a handover process that is normally handled through Xcode.

App Center telemetry and diagnostics

App Center offers advanced telemetry and diagnostic options. To start using these monitoring features, the App Center SDK needs to be installed on the application and initialized for all target platforms. Follow these steps to learn how:

1. Install the NuGet package from the public NuGet store. Use the package manager context as follows:

```
PM> Install-Package Microsoft.AppCenter.Analytics
PM> Install-Package Microsoft.AppCenter.Crashes
```

2. In this case, we are creating a Xamarin.Forms application, so the initialization does not need to be platform-specific:

```
AppCenter.Start("ios={AppSecret};android={AppSecret};
uwp={AppSecret}", typeof(Analytics), typeof(Crashes));
```

3. Once the App Center SDK has been initialized, default telemetry information, as well as crash tracking, is enabled for the application. This telemetry information can be extended with custom metrics and event telemetry using the available functionality within the SDK:

Figure 14.25 – App Center Telemetry Collection

On top of this telemetry information, App Center allows you to track two types of error information: app crashes and errors. App crash information is logged together with the telemetry events that lead to the application crashing, allowing developers to easily troubleshoot problems.

Moreover, telemetry information can be pushed to Application Insights so that it can be analyzed on the Azure portal.

Summary

In this chapter, we set up the initial build pipeline, which will be expanded on in the upcoming chapters. We also discussed the available ALM features on Azure DevOps and Visual Studio App Center, as well as how to effectively use these two platforms together. Depending on the team's size and the application type, many different configurations can be implemented on these platforms, thus providing developers with an automated and easy-to-use development pipeline.

In the next chapter, we will learn how to monitor our mobile application, as well as the Azure resources that are used with Azure Application Insights.

15
Application Telemetry with Application Insights

Agile application life cycle management dictates that after an application's release, performance and user feedback should be introduced back into the development cycle. Feedback information can provide vital clues to how to improve your application from both business and technical perspectives. Application Insights can be a great candidate for collecting telemetry data from Xamarin applications that use an Azure-hosted web service infrastructure because of its intrinsic integration with Azure modules, as well as its continuous export functionality for App Center telemetry.

In this chapter, we will be analyzing the data models and utilization of two different telemetry sources, namely App Center and Application Insights. We will take a look at the SDKs and what these platforms offer for user telemetry. The following sections will guide you through this chapter:

- Collecting insights for Xamarin applications
- Collecting telemetry data for Azure Service
- Analyzing data

At the end of this chapter, you will be able to integrate the App Center telemetry client into your Xamarin applications and collect valuable user telemetry. You will also learn how to migrate this telemetry data to Application and analyze it with advanced query models and visualizations.

Collecting insights for Xamarin applications

In this section, we will focus on App Center telemetry and how to expand the scope of user telemetry.

As we have previously discussed and set up, application telemetry within Xamarin applications is collected with the App Center SDK. This application data, while providing crucial information about the usage patterns of the application, cannot be further analyzed in the App Center. We first need to export the App Center standard as well as the custom telemetry to an Azure Application Insights resource so that further analysis can be executed with a query language.

The telemetry data model

By using the App Center SDK, telemetry information can be collected along with events, which can contain additional information about a specific user action or application execution pattern. These additional data points, also known as **dimensions**, are generally used to give the user a quick snapshot of the data that is used to execute the function that triggered the telemetry event. In simple terms, a telemetry event can be described as the event name and the additional dimensions for this event. Let's begin by creating our telemetry model:

1. First, create a telemetry event, as follows:

    ```csharp
    public abstract class TelemetryEvent
    {
        public TelemetryEvent()
        {
            Properties = new Dictionary<string, string>();
        }

        public TelemetryEvent(string eventName) : this()
        {
            Name = eventName;
    ```

```
        }

        public string Name { get; private set; }

        public virtual Dictionary<string, string> Properties
{ get;
    set; }
}
```

> **Important note**
> Any custom event will contain standard tracking metadata, such as the OS version, the request's geographical region, the device model, the application version, and so on. These properties don't need to be logged as additional dimensions. Properties should be used for event-specific data.

2. Now, implement the telemetry writer using the App Center SDK:

```
public class AppCenterTelemetryWriter
{
    public void Initialize()
    {
        AppCenter.Start("{AppSecret}", typeof(Analytics),
        typeof(Crashes));
        AppCenter.SetEnabledAsync(true).
ConfigureAwait(false);
        Analytics.SetEnabledAsync(true).
ConfigureAwait(false);
        Crashes.SetEnabledAsync(true).
ConfigureAwait(false);
    }

    public void TrackEvent(TelemetryEvent event)
    {
        Analytics.TrackEvent(event.Name, event.
Properties);
    }
}
```

3. In order to expand our event definition to include an `Exception` property, we can add an additional event for errors. In other words, we can track the handled exceptions within the application:

```
public void TrackEvent(TelemetryEvent @event)
{
    if (@event.Exception != null)
    {
        TrackError(@event);
        return;
    }

    Analytics.TrackEvent(@event.Name, @event.Properties);
}

public void TrackError(TelemetryEvent @event)
{
    Crashes.TrackError(@event.Exception, @event.Properties);
}
```

4. Now, start creating custom events and start logging telemetry data. Our initial event might be the login event, which is generally the starting location for a user session:

```
public class LoginEvent: TelemetryEvent
{
    public LoginEvent() : base("Login")
    {
        Properties.Add(nameof(Result), string.Empty);
    }

    public string Result
    {
        get
        {
            return Properties[nameof(Result)];
```

```
            }

            set
            {
                Properties[nameof(Result)] = value;
            }
        }
    }
```

5. After logging in, the user will navigate to the main dashboard, so we will log our dashboard appearing event in a similar fashion:

```
    protected override void OnAppearing()
    {
        base.OnAppearing();

        App.Telemetry.TrackEvent(new HomePageEvent()
        {
            LoadedItems = ViewModel.Items.Count.ToString()
        });
    }
```

6. Additionally, define navigation to the details view, where various actions can be executed by the user:

```
    protected override void OnAppearing()
    {
        base.OnAppearing();

        App.Telemetry.TrackEvent(new DetailsPageEvent()
        {
            SelectedItem = viewModel.Title
        });
    }
```

434 Application Telemetry with Application Insights

> **Important note**
> There are certain limitations on event structures that the App Center can track. The maximum number of custom event names cannot exceed 200. Additionally, the length of event names is limited to 256 characters, whereas property names cannot exceed 125 characters.

7. The resultant metadata can now be visualized on App Center dashboards:

Figure 15.1 – App Center Data Visualization

In this section, so far, we have created a small page tracker using custom events. In the next part of the section, we will try to organize the telemetry events delivered by our application.

Advanced application telemetry

In the previous examples, we used a static accessor for our telemetry writer instance. However, this implementation can cause serious architectural problems, the most important of which is that we would be coupling our application class with a concrete implementation of the App Center SDK.

In order to remedy architectural issues that may arise, let's create a proxy telemetry container that will divert telemetry requests to target telemetry writers. To do so, follow the following steps:

1. Start by creating an `ITelemetryWriter` interface to abstract our App Center telemetry handler:

    ```csharp
    public interface ITelemetryWriter
    {
        string Name { get; }

        void TrackEvent(TelemetryEvent @event);

        void TrackError(TelemetryEvent @event);
    }
    ```

2. Now, create a proxy container:

    ```csharp
    public class AppTelemetryRouter : ITelemetryWriter
    {
        // Removed for Brevity

        public static AppTelemetryRouter Instance
        {
            get
            {
                if(_instance == null)
                {
                    _instance = new AppTelemetryRouter();
    ```

```csharp
            }

            return _instance;
        }
    }

    public void RegisterWriter(ITelemetryWriter telemetryWriter)
    {
        if(_telemetryWriters.Any(tw=>tw.Name == telemetryWriter.Name))
        {
            throw new InvalidOperationException($"Already registered Telemetry Writer for {telemetryWriter.Name}");
        }

        _telemetryWriters.Add(telemetryWriter);
    }

    public void RemoveWriter(string name)
    {
        if(_telemetryWriters.Any(tw => tw.Name == name))
        {
            var removalItems = _telemetryWriters.First(tw =>
            tw.Name == name);

            _telemetryWriters.Remove(removalItems);
        }
    }

    public void TrackEvent(TelemetryEvent @event)
    {
        _telemetryWriters.ForEach(tw => tw.TrackEvent(@event));
```

```csharp
        }

        public void TrackError(TelemetryEvent @event)
        {
            _telemetryWriters.ForEach(tw => tw.TrackError(@event));
        }
    }
}
```

It is also important to note that the container should be created on a cross-platform project where the view models are defined, since most of the diagnostic telemetry will in fact be collected on the view models rather than the views themselves. Another advantage of this implementation is the fact that we can now define multiple telemetry writers for different platforms, such as Firebase, Flurry Analytics, and so on.

While the abstract telemetry event class provides the basic data, it does not provide any metrics about the execution time. For instance, if we are executing a remote service call or a long-running operation, the execution time can be a valuable dimension.

3. In order to collect this specific metric, create an additional telemetry object:

```csharp
public abstract class ChronoTelemetryEvent : TelemetryEvent
{
    public ChronoTelemetryEvent()
    {
        Properties.Add(nameof(Elapsed), 0.ToString());
    }

    public double Elapsed
    {
        get
        {
            return double.Parse(Properties[nameof(Elapsed)]);
        }
        set
```

```
            {
                Properties[nameof(Elapsed)] = value.ToString();
            }
        }
    }
```

4. Now, create a tracker object, which will track the execution time for events that require the execution time metric:

```
public class TelemetryTracker<TEvent> : IDisposable
    where TEvent : ChronoTelemetryEvent
{
    private readonly DateTime _executionStart = DateTime.Now;

    public TelemetryTracker(TEvent @event)
    {
        Event = @event;
    }

    public TEvent Event { get; }

    public void Dispose()
    {
        var executionTime = DateTime.Now - _executionStart;
        Event.Elapsed = executionTime.TotalMilliseconds;

        // The submission of the event can as well be moved out of
        //the tracker
        AppTelemetryRouter.Instance?.TrackEvent(Event);
    }
}
```

5. Now, using our tracker object, we can collect valuable information about time-sensitive operations within the application:

```
public async Task LoadProducts()
{
    using (var telemetry = new
TelemetryTracker<ProductsRequestEvent>(new
ProductsRequestEvent()))
    {
        try
        {
            var result = await _serviceClient.RetrieveProducts();

            Items = new ObservableCollection<ItemViewModel>(
                result.Select(item => ItemViewModel.FromDto(item)));
        }
        catch (Exception ex)
        {
            telemetry.Event.Exception = ex;
        }
    }
}
```

6. The results of the service call are measured with the `Elapsed` metric, which can be observed in the App Center's **LogFlow**:

8092425a	STARTSESSION - 7b106777-f07c-4312-9b53-5f2930c101db	14:11:03
8092425a	STARTSERVICE	14:11:03
8092425a	EVENT - Login - {"result":"Successfully Logged In!"}	14:11:08
8092425a	EVENT - HomeView - {"loadedItems":"16"}	14:11:09
8092425a	EVENT - ProductsServiceRequest - {"elapsed":"659.583"}	14:11:12
8092425a	EVENT - DetailsView - {"selectedItem":"First Item"}	14:11:57
8092425a	EVENT - HomeView - {"loadedItems":"16"}	14:11:59
8092425a	EVENT - ProductsServiceRequest - {"elapsed":"633.312"}	14:12:04

Figure 15.2 – App Center Log Flow

7. Similarly, tracker objects can be created on the `OnAppearing` events of certain views and disposed of with the `OnDisappearing` event so that we can track how much time the user spent on a certain view.

While App Center provides a convenient way to collect telemetry, in order to execute analysis on the user patterns and troubleshoot application issues, we can export the telemetry data to Application Insights.

Exporting App Center telemetry data to Azure

At this point, the application is collecting telemetry data and pushing it to App Center. However, as we discussed earlier, you won't be able to analyze this data – especially the custom event dimensions – any further.

In order to do this, we will need to create a new Application Insights resource and set up a continuous export so that App Center telemetry can be exported as Application Insights data. Let's begin:

1. Start this process by creating the Application Insights resource:

Figure 15.3 – Export to Application Insights

Notice that, for **Application Type**, we have selected **App Center application**. As a resource group, we will be using the same resource group as the previously created Azure services so that the complete Azure infrastructure can be deployed together.

2. Once the resource is created, go to the **Overview** section to find the instrumentation key. This key is the only requirement for setting up the continuous export process:

Figure 15.4 – Application Insights for Xamarin Telemetry

3. On App Center, in order to set up the export, navigate to the **Settings** section and select **Export and Application Insights** on the data export window.

In this view, you can use the **Set up standard export** option, which is used when an Azure subscription is configured to be used with App Center. Selecting the standard export will require admin access to the Azure subscription and will create a new resource. You can also select **Customize** and paste in the instrumentation key that we have from the Azure portal.

4. After this setup, the event telemetry will be pushed periodically to **Application Insights**, which can be analyzed within the Azure portal either using the standard analysis sections or using the query language:

Figure 15.5 – Application Insights User Telemetry

This section focused on App Center telemetry. We started with basic user telemetry using custom events, which expanded to advanced operation diagnostic data. As you can see, with small adjustments to the telemetry model, you can get valuable insights into the common user flows, which can help steer your application to success. Now that the telemetry data from our application has been collected and exported to Application Insights, we can start creating the Application Insights infrastructure for our remaining modules on Azure.

Collecting telemetry data for Azure Service

Application Insights is a little more tightly integrated into Azure-based services than mobile applications. In addition to the various standard, out-of-the-box, telemetries that can be collected for services such as Azure App Service and serverless components such as Azure Functions, custom telemetry, trace, and metric collection implementations are possible.

Application Insights data model

Application Insights telemetry collection can be grouped into three major groups:

- **Trace**: Trace can be recognized as the simplest form of telemetry. Trace elements generally give a nominal description of an event and are used as a diagnostic log, similar to other flat-file diagnostic log implementations. In addition to the main telemetry message, a severity level and additional properties can be defined. Trace message size limits are much larger than other telemetry types and provide a convenient way of providing large amounts of diagnostic data. Trace models are also used when standard logging extensions are used within .NET 5.0 applications.

- **Events**: Application Insights events are very similar to App Center telemetry items and are treated the same way once the App Center data is exported to Application Insights. In addition to the nominal dimensions, additional metrics data can be sent to Application Insights. Once the data is collected, the `customProperties` collection provides access to the descriptive dimensions, while the `customMeasurements` dictionary is used to access metrics.

- **Metrics**: They are generally pre-aggregated scalar measurements. If you're dealing with custom metrics, it is the application's responsibility to keep them up to date. The Application Insights client provides standardized access methods for both standard and custom metrics.

In addition to event-specific telemetry data types, operation-specific data types can also be traced and tracked with Application Insights, such as requests, exceptions, and dependencies. These are classed as more generalized, macro-level telemetry data, which can provide valuable information as to the health of the application infrastructure. Request, exception, and dependency data is generally tracked by default, but custom/manual implementation is also possible.

Collecting telemetry data with ASP.NET Core

Application Insights can easily be initialized using Visual Studio for any ASP.NET Core web application. In our case, we will be configuring the web API layer to use Application Insights. Let's see how we can do this:

1. Start by right-clicking on the web application project, then select **Add | Application Insights Telemetry**, and then click the **Get Started** link. Visual Studio automatically loads the resources that your account(s) are associated with, allowing you to choose a subscription, as well as the resource/resource group pair.

2. Use the **Configure Settings...** option on this page to assign an already existing resource group; otherwise, the Application Insights instance will be created on a default Application Insights resource group:

Figure 15.6 – Application Insights Configuration

After the **Application Insights** configuration is complete, we can see how the telemetry data is collected without deploying the web API to the Azure App Service resource.

3. In order to see the collected telemetry data, you can start a debugging session. Select **View | Other Windows | Application Insights** to open the live Application Insights data that is collected within the debug session:

Figure 15.7 – Application Insights Debug Session Telemetry

It is important to note that the data is set to use **Debug session telemetry**. The **Application Insights Search** toolset can also be used to read remote telemetry and execute quick search queries on live data.

Another useful tool window is **Application Insights Trends**, which is a quick reporting tool for various application telemetry data types, such as requests, page views, exceptions, events, and dependencies.

The same telemetry set, even if this is a debugging session, should already be available on the Azure portal as well. In other words, Application Insights does not require an Azure deployment for a server resource to be profiled and its telemetry tracked.

4. Now, if you navigate to the Application Insights overview page, you will notice the incoming data and collected telemetry data about the requests.

5. Next, navigate to the live metrics screen using the side panel navigation. The live metrics screen can provide information about the server's performance and aggregated metrics data. In order to use profiling and performance data, update the Application Insights SDK to a version higher than 2.2.0 so you can see this:

Figure 15.8 – Application Insights Live Metrics Stream

Now that the Application Insights infrastructure is set up, we can start creating custom telemetry and trace data.

6. Create a new operation context for the product retrieval API operation and include some additional telemetry data:

```
using (var operationContext = _telemetryClient.
StartOperation<RequestTelemetry>("getProducts"))
{
    var result = Enumerable.Empty<Product>();
    _telemetryClient.TrackTrace("Creating Document 
Client",
    SeverityLevel.Information);
    using (var document = GetDocumentClient())
```

```csharp
{
    try
    {
        _telemetryClient.TrackTrace("Retrieving Products",
            SeverityLevel.Information);
        result = await document.Retrieve();
    }
    catch (Exception ex)
    {
        _telemetryClient.TrackException(ex);
        operationContext.Telemetry.ResponseCode = "500";
        throw ex;
    }
}

    operationContext.Telemetry.ResponseCode = "200";
    return Ok(result);
}
```

7. Now, the resultant telemetry collection that contains trace entries is automatically grouped to the operation context, thus providing more meaningful information:

Figure 15.9 – Application Insights Operation Context

We can further granulize this telemetry data by separating the dependency telemetry. For instance, in this implementation, we call the data provider client to load all the products.

8. Using the telemetry client, create a dependency telemetry for this request:

```
using (var document = GetDocumentClient())
{
    var callStartTime = DateTimeOffset.UtcNow;

    try
    {
        _telemetryClient.TrackTrace("Retrieving Products",
            SeverityLevel.Information);
        result = await document.Retrieve();
    }
    finally
    {
        var elapsed = DateTimeOffset.UtcNow - callStartTime;
        _telemetryClient.TrackDependency(
            "DataSource", "ProductsDB", "Retrieve", callStartTime,
            elapsed, result.Any());
    }
}
```

9. Now, the application telemetry is tracked separately for the document source. This dependency is even created on the application map on the Azure portal:

Figure 15.10 – Application Insights Application Map

Under normal circumstances, dependency calls to resources such as Cosmos DB and SQL are automatically detected and tracked separately. The preceding implementation suits external dependencies or legacy systems.

As you have seen in this part, collecting custom telemetry from ASP.NET 5 applications mainly relies on using the telemetry client and the features available through the SDK. Most of the dependency telemetry, as well as the exceptions, are already collected by the client automatically. Let's now move on to Azure Functions.

Collecting telemetry with Azure Functions

When we talk about custom traces, collecting Application Insights telemetry data from Azure Functions is no different from using any other .NET application. When we created our Azure functions, we injected a `TraceWriter` instance into our methods. `TraceWriter` logs are the main source of diagnostic telemetry and are collected within an Azure function. These log entries can be filtered according to the log level using the `host.json` settings:

```
{
    "logger": {
        "categoryFilter": {
            "defaultLevel": "Information",
```

```
            "categoryLevels": {
                "Host.Results": "Error",
                "Function": "Error",
                "Host.Aggregator": "Information"
            }
        },
        "aggregator": {
            "batchSize": 1000,
            "flushTimeout": "00:00:30"
        }
    },
    "applicationInsights": {
        "sampling": {
            "isEnabled": true,
            "maxTelemetryItemsPerSecond" : 5
        }
    }
}
```

The Function section in the category levels refers to the traces that are collected within the function. `Host.Results` are automatically collected request/result telemetry data pairs, whereas aggregator data is full of aggregated metrics that the function's host collects by default, either every 30 seconds or 1,000 results. This is then used to calculate the aggregated metrics, such as count, success rate, and so on.

In addition to the basic telemetry implementation, you can also modify default telemetry data using the Application Insights telemetry client. In this context, the telemetry client is used to modify the operation context rather than creating a new `TrackRequest`.

As you can see, the telemetry client acts more like middleware rather than the source of truth in this implementation, simply modifying the existing operation context and creating additional event data.

In this section, we have looked at different telemetry models and how they can be used on ASP.NET applications as well as Azure Serverless components. We have used the telemetry client to provide custom telemetry data in our web service while using the standard configuration for Application Insights in our Azure function. Now that we have enough telemetry data collected on both mobile and web platforms, we can start analyzing this dataset.

Analyzing data

Now that we have set up Application Insights telemetry collection on both the server side and the application side, we can try and make sense of this data.

While the Azure portal provides quick insights into application telemetry data, if we want to really dive into application data, the Application Insights portal should be used for analysis. In the Application Insights portal, data can be analyzed using the query language. The query language, also known as the Kusto language, provides advanced read-only querying features that can help organize data from multiple sources and render valuable insights into the performance and usage patterns of your application.

For instance, let's take a look at the following simple query, which is executed on our Xamarin telemetry data. We are returning the first 50 custom events that are exported from App Center:

```
customEvents
| limit 50
```

These telemetry entries contain general telemetry-related data in the root:

Figure 15.11 – Application Insights Telemetry Details

Whereas the `customDimensions` object provides more Xamarin-specific data:

customDimensions	{"WrapperRuntimeVersion":"11.2.0","WrapperSdkVersion":"1.13.0","IngressTimestamp":"2019-01-27T14:11:15.7610000Z"
AppBuild	1.0
AppId	f49e730f-32de-449e-a516-5113d6d81b08
AppNamespace	com.companyname.FirstXamarinFormsApplication
CarrierCountry	None
CarrierName	None
CountryCode	None
EventId	c5129672-16ea-4377-acb2-71b467ec8ce4
IngressTimestamp	2019-01-27T14:11:15.7610000Z
Locale	en_TR
MessageType	EventLog
OsApiLevel	None
OsBuild	18C54
OsName	iOS
OsVersion	12.1
> Properties	{"elapsed":"659.583"}
ScreenSize	2436x1125
SdkName	appcenter.ios
SdkVersion	1.13.0
TimeZoneOffset	PT1H
UserId	

Figure 15.12 – Application Insights Custom Dimensions

Finally, the `Properties` node of `customDimensions` provides the actual custom telemetry data that was sent using the **AppCenter** telemetry client. We can incorporate this data in our analysis after some preprocessing:

1. Before we can dig into event-specific data, filter the telemetry events using the telemetry event name:

   ```
   customEvents
   | where name == "ProductsServiceRequest"
   ```

2. Then, order the table by timestamp:

   ```
   | order by timestamp desc nulls last
   ```

3. By deserializing the properties data into a dynamic field, use the fetched data in our queries:

   ```
   | extend Properties = todynamic(tostring(customDimensions.Properties))
   ```

4. In order to flatten the table structure, assign the properties data into its own fields:

   ```
   | extend Duration = todouble(Properties.elapsed),
   OperatingSystem = customDimensions.OsName
   ```

5. Finally, project the data into a new table so that we can present it in a simpler structure:

   ```
   | project OperatingSystem, Duration, timestamp
   ```

6. Now, the data from our telemetry events is structured and can be presented in reports and troubleshooting:

OperatingSystem	Duration	timestamp [UTC]
iOS	633.348	2019-01-27T15:23:21.593
	OperatingSystem	iOS
	Duration	633.348
	timestamp [UTC]	2019-01-27T15:23:21.593Z
iOS	633.311	2019-01-27T15:23:18.144
iOS	640.723	2019-01-27T15:23:12.933
iOS	633.312	2019-01-27T14:12:04.082
iOS	659.583	2019-01-27T14:11:12.681

Figure 15.13 – Operating System Projection

7. To take this one step further, we can also draw a chart using the final table as follows:

   ```
   | render timechart
   ```

8. This would draw a line chart with the duration values. You can also sort data by using the `summarize` function with numerous aggregate functions, such as by grouping events into hourly bins and drawing a time-based bar chart:

```
customEvents
| order by timestamp desc nulls last
| extend Properties = todynamic(tostring(customDimensions.Properties))
| summarize event_count=count() by bin(timestamp, 1h)
| render barchart
```

Application Insights data and available query operators and methods provide countless ways for developers to act proactively on application telemetry by gathering invaluable application data from staging environments or production and feeding it back to the application life cycle.

Summary

Application telemetry data that is collected from both the server and the client side can provide information that's required to improve and mold your application according to user needs. In a way, by collecting application telemetry data from various modules of the application on live environments, live application testing is executed with actual user data. This telemetry data can provide insights into the application that no other automated testing can provide. Regardless of the reality and the synthetic nature of the data, unit tests, as well as automated UI tests, should still be part of the application life cycle.

In the next chapter, we will look into various ways of testing and how we can include these tests in the development pipeline.

16
Automated Testing

Unit and coded UI tests are generally perceived by most developers as the most monotonous part of the application project life cycle. However, improving the unit test code coverage and creating automated UI tests can help save an extensive amount of developer hours, which would otherwise be spent on maintenance and regression. Especially for application projects with a longer life cycle, the stability of the project directly correlates with the level of test automation. This chapter will discuss how to create unit and coded UI tests and the architectural patterns that revolve around them. Data-driven unit tests, mocks, and Xamarin UI tests are some of the concepts that will be discussed.

In this chapter, we will be focusing on creating various types of tests for different phases of the application life cycle. We will start this chapter by looking at unit testing, before taking a look at setting up unit testing and the execution strategies in Xamarin's scope. We will then move on to integration tests and automated UI tests, which, together with unit tests, enable developers to keep their applications in check throughout the delivery pipeline.

The following topics will walk you through how to implement an automatically verified application development pipeline:

- Maintaining application integrity with tests
- Maintaining cross-module integrity with integration tests
- Automated UI tests

By the end of this chapter, you will be able to effectively use mocks and fixtures while creating strategically prepared unit tests. You will also understand the motives behind and the benefits of integration and automated testing.

Maintaining application integrity with tests

The focus of this section will be on the unit testing and strategies and tools available for unit testing Xamarin applications. We will look at unit testing fundamentals, as well as mock and fixture concepts.

Regardless of the development or runtime platform, unit tests are an integral part of the development pipeline. In fact, nowadays, **test-driven development** (**TDD**) is the most prominent development methodology and is the best choice for any agile development team. In this paradigm, developers are responsible, even before the first line of actual business logic implementation has been written, for creating unit tests that are appropriate for the current unit that is under development.

Arrange, Act, and Assert

Without further ado, let's take a look at the first view model in our application and implement some unit tests for it. The products view model is a simple view model that, upon initialization, loads the products data using the available service client. It exposes two properties; that is, the `Items` collection and the `ItemTapped` command. Using this information, we can identify the units.

The units of the application can be identified by implementing simple stubs, as shown in the following code:

```
public class ListItemViewModel : BaseBindableObject
{
    public ListItemViewModel(IApiClient apiClient, INavigationService
navigationService)
    {
        //...Load products and initialize ItemTapped command
    }

    public ObservableCollection<ItemViewModel> Items { get; set; }
```

```
    public ICommand ItemTapped { get; }

    internal async Task LoadProducts()
    {
        // ...
        var result = await _serviceClient.
RetrieveProductsAsync();
        // ...
    }

    internal async Task NavigateToItem(ItemViewModel 
viewModel)
    {
        // ...
    }
}
```

Our initial unit test will set up the mock for `apiClient`, construct the view model, verify that `RetrieveProductsAsync` is called on the service client, and verify that the `ItemTapped` command is initialized properly. An additional check can be done to see whether the `PropertyChanged` event has been triggered on the `Items` property. In the context of unit testing, these three steps of a simple unit test are generally called the triple-A or AAA – **Arrange, Act, Assert**:

1. In the `Arrange` section, prepare a set of results data and return the data with a mock client:

    ```
    #region Arrange
    
    var expectedResults = new List<Product>();
    expectedResults.Add(new Product { Title = "testProduct", 
    Description = "testDescription" });
    
    // Using the mock setup for the IApiClient
    _apiClientMock.Setup(client => client.
    RetrieveProductsAsync()).ReturnsAsync(expectedResults);
    
    #endregion
    ```

2. Now, let's execute the Act step by constructing the view model:

   ```
   #region Act

   var listViewModel = new ListItemViewModel(_apiClientMock.Object);

   #endregion
   ```

3. Finally, execute the assertions on the view model target:

   ```
   #region Assert

   // Just checking the resultant count as an example
   // Foreach with checking each expected product has a
   // matching domain entity would improve the robustness of the test.
   listViewModel.Items.Should().HaveCount(expectedResults.Count());
   listViewModel.ItemTapped.Should().NotBeNull()
       .And.Subject.Should().BeOfType<Command<ItemViewModel>>();
   _apiClientMock.Verify(client => client.RetrieveProductsAsync());

   #endregion
   ```

4. Now run the unit tests to check code coverage:

▷ ItemViewModel		50%	22/44
▷ Product		67%	4/12
▲ ListItemViewModel		80%	7/35
▷ NavigateToItem(ItemViewModel)		0%	2/2
▷ LoadProducts()		71%	4/14
▷ ListItemViewModel(IApiClient)		91%	1/11
▷ ItemTapped		100%	0/1
▷ Items		100%	0/7
▲ BaseBindableObject		100%	0/3
SendPropertyChanged(string)		100%	0/3
▷ PropertyChanged			0/0

Figure 16.1 – Code Coverage Results

With this simple unit test implementation, we have already reached ~80% of our unit test code coverage.

> **Important Note**
> The xUnit.net framework was used to implement this unit test, or so-called fact. Additionally, the `FluentAssertions` and `Moq` frameworks were utilized in order to ease the implementation and assertions. The feature sets of these frameworks are beyond the scope of this book.

The implementation is good enough for checking the initialization of the constructor. The constructor implementation we are testing looks similar to this:

```
public ListItemViewModel(IApiClient apiClient)
{
    _serviceClient = apiClient;
    ItemTapped = new Command<ItemViewModel>(async _ => await
    NavigateToItem(_));
    if (_serviceClient != null)
    {
        LoadProducts().ConfigureAwait(false);
    }
}
```

However, notice that the `LoadProducts` method is, in fact, called without `await`, so it does not merge back into the initial synchronization context. In a multi-threaded environment, when executing multiple unit tests in parallel, the constructor might be executed; however, before the asynchronous task can complete, the assertions start. This can be worked around with a poor man's thread synchronization – `Task.Delay` or `Thread.Sleep`.

This implementation is nothing more than a temporary workaround. Since we cannot and should not really wait for the task to complete within the constructor, we need to utilize the service initialization pattern:

```
public ListItemViewModel(IApiClient apiClient)
{
    _serviceClient = apiClient;
    ItemTapped = new Command<ItemViewModel>(async _ => await NavigateToItem(_));
    if (_serviceClient != null)
    {
        (Initialized = LoadProducts()).ConfigureAwait(false);
    }
}

internal Task Initialized { get; set; }
```

Now, our `Act` implementation will look similar to this:

```
#region Act

var listViewModel = new ListItemViewModel(_apiClientMock.Object);
await listViewModel.Initialized;

#endregion
```

> **Important Note**
>
> Note that we were not able to verify the `PropertyChanged` event trigger at the view model level for the `Items` property. The main reason for this is that the `ListItemsViewModel` instance immediately executes the `LoadProducts` method, and before we even have a chance to subscribe to the target event, its execution is finalized. This can also be remedied with a circuit flag within the mock object we have implemented, releasing the task once the monitor has been attached to the view model.

To execute these unit tests, as well as the IDE extensions, use the `dotnet` console command:

```
dotnet test --collect "Code Coverage"
```

This command will execute the available unit tests and generate a coverage file that can be viewed in Visual Studio:

Figure 16.2 – DotNet Test Execution

In this section, we created unit tests for a very basic view-model with the classic AAA setup. However, things can easily become complicated when the view-models have numerous dependencies on both platform and application services. So, now that we've refreshed our memory on the unit testing nomenclature and basic unit testing know-how, we can move on to mocks.

Creating unit tests with mocks

When implementing unit tests, it is important to isolate the units we are currently testing. By isolation, we are referring to the process of mocking the dependencies of the current subject under test. These mocks can be introduced in various ways, depending on the implementation of the Inversion of Control pattern. If the implementation involves constructor injection, we can mock our dependency interfaces in the first A of our test and pass it on to our target. Otherwise, frameworks such as NSubstitute can replace interfaces, as well as the concrete classes that are used by the subject.

Looking back at our view model and the unit test that we implemented, you may have noticed that we used the Moq framework to create a mock interface implementation for our `IApiClient` object. Now, let's learn how to create unit tests using Moq:

1. Extend the constructor so that it takes the `INavigationService` instance, which will be used to navigate to the details view of the selected item; in other words, isolate our `ItemTapped` command's implementation:

    ```
    public ListItemViewModel(IApiClient apiClient,
    INavigationService navigationService)
    {
        _serviceClient = apiClient;
        _navigationService = navigationService;
        ItemTapped = new Command<ItemViewModel>(async _ =>
    await
        NavigateToItem(_));
        if (_serviceClient != null)
        {
            (Initialized = LoadProducts()).
    ConfigureAwait(false);
        }
    }
    ```

2. Our navigation command will be as follows:

    ```
    internal async Task NavigateToItem(ItemViewModel
    viewModel)
    {
        if (viewModel != null && _navigationService != null)
        {
            if (await _navigationService.
    NavigateToViewModel(viewModel))
    ```

```
            {
                // Navigation was successful
                return;
            }
        }

        throw new InvalidOperationException("Target view model or
    navigation service is null");
    }
```

> **Important Note**
> In this example, we are throwing an exception, just for demonstration purposes. In a real-life implementation, it is probably a better choice to track errors internally and/or throw an exception only in debug mode. Moreover, it is not quite SOLID to throw the same type of exception as in these scenarios.

3. Now, let's implement our unit test:

```
[Trait("Category", "ViewModelTests")]
[Trait("ViewModel", "ListViewModel")]
[Fact(DisplayName = "Verify ListViewModel navigates on ItemTapped")]
public async Task ListItemViewModel_ItemTapped_
ShouldNavigateToItemViewModel()
{
    #region Arrange

    _navigationServiceMock.Setup(nav => nav.NavigateToViewModel(
                    It.IsAny<BaseBindableObject>()))
                    .ReturnsAsync(true);
    var listViewModel = new ListItemViewModel(
                    _apiClientMock.Object,
                    _navigationServiceMock.Object);
    await listViewModel.Initialized;
    var expectedItemViewModel = new ItemViewModel() {
```

```
    Title = "Test
        Item" };

    #endregion

    #region Act

    listViewModel.ItemTapped.
Execute(expectedItemViewModel);

    #endregion

    #region Assert

    _navigationServiceMock.Verify(
        service => service.NavigateToViewModel(It.
IsAny<ItemViewModel>()));

    #endregion
}
```

4. We have implemented the unit test to check the so-called happy path. We can also take this implementation one step further by checking whether the navigation service was called with `expectedItemViewModel`:

```
Func<ItemViewModel, bool> expectedViewModelCheck = model
=>
    model.Title == expectedItemViewModel.Title;

_navigationServiceMock.Verify(
    service => service.NavigateToViewModel(
        It.Is<ItemViewModel>(_ =>
expectedViewModelCheck(_))));
```

In order to cover the possible outcomes (remember, we are dealing with the view model as if it were a deterministic finite automaton), we will need to implement two more scenarios where the navigation service is `null` and where the command parameter is `null`, both of which will throw `InvalidOperationException`.

5. Now, modify the `Arrange` section of the initial set:

    ```
    var listViewModel = new ListItemViewModel(_apiClientMock.
    Object, null);
    ```

    In this specific case, the command (that is, `ICommand`) is constructed from an asynchronous task (that is, `NavigateToItem`). Simply calling the `Execute` method on the command will swallow the exception, which means we will not be able to verify the exception.

6. Because of this, modify the execution so that it uses the actual view model method so that we can assert the exception:

    ```
    #region Act
    // Calling the execute method cannot be asserted.
    // Action command = () => listViewModel.ItemTapped.
    Execute(expectedItemViewModel);
    Func<Task> command = async () => await listViewModel.
    NavigateToItem(expectedItemViewModel);
    #endregion

    #region Assert
    await command.Should().
    ThrowAsync<InvalidOperationException>();
    #endregion
    ```

    Notice that, in both test cases, we are still using the same `IApiClient` mock without a setup method. We can still execute this mock since it was created with a loose mock behavior, which returns an empty collection for collection return types instead of throwing an exception for methods without a proper setup.

7. This brings the tally to ~90% unit test code coverage on `ListViewModel`, as shown in the following screenshot:

ListItemViewModel	0	0.00%	19	100.00%
ListItemViewModel.<>c	0	0.00%	2	100.00%
ListItemViewModel.<LoadProducts>d_...	3	15.79%	16	84.21%
ListItemViewModel.<NavigateToItem>...	2	16.67%	10	83.33%

Figure 16.3 – Visual Studio Code Coverage Results

All the tests so far have been implemented for the view models. These modules in an application are, by definition, decoupled from the UI and platform runtime. If we were to write unit tests that are targeting a Xamarin.Forms view specifically, or the targeted view model specifically requires a runtime component, the runtime and runtime features would need to be mocked because the application will not actually be executed on a mobile runtime, but rather on the .NET Core runtime. The `Xamarin.Forms.Mocks` package fills this gap by providing a mock runtime that the Xamarin.Forms views can initialize and test.

Fixtures and data-driven tests

As you might have noticed in the previous tests we implemented, one of the most time-consuming parts of writing a unit test is implementing the arrange portion of the implementation. In this portion, we are essentially setting up the system under test that will be used by the test target. In this setup, our goal is to bring the system to a known state so that the results can be compared with the expected results. This known state is also known as a **fixture**.

In this context, a fixture can be as simple as a mock container that contains the determinate set of components that defines the **System Under Test (SUT)**, or a factory that is driven with a predictable behavioral pattern.

For instance, if we were to create a SUT factory for our `ListItemViewModel` object, we can do so by registering the two dependencies with the fixture. Let's begin:

1. Start the implementation by initializing our fixture and adding `AutoMoqCustomization`:

    ```
    _fixture = new Fixture();
    _fixture.Customize(new AutoMoqCustomization());
    ```

2. Now, set up our mocks for the two service interfaces and freeze them (that is, register them so that they have a singleton life cycle):

    ```
    // Generating 9 random product items
    _expectedProductData = _fixture.CreateMany<Product>(9);

    _apiClientMock = _fixture.Freeze<Mock<IApiClient>>();
    _apiClientMock.Setup(service => service.RetrieveProductsAsync())
        .ReturnsAsync(_expectedProductData);
    ```

```
_navigationServiceMock = _fixture.
Freeze<Mock<INavigationService>>();
_navigationServiceMock.Setup(nav => nav.
NavigateToViewModel(It.IsAny<BaseBindableObject>()))
    .ReturnsAsync(true);
```

3. Now that the mocks have been set up, let's take a look at the Arrange block of our navigation test:

```
#region Arrange

var listViewModel = _fixture.Create<ListItemViewModel>();
var expectedItemViewModel = _fixture.
Create<ItemViewModel>();

#endregion
```

As we can see, mock interface injection is already taken care of by `AutoMoqCustomization`, and the registered frozen specimens are used for the instances.

However, what if the data object we were using to execute the test target actually affected the outcome so much that we were to need an additional test case? For instance, the navigation method could have two different routes, depending on the data contained in the view-model:

```
if (viewModel.IsReleased)
{
    if (await _navigationService.
NavigateToViewModel(viewModel))
    {
        return;
    }
}
else
{
    await _navigationService.ShowMessage("The product has not been released yet");
    return;
}
```

In this case, we will need at least two states of the `ItemViewModel` object (that is, released and not). The easiest way to achieve this is to use inline data rather than the fixture, using the provided inline data attributes:

```
[Trait("Category", "ViewModelTests")]
[Trait("ViewModel", "ListViewModel")]
[Theory(DisplayName = "Verify ListViewModel navigates on ItemTapped")]
[InlineData(true, "Navigate")]
[InlineData(false, "Message")]
public async Task ListItemViewModel_ItemTapped_
ShouldNavigateToItemViewModel(
        bool released,
        string expectedAction)
```

4. Using the inline feed of data, create a composer that will create the `ItemViewModel` data items using the inline data feed:

```
var expectedItemComposer = _fixture.
Build<ItemViewModel>()
    .With(item => item.IsReleased, released);
var expectedItemViewModel = expectedItemComposer.
Create();
```

5. Now, just make sure you verify that the correct `navigationService` method is executed:

```
if (expectedAction == "Navigate")
{
    _navigationServiceMock.Verify(
        service => service.NavigateToViewModel(
            It.IsAny<ItemViewModel>()));
}
else
{
    _navigationServiceMock.Verify(service => service.
ShowMessage(It.IsAny<string>()));
}
```

This way, both outcomes of the `ItemTapped` command are, in fact, covered by unit tests.

As we saw in the AAA description, unit tests are only about setting up a unit for testing it with all its dependencies isolated, executing the unit, and then verifying its outcome. Even though it might look like overhead for fast-paced projects, unit tests coupled with mocks and fixtures can provide a valuable foundation to lean on. Unit tests make up the first line of defense for isolated modules. Nevertheless, without checking how these modules work together, we would just be creating silos within our application. The next section provides insights into integration testing.

Maintaining cross-module integrity with integration tests

Most of the time, when we are dealing with a mobile application, there are multiple platforms involved, such as the client app itself, maybe local storage on the client application, and multiple server components. These components may very well be implemented in the most robust fashion and have deep code coverage with unit tests. Nevertheless, if the components cannot work together, then the effort that's put into individual components will be in vain.

To make sure that two or more components work well together, the developers can implement end-to-end or integration tests. While end-to-end scenarios are generally covered by automated UI tests, integration tests are implemented as a pair of permutations of the target system. In other words, we isolate two systems that depend on one another (for example, a mobile application and the web API facade) and prepare a fixture that will prepare the rest of the components so that they're in a known state. Once the fixture is ready for the integration pair, the implementation of integration tests is no different than it is for unit tests.

To demonstrate the value of integration tests, let's take a look at a couple of examples.

Testing client-server communication

Let's assume that we have a suite of unit tests for testing the view models of our client app. We have also implemented unit tests that control the integrity of the `IApiClient` implementation, which is our main line of communication with the service layer. In the first suite, we will be mocking `IApiClient`, while in the latter suite, we will be mocking the HTTP client. In these two suites, we have covered all the tiers, from the core logic implementation down until the request is sent over the transport layer.

At this point, the next order of business is to write integration tests that will use the actual implementation of `IApiClient`, which will send service requests to the service API facade (also known as the gateway). However, we cannot really use the actual gateway deployment since multiple modules on the server side would be involved in this communication, and the system under test would be too unpredictable.

In this scenario, we have two options:

1. Create a fixture controller that will maintain the database and other moving parts involved in a known state (for example, a pre-test execution that will clean a sample database and insert the required data to be retrieved from it).
2. Create a rigged deployment of the complete gateway, possibly with mocked modules as dependencies, and execute the integration tests on this system.

For the sake of simplicity, let's go with the first option and assume we have a completely empty document collection deployed to run the integration tests. In this case, we can adapt our fixture to register a set of products in a predetermined document collection (that is, the one that the server side is expecting to find), execute our retrieve calls from the application client, and clean up the database.

We will start by implementing our custom fixture:

```
public class DataIntegrationFixture : Fixture
{
    public async Task RegisterProducts(IEnumerable<Product> products)
    {
        var dbRepository = this.Create<IRepository<Product, string>>();
        foreach (var product in products)
        {
            await dbRepository.AddItemAsync(product);
        }
        this.Register(() => products);
    }

    public async Task Reset()
    {
        var dbRepository = this.Create<IRepository<Product, string>>();
```

```
            var items = this.Create<IEnumerable<Product>>();
            foreach (var product in items)
            {
                await dbRepository.DeleteItemAsync(product.Id);
            }
        }
    }
```

We have two initial methods, `RegisterProducts` and `Reset`:

- `RegisterProducts` is used for inserting the testing data and registering the product data within the fixture.
- `Reset` is used to clear the inserted test data. This way, the test execution will yield the same results – at the database level, at least. In other words, the execution of the tests will be idempotent.

Note that the repository is created using the `Create` method so that we can delegate the responsibility of injecting the correct repository client to the test schedule.

Now, let's start working on our tests:

1. Start by creating the test initialization (that is, the constructor in xUnit) and test teardown (that is, the `Dispose` method in xUnit).

2. In the constructor, register the repository client implementation that the fixture will be using and register the products using this client:

```
public ClientIntegrationTests()
{
    _fixture.Register<IRepository<Product, string>>(() => _repository);
    var products = _fixture.Build<Product>().With(item => item.Id, string.Empty).CreateMany(9);
    _fixture.RegisterProducts(products).Wait();
}
```

3. Next, implement the `Dispose` method of the `IDisposable` interface. This will be our test teardown function:

```
public void Dispose()
{
    _fixture.Reset().Wait();
}
```

4. Now that we have set up our initialization and teardown procedures, we can implement our first test:

```
[Fact(DisplayName = "Api Client Should Retrieve All Products")]
[Trait("Category", "Integration")]
public async Task ApiClient_GetProducts_RetrieveAll()
{
    #region Arrange
    var expectedCollection = _fixture.Create<IEnumerable<Product>>();
    #endregion

    #region Act
    var apiClient = new ApiClient();
    var actualResultSet = await apiClient.RetrieveProductsAsync();
    #endregion

    #region Assert
    actualResultSet.Should().HaveCount(expectedCollection.Count());
    #endregion
}
```

Similar tests can be implemented to test the interaction between the server and the database or other components of the system. The key is to control the modules that are not under test and make sure the tests are executed for the target interaction.

Implementing platform tests

As we mentioned earlier, integration tests don't necessarily need to be the assertion of two separate runtimes interacting with each other. They can also be used to test two distinct modules of an application in a controlled environment. For instance, when dealing with mobile applications, certain features are implemented that require interaction with the mobile platform (for example, the local storage API implementation would use the native platform filesystem; even the core SQLite implementation is abstracted to .NET Core).

For integration tests that must be executed on a specific mobile platform (such as iOS, Android, and UWP), the Devices.xUnit framework can be used. The Devices.xUnit framework is managed by the .NET Foundation. The multi-project template that's included as part of the SDK creates test harness projects for the target platform and the library projects. Once the execution starts, the tests are executed on the test harness application providing the real or emulated target platform, hence allowing the developers to execute integration tests on platform-specific features.

Whether you are testing integration health between modules or integration with external services, integration testing is an invaluable member of the delivery pipeline. In this section, we worked out a sample testing scenario where an API client is retrieving data from a remote service that has a predetermined set of data controlled by the unit test fixture. While this implementation can be construed as a system test rather than integration, the complete system tests would refer to a testing infrastructure that would execute tests on a mobile device without isolating any dependency. For mobile platforms, automated UI testing can fill this gap.

Automated UI tests

Arguably one of the most painstaking and costly stages of the development cycle is manual certification testing, also called acceptance testing. In a typical non-automated verification cycle, certification testing can take up to 2-3 times longer than developing a certain feature. Additionally, if previously implemented features are at risk, regression in those areas would have to be executed. In order to increase the release cadence and decrease the development cycles, it is essential that automated UI (or end-to-end) tests are implemented. This way, the automated pipeline can be verified once and reused to verify the application's UI and integration with other systems, rather than us executing manual testing in each release cycle.

App Center allows us to execute these automated tests on several real devices and includes automated runs in the development pipeline:

Figure 16.4 – App Center Test Results View

Xamarin.UITests is one of the supported automation frameworks that can be used to create these automated acceptance tests.

Xamarin.UITests

Xamarin.UITests is an automated UI test framework that integrates tightly with Xamarin target platforms. In addition to applications that have been created using the Xamarin framework, it can also be used to create automated tests for mobile applications created with Java and Objective-C/Swift. NUnit is used together with the automation framework to execute assertions and create test fixtures.

The framework allows developers to interact with mobile platforms using queries and actions. A query can be described as a `select` command that is executed on the current instance of an `IApp` interface, whereas the actions are user interactions that are simulated with the selected elements (that is, as a result of the query). The `IApp` interface, which makes this interaction possible, provides the required abstraction among the target platforms and facilitates user interaction with them.

You can initialize the implementation of the `IApp` interface (in other words, the simulated interaction platform) in various ways, depending on the target device and platform.

Here are some examples:

- Initializing the app using an iOS app bundle can be done as follows:

  ```
  IApp app = ConfigureApp .iOS .AppBundle("/path/to/iosapp.
  app") .StartApp();
  ```

- Initializing it to be run on an iOS simulator with an already-installed application can be done as follows:

  ```
  IApp app = ConfigureApp.iOS
      .DeviceIdentifier("ABF03EF2-64FF-4206-899E-
  FB945ACEA4F2").StartApp();
  ```

- Initializing it for an Android device that is currently connected to ADB can be done as follows:

  ```
  IApp app = ConfigureApp.Android.ApkFile("/path/to/
  android.apk")
       .DeviceSerial("03f80ddae07844d3") .StartApp();
  ```

Once the IApp instance has been initialized, the simulated user interaction can be executed with the aforementioned queries and actions.

Queries can be written using the various available selectors. The most prominent queries are as follows:

1. **Marked**: This refers to x:Name of a Xamarin.Forms element, or an element with the given AutomationId object. This is done in a similar fashion for native UI implementations, with AccessibilityIdentifies or AccessibilityLabel on iOS and a view's Id, ContentDescription, and Text on Android are used for this query.
2. **Class**: This queries the current UI for a specified class name. It's generally used with nameof(MyClass).
3. **Id**: This refers to the Id part of the element that we are trying to locate.
4. **Text**: This is any element that contains the given text.

For instance, if we were looking to tap on an element marked as ProductsView and select the first child in this list, we'd use the following code:

```
app.Tap(c => c.Marked("ProductsView").Class("ProductItemCell").
Index(0));
```

It is important to note the fluent execution style of the queries, where each query returns an `AppQuery` object, whereas the app actions use a `Func<AppQuery, AppQuery>` delegate.

The easiest way to create structured queries for a certain view is to use the **Read-Eval-Print-Loop** (**REPL**) provided by the Xamarin.UITests framework. To start the REPL, you can make use of the associated `IApp` method:

```
app.Repl();
```

Once the REPL has been initialized on the Terminal session, the `tree` command can provide the complete view tree. You can also execute app queries and actions using the same `IApp` instance:

```
App has been initialized to the 'app' variable.
Exit REPL with ctrl-c or see help for more commands.

>>> tree
[UIWindow > UILayoutContainerView]
    [UINavigationTransitionView > ... > UIView]
        [UITextView] id: "CreditCardTextField"
            [_UITextContainerView]
        [UIButton] id: "ValidateButton"
            [UIButtonLabel] text: "Validate Credit Card"
        [UILabel] id: "ErrorrMessagesTestField"
    [UINavigationBar] id: "Credit Card Validation"
        [_UINavigationBarBackground]
            [_UIBackdropView > _UIBackdropEffectView]
            [UIImageView]
        [UINavigationItemView]
            [UILabel] text: "Credit Card Validation"
>>>
```

The actions differ, depending on the selected view element, but the most commonly used actions are as follows:

1. `Tap`: This is used for simulating the user tap gesture.
2. `EnterText`: This enters the text in the selected view. It is important to note that, on iOS, a soft keyboard is used to enter text, while on Android, data is directly passed onto the target view. This might cause issues when you're interacting with elements that are hidden under or offset by the keyboard.
3. `WaitForElement`: This waits for the element defined by the query to appear on the screen. At times, with a shorter timeout period, this method can be used as part of the assertion of the element.
4. `Screenshot`: This takes a screenshot with the given title. This represents a step in the App Center's execution.

Page Object Pattern

Implementing UI tests within a certain test method can become quite tedious. The automation platform's queries and actions would, in fact, become closely coupled and unmaintainable. To avoid such scenarios, it is advised to use the **Page Object Pattern** (**POP**).

In POP, each view or distinct view element on the screen implements its own page class, which implements the interaction with that specific page, as well as the selectors for the view components within that page. These interactions are implemented in a simplified, lexical manner so that the complex automation implementation behind the scenes is not reflected in the actual test implementation. In addition, for interactions and queries, the page object is also responsible for providing a method of navigation to and from another page.

Let's learn how to implement our POP structure:

1. Let's start by creating our `BasePage` object:

    ```
    public abstract class BasePage<TPage> where TPage :
    BasePage<TPage>
    {
        protected abstract PlatformQuery Trait { get; }

        public abstract TPage NavigateToPage();
    ```

```csharp
        internal abstract Dictionary<string, Func<AppQuery,
AppQuery>>
        Selectors { get; set;}

        protected BasePage() {}

        // ,..
        // Additional Utility Methods for ease of execution
}
```

The base class dictates that each implementation should implement a `Trait` object that defines the page itself (to verify that the application has navigated to the target view) and a navigation method that will take the user (from the home screen) to the implementing view.

2. Now, let's implement a page object for the `About` view:

```csharp
    public class AboutPage : BasePage<AboutPage>
    {
        public AboutPage()
        {
            Selectors = new Dictionary<string, Func<AppQuery,
AppQuery>>()

            Selectors.Add("SettingsMenuItem", x =>
            x.Marked("Settings"));
            Selectors.Add("SettingsMenu", x =>
            x.Marked("CategoryView"));
            Selectors.Add("AboutPageMenuItem", x =>
            x.Marked("Information"));
            Selectors.Add("Title", x => x.Marked("Title"));
            Selectors.Add("Version", x =>
x.Marked("Version"));
            Selectors.Add("PrivacyPolicyLink", x =>
            x.Marked("PrivacyPolicyLink"));
            Selectors.Add("TermsOfUseLink", x =>
            x.Marked("TermsOfUseLink"));
            Selectors.Add("Copyright", x =>
```

```csharp
        x.Marked("Copyright");
    }

    internal override Dictionary<string, Func<AppQuery, AppQuery>>
        Selectors { get; set;}

    protected override PlatformQuery Trait => new PlatformQuery
    {
        Android = x => x.Marked("AboutPage"),
        iOS = x => x.Marked("AboutPage")
    };

    public override AboutPage NavigateToPage()
    {
        // Method implemented in the base page using the App
        OpenMainMenu();

        App.WaitForElement(Selectors["SettingsMenuItem"],
            "Timed out waiting for 'Settings' menu item");

        App.Tap(Selectors["SettingsMenuItem"]);
        App.WaitForElement(Selectors["SettingsMenuItem"],
            "Timed out waiting for 'Settings' menu");

        App.Screenshot("Settings menu appears.");

        App.Tap(Selectors["AboutPageMenuItem"]);

        if(!App.Query(Trait).Any())
        {
            throw new Exception("Navigation Failed");
        }
```

```
            App.Screenshot("About page appears.");

            return this;
        }

        public AboutPage TapOnTermsOfUseLink()
        {
            App.WaitForElement(Selectors["TermsOfUseLink"],
                "Timed out waiting for 'Terms Of Use' link");

            App.Tap(Selectors["TermsOfUseLink"]);
            App.Screenshot("Terms of use link tapped");

            return this;
        }
    }
```

So, now, using the `AboutPage` implementation and executing actions on `AboutPage` is as easy as initializing the `Page` class and navigating to it:

```
new AboutPage()
    .NavigateToPage()
    .TapOnTermsOfUseLink()
```

The community is divided on including the assertions within the page itself, or simply exposing the selectors so that the assertions are implemented as part of the tests. Either way, implementing POP helps developers and QA teams create easily maintainable tests in a short amount of time with ease.

Summary

In this chapter, we looked at various testing strategies for automating the testing and verification process. Creating automated tests helps us control the technical debt that's created throughout the development life cycle and keeps the source code in check, hence increasing the quality of the code and the pipeline itself. As you have seen, some of these tests are as simple as unit tests that are implemented at the beginning of the application life cycle and executed almost at every code checkpoint, while some are elaborate, such as the integration and coded UI tests, which are generally written at the end of the development stage and executed only at certain checkpoints (that is, nightly builds or prerelease checks). Regardless, the goal should always be to create a certifiable pipeline for code rather than to create code for certification.

With the testing covered, we can say that the continuous integration part of our delivery pipeline is covered. Next, we will be moving on to the continuous delivery phase, where we will focus on infrastructure as code by means of using Azure Resource Manager to manage the desired state.

17
Deploying Azure Modules

Azure services are bundled into so-called resource groups for easy management and deployment. Each resource group can be represented by an **Azure Resource Manager** (**ARM**) template, which, in turn, can be used for multiple configurations and specific environment deployments. In this chapter, we will be configuring the ARM template for Azure-hosted web services, as well as other cloud resources (such as Cosmos DB, Notification Hubs, and others) that we have used previously so that we can create deployments using the Azure DevOps build-and-release pipeline. Introducing configuration values into the templates and preparing them to create staging environments is our main focus in this chapter.

The following sections will take you through the creation of a parameterized, environment-specific resource group template:

- Creating an ARM template
- ARM template concepts
- Using Azure DevOps for ARM templates
- Deploying .NET Core applications

By the end of this chapter, you will have a deeper understanding of ARM templates and will be able to create resource group templates and deploy them through Azure DevOps pipelines, in other words, managing your infrastructure as code.

Creating an ARM template

In this section, we will be discussing how you can manage your Azure infrastructure as code and create reusable templates to manage and recreate your cloud environment.

One of the cornerstones of the modern DevOps approach is the ability to manage and provision the infrastructure for a distributed application with a declarative or even procedural set of definition files that can be versioned and stored together with the application source code. In this **Infrastructure-as-Code** (**IaC**) approach, these files should be created in such a way that whatever the current state of the infrastructure, executing these resources should always lead to the same desired state (that is, idempotency).

In the Azure stack, the infrastructure resources created within a subscription are managed by a service called ARM. **Azure Resource Manager** (**ARM**) provides a consistent management tier that allows developers to interact with it to execute infrastructure configuration tasks using Azure PowerShell, the Azure portal, and the available REST API. Semantically speaking, ARM provides the bridge between numerous resources providers and developer subscriptions.

The resources that we manage using ARM are grouped using resource groups, which are logical sets for identifying application affinity groups. ARM templates, which define the set of resources in a resource group, are declarative definitions of this infrastructure as well as configurations that can be used for provisioning the application environment.

Creating an ARM template 485

If we go back to our application and take a look at the resource group we have been using for this application, you can see the various types of Azure resources that were introduced in previous chapters:

NAME	TYPE	LOCATION
documentdb	API Connection	North Europe
outlook	API Connection	North Central US
HandsOnCrossFunctions	App Service	Central US
NetCoreUserApi-Dev	App Service	Central US
NetCoreWebUsersApi20190330084814Plan	App Service plan	Central US
HandsOn.Azure.Service	Application Insights	East US
XamarinTelemetry	Application Insights	East US
handsoncore	Azure Cache for Redis	Central US
handsoncrossplatform	Azure Cosmos DB account	West Europe
EmailProcessor	Logic app	North Europe
handsoncrossstorage	Storage account	North Europe

Figure 17.1 – Azure Resource Group

While all of these resources could be created using a set of Azure PowerShell or CLI scripts, it would be quite difficult to maintain them without compromising the idempotency of these scripts.

Fortunately, we can export this resource group as an ARM template and manage our infrastructure using the generated JSON manifest and environment-specific configuration parameters. In order to create the initial ARM template, execute the following steps:

1. Navigate to the target resource group and select the **Export template** blade on the Azure portal:

Figure 17.2 – : Export Azure Resource Group Template

2. Once the resource group template is created, head back to Visual Studio and create an Azure Resource Group project and paste the exported template. When prompted to select an Azure template, select the **Blank Template** option to create an empty template.

> **Important note**
> It is important to understand that the templates can be created using the schema provided. Exporting the template does produce quite a number of redundant parameters and resource attributes that would not occur if the template was created manually, or if we used a base template available on GitHub.

When the blank ARM template is created, it has the following schema, which defines the main outline of an ARM template:

```
{
    "$schema": "https://schema.management.azure.com/schemas/2015-01-01/deploymentTemplate.json#",
    "contentVersion": "1.0.0.0",
    "parameters": {},
    "variables": {},
    "resources": [],
    "outputs": {}
}
```

In this schema, while the parameters and outputs define the input and output parameters of the Azure deployment, the variables define the static data that we will be constructing and referencing throughout the deployment template. Finally, the resources array will be used to define the various Azure resources that will be included in our resource group.

> **Important note**
> While dealing with ARM templates, Visual Studio provides the JSON outline view, which can help in navigating through the sections of the template, as well as in adding and removing new resources.

3. Without further ado, let's start by copying our first resource from the exported template into our Visual Studio project. We will start by importing the Redis cache resource:

```
{
    "type": "Microsoft.Cache/Redis",
    "apiVersion": "2017-10-01",
    "name": "[parameters('Redis_handsoncore_name')]",
    "location": "Central US",
    "properties": {
        "sku": {
            "name": "Basic",
            "family": "C",
            "capacity": 0
        },
```

```json
            "enableNonSslPort": false,
            "redisConfiguration": {
                "maxclients": "256",
                "maxmemory-reserved": "2",
                "maxfragmentationmemory-reserved": "12",
                "maxmemory-delta": "2"
            }
        }
    }
```

In this resource, the `name` attribute is referencing a parameter called the `Redis_handsoncore_name` parameter, which we will need to add to the parameters section. Aside from the name, some basic resource metadata is defined, such as `apiVersion`, `type`, and `location`. Additionally, resource-specific configuration values are defined in the `properties` attribute.

4. Let's continue by adding the parameter to the parameters section, with a number of modifications:

```json
"resourceNameCache": {
    "defaultValue": "handsoncore",
    "type": "string",
    "minLength": 5,
    "maxLength": 18,
    "metadata": {
        "description": "Used as the resource name for Redis cache resource"
    }
}
```

We have added the metadata, which, in a certain sense, helps us to document the resource template so that it is more maintainable. In addition to the metadata, we have defined the `minLength` and `maxLength` attributes so that the parameter value has some validation (if we decide to use a generated or calculated value). Additionally, for a string type parameter, we could have defined allowable values.

5. Finally, let's add an output parameter that outputs the Redis resource connection string as an output parameter:

```json
"redisConnectionString": {
    "type": "string",
```

```
      "value": "[concat(parameters('resourceNameCache'),
  '.redis.cache.windows.
  net:6380,abortConnect=false,ssl=true,password=',
  listKeys(resourceId('Microsoft.Cache/Redis',
  parameters('resourceNameCache')), '2017-10-01').
  primaryKey)]"
    }
```

Here, we are creating the Redis connection string using an input parameter, as well as a reference to an attribute of the given resource (that is, the primary access key of the Redis cache instance). We will take a closer look at ARM functions and references in the next section.

6. Now that our basic template for the resource group (that is, only the partial implementation that includes the Redis cache resource) is ready, start by deploying the template using Visual Studio.

7. After you create a new deployment profile and designate the target subscription and resource group, edit the parameters, and see how the parameter metadata that we have added reflects on the user interface:

Figure 17.3 – Resource Group Template Parameters

8. Once the deployment is complete, you can see the output parameters on the deployment details:

```
09:27:19 - DeploymentName  : azuredeploy-0421-0713
09:27:19 - CorrelationId   : 4ec72df5-00d3-4194-9181-
161a5967235b
09:27:19 - ResourceGroupName : NetCore.Web
09:27:19 - ProvisioningState : Succeeded
```

```
09:27:19 - Timestamp : 4/21/2019 7:27:20 AM
09:27:19 - Mode : Incremental
09:27:19 - TemplateLink :
09:27:19 - TemplateLinkString :
09:27:19 - DeploymentDebugLogLevel :
09:27:19 - Parameters : {[resourceNameCache,
09:27:19 -        Microsoft.Azure.Commands.
ResourceManager.Cmdlets.SdkModels.DeploymentVariable]}
09:27:19 - ParametersString :
09:27:19 - Name              Type
Value
09:27:19 - ===============   ==========================
==========
09:27:19 - resourceNameCache   String
handsoncore123
09:27:19 -
09:27:19 - Outputs : {[redisConnectionString,
09:27:19 -     Microsoft.Azure.Commands.ResourceManager.
Cmdlets.SdkModels.DeploymentVariable]} 09:27:19 -
OutputsString :
09:27:19 - Name              Type
Value
09:27:19 - ===============   ==========================
==========
09:27:19 - redisConnectionString String
handsoncore123.redis.cache.windows.net:6380
09:27:19 -
,abortConnect=false,ssl=true,password=JN6*******kg=
09:27:19 -
09:27:20 -
09:27:20 - Successfully deployed template 'azuredeploy.
json' to resource group 'NetCore.Web'.
```

In template deployment, one of the key parameters is deployment mode. In the preceding example, we were using the default deployment mode, namely, `Incremental`. In this type of deployment, Azure resources that exist in the resource group but not in the template will not be removed from the resource group, and only the items in the template will be provisioned or updated, depending on their previous deployment state. The other deployment option available is so-called complete deployment mode. In this mode, any resource that exists in the resource group but not in the template is removed automatically.

> **Important note**
> The resources that exist in the template, but are not deployed because of a condition, will not be removed from the resource group.

We have now successfully created and deployed our resource group template using the template export feature of ARM. During this process, we have used several parameters and discussed the resource attributes. This type of creation could work for smaller infrastructure setups, however, as the number of resource groups increases, we would need to restructure our resource template using somewhat advanced concepts of the templates.

ARM template concepts

So, now that we have successfully deployed our first resource, let's continue with expanding our template to include other resources. In this section, we will take a look at dependent resources within the same template and how to use template functions to create configuration values for these resources.

In order to demonstrate the dependencies between resources, let's introduce next the app service instance, which will be hosting the user's API. Technically, this app service only has a single dependency — the app service plan — that will be hosting the app service (that is, the `ServerFarm` resource type):

```
{
    "type": "Microsoft.Web/serverfarms",
    "name": "[parameters('resourceNameServicePlan')]",
    "kind": "app",
    // removed for brevity
},
{
    "type": "Microsoft.Web/sites",
    "name": "[parameters('resourceNameUsersApi')]",
    "dependsOn": [
        "[resourceId('Microsoft.Web/serverfarms', parameters('resourceNameServicePlan'))]"
    ],
    "kind": "app",
    "properties": {
        "enabled": true,
        "serverFarmId": "[resourceId('Microsoft.Web/serverfarms', parameters('resourceNameServicePlan'))]",
        // removed for brevity
    }
}
```

In this setup, the `sites` resource has a dependency on the `serverfarms` resource type (that is, the deployment order will be evaluated depending on these dependencies). Once the `serverfarms` resource is deployed, the `resourceId` function of the created resource is going to be used as the `serverFarmId` for the `sites` resource.

Additionally, the user's API, from an architectural perspective, has two main dependencies: Redis Cache and Cosmos DB. The resultant resource instances should produce values that should be added to the application configuration of the app service (that is, connection strings).

Since we have already created an output parameter for the Redis Cache instance, create a dependency and add the connection string.

The connection string can be added as part of the `siteConfig` attribute of a `sites` resource or by creating an additional resource specifically for the site configuration:

```
"properties": {
    "enabled": true,
    // removed for brevity
    "siteConfig": {
        "connectionStrings": [ {
            "name": "AzureRedisCache",
            "type": "custom",
            "connectionString":
"[concat(parameters('resourceNameCache'), '.redis.cache.
windows.net:6380,abortConnect=false,ssl=true,password=',
listKeys(resourceId('Microsoft.Cache/Redis',
parameters('resourceNameCache')), '2017-10-01').primaryKey)]"
        } ]
    }
}
```

Now, when the site is deployed, the Redis cache connection string is automatically added to the site configuration:

Connection strings

Name	Value	Type
AzureRedisCache	Hidden value. Click show values button above	Custom

Figure 17.4 – Connection strings

Notice that when preparing the connection string, we are making use of the `concat` function to compose the value, and we use the `listKeys` function to get a list of values from the resource instance that is retrieved according to type and name using the `resourceId` function.

These functions and other user-defined functions can be used throughout the resource template, either while constructing reference values or defining conditions. Some of these functions according to the parameter type are listed here:

String	base64, base64ToJson, base64ToString, concat, contains, dataUri, dataUriToString, empty, endsWith, first, format, guid, indexOf, last, lastIndexOf, length, newGuid, padLeft, replace, skip, split, startsWith, string, substring, take, toLower, toUpper, trim, uniqueString, uri, uriComponent, uriComponentToString, utcNow
Array	array, coalesce, concat, contains, createArray, empty, first, intersection, json, last, length, max, min, range, skip, take, union
Comparison	equals, greater, greaterOrEquals, less, lessOrEquals
Deployment	deployment, parameters, variables
Logical	and, bool, if, not, or
Numeric	add, copyIndex, div, float, int, max, min, mod, mul, sub
Resource	listAccountSas, listKeys, listSecrets, list*, providers, reference, resourceGroup, resourceId, subscription

Figure 17.5 – Azure Template Functions

Using these functions, complex variables can be constructed and reused using parameters and references to other deployed resources. These constructs can then be exposed as functions so that they can be reused throughout the template declarations.

As you may have noticed, every time we deploy the ARM template, according to the parameters we define, the `azuredeploy.parameters.json` file is updated. These are the parameters that are provided to the template, and in a multi-stage environment (that is, DEV, QA, UAT, PROD), you would expect to have multiple parameters' files assigning environment-specific values to these resources:

```
{
    "$schema": "https://schema.management.azure.com/schemas/2015-01-01/deploymentParameters.json#",
    "contentVersion": "1.0.0.0",
    "parameters": {
        "environment": { "value": "DEV" },
        "resourceNameCache": { "value": "dev-handsoncoreCache" },
        "resourceNameServicePlan": { "value": "dev-handsoncorePlan" },
        "resourceNameUsersApi": { "value": "dev-
```

```
handsoncoreusers" }
    }
}
```

With multiple parameters' files, unique resource names and addresses can be constructed so that during deployment, duplicate resource declarations can be avoided. Another method that is generally used to avoid resource name/address clashes is to include the current resource group identifier as part of the resource names, making sure that the resources are specific and unique.

In this section, we expanded our template with an app service, and created a configuration value for the app service using the template functions so that it can utilize the Redis cache instance that is included in the same template. We finally converted our template to be environment dependent so we can manage multiple environments with the same resource template, ensuring that the infrastructure is consistent across these environments.

Using Azure DevOps for ARM templates

Once the template is ready and we are sure that all Azure resources that are required by our application are created, we can continue with setting up automated builds and deployments. In this section, we will be creating a release pipeline on Azure DevOps to deploy our infrastructure.

In order to be able to use Azure DevOps for cloud deployments, our first action will be to create a service principal that will be used to deploy the resources. A service principal can be described as a service identity that has access to Azure resources within a certain subscription and/or resource group.

496　Deploying Azure Modules

So, let's begin:

1. Create a service principal by adding a new ARM service connection within the Azure DevOps project settings:

Figure 17.6 – Azure Resource Manager Service Connection

Creating the connection will create an application registration for Azure DevOps and assign this service principal the contributor role on the selected subscription.

2. Another way to do this is by using the **Authorize** button when creating an **Azure Deployment** task. The **Authorize** button becomes available if an Azure subscription is selected, instead of a service principal:

Figure 17.7 – Azure Resource Group Deployment with Subscription

3. Once the service principal is created, continue with setting up the deployment for the resource group.

   Azure DevOps offers multiple deployment options for deploying Azure Resource Group templates, such as the following:

   a) **Azure PowerShell**: To execute inline or referenced Azure PowerShell scripts

   b) **Azure CLI**: To execute inline or referenced Azure CLI scripts

   c) **Azure Resource Group Deployment**: To deploy ARM templates with associated parameters

   For this example, we will be using the **Azure Resource Group Deployment** task:

Figure 17.8 – Azure Resource Group Deployment Task

4. For this task, other than the service principal settings, the **Template** section provides the main configuration area. Here, select the ARM template and provide the parameters file designated for this environment:

Figure 17.9 – ARM Template Parameters

5. Additionally, define configuration values such as deployment name and deployment outputs.

> **Important note**
> The **Azure Resource Group Deployment** task allows the selection of three deployment modes. In addition to the Azure deployment modes (that is, complete, and incremental), the **Validate** option provides the ability only to validate the template. The **Validate** option can be used to validate pull requests and can only execute during continuous integration builds.

Now, the ARM deployment can be triggered whenever an update is merged into the master branch that keeps the development (or higher) environment up to date with the ARM template definition:

Figure 17.10 – ARM Deployment pipeline

So far, we have created a resource template that defines the desired state for our infrastructure. We then created an Azure DevOps pipeline that will be deploying this infrastructure to a designated resource group. The next step for us is to expand our release pipeline to include the deployment of the actual application so that we have a fully automated pipeline that can create the application as well as the host infrastructure from scratch.

Deploying .NET Core applications

Once the ARM template is deployed and the Azure resources are created, our next step is to deploy .NET Core applications (that is, microservice applications as well as our functions app).

Azure DevOps provides all the necessary tasks to build and create the deployment package for an app service/web app. The trifecta of creating a .NET Core web deployment package is composed of restore, build, and publish. All these dotnet CLI commands can be executed using the built-in tasks within the build-and-release pipeline. So, let's begin:

1. We will start by restoring the NuGet packages for our user's API microservice:

Figure 17.11 – DotNet Restore Task

2. The next step is to build the application using a specific build configuration (a pipeline variable can be used for this):

Figure 17.12 – DotNet Build Task

3. After the project is built, prepare the web deployment package to be able to push it to the app service resource that was created in the ARM deployment step. In order to prepare the deployment package, we will use the **publish** command:

Figure 17.13 – DotNet Publish Task

4. Finally, as regards deployment, make use of the **Azure App Service Deploy** task:

Figure 17.14 – Azure App Service Deploy Task

In the deployment step, it is imperative that the package or folder parameter matches the folder that was used as the output directory in the publishing step (that is, `$(build.artifactstagingdirectory)`).

In the last task, we have used a hardcoded name for the app service name parameter. This means that each time the ARM parameter file is modified, we need to update the build definition, or, if we were using a YAML file for the build definition, the YAML definition. This could prove to be a maintenance nightmare, since every time a new environment is created, the build-and-release definitions would need to be updated.

One possible solution to integrating the ARM deployment with the actual application deployment would be to output the target application name from the ARM template and use it as the app service's name parameter:

```
"outputs": {
    "redisConnectionString": { //... },
    "userApiAppResource": {
        "type": "string",
        "value": "[parameters('resourceNameUsersApi')]"
    }
}
```

5. Next, assign the output from the ARM deployment to a variable named `armOutputVariables`, using the **Deployment outputs** option from the **Azure Resource Group Deployment** task:

Figure 17.15 – Deployment Outputs Parameter

6. Now, add a PowerShell script task (that is, not Azure PowerShell) to parse the output into JSON format and assign the required app service name to a pipeline variable:

```
$outputs = ConvertFrom-Json $($env:armOutputVariables)

Write-Host "##vso[task.setvariable
variable=UsersApiAppService]$($outputs.
userApiAppResource.value)"
```

7. At this point, the app service resource name can be accessed like other pipeline variables (that is, with `$(UsersApiAppService)`) and can be assigned to the **Azure App Service Deploy** step.

The rest of the build templates can be created in the same manner, using the same or similar .NET Core and Azure tasks.

Summary

In this chapter, we have gone through the basic steps of creating an ARM template so that the cloud infrastructure required for our application can be provisioned and managed in line with IaC concepts. Having set up our cloud resources as a declarative JSON manifest, we can easily version and keep track of our environment(s) without environment drift and infrastructure-related deployment issues. The .NET Core build and publish steps that are part of the Azure DevOps services are then used to create the deployment artifacts, which seamlessly integrate with the Azure cloud infrastructure.

We have managed to prepare our build-and-release pipeline for one of the .NET Core services in this chapter. However, what we are actually after is to create the deployment artifacts during the continuous integration build and use a release pipeline to deploy the infrastructure, followed by deployment of the app service artifacts. We will create the release pipeline in the next chapter.

18
CI/CD with Azure DevOps

Continuous Integration (**CI**) and **Continuous Delivery** (**CD**) are two concepts that are deeply rooted in the Agile project life cycle definition. In the agile methodology, the DevOps effort is mostly spent on decreasing the CD cycle so that smaller sprints and smaller change sets can be periodically delivered to users. In return, the smaller the change, the smaller the risks, and the easier adoption will be for the users. In order to minimize the length of delivery cycles, an automated delivery pipeline is vital. Using the toolset provided with Azure DevOps, developers can create fully automated templates for builds, testing, and deployments. In this chapter, we will set up the build and release pipeline for Xamarin in line with the Azure deployment pipeline.

In this chapter, we will be mainly dealing with implementing a proper application life cycle and an automated delivery pipeline using the toolset provided by Azure DevOps. We will take a short look at CI/CD using Azure DevOps and how it is implemented using Git and GitFlow as the branching strategy. We will then move on to quality assurance of the delivered application using automated tools. Finally, we will be releasing application packages using release templates for the web backend as well as our mobile application. The following topics will guide you through these DevOps concepts:

- Introducing CI/CD
- CI/CD with GitFlow

- **Quality Assurance (QA)** of branches
- Creating and using release templates

By the end of this chapter, you will be able to set up a proper delivery pipeline for your web and mobile applications using the intrinsic toolset available on Azure DevOps.

Introducing CI/CD

Let's start the chapter with CI and CD pipelines. In this section, we will be focusing on understanding the foundational concepts for a properly set-up development and delivery pipeline.

In the previous chapters, we have set up various build definitions to create application binaries and packages that can be used as deployment artifacts. While preparing these artifacts, we implemented automated tests that can be included in automated build definitions. This process of automating the building and testing of code every time a team member introduces changes to version control is generally referred to as CI. CI, coupled with a mature version control system and a well-defined branching strategy, is the primary factor in encouraging developers to be bolder and more agile with their commits, contributing to a high release cadence.

On the other hand, CD is the (generally) automated process of building, testing, and configuring your application and finally deploying that specific version of your application to a staging environment. Multiple testing or staging environments are generally used, with the automated creation of infrastructure and deployment, right up until the production stage. In a healthy CD pipeline, the success of the sequential set of environments is measured by progressively longer-running activities of integration, load, and user acceptance testing. CI starts the CD process, and the pipeline stages each successive environment upon the successful completion of the previous round of tests.

In CD, a release definition is composed of a collection of environments. An environment is a logical container that represents where you want to deploy your application. Physically, an environment can refer to a cluster of servers, a resource group on cloud infrastructure, or a mobile application distribution ring. Each environment (sometimes referred to as stage) has its purpose, and a subset of the stakeholders from the development pipeline are assigned as owners for that specific environment:

Figure 18.1 – Application Development Life cycle

The configuration of the web services and mobile application for each environment could differ depending on the purpose of that specific environment. Nevertheless, it is important to keep in mind that the environments should, at any point in the CI/CD pipeline, host the same application release version and binaries. This way, we can make sure that, once the application is promoted to a higher environment (that is, closer to production), it will function as it did in the previous stage.

As you can see, in DevOps terms, deployment does not always mean release or production. As part of CD, various deployment pipelines are triggered by commits from the development team. If the committed code is verified by unit tests and integration builds, the artifacts from these branches are deployed to the staging environments. In staging environments, smoke and acceptance tests are executed. If the application integrity and new features are verified by these tests on various stages, the new release can be rolled out across the production environment.

In Azure DevOps terms, as you have seen from the previous examples, CI is implemented using Git and Azure DevOps Build templates. CD, on the other hand, is handled by release definitions using the build artifacts prepared with the triggered CI builds.

> **Important note**
> CI/CD pipelines can, in fact, be prepared to use TFVC and associated branching strategies; however, Git and its associated branching strategies such as GitFlow provide a more flexible and agile setup.

Using Azure DevOps, the transition between the environments (that is, the promotion process) can be controlled with pre-deployment and post-deployment gates. These gates can be set up to require approval from specific stakeholders in the development pipeline (for example, the environment owner). In addition to manual approval, remote services can be used for gate approvals. For instance, it is possible to synchronize the release of a module for an application with another dependent module or delay a deployment stage until certain tests are executed.

The examples provided here are only one of the possible designs, and the version control implementation, branching strategy, and the associated release pipeline setup should be designed and executed according to the needs of the development team and business requirements.

In our example application, for creating the pipeline, we will be using Git and GitFlow as our version control and branching strategy, respectively. For the release pipeline, we will create a development release that will be automatically deployed with each commit/merge to the development branch (that is, the next version), whereas QA, UAT, and production environments will be deployed from release branches (that is, the current version).

CI/CD with GitFlow

The easiest way to illustrate CI/CD would be to walk through the policies and procedures, starting with GitFlow. Here, we are dealing with two separate repositories, namely, web and application, and each of these repositories has its own life cycle.

In other words, while it is not advised, it is possible to have unsynchronized releases and versions of our web application (that is, the service infrastructure) and application (that is, mobile platform releases); hence, it is important to create backward-compatible modules and communicate releases to development team members.

The following subsections will illustrate a default development cycle and explain what the developers would generally need to do to maintain the quality of the application without jeopardizing the release cadence.

Development

Development of the application or web modules starts with the creation of a feature branch (for example, `feature/12345`). The feature branch can be shared between multiple developers or handled by a single developer. If the feature branch is being worked on by multiple developers, user branches can be created following a similar convention along the lines of `user/<user identifier>/<feature id>` (for example, `user/cbilgin/12345`). Once each developer is done with their implementation, a pull request can be executed on the main feature branch.

An important factor for determining the health of a feature branch is the commit differences between the development branch and the feature branch. Ideally, the feature branch should always be ahead of the development branch, regardless of the number of pull requests completed on the development branch while the feature branch is being worked on. In order to achieve this, the feature branch should be periodically rebased on the current development tree, retrieving the latest commits from other features.

The work done on a feature branch can be tested locally by developers through locally running the web application and running the mobile application on the desired emulator/simulator. While iOS and UWP simulators can use the localhost prefix, since the local machine network is shared by the simulator, Android emulators use their own NAT table, where localhost refers to the mobile device, not the host machine. In order to access a hosted web service on the host machine, you should use the `10.0.2.2` IP interface. The following table shows the different IP addresses and how they can be used in the context of an Android emulator:

Network address	Description
10.2.2.1	Router/gateway address
10.2.2.2	Special alias to your host loopback interface (that is, 127.0.0.1 on the host machine)
10.0.2.3	First DNS server
10.0.2.4-6	Optional additional DNS servers
10.0.2.15	The emulated device network/Ethernet interface
127.0.0.1	The emulated device loopback interface

Figure 18.2 – Android Emulator NAT

If the application and web services are handled on separate repositories with their own release cycles, the local web server instance should use the latest commit on the development (or master) branch, making sure that the development is done with the latest service infrastructure.

Once the feature is ready to be integrated into the next release, the developer is responsible for creating a pull request with the associated work item that this feature branch represents.

Pull request/merge

In an ideal setup, the only way a feature branch is merged into the development branch should be through a pull request. Pull requests are also used to execute quick sanity checks and code reviews.

The quality of the code that is delivered by the developers can be verified by the branch policies of the target branch (that is, the development branch). In this example, for the development branch, we will make use of four policies:

- **Work items to be attached to the pull request (feature and/or user story or bug)**: The tasks and user stories are generally attached to the commits within the feature branch. The feature, user story, and/or bug work items (these are parent work items to the tasks) have to be attached to the pull request so that, once the release pipeline is created, these work items can be determined from the release build.

- **Review by two team members**: To encourage the peer review process, a minimum of two team members are responsible for reviewing the pull request. One of these team members is generally the team lead, who is a mandatory reviewer of any pull request targeting either the development or release branches. Each reviewer is responsible for commenting the code changes, which are then corrected by the owner of the pull request.

- **Review by team lead (included in the minimum count)**: The architect or team lead is generally the person ultimately responsible for the quality of the code introduced into the development or release branches, so he/she is a mandatory reviewer for the pull requests.

- **Branch evaluation build**: For the mobile project, the branch evaluation build can be a build of the Android project (since Android builds can be executed on a Windows build agent, as opposed to the iOS builds having to be executed on a Mac agent). This build should execute the unit tests and run static code analysis using a platform such as SonarQube or NDepend.

CI/CD with GitFlow 511

> **Important note**
> In such a setup, it is wise to allow team leads or other accountable stakeholders to have override authority over the policies in cases of emergency, bypassing the evaluation build (rarely) and the review requirements (more common).

Using Azure DevOps, in order to set up policies and enforce developers to create pull requests, the target branch (that is, the development branch) should be configured with the following branch policies:

Figure 18.3 – Branch Policies

Any policy requirement on the target branch should enforce the use of pull requests when updating a branch.

Once the policy validations are satisfactory (that is, all required policies are met), the code is ready to be merged to the development branch. Azure DevOps allows the selection of a merge strategy during completion. This merge strategy should be in line with the branching strategy and design. In our example, we will be using Rebase; however, any of the other three merge options can be used:

Figure 18.4 – Merge Types

Once the pull request is merged into the development branch, the CI phase can commence, which will be covered in the next section.

The CI phase

Any update on a CI-enabled branch triggers the build(s) to build the application and/or web services package. For instance, for the mobile application development pipeline, multiple builds can be triggered for target mobile platforms with development stage configurations (for example, DevDroid and DeviOS configurations). These builds can prepare the application packages as build artifacts and publish them with the next application version and minor revision.

The trigger for the CI build can be set up in the build properties:

Figure 18.5 – Build Triggers

In addition to the triggering branch, path filters can be set so that, depending on the changes introduced to the application code base, different CI builds can be triggered and artifacts prepared.

Additionally, the CI build should execute any available unit tests, along with simple integration tests, that can be run on the build agent, and these results can be published with code coverage to the pipeline. Another round of static code analysis with the current artifact version annotation can be executed and published on the static analysis platform (for example, a SonarQube server). This would help to correlate the source code delta and possible issues occurring with this version of the application.

514 CI/CD with Azure DevOps

When the CI build is successfully completed, depending on trigger setup, a release pipeline can be created, deploying the prepared artifact(s) to the target environment (that is, the development environment in this case):

Figure 18.6 – Release Stage Artifact Trigger

This example deploys the microservice packages prepared by the CI build and deploys them to the development environment. The environment is updated by the **Azure Resource Manager** (**ARM**) deployment to target the resource group. It is common practice to have the development environment release setup without any pre-approval gate so that any code integrated into the development branch is automatically deployed to the development environment.

Azure DevOps offers two tasks to publish the build pipeline artifacts, and created artifacts can be used as the trigger or a secondary artifact for a release pipeline:

Figure 18.7 – Artifact Tasks

The general rule of thumb for artifact publishing is to use the staging directory for the build:

Figure 18.8 – Publish Pipeline Artifact Task

Before the artifact publishing task, for the web application, a .NET publishing task can be used with the same output directory. For the Xamarin packages, a copy task can be created, copying the application package(s) to the staging directory.

Artifacts from merged feature branches can already be deployed to a certain environment for verification or they can be included in a release scope to be verified as part of the release.

Release branch

Once the development branch is verified and the current feature set matches the predetermined release scope, a release branch is created (for example, release/1.8). The creation of the release branch goes hand in hand with the triggering of the release build that will prepare the complete set of artifacts required for the release of a certain environment. The associated release pipeline will, in turn, be triggered by the builds on this branch.

We should dedicate a paragraph here to Xamarin application packages because of the environment-specific configuration structure and multiple application artifacts. As previously mentioned, for a native app to support multiple configurations, we would need to create multiple application packages. If you consider a minimal support scenario, such as only supporting the iOS platform, in order to have QA, staging, and production environments in our release pipeline, we will need to have three separate application packages that are created from the same source code version. If we also want to support Android, this will mean for a single environment (for example, QA), we will need to deploy an IPA and an APK to Visual Studio App Center (two separate application rings) and verify these applications using the same web infrastructure. The synchronization of these builds and release stages should be carefully designed and executed. Multi-configuration builds for a single platform can be used in conjunction with multi-agent build templates to create a single artifact with multiple packages, so that the release pipeline is triggered only after all of the required builds are finalized.

Finally, the build template for the release artifacts can also be used to check the quality and process the scope introduced by the release to be created. Release pipelines also support the execution of automated tests so that the validation process can be automated within a release environment. For instance, after a certain service API package is deployed, it would be a good idea to execute functional tests against the deployment URL to verify the success of the deployment. In a similar fashion, before the application package is deployed to a certain App Center ring (for example, staging), Xamarin Test Cloud tests can be executed to verify the application features.

Hotfix branches

After the release pipeline is used to deploy the application to either the fast or slow ring (QA or UAT), depending on the testing agreement, the QA team can start testing the application.

At this phase, any bugs created or additional feature requests that are pulled into the current release scope should be introduced by the development team using hotfix branches. Hotfix branches originate from the current release branch and are merged back into the release branch (for example, `release/1.8 -> hotfix/12324 -> release/1.8`) with the user of pull requests. Once the hotfix is merged back into the release branch (that is, it has passed the validation), it will need to be merged back to the development branch as well to propagate the code changes and avoid regression in the following releases.

The merges and pull requests to the release branch follow a similar (although not identical) methodology as that in the development branch. This way, we can push the hotfix modifications through the same quality validation process.

Production

In the release pipeline, a certain version of the artifact(s) can be promoted from one environment to higher ones until the production release is complete and the new version of the application is delivered to the end users.

According to the pipeline design, the production environment can also utilize a staging or phased release strategy with release rings using deployment slots (that is, on Azure App Service), native staging with TestFlight (that is, for iOS applications), or even incremental releases, which both Apple and the Google Play Store support. This way, application telemetry from the release environments can be collected from beta users and introduced back into the development pipeline.

In this section, we started our analysis by talking about the "left side" of the delivery pipeline and looking at the pipeline from the development team's perspective: how the application source is created, reviewed, merged, and possibly delivered to a testing environment. We then talked about the release scope and delivery pipelines, in other words, moving toward the "right side" of the delivery pipeline. In this setup, we of course need verification and quality checks starting as early on the left side as possible so that we do not have bottlenecks in our pipeline. In the next section, we will be taking a look at these various quality verification checkpoints throughout this pipeline.

The QA process

In each phase of a CD process, the quality of the features should be verified preferably with an automated process or, at the very least, with proper code reviews. This is where the pull request creation and validation process become even more important. Nevertheless, as mentioned, the QA of an artifact or a branch is not limited to the CI phases of the process but runs throughout the CI/CD pipeline.

As you can see, we can have various quality checks for both the source code and the produced artifacts such as code reviews, automated tests, and even static code analysis for identifying both code smells and coding convention issues. Let's take a closer look at these QA steps.

Code review

A healthy development team should be driven by collaboration. In this context, the concept of peer review is extremely important, since it gives the chance for the development team to suggest and advise on improvements of a colleague's work. Azure DevOps has two branch policies that directly encourage or even enforce the peer review process. One of these policies is the minimum number of reviewers, and the second one is the automatic code reviewer policy:

Automatically include code reviewers
Include specific users or groups in the code review based on which files changed.

+ Add automatic reviewers

Reviewer(s)	Requirement	Path filter	
Can Bilgin	Required	**/Controllers/*	Enabled

Figure 18.9 – Code Review Policy

Using the Automatic Code Reviewer policy, multiple optional and/or mandatory reviewers can be automatically added to the pull request review process for different source paths.

This allows the developers to collaborate on the Azure DevOps web portal, creating comments on certain lines, sections, or even files from the commits included in the pull request.

The review process is not only limited to manual developers' feedback, but some partial automation can even be introduced. If included as part of a validation build policy, SonarQube and the Sonar C# plugin can detect that the containing build is executed on a pull request, and the code issues, found as the result of static analysis on the new code, are added to the pull request as comments to be resolved before the pull request is completed.

The review comments added by peers or automated tools can be enforced (that is, they must be resolved before the pull request is complete) using the comment resolution policy:

☐ **Check for comment resolution**
Check to see that all comments have been resolved on pull requests.

Figure 18.10 – Comment resolution policy

Overall, it is fair to say that code review makes up an important part of code quality maintenance in a CI/CD pipeline.

Testing

As you have seen in *Chapter 16*, *Automated Testing*, various tests can be automated and introduced into the CD pipeline. The tests executed on any CI build can be displayed in the build results summary in a separate section with aggregated report values (taking the previous runs into consideration), giving developers the chance to identify issues before the application artifacts are deployed to the target environment.

Any (failed) test can be used as the starting point to create a work item (for example, a bug or an issue depending on the process template used) in the product backlog with any associated debugging information, if available. Moreover, automated tests can be associated with actual work items such as features or user stories, allowing the CI process to create meaningful correlations with the project management metadata:

Figure 18.11 – Test and work item association

As a result, automated tests can be used not only to identify problems early on but can also help with the analysis and triage processes. This way, the development team can improve two important DevOps KPIs: **Mean Time To Detect (MTTD)** and **Mean Time To Restore (MTTR)**, creating and maintaining a healthy CD pipeline.

Static code analysis with SonarQube

Because of the compiled nature of C# and .NET Core, static analysis and quality metrics of the source code can help the development team to maintain a healthy development pipeline. Similar to older tools such as StyleCop, and more popular Visual Studio extensions such as ReSharper, SonarQube is an open source static analysis platform providing valuable KPIs and history about the application source. Using SonarQube, certain traits and trends on quality metrics such as complexity, code smells, and duplications can be used to identify issues early in the development cycle, helping the development team to steer the application in the right direction.

SonarQube supports a number of platforms and languages, including C#, and is deeply integrated with MSBuild and Azure DevOps infrastructure, which makes it an ideal choice for any .NET Core development project. The server component can be hosted on-premises or as part of a cloud setup. On the other hand, SonarCloud is offered as a hosted version of the Java-based platform.

Once the SonarQube server is set up and the required plugins installed (namely, SonarCSharp), the quality profile for a given project can be set up. A quality profile is composed of the quality rules that the source code should abide by, and each rule defines various warning and error levels:

Figure 18.12 – SonarCloud issues view

Using the quality profile, a so-called quality gate can be defined, identifying which type of change in source code would trigger gate failure, alerting the development team to possible issues. A quality gate is generally defined on the new code that is introduced into the repository within the leak period (that is, the period in which you calculate the *new* code); however, some aggregate values throughout the project can also be included.

Here, it is important to mention that SonarQube uses a Git extension to access the source code revision history and annotates the code tree so that the code delta and the owner of the commits can be easily identified. A simple quality gate might look similar to the following:

Metric	Operator	Error
Coverage on New Code	is less than	80.0%
Duplicated Lines on New Code (%)	is greater than	3.0%
Maintainability Rating on New Code	is worse than	A
Reliability Rating on New Code	is worse than	A
Security Rating on New Code	is worse than	A

Figure 18.13 – SonarCloud quality gate

Execution of SonarQube analysis can take place during the CI phase, as well as the CD phase. While the Azure DevOps SonarScanner extension provides a convenient integrated build and analysis experience, SonarLint and the associated Roslyn analyzers provide insight and assistance to the developers within the Visual Studio IDE.

Local analysis with SonarLint

SonarLint is a Visual Studio extension that allows developers to bind a local project to the designated SonarQube server and its associated quality profile. Once the source is associated with a SonarQube project, it downloads the ruleset and these rules are applied to the source using Roslyn analyzers, providing a fully integrated editor experience with highlighting and issue solution options.

Using SonarLint together with SonarQube allows the central management of coding conventions and rules and helps to maintain the code quality within bigger development teams. While the rule definitions are provided by the aforementioned analyzers, the severities defined by the quality profile are included in the project using the ruleset files:

```xml
<?xml version="1.0" encoding="utf-8"?>
<RuleSet Name="SonarQube - App Sonar way" Description="This rule set was automatically generated from SonarQube.
http://****.northeurope.cloudapp.azure.com:9000/profiles/show?key=cs-sonar-way-35075" ToolsVersion="15.0">
    <Rules AnalyzerId="SonarAnalyzer.CSharp"
    RuleNamespace="SonarAnalyzer.CSharp">
        <Rule Id="S100" Action="Warning" />
        <Rule Id="S1006" Action="Warning" />

        <!-- Removed for brevity -->

        <Rule Id="S103" Action="Warning" />
        <Rule Id="S4027" Action="None" />
        <Rule Id="S907" Action="Warning" />
        <Rule Id="S927" Action="Warning" />
    </Rules>
</RuleSet>
```

These rules are periodically synced with the SonarQube server and can be combined with ruleset files that might be defined for other analyzers, such as StyleCop analyzers.

CI analysis

Once the developer commits their changes and creates a pull request, SonarScanner for CSharp can be executed using the Azure DevOps extensions available in the marketplace.

After the extension is installed on your Azure DevOps instance, the setup of the extension is quite straightforward. The initial step is to create an access token on a SonarQube server of your choice (that is, SonarQube or SonarCloud depending on the variant used), and create a service connection on Azure DevOps using this token:

Figure 18.14 – SonarCloud service connection

The integrated build tasks will then be included in the desired pull request validation build (or the CI build) as a pair of tasks: Prepare Analysis and Run Analysis.

The Prepare Analysis task downloads the required analysis configuration and prepares the integrated MSBuild execution targets. The Run Analysis task, on the other hand, collects the results that are gathered during the build execution and uploads them to the server. It is important to place the preparation task before any compilation takes place so that the Sonar configuration is ready while the compilation is being executed. A simple build sequence might look like the following:

Figure 18.15 – SonarCloud CI pipeline tasks

Finally, the optional Publish Analysis task can wait for the analysis results and then publish them within the current pipeline.

> **Important note**
> .NET Core projects do not require a `ProjectGuid` property, unlike the classic .NET projects. However, the Sonar scanner uses `ProjectGuid` to identify the projects and execute analysis on them. In order to make sure the Sonar scanner can be executed successfully, the `ProjectGuid` property should be manually created on each `.csproj` file and set to a random `Guid`.

With this setup, Sonar rules would be used by the sonar analyzers during the build to identify code issues with varying severities. However, if we need or want to include additional Roslyn analyzers, we probably would want to run the sonar analysis and calculate metrics on the aggregated set of code issues.

External Roslyn analyzers

In addition to the built-in set of analysis rules, SonarQube can also consume the warnings and errors that are identified by other Roslyn analyzers, such as the available StyleCop analyzers.

In order to include StyleCop rules into a .NET Core project, it is enough to reference the publicly available NuGet package:

```xml
<ItemGroup>
    <PackageReference Include="StyleCop.Analyzers" Version="1.1.118" PrivateAssets="All" />
</ItemGroup>
```

At this point, the coding convention-related issues would be identified and flushed through the build output as warnings. Additionally, the IDE would provide annotations and solutions using the Roslyn infrastructure.

Finally, once the project is put through SonarQube server analysis, the issues identified by `StyleCop.Analyzers` would also be stored and included in the quality gate calculations. For instance, the following issues are identified by StyleCop rules but are included in SonarQube:

Figure 18.16 – SonarCloud Roslyn analyzers

Overall, SonarQube provides a complete code quality management platform that, coupled with Azure DevOps and .NET Core, provides an ideal automated development pipeline and secures the CI process.

Creating and using release templates

As previously discussed, once the CI is complete, published build artifacts should ideally be transferred into the release pipeline, starting the CD phase. Azure DevOps release templates and infrastructure provide a complete release management solution that, without the need for any additional platform such as Jenkins, Octopus, or TeamCity, can handle the CI/CD pipeline.

In this section, we will take a look at the basic release template elements and work out details for both Xamarin and Azure web application releases within separate release templates.

Azure DevOps releases

A release definition is made up of two main components: artifacts and stages. Using triggers and gates, the deployment of artifacts to target stages is organized and managed.

Release artifacts

Release artifacts are the elements that provide the components for the release tasks. These artifacts can vary from simple compiled application libraries to source code retrieved directly from the application repositories:

Figure 18.17 – Release Artifacts

Let's take a closer look at these artifact types:

- **Azure Pipelines**: This is the most commonly used artifact type, which allows the build pipelines to pass the compilation results as packaged components to the release pipeline. Using this artifact type allows the release pipeline to detect the work items that are introduced with the artifacts, creating a direct relationship between project work items and release details. The creation of the new version of an artifact can be used as the trigger for the release.

- **TFVC, Git, and GitHub**: If static content from the source code repository, such as configuration files, media content, or the source code itself, is required for the release pipeline tasks, various repositories can be used as artifacts. Incoming commits to the repository can be used as triggers for the release.

- **Jenkins**: If multiple build and release pipelines are involved in a setup, a service connection can be created for a Jenkins deployment and Jenkins build artifacts can be consumed by Azure DevOps release pipelines.

- **Azure Container Registry, Docker, and Kubernetes**: When dealing with containerized application packages, the images prepared can be pushed to a private container registry and these images can then be retrieved during the release process.

- **Azure Artifacts (NuGet, Maven, and npm)**: Azure package management artifacts can be retrieved and used to trigger new releases using this source, allowing various packaged components to be included in the release pipeline.
- **External or on-premises TFS**: On-premises TFS infrastructure can also be included in an Azure DevOps release pipeline. In order for this type of integration to work, the on-premises TFS server should be equipped with an on-premises automation agent.

Additional artifacts such as TeamCity can be introduced into release pipelines using the Azure DevOps extensions available on the marketplace.

In our application pipelines, we would be using the build artifact type that will contain the ARM definition, web API service packages, and the multiple configuration application packages for various environments.

Release stages

In layman's terms, **release stages** roughly translate to the environments in which we want the application to be deployed. It is important to emphasize the fact that a stage is only a logical container and does not need to refer to a single server environment. It can refer to various environment infrastructures, as well as a managed distribution ring for mobile applications.

A release stage contains the release jobs that will be executed on release agents. For instance, if we are deploying a build artifact to Azure Stack or a mobile application package to App Center, we can use an agent job on a hosted agent. Nevertheless, if the deployment target is an on-premises server, we would need to use a specific deployment agent or a deployment group.

As mentioned, a release stage can contain multiple release jobs, which can be executed in parallel or sequentially, depending on the dependencies between the components. For instance, in order to deploy the iOS component to the QA distribution ring simultaneously with the Android or UWP packages, we can utilize parallel agent jobs that would select the specific artifacts to download and release. Each job can define which specific artifact it requires. Another example for a multi-job release setup could be a microservice package deployment setup where each service is deployed independently:

Figure 18.18 – Artifact Downloads for Stages

In this example, the API deployments could have been configured so that the services are deployed to related to app services only after the main ARM deployment takes place.

Release gates and triggers

In an Azure DevOps release, the transition between stages is controlled by triggers and gates. The release train, as well as manual or external service gates, can be configured using these components.

The main trigger for a release is set up through the artifacts introduced in a release. As mentioned, a build artifact can be set up to trigger a new release with each new version.

The following trigger will be executed every time a build artifact is created from a source branch matching the given wildcard expression (that is, `/release/*`):

Figure 18.19 – Continuous Deployment Triggers

This scenario can be extended to include build tags and additional `exclude` expressions.

On top of the main release trigger, each stage can define a separate trigger. These triggers can refer to the actual release trigger or the completion of another stage. Manual deployment is also included to separate a stage from the main release train. The following trigger defines the QA stage as the trigger for the UAT stage, chaining the two releases:

Figure 18.20 – Stage Dependencies

This automatic transition between the stages can be set to expect input from a specific user (manual approval) or an external server. These so-called gates can be defined as pre-deployment or post-deployment gates, with one verifying the availability of an environment to receive the release, and the other verifying the success of the deployment.

The most common application of gates is the manual approval pre-deployment configuration for higher environments, so that ongoing testing or actual public web application is not jeopardized. Manual approval can be done by any user within the Azure DevOps organization. Approval can be set to expire after a certain time and the selected approvers can delegate to other users.

External gates can be various service endpoints, such as Azure functions, external web services, or even a custom work item query within the same Azure DevOps project:

Figure 18.21 – Release Gates

Using the intrinsic trigger and gate capabilities, complex release workflows can be set up and executed on-demand or in an automated manner.

Xamarin release template

In the Xamarin release pipeline, we would be receiving multiple application packages for multiple platforms and environments as build artifacts. For instance, consider the following CI build setup for Xamarin Android, in which we would receive three packages for QA, UAT, and PROD:

Figure 18.22 – Publishing a Xamarin Artifact

532   CI/CD with Azure DevOps

If we were to create a similar multi-agent build for iOS and set these builds to trigger on incoming commits to any release branch, we would be creating a new application for each deployment environment with every new push:

☑ Enable continuous integration

☑ Batch changes while a build is in progress

Branch filters

Type	Branch specification
Include	release/*

+ Add

Figure 18.23 – Continuous Integration Trigger

The release pipeline for the App Center releases can now reference these artifacts and deploy them to a specific App Center ring. App Center is capable of pushing the application package to target the App Store, so we can create a production ring on App Center and deploy the package to production from App Center.

The deployment to parallel rings for different mobile platforms can be parallelized as parallel jobs or as parallel stages converging on synchronization stages:

Figure 18.24 – Xamarin Release Template

Gates on the synchronization stages (for example, **Beta-Start** and **Beta-Finish**) can be used to control the deployment to certain distribution rings.

Azure web application release

For Azure infrastructure, we would also be receiving multiple packages. The foremost important package of the Azure deployment pipeline is the ARM template and the associated configuration parameters files defining our application configuration. These resources can be retrieved directly from the source repository or they can be packaged during the CI build using the basic utility tasks used to copy files and package them (optionally) in a ZIP container.

> **Important note**
> Another useful tool that can be used during the CI build is the validation mode of the Azure Resource Group Deployment task. This way, the CI build can validate the ARM template changes introduced against at least one of the available environments.

The API services, depending on the hosting option selected (that is, containerized, or packaged as a web deployment, and so on), would also be created as deployment artifacts.

The release pipeline would then deploy the ARM template to the target resource group(s). Once the resource manager deployment is completed, the web application packages can be released to the target app service instances or app service slots, depending on the deployment strategy.

Similar to the Xamarin deployment, the release pipeline can be configured to use multiple stages to define an environment or multi-agent stage with multiple deployments. For instance, a sample release pipeline with deployment components separated into stages would look like the following:

Figure 18.25 – Azure Release Template

In either scenario, the release management flow should be the same: deploy the infrastructure and configuration, then continue with service package deployments.

Summary

In this chapter, we completed the CI/CD pipelines for both the Xamarin repository and the Azure web infrastructure. We have seen that the toolset offered by Azure DevOps is perfectly suitable for implementing a GitFlow branching strategy. This toolset is also used for managing the application life cycle by implementing branch policies and setting up CI triggers. Additionally, we have seen how the CI phase should also be used to maintain the code quality and technical debt. Finally, we discussed strategies for implementing release pipelines for both distributed Azure and native mobile applications.

Summary

With this final chapter, we have reached the end of the development of our project. At the beginning of the book, after refreshing our knowledge about various .NET concepts, runtimes, frameworks as well as platforms, we moved on to Xamarin development. We created and customized Xamarin applications using the .NET Standard framework and Xamarin platform runtimes. Hopefully, you have learned where to use which type of customization on the Xamarin.Forms framework. Once we completed the Xamarin project, our focus shifted to the Azure cloud stack and how we can utilize .NET Core on various Azure services that can be used in conjunction with Xamarin mobile applications. The Azure stack discussion mainly focused on Platform as a Service offerings such as App Service, serverless components, and finally data storage services such as Cosmos DB. In addition, we learned how we can engage our users in better ways with the help of external services such as push notifications, Graph API, and Cognitive Services. We slowly created the mobile application as well as the backend infrastructure, and the last section was about how to effectively manage the life cycle of our projects using Microsoft Azure DevOps and Microsoft Visual Studio App Center. Using Azure DevOps, we have tried to realize modern DevOps concepts by creating automated CI/CD pipelines.

While the implementations and practical examples were quite generalized, the hands-on concepts we have discussed throughout the book would be a good starting point for any cross-platform development project you and your team are planning to undertake. For any .NET developer, understanding .NET Core and other implementations of .NET Standard is the key to unlock multiple platforms and create user experiences that span platforms.

Packt.com

Subscribe to our online digital library for full access to over 7,000 books and videos, as well as industry leading tools to help you plan your personal development and advance your career. For more information, please visit our website.

Why subscribe?

- Spend less time learning and more time coding with practical eBooks and Videos from over 4,000 industry professionals
- Improve your learning with Skill Plans built especially for you
- Get a free eBook or video every month
- Fully searchable for easy access to vital information
- Copy and paste, print, and bookmark content

Did you know that Packt offers eBook versions of every book published, with PDF and ePub files available? You can upgrade to the eBook version at packt.com and as a print book customer, you are entitled to a discount on the eBook copy. Get in touch with us at customercare@packtpub.com for more details.

At www.packt.com, you can also read a collection of free technical articles, sign up for a range of free newsletters, and receive exclusive discounts and offers on Packt books and eBooks.

Other Books You May Enjoy

If you enjoyed this book, you may be interested in these other books by Packt:

ASP.NET Core 5 and React - Second Edition

Carl Rippon

ISBN: 978-1-80020-616-8

- Build RESTful APIs with .NET 5 using API controllers
- Secure REST APIs with identity and authorization policies
- Create strongly typed, interactive, and function-based React components using Hooks
- Understand how to style React components using Emotion.js
- Perform client-side state management with Redux

Customizing ASP.NET Core 5.0

Jürgen Gutsch

ISBN: 978-1-80107-786-6

- Explore various application configurations and providers in ASP.NET Core 5
- Understand dependency injection in .NET and learn how to add third-party DI containers
- Discover the concept of middleware and write your own middleware for ASP.NET Core apps
- Create various API output formats in your API-driven projects
- Get familiar with different hosting models for your ASP.NET Core app
- Develop custom routing endpoints and add third-party endpoints

Packt is searching for authors like you

If you're interested in becoming an author for Packt, please visit `authors.packtpub.com` and apply today. We have worked with thousands of developers and tech professionals, just like you, to help them share their insight with the global tech community. You can make a general application, apply for a specific hot topic that we are recruiting an author for, or submit your own idea.

Leave a review - let other readers know what you think

Please share your thoughts on this book with others by leaving a review on the site that you bought it from. If you purchased the book from Amazon, please leave us an honest review on this book's Amazon page. This is vital so that other potential readers can see and use your unbiased opinion to make purchasing decisions, we can understand what our customers think about our products, and our authors can see your feedback on the title that they have worked with Packt to create. It will only take a few minutes of your time, but is valuable to other potential customers, our authors, and Packt. Thank you!

Index

Symbols

.NET
  using, with Xamarin 35-37
.NET 5.0
  applications, developing with 9
.NET Core 7, 8
.NET Core applications
  deploying 499-503
.NET Native
  using, with UWP 54
.NET Standard
  using, with UWP 54
.NET vNext 3

A

AbsoluteLayout 121
acceptance testing 473
advanced application telemetry 435
Android platform
  services 349, 350
AOT compilation 35
App Center
  diagnostics option 425, 426
  distributing with 422
  telemetry option 425, 426
App Center distribution
  to production stage 424, 425
App Center distribution groups 423, 424
App Center, for Xamarin
  about 417
  builds, integrating with 418, 419
  distribution rings, setting up 420-422
  source repository, integrating
    with 418, 419
App Center releases 422, 423
App Center telemetry data
  exporting, to Azure 440-443
append blobs 203
Apple Push Notification Service
    (APNS) 377, 378
application
  securing 277-279
Application Insights data model
  about 443, 444
  events 443
  metrics 443
  Trace 443
application integrity
  fixtures and data-driven tests 466-469
  maintaining, with unit tests 456
  unit tests, creating with mocks 462-466

application layout
  about 88
  consumer expectations 88, 89
  development cost 93
  platform imperatives 91, 93
Application Lifecycle Management
    (ALM) 210
applications, developing with .NET 5.0
  about 9
  framework, defining 17-19
  runtime-agnostic application,
    creating 9-14
  runtime, defining 14-17
  self-contained deployment,
    defining 14-17
application-wide authentication scheme
  setting, up with Azure AD B2B 281, 282
app model
  selecting 248
APT and LLVM, for Xamarin.
    iOS applications
  transcompilation process 35
architectural patterns
  about 83
  decorator pattern 85
  event aggregator 84
  for unidirectional data flow 81, 82
  Inversion of Control (IoC) 83
ARM template
  Azure DevOps, using for 495-499
  concepts 491-495
  creating 484-491
Arrange, Act, and Assert (AAA) 456-461
ASP.NET Core
  telemetry data, collecting with 444-449
ASP.NET Core Identity 279, 280
asynchronous command 346-348
asynchronous event handling 344-346

asynchronous execution patterns
  about 342
  service initialization pattern 342-344
Asynchronous Programming
    Model (APM) 345
Atomic, Consistent, Isolated,
    Durable (ACID) 201
attached properties
  using 154-156
automated UI tests 473, 474
awaitables
  utilizing 320, 321
Azure
  App Center telemetry data,
    exporting to 440-443
  containers 250
Azure AD 280
Azure AD B2B
  used, for setting up application-wide
    authentication scheme 281, 282
Azure AD B2C 285
Azure App Service 252
Azure blobs 202
Azure Cache for Redis 205
Azure Container Service (ACS) 250
Azure DevOps
  about 210, 211
  Git repository, creating with 400, 401
  using 400
  using, for ARM templates 495-499
Azure DevOps releases 525
Azure ecosystem
  service offerings 198, 199
Azure Event Grid 209
Azure files 203
Azure Function Runtimes
  using 289-293

Index   543

Azure Functions
  about 205-207
  bindings 294, 295
  configuring 295, 296
  creating 297-300
  developing 288, 289
  execution models 205
  hosting 296
  telemetry, collecting with 449, 450
  triggers 294, 295
Azure Logic apps 208
Azure Notification Hubs
  about 379
  infrastructure 379
  notification 382
  registration 381
Azure PaaS setup 189
Azure queues 203
Azure repository models
  Azure Blob Storage 314
  Azure Table Storage 314
  Cosmos DB 313
  SQL Server 313
Azure Resource Manager
    (ARM) 200, 484, 514
Azure Serverless 205, 288
Azure Service
  telemetry data, collecting for 443
Azure Service Bus 314
Azure Service Fabric 251
Azure services
  integration with 313
  overview 186
Azure SQL databases
  security features 201
Azure SQL Data Warehouse 313
Azure storage 202
Azure tables 203

Azure virtual machines 249
Azure Web App
  for App Service 271-273
Azure web application release 533, 534

B

Base Class Library (BCL) 54
behaviors
  creating 148-153
binding 72
block blobs 202

C

calculator application
  with Xamain.Android 26-31
  with Xamarin.iOS 32-34
Cassandra 224
change feed 245
CI analysis 522, 523
CI/CD 506-508
CI/CD, with GitFlow
  about 508
  CI phase 512-515
  development 509, 510
  hotfix branches 516
  production 517
  pull request/merge 510-512
  release branch 515, 516
client cache aside
  HTTP performance, improving
    with 355-357
Client URL (curl) 254
cloud architecture
  about 190
  backends, for frontends 192
  cache-aside pattern 194, 195

Index

circuit breaker pattern 197, 198
competing consumers 196, 197
gateway aggregation 190, 191
materialized view 193, 194
publisher/subscriber pattern 197
queue-based load leveling 195, 196
retry pattern 197, 198
collection views 138, 139
command pattern 332-335
Common Language Infrastructure (CLI) 7, 22
composite customizations 164-168
consumers
  creating 335, 336
containers
  about 274
  in Azure 250
Continuous Delivery (CD) 506
Continuous Integration (CI) 506
control statements
  condition 310
  foreach 310
  scope 310
  switch 310
  terminate 310
  until 310
Core Common Language Runtime (Core CLR) 54
Cosmos DB
  about 204, 236
  change feed 245
  indexing 239-241
  partitioning 236-238
  programmability 241-245
Cosmos DB basics
  about 214, 215
  consistency spectrum 216-218
  global distribution 216

pricing 219, 220
cross-module integrity
  client-server communication, testing 469-472
  maintaining, with integration tests 469
  platform tests, implementing 473
cross-platform application development 4
cross-platform applications
  fully native applications 5
  native cross-platform frameworks 6
  native hosted web applications 5
custom control
  creating 168
custom renderer
  creating 172-177
custom Xamarin.Forms control
  creating 178-181

D

data
  analyzing 451-454
data access model
  about 220
  Cassandra 224
  Gremlin 224
  MongoDB API 220-224
  SQL API 220
data access patterns
  about 364, 365
  observable repository 367-373
Database Transaction Unit (DTU) 201
data binding 38
data binding essentials 128, 129
data denormalization
  data modeling 232-234
data-driven views
  creating 128

triggers 133-135
value converters 130-132
visual states 135, 137
data-driven views, triggers types
  data trigger 133
  event trigger 133
  multi-trigger 133
  property trigger 133
data modeling
  about 224
  data denormalization 231, 232
  documents, accessing 225-231
  documents, creating 225-231
  referenced data 234-236
data stores 201
data streams
  using 337-341
Data Transaction Unit (DTU) 219
Data Transfer Object (DTO) 64
Data Transformation Object (DTO) 225
decorator pattern 85
DependencyService 83
design techniques, for Xamarin applications
  fluid layout 91
  orientation change 92
  resize 92
  restructure 92
Desired State Configuration (DSC) 249
development branch
  about 402
  managing 404-408
development services
  about 209
  Azure DevOps 210, 211
  Visual Studio App Center 211, 212
device relay 394

Devices.xUnit framework 473
diagnostics option
  in App Center 425, 426
dimensions 430
distributed systems
  about 186
  with on-premises n-tier application setup 187, 188
distribution rings
  setting up 420-422
Docker 274
Dynamic Link Library (DLL) 12

E

Electronic Data Interchange (EDI) 304
Enterprise Application Integration (EAI) 304
Enterprise Integration Pack (EIP) 208, 304
Entity Data Model (EDM) 260
Entity Framework Core 363, 364
Entity tag (ETag)
  HTTP performance, improving with 357-359
event aggregator 84
Event Grid 315
Event Hubs 315
eventual consistency 218
EXtensible Application Markup Language (XAML)
  about 51
  differences 51, 53
  layout structure 52
external Roslyn analyzers 524

F

Firebase Cloud Messaging
  (FCM) 377, 378
fixture 466
FlexLayout 117
fully native applications
  developing 5

G

Git
  using 400
Git, branching strategy
  about 402
  development branch 402
  flow 402, 403
  master branch 403
Git repository
  creating, with Azure DevOps 400, 401
Global System for Mobile
  Communications (GSM) 354
Graph API 393
Gremlin 224
Grid layout 118-120

H

HTTP performance
  improving, with client cache
    aside 355-357
  improving, with Entity tag
    (ETag) 357-359
  improving, with key/value store 359, 360
  improving, with transient caching 354
hybrid applications 5

I

IApp interface
  example 475
Identity as a Service (IDaaS) 280
idioms 91
indexing 239-241
Infrastructure as a Service (IaaS) 248
Infrastructure-as-Code
  (IaC) 188, 249, 484
integration options, for Azure serverless
  components with Azure resources
  event aggregation 315
  queue-based processing 314
  repository 313, 314
integration tests
  used, for maintaining cross-
    module integrity 469
interaction models
  Item Context Actions 90
  List Context Actions 90
  List/Detail View 89, 90
Intermediate Language (IL) 54
internal execution method
  implementing 329, 330
Inversion of Control (IoC) 83
iOS platform
  background mechanisms 350-352

K

key-value pair (KVP) 203
key/value store
  HTTP performance, improving
    with 359, 360

L

layouts 116
Line of Business (LOB)
    application 143, 285
local analysis
  with SonarLint 522
logical tasks 331, 332
Logic App
  connectors, checking 304
  control statements 310
  creating 305-309
  developing 300, 301
  implementing 301-304
  workflow execution control 310-312
Long Term Evolution (LTE) 354

M

master/detail view 109-113
Mean Time To Detect (MTTD) 519
Mean Time To Restore (MTTR) 519
Mediating Controller 68
microservice
  creating 253
  initial setup 253-256
  retrieval actions, implementing 256-264
  soft delete, implementing 267, 268
  update methods, implementing 264-267
  with Azure Service Fabric 251
microservice setup 188
Microsoft Authentication Library (MSAL)
    used, for implementing authentication
        on client application 283-285
Microsoft Azure
  providers 199, 200
Microsoft Developer Network
    (MSDN) 211

Microsoft Intermediate
    Language (MSIL) 34
mocks
  used, for creating unit tests 462-466
Model-View-Adapter (MVA) 68
Model-View-Controller (MVC)
  implementing 68-72
Model View Intent (MVI) 332
Model-View-Presenter (MVP) 68
Model-View-ViewModel (MVVM)
  about 38
  implementing 72-80
Model-View-ViewMode (MVVM) 332
MongoDB API 220-224
Mono 22
multi-page views 103-108

N

native asynchronous execution
  about 349
  Android services 349, 350
  iOS backgrounding 350-352
native components 126, 127
native cross-platform frameworks 6
native cross-platform frameworks, tiers
  application model 6
  framework 6
  platform abstraction 6
native domains
  composite customizations 164-168
  customizing 159
  platform specifics 159, 160
  Xamarin.Forms effects 160-164
native hosted web applications 5
Native Notification Services
  about 376
  general constraints 378

navigation strategies
  master/detail view 109-113
  multi-page views 103-108
  simple navigation 100-103
  single-page view 94-100
navigation structure
  implementing 94
nearby sharing 395
Network Link Conditioner tool 354
Network type option 354
notification hub 379
notification namespace 380, 381
notification providers
  about 376, 377
  issues, for cross-platform
    application 377
notifications
  Azure Notification Hubs, using 381
  sending, with Platform Notification
    Systems (PNS) 377, 378
notification service, advanced scenarios
  about 391
  Push-to-Pull pattern 391
  rich media, for push messages 391, 392
notification service, creating
  about 383
  broadcasting, to multiple
    devices 390, 391
  device, registering 384-387
  notifications, transmitting 388- 390
  requirements, defining 383, 384

O

observable repository 367-373
observables
  using 337-341
OpenID Identity Connect (OIDC) 279

P

page blobs 202
Page Object Pattern (POP) 477
partitioning 236-238
partition key 236
persistent relational data cache 361
Personal Access Token (PAT) 401
Platform Abstraction Layer (PAL) 7
Platform extensions
  working with 55, 56
Platform Invoke (P-Invoke) statement 46
Platform Notification System (PNS)
  about 376, 379
  notifications, sending with 377, 378
POP structure
  implementing 477-480
Portable Class Libraries (PCLs) 36, 361
presentation architecture
  architectural patterns, for
    unidirectional data flow 81, 82
  Model-View-Controller (MVC) 68-72
  Model-View-ViewModel
    (MVVM) 72-80
  selecting 67
producers
  creating 335, 336
programmability 241-245
Progressive Web Apps (PWAs) 5
Project Rome 393
Project Rome, API
  about 393
  device relay 394
  nearby sharing 395
  notifications 395
  Remote Sessions 395
  user activities 394
Project Rome notifications 395

Index 549

proxy telemetry container
  creating 435-440
push notifications 376

Q

QA process
  about 517
  code review 518, 519
  static code analysis, with
    SonarQube 520
  testing 519

R

Read-Eval-Print-Loop (REPL) 476
Redis cache
  integrating with 268-271
reference data 364
relational databases 201
RelativeLayout 121, 123
release artifacts 526
release gates 528, 530
release stages 527, 528
release templates
  creating 525
  using 525
release trigger 528, 529
Remote Sessions API 395
repository pattern
  implementing 365-367
Request Unit (RU) 219
Runtime Identifier (RID) 15

S

ScrollView 121
Security Token Service (STS) 278
self-contained package 15
Server Message Block (SMB) 203
Service Fabric Mesh 250
service initialization pattern 342-344
Service-Oriented Architecture (SOA) 188
services
  containerizing 274-277
  hosting 271
session consistency 217
Shared Source Common Language
    Infrastructure (SSCLI) 7
Shell Navigation
  implementing 113-116
simple navigation 100-103
Single Page Application (SPA) 5
single-page view 94-100
Software-Defined Networking (SDN) 251
SonarLint
  about 521
  using, for local analysis 522
SonarQube
  using, for static code analysis 520, 521
SQL API 220
SQLite.NET 361, 362
StackLayout 116
static code analysis
  with SonarQube 520, 521
static data 364
strong consistency 217
styles
  using 144-148
synchronization context 327, 328
System Under Test (SUT) 466

T

Task Asynchronous Programming
 (TAP) 321
task-based execution 321-326
tasks
 utilizing 320, 321
Team Foundation Version
 Control (TFVC) 400
telemetry
 collecting, with Azure
 Functions 449, 450
telemetry data
 collecting, for Azure Service 443
 collecting, with ASP.NET Core 444-449
telemetry data model
 about 430
 creating 430- 434
telemetry option
 in App Center 425, 426
test-driven development (TDD) 456
Time-Based One-Time Password
 (TOTP) 279
Time To Live (TTL) property 268
Tizen implementation 42
transient caching
 HTTP performance,
 improving with 354
transient data 364
triggers 133-135
trunk 402

U

unit tests
 creating, with mocks 462-466
 used, for maintaining application
 integrity 456

Universal Windows Platform (UWP)
 .NET Native, using 54
 .NET Standard, using 54
 about 46, 47
 application, creating 47-51
user activities 394
User experience (UX) 320

V

value converters 130-132
view elements 123-125
virtual machines (VMs) 249
Visual State Manager (VSM) 135
visual states 135, 137
Visual Studio App Center 211, 212

W

Windows Notification Service (WNS) 376
Windows Presentation
 Foundation (WPF) 72
Windows Runtime (WinRT) 46

X

Xamain.Android
 calculator application 26-31
Xamarin
 .NET, using with 35, 37
 about 22
 App Center 417
 development environment,
 setting up 22-25
 versus Xamarin.Forms 42, 62, 63
Xamarin.Android build 410-412
Xamarin application
 creating 25

Xamarin application packages
  artifacts, creating 416
  artifacts, utilizing 416
  creating 408
  environment-specific configurations 416
Xamarin applications
  insights, collecting for 430
Xamarin build templates
  using, for Xamarin applications 409
Xamarin.Forms
  about 37, 62, 63
  native components 126, 127
  using 116
  view elements 123-125
Xamarin.Forms application
  creating 38-41
Xamarin.Forms application projects
  organizing 64-67
Xamarin.Forms control
  creating 168-171
Xamarin.Forms development
    domains 142, 143
Xamarin.Forms effects 160-164
Xamarin.Forms, layouts types
  AbsoluteLayout 121
  FlexLayout 117
  Grid layout 118-120
  RelativeLayout 121, 123
  ScrollView 121
  StackLayout 116
Xamarin.Forms, native controls
  using 116
Xamarin.Forms shared domains
  about 144
  attached properties 154-156
  behaviors, creating 148-153
  styles, using 144-148
  XAML markup extensions 156-159

Xamarin.iOS
  calculator application 32-34
Xamarin.iOS pipeline 413-416
Xamarin release template 531-533
Xamarin.UITests 474-477
XAML markup extensions 156-159

Printed in Great Britain
by Amazon